The Complete Unraveling of the JFK Assassination

Also by Brian T. Kelleher

Drake's Bay: Unraveling California's Great Maritime Mystery (1997)

The Complete Unraveling of the JFK Assassination

A Lost Bullet's Deadly Trail

Brian T. Kelleher

Kelleher & Associates Environmental Mgmt LLC

San Jose, California

Kelleher & Associates Environmental Mgmt LLC

San Jose, California

Library of Congress Catalogue Card Number: Pending

ISBN: 978-0-9863096-1-8 (print on demand edition 6, December 2016 with additions and corrections)

Copyright 2015 by Kelleher & Associates Environmental Mgmt LLC

All rights reserved

No part of this publication may be reproduced, stored in a retrieval system, or transmitted in any form or by any means without written permission of the copyright holder, except for brief quotations in a review.

The Complete Unraveling of the JFK Assassination

Dedication

To those who remain profoundly impacted and Phuong Kim Vu.

The Kennedys and Connallys arrive at Love Field, Dallas, shortly before noon, November 22, 1963 - George Reid motion picture frame, The Sixth Floor Museum at Dealey Plaza http://www.jfk.org.

Acknowledgments

I thank my brothers Michael, the Doctor, Kevin, the Mechanical Engineer, and Peter, the Nuclear Engineer, for reviewing the manuscript and providing some excellent suggestions with respect to content and presentation. I thank my mother Louise for doing her usual excellent editing work and my friend Vic LoBue for proofing multiple drafts and providing much useful input especially on the front and rear covers, preface and introduction. My brother's wife Catherine Benedict Kelleher did the final proofing and some restructuring and rewriting that was very much to the benefit of the reader. I thank my clients for their patience.

I am amazed at the amount of assassination resources that are available on the internet. I used on-line resources provided on the following web sites and am very grateful to those who have assembled this information and are hosting the sites.

Rex Bradford's History-Matters and Mary Ferrill Foundation

Debra Conway's JFK Lancer Research

John Costella's JFK Assassination

John McAdams' Kennedy Assassination Home Page

Jefferson Morley's JFKfacts.org

Dale Myers' JFK Files

Don Roberdeau's: Men of Courage + Kennedy Assassination Evidence . . .

Sixth Floor Museum at Dealey Plaza's JFK.org

Robin Unger's JFK Assassination Forum

David Von Pein's Assassination of President Kennedy: A Lone-Gunman's View Point

Photo Credits

There are 100 illustrations in this book. I found all the photographs and existing illustrations that I used in creating these illustrations within the public domain. I made fair use of these materials in presenting, explaining and unraveling the JFK assassination conundrum. With each caption, I provided, to the extent of my knowledge, relevant information as to the author of any reproduced images and the current copyright holder.

The front cover includes cropped images from the November 22, 1963, Orville Nix and Marie Muchmore motion picture sequences of the assassination. The copyrights are respectively held by The Sixth Floor Museum at Dealey Plaza and *Associated Press Television News*, respectively.

The rear cover includes cropped images from one of a series of November 22, 1963, Dealey Plaza photographs taken by *AP* photographer James Altgens. The copyright is held by Bettmann/CORBIS.

Front and rear cover artwork and design is by artist/composer/vocalist/instrumentalist, April Gee d.b.a. "Containher," San Jose, California.

Table of Contents

Dedication	v	
Acknowledgments	vi	
Photo Credits	vi	
Preface	xix	
List of Acronyms and Abbreviations	xx	
Chapter 1	Introduction and Summary	1
Chapter 2	The Zapruder Assassination Sequence	31
Chapter 3	The Wiegman Assassination Sequence	57
Chapter 4	The Dorman Assassination Sequences	77
Chapter 5	The Muchmore Assassination Sequence	97
Chapter 6	The Nix Assassination Sequence	111
Chapter 7	The Bronson Assassination Sequence	127
Chapter 8	Jiggle Analysis	133
Chapter 9	Evidence on Minimum Firing Time	149
Chapter 10	Key Evidence on the Location of the Assassin	153
Chapter 11	Key Witness Testimony for the First Shot	163
Chapter 12	Key Witness Testimony for Final Two Shots	177
Chapter 13	Tracking Down the "Lost Bullet"	197
Chapter 14	Resolving the Evidence on Wound Locations	209
Chapter 15	Oswald Acted Alone	239
Conclusions and Recommendations		245
List of References Cited		249

Chapter Index 253

Name Index 259

List of Tables

Table 1 - Signature two-frame jolts and cranial eruptions due to a bullet striking the president or governor or a bullet shock wave passing under and striking a camera at Mach 1 speed 21

Table 2 - Observable first shot reflex and alarm reactions for the Zapruder and Dorman films 21

Table 3 - Observable second shot reflex and alarm reactions for the Zapruder, Dorman, Wiegman, Muchmore, Nix and Bronson films 23

Table 4 - Observable Z328 third shot reflex and alarm reactions for the Zapruder, Dorman, Wiegman, Muchmore, Nix and Bronson films 25

Table 5 - First shot jiggle analysis for the Zapruder and Dorman assassination sequences and the Bronson Z227 photo of the limo under fire confirms it was fired from the TSBD sniper's nest at Z221/M371 (muzzle blast noise in all cases) 27

Table 6 - Second shot jiggle analysis for the Zapruder, Dorman, Wiegman, Muchmore, Nix and Bronson assassination sequences confirm it was fired from the TSBD sniper's nest at Z310/W073/D394/M39/N20/B10 27

Table 7 - Third shot jiggle analysis for the Zapruder, Dorman, Wiegman, Muchmore, Nix and Bronson assassination sequences confirms it was fired from the TSBD sniper's nest at Z328/W098/D409/M57/N038/B22 28

Table 8 - Signature two-frame jolts and cranial eruptions due to a bullet striking the president or governor and transferring momentum to the wounded area or a bullet shock wave passing under and striking a camera at Mach 1 speed 46

Table 9 - Observable first shot reflex and alarm reactions for the Zapruder film 47

Table 10 - Observable second shot reflex and alarm reactions for the Zapruder film 48

Table 11 - Observable third shot reflex and alarm reactions for the Zapruder film 49

Table 12 - Observable second shot reflex and alarm reactions for the Wiegman film 67

Table 13 - Observable third shot reflex and alarm reactions for the Wiegman film 67

Table 14 - Scientific evidence that the second shot came from the TSBD at Z310/W073 68

Table 15 - Scientific evidence that the third shot came from the TSBD at Z328/W098 69

Table 16 - Observable first shot reflex and alarm reactions for the Dorman Film 86

Table 17 - Observable second shot reflex and alarm reactions for the Dorman film 86

Table 18 - Observable third shot reflex and alarm reactions for the Dorman film 87

Table 19 - Scientific evidence that the first shot came from the TSBD at Z221/D370 88

Contents

Table 20 - Scientific evidence that the second shot came from the TSBD at Z310/D393   89

Table 21 - Scientific evidence that the third shot came from the TSBD at Z328/D409   90

Table 22 - Signature two-frame jolts and cranial eruptions due to a bullet striking the president or governor and transferring momentum to the wounded area   104

Table 23 - Observable second shot reflex and alarm reactions for the Muchmore film   104

Table 24 - Observable third shot reflex and alarm reactions for the Muchmore film   105

Table 25 -Signature two-frame jolts and cranial eruptions due to a bullet striking the president or governor and transferring momentum to the wounded area   119

Table 26 - Observable second shot reflex and alarm reactions for the Nix Film   120

Table 27 - Observable third shot reflex and alarm reactions for the Nix film   121

Table 28 - First shot jiggle analysis for the Zapruder and Dorman assassination sequences and the Bronson Z227 photo of the limo under fire confirms it was fired from the TSBD sniper's nest at Z221/M371   144

Table 29 - Second shot jiggle analysis for the Zapruder, Dorman, Wiegman, Muchmore, Nix and Bronson assassination sequences confirm it was fired from the TSBD sniper's nest at Z310/W073/D394/M39/N20/B10   145

Table 30 - Third shot jiggle analysis for the Zapruder, Dorman, Wiegman, Muchmore, Nix and Bronson assassination sequences confirms it was fired from the TSBD sniper's nest at Z328/W098/D409/M57/N038/B22   146

List of Figures

Figure 1 - Dealey Plaza scaled drawing: presidential limo's path on Elm showing the president's location and speed at key Z frames, the six key filmmakers Zapruder, Nix, Muchmore, Bronson, Dorman and Wiegman, and the points of impact for the missing Z328 bullet   29

Figure 2 - Dealey Plaza from the air circa 1967   30

Figure 3 - Zapruder's field of vision from Z225 to Z350   50

Figure 4 - Abraham Zapruder's live interview by Jay Watson, WFAA TV, 2:30 P.M. Dallas time, November 22, 1963 and his camera   50

Figure 5 - Signature jolts and reflex reactions for the Z221 first shot: Z frames Z222-Z224 and Z228   51

Figure 6 - Signature jolts, cranial eruptions and reflex reactions for the Z310 second shot: Z frames Z312-Z315 and Z317   52

Figure 7 - Signature jolts and cranial eruptions for the Z328 third shot: Z frames Z330, Z331, Z332, and Z333   53

Figure 8 - Reflex and alarm reactions for the Z328 third shot and visible brain matter fallout: Z frames Z330-Z335, Z337 and Z340   54

Figure 9 - Zooming in on reflex reactions for the Z328 shot: Zapruder frames Z333 and Z335   55

Figure 10 - The presidential limo traveling west on Main minutes before the assassination   56

Figure 11 - Syncing the Wiegman and Zapruder films: W265=Z447   70

Figure 12 - Syncing the Wiegman and Zapruder films: W001=Z259   71

Figure 13 - Reflex reactions for the Z310 shot: Wiegman frames W075 and W079 (Z312/Z314)   72

Figure 14 - Alarm reactions for the Z310 shot: Wiegman frames W084 and W089 (Z318/Z322)   73

Figure 15 - Reflex reactions for the Z328 shot: Wiegman frames W102 and W106 (Z331/Z334)   74

Figure 16 - Alarm reactions for the Z328 shot: Wiegman frames W111 and W125 (Z337/Z347)   75

Figure 17 - Photograph (cropped) of the Kennedys' arrival at Love Field taken by White House Photographer Cecil Stoughton, with NBC cameraman Dave Wiegman in the background wearing his trademark black Fedora hat   76

Figure 18 - Syncing the Dorman and Wiegman films: D377=W046=Z291   91

Figure 19 - Syncing Dorman's fourth sequence to the Zapruder film (D337=Z182)   92

Figure 20 - Reflex reactions for the Z310 shot: Dorman frames D395 and D399 (Z312/Z316)   93

Figure 21 - Alarm reactions for the Z310 shot: Dorman frames D405 and D409 (Z323/Z328)   94

Figure 22 - Reflex reactions for the Z328 shot: Dorman Frames D413 and D415 (Z332/Z335)   95

Figure 23 - Alarm reaction for the Z328 shot: Dorman frames D417, D420 and D426 (Z/337Z340/Z347)   96

Figure 24 - Muchmore's field of vision from Z272 to Z337   106

Figure 25 - Reflex reactions for the Z310 second shot: Muchmore frames M44, M45, and M47 (Z315/Z316/Z318   107

Figure 26 - Signature jolts and cranial eruptions for the Z328 third shot: Muchmore frames M58, M60, and M61 (Z329/Z331/Z332)   108

Figure 27 - Reflex reactions for the Z328 third shot and visible brain matter fallout: Muchmore frames M60, M61, M64 and M65 (Z331/Z332/Z335/336)   109

Figure 28 - Zooming in on reflex reactions for the Z328 shot: Muchmore frames M61 and M64 (Z332/335)   110

Figure 29 - Nix's field of vision from Z291 to Z370 122

Contents

Figure 30 - Reflex reactions for the Z310 second shot: Nix frames N026 and N028 (Z316/318) 123

Figure 31 - Signature jolts and cranial eruptions for the Z328 third shot: Nix frames N039, N040, and N041 (Z329/Z330/Z331) 124

Figure 32 - Reflex reactions for the Z328 third shot: Nix frames N042, N043 and N046 (Z332/333/336) 125

Figure 33 - Zooming in on reflex reactions for the Z328 shot: Nix frames N042, N043, N045 and N046 (Z332/Z333/Z335/Z336) 126

Figure 34 - Charles Bronson's field of vision and key sightlines for his Z227 photo and assassination sequence 130

Figure 35 - The Bronson Z227 photo of the limo under fire 131

Figure 36 - Bronson frame B21/Z325 and Agent Clint Hill's sprint and revealing testimony 132

Figure 37 - Scaled drawing of Dealey Plaza used for jiggle analysis 147

Figure 38 - The Croft Z160 photo of the presidential limo heading west on Elm refutes the mythical Z152-first-shot miss 148

Figure 39 - Location of key witnesses to the source of the three shots 159

Figure 40 - Altgens Z253 photo head turning toward the TSBD sniper's nest (cropped) 160

Figure 41 - Muchmore frame M66/Z337 Flying Tackle Man heads for shelter in the alleged picket-fence shooter area as Officers Martin and Chaney look right rear (cropped) 160

Figure 42 - Wiegman frame W111/Z337 head turning toward the TSBD sniper's nest (cropped) 160

Figure 43 - Dorman frame D421/Z342 head turning and looking up toward the TSBD sniper's nest (cropped) 160

Figure 44 - Tom Dillard photo of the TSBD sniper's nest taken 10 to 15 seconds after the last shot 160

Figure 45 - James Powell photo of the TSBD sniper's nest taken about 30 seconds after the last shot (cropped) 160

Figure 46 - Dallas police crime lab photo of the sniper's nest 11/25/63 with the boxes repositioned after they were moved 161

Figure 47 - Press photo showing Dallas police crime lab's Lieutenant Carl Day holding Oswald's Carcano rifle above his head, 11/22/63 161

Figure 48 - Dallas police crime lab photo of the sniper's nest showing three spent shell casings, 11/23/63 161

Figure 49 - Dallas police crime lab photo of the sniper's rifle just after it was discovered, 11/23/63 161

Figure 50 - Dallas police crime lab photo of the sniper's nest from the rear, 11/23/63 161

The Complete Unraveling of the JFK Assassination

Figure 51 - Couch film frame 83 showing officer Marion Baker and Roy Truly heading for the TSBD entrance as Stetson Hat Man looks up at the TSBD sniper's nest   162

Figure 52 - Key first-shot witness locations   173

Figure 53 - Photographic evidence refuting a first-shot miss at Z151   174

Figure 54 - The Betzner Z186 photo of the presidential limo and Queen Mary heading west down Elm   175

Figure 55 - The Phil Willis Z201 photo of the presidential limo and Queen Mary heading west down Elm   176

Figure 56 - Locations of key second-and-third-shot witnesses   193

Figure 57 - The Mary Moorman Z316 photograph of the limo under fire and the revealing testimony of Motorcycle Officers Hargis and Chaney   194

Figure 58 - The James Altgens Z253 photo of the limo under fire showing the Queen Mary and the police motorcycle escort and alarm reactions to the Z221 first shot, and the misperceptions of Agent Glen Bennett   195

Figure 59 - Life Magazine Photographer, Art Rickerby's post-assassination photo of a mix of key grassy knoll eyewitnesses and press photographers taken from camera car 2 within a minute of the shooting   196

Figure 60 - Three pictures of the bullet-strike investigations of the storm-sewer catch-basin area taken November 22, 1963   203

Figure 61 - The bullet-strike gouge at the Z400-storm-sewer catch basin's SW corner as it appears today   203

Figure 62 - The bullet strike on the south of Main curb 23 feet east of the triple underpass abutment   204

Figure 63 - Lateral trajectories of the Z328 strikes on the curbs   205

Figure 64 - Which of James Tague's cheeks were wounded?   206

Figure 65 - The true location of the wound to James Tague's cheek and its significance   206

Figure 66 - Concrete photographic evidence of the "Lost Bullet"   207

Figure 67 - Possible bullet and or fragment strikes on the triple underpass concrete abutment   208

Figure 68 - Vertical trajectory analysis for the Z310 shot using Zapruder frame Z312 reveals it struck the back of the governor's forearm as well as the president's head   221

Figure 69 - Vertical trajectory analysis using Zapruder frame Z222 confirms the Z221 shot did not cause the wounds to the governor's right forearm or wrist   222

Figure 70 - Vertical trajectory analysis using Zapruder frame Z225 confirms the Z221 shot caused the wounds to the base of the president's neck and the governor's torso and left inner thigh   223

Figure 71 - WC Exhibits CE-567 and CE-569 mangled bullet fragments and four pieces of skin and underlying flesh   223

Contents

Figure 72 - HSCA Exhibit F-83 X-ray of Governor Connally's right forearm   223

Figure 73 - CE-894 and HSCA Exhibit F-142 showing the incorrect slope of bullet causing JFK back and neck wounds   224

Figure 74 - Dale Myers' 3-D computer-graphics simulation of the president's and governor's position in the limo at Z223   224

Figure 75 - CE-399, 840, and 842 showing the the magic bullet, three bullet fragment recovered from under the left jump seat, and the bullet fragments recovered from Connally's forearm   225

Figure 76 - WC Exhibit Shaw # 1 showing the governor's wounds (cropped)   225

Figure 77 - Photographic evidence in the Z Film images that Connally's wounds to his right forearm and wrist occurred at Z313   225

Figure 78 - Unraveling misunderstood autopsy view 6 of the entrance wounds in the back of the head using HSCA Exhibit F-307   226

Figure 79 - Syncing autopsy views 6 and 7, the entrance wounds without and with the scalp reflected   227

Figure 80 - Close-ups of the view 6 and view 7 same Z313 scalp defect   227

Figure 81 - The exact location of the two inshoot and two outshoot wounds on the lateral X-ray and HSCA Exhibit F-307   228

Figure 82 - The path of the bullet through the president's head at Z313 and HSCA Exhibit F-66   228

Figure 83 - Syncing the anterior-posterior and lateral X-rays to identify the entrance and exit wound locations and to explain the 6.5 mm lead fragment   229

Figure 84 - WC Exhibit CE-843 and its FBI photo, lead fragments recovered from the president's brain tissues   230

Figure 85 - Sculpting the photo of CE-843 to confirm it is the "6.5 mm" fragment in the AP X-ray   230

Figure 86 - WC Exhibits 386 and 388: the Rydberg Drawings of the head wounds   231

Figure 87 - HSCA Exhibit F-66, the Dox drawing of the bullet's path through the president's head (cropped)   231

Figure 88 - Boswell sketch of the top of the president's head   231

Figure 89 - HSCA Exhibit F-44, JFK autopsy face-sheet   231

Figure 90 - Markup of HSCA Exhibit F88 (Dox drawing) showing the locations of the greater exit defect and main fractures   232

Figure 91 - Autopsy view 2, right side of the president's head and clarification of the so-called v-shaped notch via the AP X-ray   232

Figure 92 - Source of 2 percent error in the WC/FBI trajectory analysis for Z313   233

Figure 93 - Source of 5 percent error in the HSCA trajectory analysis for Z313   233

Figure 94 - A simple lateral trajectory analysis for the Z310 shot using HSCA exhibits 137, 138 (in part) and 147   234

Figure 95 - A simple lateral trajectory analysis for the Z221 shot using HSCA Figure II-23   235

Figure 96 - Zapruder sightlines for Z183, Z186 and Z193 for positioning the president and governor for the Z221 shot and WC Exhibit CE-689 showing the correct and incorrect wound locations and bullet path through the governor's torso   236

Figure 97 - Lateral trajectory analysis for the Z328 shot   237

Figure 98 - Vertical trajectory analysis for the Z328 shot   238

Figure 99 - Hunter of Fascists: backyard photo CE-133-A   243

Figure 100 - White House Photographer Cecil Stoughton's picture of President Kennedy's casket being taken aboard Air Force One   244

Preface

This sixth edition of "The Complete Unraveling of the JFK Assassination" is a print-on-demand soft-cover book targeted for general readers/colleges. It comes in the aftermath of my July 11, 2016, fortuitous discovery of the exact recording speed of a behind the scene assassination-day film sequence shot by *NBC-TV* Cameraman Dave Wiegman at 12:30 p.m. at the intersection of Houston and Elm in Dealey Plaza. This new piece of evidence scientifically confirms the forensic value of what I refer to below as "visual shot identifiers." The fifth edition includes significant updates to Chapters 1 through 8 incorporating this new evidence. The sixth provides minor repairs and improvements throughout. I issued editions 1 through 4 of this book in February through July 2015 in soft cover print-on-demand format via CreateSpace and sold just a few copies on Amazon. There are quite a few errors/omissions and they are no longer available. The next edition will be a hard cover book for collectors and libraries. The hard and soft cover editions will eventually be available only on my web site kelleherassoc.com along with links to a future *YouTube* channel.

Chapter 1 is intended to be a concise readable summary for the layperson explaining exactly what happened during the JFK assassination. The subsequent chapters are written in the first person as if I were preparing them for a federal court special master who was attempting to help litigating parties settle a lawsuit without going to trial (this would never happen in a murder trial and I never put my findings in writing).

In 1964 I achieved a tie by class vote in a debate with my seventh-grade English classmate and appointed Warren Commission defender Jeff Lee on whether there was a shot from the grassy knoll. My interest in the JFK assassination has never waned. I obtained a copy of the MPI version of the Zapruder film soon after its release in 1998. I have been conducting research for this book since then.

With so many other books filling the libraries and book-store shelves and all that has already been said and repeated five hundred times over in these books, not to mention magazine articles, web sites, news groups, radio debates, TV documentaries, etc., am I really offering anything worthwhile or important here?

With the new lines of visual evidence I am presenting in this book that I refer to collectively as "visual shot identifiers," I have solved every aspect of the JFK assassination case. Specifically, I have found in the massive photographic record of the assassination, hard scientific proof that establishes without any reasonable doubt, where the shots came from and exactly what damage they did to the president and governor. While most Americans and the Department of Justice have become resigned to the opinion that we will never know the truth of what happened during the JFK assassination, I have put together enough pieces of visual evidence so that everyone can easily see for themselves exactly what happened.

Why was I able to do this?

By trade, I am an environmental engineer/scientist who, since the early 1990s, has done most of my work for the California Superior Court special master program. I am retained as a neutral court-consultant to assist the special masters in the technical aspects of cases involving liability disputes associated with contaminated properties. In a typical project, I am handed many linear feet of technical reports prepared by consultants as well as any documents prepared by experts for the antagonists. My job is to review the scientific data objectively and help the special master resolve the lawsuit without going to trial. I have the right combination of scientific/technical abilities and communication skills to do this very difficult and challenging work with a considerable degree of competence.

I believe that my many years of experience working as a neutral court consultant has sharpened my eye for subtle details giving me an advantage over all previous assassination researchers irrespective of their professional qualifications in any of the associated fields of expertise that the assassination evidence touches. Because the devil is in the detail and things are not always as they first appear, I am very much on my toes when evaluating scientific data and alleged evidence. I also had the advantage of taking my time in conducting my research on the assassination. The government experts had to do their work under tight deadlines.

The approach that I used to make the evidence readily accessible and understandable, is that generally taken by professionals that work in the fields of applied environmental science: I organized and synthesized data by putting it into tables and figures. The good news is that this technique works very nicely in resolving the assassination evidence. The bad news is that it tends to give the book, in places, the look and feel of a technical report. With the help of my editors, I have tried to find a balance, providing plenty of pictorial support to break up the monotony of grinding through the voluminous data. The key evidence is presented in still-evolving video format at kelleherassoc.com.

List of Abbreviations and Acronyms

AP	Associated Press
B film	Bronson assassination sequence
CE	Commission exhibit
D film	Dorman film
EOP	External Occipital Protuberance
FBI	Federal Bureau of Investigation
HSCA	House Select Committee on Assassinations
M film	Muchmore assassination sequence
NAA	Neutron Activation Analysis
NBC	National Broadcasting Company
N film	Nix assassination sequence
JFK	John Fitzgerald Kennedy
Sniper's nest	The TSBD's southeast corner sixth-floor window
SS	Secret Service
TSBD	Texas School Book Depository
UPI	United Press International
WC	Warren Commission
WR	Warren Report
W film	Wiegman assassination sequence
Z film	Zapruder assassination sequence
Z221 shot	The shot fired from the TSBD at Z221 that hit the president at Z223
Z310 shot	The shot fired from the TSBD at Z310 that hit the president at Z313
Z328 shot	The shot fired from the TSBD at Z328 that hit the president at Z330

Chapter 1

Introduction and Summary

At 12:30 p.m., November 22, 1963, the warm and friendly reception the presidential party had so far received in Dallas was shattered by a loud explosion that most of those present in Dealey Plaza thought was a firecracker or backfire. Within six seconds, the dashing and charismatic 44-year-old president of the United States lay dying in the rear seat of the presidential limo. The 56-year-old governor of Texas lay critically wounded in the jump seat in front of him. Will we ever know what really happened?

At long last - Given the extent of the motion-picture evidence at hand, it was only a matter of time before a sharp-eyed researcher completely unraveled the JFK assassination. With my fortuitous discovery on July 11, 2016, of the exact recording speed of a heretofore largely unappreciated *NBC-TV News* assassination-day film sequence that captured spectators standing almost directly below the sniper's nest as the last two shots rang out, we now know for certain exactly when the shots were fired and where they came from. Here is why. (1) With knowledge of *NBC'* recording speed, we now have the information needed to sync all five key assassination-day films to the nearest 0.05 second (1 Z frame); (2) During a recreation of the assassination in August 1978, acoustics experts measured the amplitude of shot noise at all relevant locations on Elm Street and recorded muzzle blast levels of 115 to 135 decibels and a 130 decibel "crack" within 10 feet of the bullet's path; (3) Because these noise levels far exceed what is needed to trigger the human auditory reflex reaction—a survival instinct—each time the sniper fired his high-powered rifle at the president, most if not all of those located on or along Elm Street between the sniper's nest and the front seat of the presidential limo, exhibited an involuntary auditory reflex reaction—typically a telltale flinch-like dart of the head in the perceived direction of the sound. (4) In all cases, it is readily apparent from closely examining the images of five assassination-day films taken from five different locations, that for everyone in reasonably clear camera view the concurrent darting of heads, etc., started within 0.15 second +/- 0.05 second of the shot noise reaching their ears, and ended within the next 0.17 second (3 Z frames). (5) the observed reflex-reaction latency period and duration that scientifically marks three loud rifle shots in each of the five assassination-day films, is 100 percent consistent with what is reported in extensive scientific literature on the subject. (6) The onset of the reflex reaction for the person reacting—including the filmmakers—is exactly as mathematically predicted to the nearest 0.05 second (1 Z frame) based on the distance of the person to the sniper's nest at the speed of sound. (7) The bang . . . . . bang, bang shooting sequence and its deadly effects is corroborated by a very extensive body of multiple lines of forensic evidence including visual shot identifiers, eyewitness testimony and wound ballistics. I am providing irrefutable evidence in this book that three shots were fired from the sniper's nest at Z220.5, Z309.5 and shockingly, Z327.5, plus or minus a Zapruder film frame (Z frame).

Accordingly, in consideration of the many still-unanswered questions in the wake of all that has been written or claimed over the past five decades, this book's aim is to fit the many pieces of the JFK assassination evidence together and explain, for the first time, EXACTLY what happened during the six seconds the shots rang out, fully compliant with the dictates of this evidence. It is a completely fresh look at the evidence in minute detail conducted by a highly experienced neutral court consultant who routinely conducts this type of analyses and has a knack for it. My opinions do not count in court and cannot be used at trial. They are for consideration of the special masters and litigating parties. My objective was to solve a stubborn historical mystery and satisfy my own desire to understand exactly what happened and why. I was surprised by what I found. See kelleherassoc.com for video images of all the "visual shot identifiers" mentioned above and hereafter.

As my analysis unfolds, the reader will come to realize that the government's investigators and experts made critical oversights and mistakes. The experts failed to recognize the strength of the collective motion-picture evidence in establishing shot timing and source. Investigators should have more closely listened to what they were being told by the key witnesses and should have more closely examined their reactions on film. The experts went astray by rejecting or ignoring the testimony of key ear/eyewitnesses particularly those lining Elm Street, as well as those among the presidential entourage. They heard the explosions as the bullets entered or passed over the vehicles. Clearly, the first shot did not miss. Clearly, the second shot did not miss. Clearly, the third shot did not miss.

Consistent with what critics have been stating since the first official government reports were released in December 1963, I found that the lone gunman shooting sequence provided by the U.S. Department of Justice, including the controversial single bullet theory, was not supported by the photographic evidence, the autopsy report/face-sheet/X-rays/photos, nor the key ear/eyewitness testimony. Given the evidence as it is presented in the government's investigative reports, it becomes easy to understand why the public continues to believe there were multiple gunmen, a conspiracy, and a cover-up when there actually were none.

This book provides compelling proof of a lone-gunman while refuting the government's severely flawed explanation of the shooting scenario. It concludes that Oswald acted alone.

During my research, I turned up evidence that has been long overlooked that I call "visual shot identifiers." I have also tentatively identified the location of the so-called "lost bullet" and have provided the location to the Dallas FBI and Police Department and copied the *Dallas Morning News* and The Sixth Floor Museum at Dealey Plaza on the communication.

Some insights on my thought processes and approach and why I am so confident in my conclusions

In taking on the massive body of JFK assassination evidence, I applied the common-sense logic of what is often referred to as Occam's razor. William of Ockham, England, was a 14th-century Franciscan friar who espoused that the simplest solution to a problem is apt to be the correct solution. Applying this principal to the JFK assassination, I identified and followed the simplest line of evidence available and did not allow myself to be caught up in the extraneous details.

It was clear to me from the start that the answers to almost all the lingering questions were to be found in the images of the motion pictures that were taken while the presidential limo was under fire. Because of the involuntary auditory human reflex reaction to loud noise genetically built into the central nervous systems of human beings and all other mammals, I expected to find visual shot identifiers in the assassination sequences. I found exactly what I was looking for and then built from there. As a result of taking this approach, I am able to back all of my astonishing conclusions with irrefutable photographic evidence.

Introduction and Summary

Thanks to Abraham Zapruder, Dave Wiegman and the other motion-picture takers who had the presidential limo or spectators in view as the shots rang out, the timing and sequence of the shots is in full view for anyone to see <u>if one knows what to look for</u>.

With this book, I am showing anyone who is interested exactly what to look for. The collective motion-picture evidence is totally convincing. It is not just the Zapruder film images that are telling us exactly what happened, all the assassination sequences, once they are in sync with Zapruder's, are telling the same story. With the shot sequence correctly identified, all the other evidence in the case easily falls into place.

The simple common-sense logic I employed to figure out the all-important shot timing/sequence - Since the three bullets were traveling toward the presidential limo at supersonic speed, their shock-wave noise arrived with the bullets at very high amplitude (over 130 decibels). The involuntary reflex-reaction time for human beings to sudden and unexpected loud noise has been scientifically established and the range is tight: 0.14 to 0.16 second with an average of 0.15. This is exactly the interval that the third of three consecutive Zapruder frames (Z frames) covers. Thus, <u>when a bullet enters the limo, everyone in Zapruder's camera view, unless they are unconscious, will exhibit a spontaneous involuntary reflex reaction that lasts just 2 or 3 Z frames commencing exactly within the equivalent of 3 Z frames later</u>. These 2 to 3-frame duration concurrent spontaneous reactions are apparent between Z226-28 for those presidential-limo occupants in clear view and two spectators on the south side of Elm just as the president comes into view from behind a sign raising his hands to his neck. The spontaneous reactions are also conspicuous at Z316-18, exactly three frames after the president's head jolts downward and forward and explodes at Z313. Surprisingly, the reactions are also readily apparent at Z333-35 three frames after the president's head jolts forward at Z330/331 and jettisons brain matter forward onto Nellie Connally's head and rearward onto the lid of the trunk where large masses land from Z331 through Z337. These concurrent reactions by the limo occupants to the last two shots and the associated head jolts and cranial eruptions can also be readily seen in the Muchmore and Nix assassination sequences (so much for the notion that the Z film has been altered).

The simple logic I employed to figure out which bullets hit whom and where and when - Given that there is every good reason to believe that the shots were fired from the TSBD sniper's nest, <u>a bullet striking the president or governor from the high right rear will transfer its momentum and cause a sudden downward and forward jolt in the area of bodily impact, with the movement occurring during the frame the bullet struck and the next frame</u>. Focusing in on the three instances I found of concurrent spontaneous head turning/arm jerking among presidential limo occupants, I checked very carefully the interval two to four Z frames prior, looking for and finding the signature forward jolts. When one sees the governor's wounded right wrist jump an inch forward and away from him three frames before the concurrent reflex reactions commencing at Z316, he/she knows for sure that this is when his wrist was struck (so much for the single bullet theory). When one sees the president's head jolt forward 3 inches amidst a low-trajectory cranial eruption three frames before the concurrent reflex reactions commencing at Z333, he/she knows for sure that the president was struck a second time in the head from the high right rear (so much for a missed shot). The Zapruder film images show three key eyewitnesses (Agent Clint Hill, Motorcycle Officer Hargis, and *AP* photographer James Altgens) who were looking directly at the president from within 10 to 30 feet as of Z330 and all three, among others, described the exact same forward head jolt and cranial eruption we see on film.

The ease of tracking the lost bullet - Once one knows exactly when all three shots were fired and whom they struck, he/she will find him/herself hot on the trail of the so-called lost bullet given that it created two curb strikes and a linear scratch on the left side of a spectator's cheek. The only reason there is a "lost bullet" is because the government experts incorrectly concluded that one of the shots missed.

The Complete Unraveling of the JFK Assassination

The simple logic I used, in part, to confirm that each of the three shots came from the TSBD sniper's nest - A scaled drawing of Dealey Plaza shows Mr. Zapruder was 260 feet from the TSBD sniper's nest and that TSBD-employee Elsie Dorman was only 36 feet away filming from an open window on its fourth floor. Zapruder was 224 feet further from the sixth floor window than Dorman. Knowing each of them had no choice but to spontaneously jiggle or jerk their cameras commencing 2.5 Z frames after the shot noise arrived at their ears plus or minus a frame, Ms. Dorman's startle-induced blurring of film images would come earlier than Zapruder's by a mathematically predictable interval. In this case, the interval is 0.2 second (224 feet divided by the speed of sound at 1,125 feet per second). Knowing Zapruder's camera was recording at 18.3 frames per second, this is the equivalent of about four Z frames plus or minus a Z frame. In checking the film images for signature blurring, for the shots that hit the president at Z223, Z313 and late Z330, Zapruder's shot-induced blurring occurs at Z227, Z318 and Z336. Dorman's occurs four to five frames earlier at the equivalent of Z224, Z313, and Z330 consistent with an expected faster reaction time.

To lock in the location of the assassin, I applied the same simple logic and arithmetic, taking advantage of the fact that Ms. Dorman captured the movements of the spectators standing directly in front of the TSBD on the south side of Elm. These spectators were positioned on average 115 feet from the sixth floor SE corner window whereas Dorman was only 36 feet away. Her predicted signature blurred images came three frames after a given shot and a predictable two Z-frame equivalents before the spontaneous head turns of the spectators in her view. The timing of the spectator reactions across the street from the TSBD at five Z-frame equivalents from a given shot is in sync with shots fired in close proximity to Dorman and further distant from Zapruder and the other filmmakers.

Resolving the rest of the unanswered questions and controversies - As was just explained, most of the "solving" was surprisingly simple. The devil, however, is in the detail. The stubborn assassination riddles that I am most proud of solving include: (1) pinning down the recording speed of *NBC*'s Dave Wiegman's camera in July 2016; (2) figuring out how bullet shock waves created Zapruder camera movement all by themselves and ended up obscuring photographic evidence of the second lower-trajectory cranial explosion; (3) spotting the Z330/331 signature head jolt and signs of a second cranial eruption in the Zapruder film images and then verifying the head jolt and cranial eruption in the Muchmore and Nix film images; (4) tracking down the lost bullet without ever having been to Dealey Plaza; (5) conclusively debunking the single-bullet theory and first-shot miss theory using multiple lines of evidence; (6) figuring out the 45 degree left to right path that the un-deflected not-so-magic bullet took through the governor's torso; (7) unraveling autopsy view 7 including an explanation of why it is so hard to decipher; (8) syncing autopsy views 6 and 7 in identifying both inshoot wounds to the head; (9) identifying the significance of the alignment of the 6.5 by 15 mm gash in the back of the president's head; (10) unraveling the 6.5 mm fragment and syncing the head X-rays using Play-Doh™; (11) vindicating the three autopsy surgeons Humes, Boswell and Finke; (12) generating the first ever accurately drawn vertical and lateral trajectories for the three shots; (13) vindicating Nellie Connally and SSA Clint Hill; (14) showing the heart-wrenching cause of Jackie Kennedy's spontaneous rise from her seat and the nature and significance of her spontaneous right-arm-jerk reaction to bullet shock-wave noise; (15) syncing the Dorman and Wiegman films to the other assassination sequences; (16) syncing the key stationary and motorcade ear/eyewitness testimony to the visual shot identifiers, especially three of the motorcycle escort policemen; (17) spotting the glare radiating off the lenses of the Babushka Lady's (Francine Burrows) opera binoculars; and (18) via a tip provided by key assassination witness and D-day participant, Charles Brehm, figuring out how Oswald used the rifle's full sling to score a rapid-fire hit with the so-called lost bullet exactly one second after Z313.

Introduction and Summary

Official investigations and their findings in brief

According to the findings of six government investigations conducted in the aftermath of the assassination, 24-year-old Lee Harvey Oswald, ex-Marine, communist defector, and self-described radical-Marxist idealist did all the shooting that day taking advantage of a sniper's lair his fellow workers had inadvertently constructed on the sixth floor, southeast corner of the TSBD during the course of laying new floor on the other side of the sixth floor. He allegedly fired three shots with an Italian-made World War II-vintage rifle mounted with a four-power scope.

This tally includes the Secret Service's (SS) December 1963 report although it does not include a formal evaluation of the evidence in the case. The Secret Service's report simply states that the first shot rang out after the limo had traveled about 200 feet west on Elm, and provides the testimony of the witnessing agents. The other six investigations were conducted by: the FBI in 1963; the Warren Commission (WC) in 1964; the Clark Panel in 1968; the Rockefeller Commission in 1975, and the House Select Committee on Assassinations (HSCA) in 1978. The Assassination Records Review Board (ARRB) in 1994-98 compiled and declassified most of the evidence collected during the Federal investigations and took additional depositions relating to the medical evidence. The Dallas Police Department started an investigation in 1963 but was asked to stop by the FBI. The reports of these investigations were issued between December 1963 and September 1998.

The FBI, WC, and HSCA all concluded that the last of the three shots struck the president in the head. The FBI and Secret Service concluded the first shot struck the president causing his back and neck wounds. The FBI concluded the second shot entered the governor's back causing all his wounds but could not account for the bullet that caused the president's wounds. The WC concluded the same bullet caused the president's back and neck wounds and all the governor's wounds (right side, chest, wrist, and thigh) with the implied qualification that a fragment from the head shot could have caused Connally's wrist wound. The WC further concluded it was most likely the second shot that missed without committing to it. The HSCA agreed with the WC on the "single-bullet theory" but firmly concluded the first shot missed without committing to when and that the second was fired at about Z190. All the investigators except the FBI had trouble reconciling the testimony of those in the presidential entourage with a missed first shot. Governor Connally and his wife Nellie, in particular, were adamant that there was no missed shot. They insisted they knew better than the WC and HSCA investigators. My findings show the Connallys were right.

The HSCA tentatively concluded there was a missed third shot fired from behind the perimeter fence running along the northern end of the plaza (grassy knoll area) with the shots heard in the limo at Z166, Z196, Z296 and Z312. This dubious conclusion, however, was subject to confirmation of the results of a study conducted by acoustics experts toward the very end of the proceedings. The experts had been retained to examine a dictabelt obtained from the Dallas Police Department archives, which included the Department's radio communications during the assassination. Underlying the communications were 5-1/2 minutes of feed from a stuck-open microphone on a police motorcycle originally thought to be in Dealey Plaza when the shots rang out. The acoustics experts identified four sharp cracking noises on the belt as rifle-shot noise recorded on Houston Street. Despite assurance from the experts that their conclusions were statistically proven, it was subsequently determined that the motorcycle with the open microphone was not on Houston Street in Dealey Plaza after all and that the microphone got stuck at a point shortly after the assassination.

The Kennedy family had not allowed the WC to review the autopsy records leading to allegations of cover-up. This led to the limited reopening of the investigations in 1968 and 1975. In 1968, then Attorney General Ramsey Clark appointed a panel composed of four renowned medical experts to review the autopsy report, photos and X-rays. The panel reportedly found everything in order but came to the astonishing conclusion that the autopsy surgeons had misplaced the location of the inshoot wound to the back of the president's head and overlooked evidence of a conspicuous exit wound in the forehead. Medical experts retained by the Rockefeller Commission in 1975 and the HSCA in 1978 agreed with the collective medical experts over the protests of the maligned autopsy surgeons. The experts found alleged evidence in the autopsy X-rays and/or photos of an inshoot wound in the cowlick area rather than in the occipital bone as well as the lower quarter of a conspicuous 1-inch-diameter exit hole a few inches above the right eye.

Using the 486 frames of Abraham Zapruder's 26.5-second home movie of the assassination as a reference point in time, those who currently support the official government position that Lee Harvey Oswald did all the shooting from the Texas School Book Depository Building (TSBD) hold as follows: (1) while the presidential limo was heading west on Elm Street and was about 130 feet [sic] due south of Oswald's sixth-floor southeast-corner-window sniper's nest, he fired a first shot at Zapruder frame # 152 (Z152) that missed the limo and vanished without a trace; (2) with the president further down Elm and about 190 to 200 feet [sic] from his location, Oswald fired a second shot (magic bullet) at about Z220 that passed through the base of the president's neck and then went on to cause all five of the governor's wounds; (3) with the president about 274 feet [sic] from his location and opposite Zapruder on the grassy knoll, Oswald fired a final shot at about Z310 that hit the back of the president's head in the cowlick area and exited about 4 inches above his right temple making his head recoil to the rear. Given Zapruder's recording speed of 18.3 frames per second, this alleged shooting sequence occurred over an interval of about 9 seconds with slightly less time between the first and second shots than the second and third.

Along with the deluge of conspiracy related literature, film, and web material that has been published since the assassination, there are relatively few who have published books supporting the government's case against Oswald. Gerald Posner's 1994 *Case Closed* and Larry Sturdivan's 2005 *The JFK Myths* cover all the lone-gunman arguments and defend the government's single bullet theory and lone-gunman shooting scenario. So does the Dale Myers web site, "The JFK Files"; the John McAdams web site, "The Kennedy Assassination Home Page"; and the David Von Pein web site: "The Assassination of President Kennedy: A Lone-Gunman's View Point." All three web sites include many articles and research materials. Vincent Bugliosi's massive 2007 *Reclaiming History* summarizes and rebuts the prevalent conspiracy theories.

Something is wrong

Notwithstanding the impressive list of experts involved in the collective investigations and the efforts of the supporters of the government's case, the American public has been skeptical from the time the WC's report was issued in September 1964 and remains so. Theories of multiple shooters, conspiracy, and cover-up that have been floated since 1964 still abound.

Why?

Simply put, there is a great deal of credible evidence as to exactly what happened as the three shots rang out and not one of the official government investigations has been able to satisfactorily piece it all together and make it fit. How could so many key eyewitnesses including those in the presidential entourage be so far off in recalling the timing and effects of the shots they heard? The situation was made worse by the disparate findings of the official follow-up investigations. How could the autopsy doctors have been so far off in locating the head wounds? Something is wrong.

Introduction and Summary

Overall findings and some words about the realities of subtle bias in selecting and presenting evidence in a judicial setting

Examining the huge body of evidence in this case from the perspective of a neutral court consultant, I found massive photographic/scientific/visual proof that led me to the inescapable conclusion that Lee Harvey Oswald assassinated President Kennedy from his place of employment in Dealey Plaza and acted alone. I found no evidence of any conspiracy or cover up. The findings of my neutral reevaluation of the evidence, however, differ to a substantial extent with all versions of the U.S. Justice Department's official findings.

In examining the evidence, I found that the experts the government retained to prove the case against Oswald made so many accidental mistakes and oversights that they ended up inadvertently creating an extensive body of what I will call mythical evidence. They built a case around a non-existent missed shot and its non-existent "lost bullet," the wrong minimum firing time for Oswald's rifle, misinterpreted autopsy photos and X-rays, severely flawed trajectory analyses, wandering wound locations, improperly scaled maps, and a so-called "magic bullet" defying the laws of geometry.

I found in the government reports summarizing the investigation findings what I will refer to as subtle bias in the selection of evidence similar to what I typically find in expert reports representing antagonists in litigation. For example, creating the outward appearance of a cover-up or a rush to judgment, evidence that did not fit the flawed "single bullet theory" or the flawed lone-gunman shooting scenario was cast aside including the testimony of key eyewitnesses and key film images. Due to a flawed expert opinion on minimum firing time, the Warren Commissions experts tossed aside any and all evidence of a shot if it was inside of 2.3 seconds of the Z313 cranial eruption. As I already touched on, there is a lot of compelling evidence that falls into this category.

I found in the government reports summarizing the investigation findings what I will refer to as subtle bias slanting in the presentation of ambiguous evidence similar to what I typically find in expert reports representing antagonists in litigation. For example, to make a convincing argument that the wounds to the governor's right forearm and the bottom of his wrist were caused by the same bullet that caused the wounds to the governor's torso and left thigh, the geometry must work. In their efforts to get the geometry to work, I found HSCA experts exhibiting subtle single-bullet-theory bias by interpreting the evidence in such a way as to locate the president's outshoot wound in the neck a little too far to the left, the governor's inshoot wound to his right shoulder a little too low and too far left, and the outshoot wound to his chest about 1.5 inches too far right. They also exhibited bias by interpreting the sightline evidence in such a way as to position Connally's right shoulder a tad bit too far inboard in the limo. In conducting a trajectory analysis, they used a slightly altered topo survey map that was scaled to reduce the right-to-left angle at which the magic bullet arrived in the limo.

In conjunction with these observations on subtle bias, I need to emphasize that I found no evidence of any wrong doing by any government committee or individual investigator or anything even close. The fact that the single bullet theory has always been earnestly defended and endorsed by highly intelligent and qualified private individuals with no vested interest in proving the government right demonstrates there was no wrong-doing in its development. This also demonstrates how difficult it can be to recognize the subtle slanting of evidence.

The government investigators were obviously convinced for good reason that Oswald assassinated President Kennedy. Accordingly, in carrying out their respective duties, they did the best job they could under tight deadlines to build a convincing case against him. Given the nature of litigation, they are expected to select the evidence that best suits their arguments and spin any ambiguous evidence in the direction of Oswald's guilt so long as the selectivity and spinning is defensible. In this particular situation, however, the subtle bias exhibited in selecting and evaluating the evidence, though defensible and well within reason, explains where the investigations into shot timing and sequence went astray.

On the other side of the coin, as far as I can tell, any and all arguments critics have raised that profess that Oswald was innocent or framed or had an accomplice are highly dubious given the massive credible evidence of his guilt and his lack of opportunity to conspire. This is not to say that there are no reasonable arguments to be raised for conspiracy and cover-up, especially given the conflicting and dubious findings of the government's various investigative reports. Had he lived, Oswald would have received the rigorous defense to which he was entitled.

My detailed investigation findings in brief

In this book, via "visual shot identifiers, I am providing hard scientific/photographic proof that three rifle shots were fired that day in Dallas within a period of 6 seconds; that they all came from Oswald's TSBD sniper's nest; that all three hit the president, the last two in the head; and that the first two also hit the governor. I am providing hard scientific/photographic proof that the shots were fired in a bang . . . . . bang/bang sequence exactly when Zapruder recorded mid frames Z221, Z310 and Z328, plus or minus a Z frame (0.055 second). I hereafter refer to them as the Z221, Z310 and Z328 shots.

I am demonstrating that the testimony of the key ear/eyewitnesses provides overwhelming support for this alternative-shooting scenario. I am pointing at rifle test-firing results showing that Oswald could have fired the last two of the three shots in 1 second, easily hitting his target with carefully aimed first and second shots fired 5 seconds apart and scoring a lucky hit with a rapid-fire third solely because he simply maintained his second-shot aim taking advantage of the rifle's sling and stacked boxes of books for arm support.

I am providing concrete ballistics evidence confirming the final shot fired at Z328 deflected slightly upwards in passing through the top of the president's head and hit curbs twice before striking the triple underpass concrete abutment separating Main Street and Commerce Street where the slug remains lodged in the cement, possibly in pieces, about 17 feet above the west-bound lane of Main Street.

On top of using "visual shot identifiers" in the collective motion pictures taken during the shooting to arrive at the above conclusions, I was able to decipher two autopsy photos of the back of the president's head and the X-rays to the extent needed to prove that there are indeed two inshoot wounds to the president's head. The Z313 inshoot is located just where the Warren Commission concluded it was based on the official autopsy report and its face-sheet. The Z330 inshoot is located slightly above where the Clark Panel, the Rockefeller Commission medical panel and the HSCA forensic panel identified an inshoot wound.

In providing the correct interpretation of autopsy views 6 and 7 for the first time ever, I am providing further scientific proof that the bullet that entered halfway up the back of the president's head at Z313 was fired from the TSBD sniper's nest. The proof lies in the fact that the bullet created a 6.5 mm wide, by 15 mm long gash through the thick layers of tissue comprising the scalp. The orientation of the gash relative to the position of the president's head at Z312 reveals the direction and angle from which the bullet arrived.

I have identified the precise location of the two entrance and exit defects in the lateral and anterior/posterior X-rays and fully explained the so-called "6.5-mm fragment." Using an overlooked/misunderstood photograph of the fragment taken upon its receipt at the FBI crime lab, I have identified it as the tip of the bullet's nose with an actual diameter of about 5.3 mm.

Introduction and Summary

I am demonstrating that the evidence shows without any reasonable doubt, that it was the bullet exiting the president's head at Z313 that caused the wounds to the top and bottom of the governor's right forearm and wrist. For example, I conducted a vertical trajectory analysis based on revised head wound locations that confirms that the bullet entering the president's head at Z313 deflected downward 7 degrees and struck the top of governor's right forearm. I conducted a lateral trajectory analysis for the Z221 shot and found no evidence of any defection to the right as the bullet passed through the base of the president's neck and the right side of the governor's chest. I am providing photographic evidence that the governor's right wrist jolted at least an inch forward and away from him between Z312 and Z314 and that his shirt cuff quickly became a bloody mess. The Warren Commission's single bullet theory is partly wrong.

I am providing photographic evidence that the president's head jolted down and forward about 3 inches at Z330/Z331 amidst a second lower-trajectory cranial eruption that showered the Connallys with brain matter exactly as the vindicated Nellie Connally steadfastly testified. The Muchmore and Nix assassination-sequence images serve to confirm this jolt and second cranial eruption.

In preparing this book, I was able to accurately synchronize to a single Zapruder frame all seven motion-picture sequences that were taken in Dealey Plaza while the presidential limo was under fire. In so doing I was able to provide what I contend is the most comprehensive and precise analysis of the shooting sequence ever made.

The Zapruder film images show Jackie Kennedy reacting in similar fashion to the loud cracks of the bullets that entered the limo at Z313 and Z330. In both instances, she jerked her right forearm upward and to the rear commencing three Z frames after the bullet arrived. The proof that Ms. Kennedy's spontaneous arm movements caused the president's head to snap back commencing Z316 is that we see her right forearm flipping up behind the president's head the moment it lost contact with the top of his left shoulder. The Nix film images support this conclusion. If the whiplash-type head movement was caused by any other force, Ms. Kennedy's right hand would have either dropped down onto her lap commencing Z316, or stayed put.

The Zapruder film images show Nellie Connally being showered with brain matter between Z331 and Z337 yielding photographic proof of why she felt the impact and why she thought the president was hit in the head by just the Z328 final shot and her husband by just the Z310 second shot. Frames Z320 to Z330 reveal her husband slammed his head into a metal bar atop the front seatback at Z324 and was unconscious when the final shot was fired consistent with and explaining his sworn WC testimony.

Extracting and piecing together the evidence showing exactly what happened

We start by appropriately focusing minute attention on the all-important evidence contained in the six key motion-picture sequences that were taken within the confines of Dealey Plaza as the three shots rang out. In particular, we examine critical evidence as to shot source and sequence that has lain dormant for five decades in the images of motion-picture sequences taken by Abraham Zapruder, Dave Wiegman, Elsie Dorman, Marie Muchmore, Orville Nix, and Charles Bronson. The ability to formulate definitive conclusions on the source and sequence of the shots relies to some extent on the precise synchronization of the images that these six filmmakers recorded, something that has never been accurately done for the overlooked Wiegman and Dorman film sequences. My July 2016 finding that *NBC*'s Dave Wiegman was filming the spectators right below the sniper's nest at 32 frames per second as the final two shots rang out proves the validity of using visual shot identifiers to time the shots to the nearest tenth of a second.

Chapters 1 through 8 cover the above film sequences and camera jiggling. Chapters 9 through 12 explain how investigations on minimum-firing time for Oswald's rifle and key ear/eyewitness testimony on the source and sequence of the shots provides overwhelming support for the conclusions drawn from the motion-picture evidence and fully explains the perplexing testimony of the Connallys. Chapter 13 unravels the concrete ballistics evidence that confirms that the Z328 final shot fired from the TSBD sniper's nest passed through the president's head and exited the limo at Z330. Chapter 14 covers the disputed wound locations also with an eye toward confirming the shooter's location. In the final chapter, I explain and defend my conclusion that Oswald acted alone and present visual evidence as to why he did it. I end the book with some conclusions and recommendations for consideration by the U.S. Department of Justice.

Summary of motion-picture evidence as to the sequence and effects of the three shots (Chapters 2 through 7)

I started off my neutral evaluation by conducting a careful analysis of the extensive motion-picture evidence in the case commencing with the Zapruder film. I took advantage of the fact that in 2003 *Discovery Channel* had broadcast a documentary and published a DVD titled "Death in Dealey Plaza" which included the best copies available of all the assassination films of interest except the Zapruder film. I used the four photo-enhanced digital versions of the Zapruder film on a DVD published in 1998 by *MPI Media Group* under the title "Image of an Assassination" as well as the complete set of photos of individual frames published on-line by assassination researcher John Costella.

Visual shot identifiers in general - Given the redundant motion-picture evidence in the case, and particularly the Zapruder film, I am astounded that government experts and all the other independent researchers failed to realize for all these years, the strength of the involuntary auditory reflex reaction to shot noise in establishing shot timing, sequence and source. The most common visible reactions to shot noise are evidenced in subtle to overt head turns, flinches or arm jerks. Due to the laws of nature/biological evolution, every time a shot was fired at the president, every single person in Zapruder's camera view as well as Zapruder himself would have exhibited a spontaneous involuntary flinch, head turn or arm jerk within 2.5 Z frames plus or minus a frame of the shot noise reaching their ears, no more, no less.

The same goes for the conspicuous visual jolts that occur when a bullet makes impact with the human body and transfers at least part of its momentum to the area of impact. This motion commences in the very same frame the bullet makes contact. Likewise for the cranial eruptions that occur when a bullet enters the head and causes blood and/or brain matter to jettison out the exit wound at the very frame of impact.

Finally, the same also applies for the impacts of high pressure shock waves (N-waves) on the hand-held cameras as vindicated Nobel Prize winning physicist Luis Alvarez first asserted to deaf ears.

The digitized and photo-enhanced Zapruder film images confirm the bang . . . . . bang/bang three-shot assassination sequence that the vast majority of the key ear/eyewitnesses described. These spontaneous physical reactions can be easily observed with the naked eye using frame-labeled versions of the film provided in the DVD "Image of an Assassination" (MPI Media Group 1998). Some of the same telltale movements and/or others can be verified in the other five film sequences that were taken when the shots rang out once their recording speeds are established and accurate correlations/synchronizations are made to the Zapruder film timeline.

Signature jolts and cranial eruptions due to transfer of a bullet's momentum - First and foremost, Zapruder's film images clearly indicate that whenever a bullet struck the president or governor from the rear,

Introduction and Summary

it produced a signature jolt as the bullet transferred a portion of its momentum to the stricken area. The jolts occur in just the Z frame of impact and the next frame thereafter and are identifiable in the following frames: Z223/Z224 wherein the governor's right shoulder dips; Z313/Z314 wherein the president's head jolts forward and downward about an inch or two amidst a conspicuous vertical cranial explosion, and the governor's right wrist jolts forward and to the right at least an inch; and Z330/Z331 wherein the president's head jolts forward approximately 3 inches amidst a second less-conspicuous, lower-trajectory cranial eruption that visibly disrupted the scalp of the cowlick area. The jolts for the second and third shots are confirmed by Muchmore and Nix film images both of which show the movement and eruption commencing at the equivalent of Z330/331. The initial forward and rearward jettisons of brain matter from the cowlick area at Z330/331 are easiest to see in the Nix film when the dark grainy images are photo enhanced to increase brightness and contrast. The subsequent fallout inside the limo from Z332 to Z337 is easiest to see in the Muchmore and Zapruder film images. The Zapruder and Nix film images collectively show Ms. Connally being showered with brain matter from Z331 to Z337 with the initial impact knocking her head downward and forward between Z330 and Z331 consistent with her testimony that she felt the impact. All three show brain matter landing on the lid of the trunk from Z332 to Z337. The Muchmore and Nix film images respectively show fallout reaching Motorcycle Officer Bobby Hargis and Agent Clint Hill from about Z335 to Z338 consistent with their testimony that they felt the impact. The Zapruder and Nix film images show Ms. Kennedy's upper body driven backward at Z330-31 as a result of the president's head slamming into her right shoulder. Because it was near vertical and just a few feet high, the Z313 cranial eruption of brain matter did not appear to create significant fallout outside of the rear-seat area with most of it landing on the president by Z319.

Signature camera jolts and jiggles from ballistic shock-wave impacts - After doing some checking to make sure it was physically possible, I was able to confirm Professor Alvarez's finding that high/low pressure ballistic shock waves radiating outward and forward at a 56 degree angle from the nose of the speeding bullets at the speed of sound created enough turbulence to cause blurred images at Zapruder frames Z313/314 during the first cranial eruption. The confirmation lies in the fact one can see the exact same two-frame signature blurring at Z331/332 during the second cranial eruption. The last of the shock waves for the Z221 shot passed by Zapruder about 13 feet to his north. I similarly concluded that bullet shock waves that were propagated just 13 feet from the sniper's lair and 28 feet from Ms. Dorman caused signature blurring in Dorman frame D371/Z221 which is the same frame the shot was fired. According to my protractor, Bronson was struck by all three sets of bullet shock waves. Muchmore and Nix would have been too except for the fact they were sheltered by the north peristyle colonnade. Wiegman was located too far east. Dorman's camera was apparently too far back from the window opening during the last two shots.

Signature reflex and alarm reactions to the bullet shock-wave noise generated in the limo - The Zapruder film images are telling us that as the three bullets entered the limo at mid Z223, early Z313 and late Z330, the shock waves that arrived with them produced at least one and sometimes two signature patterns of reactions amongst all the limo occupants and security forces in view and all the spectators in view as well.

Reflex reactions - With respect to presidential limo occupants, these are spontaneous reactions commencing 2.5 Z frames (0.14 second) plus or minus a frame (0.055 second) after the bullet's arrival in the limo and include grimacing, flinching, cringing, and rapid head and arm movements. With respect to spectators or motorcade participants, these are spontaneous reactions commencing 2.5 Z frames plus or minus a frame after shot-related sound waves reach them, typically a dart of the head toward the perceived direction of the sound. With respect to Zapruder and the rest of the assassination filmmakers, this is a flinch or camera jerk that created signature blurring of the film images 2.5 frames plus or minus a frame after the noise reached their ears. The reactions are typically complete within 3 Z frames (0.15 seconds), but five frames after they commence, reflex reactions commonly morph into alarm reactions.

Alarm reactions - With respect to presidential limo occupants, these are conscious reactions commencing eight Z frames (0.4 second) plus or minus two frames after the bullet's arrival in the limo and include head turning, ducking, diving, recoiling, fleeing and stopping. With respect to spectators or motorcade participants, these are reactions commencing eight Z frames plus or minus two frames after the first shot-related sound waves reach them. Neurologically speaking, whenever an alarm reaction occurs in response to shot noise, it commences as a reflex reaction, but not all reflex reactions morph into alarm reactions.

Negative visual evidence of any more than three shots - There is nothing to point to anywhere else in the film where there are concurrent movements or reactions among multiple motorcade participants, spectators, and in particular presidential security that are in any way indicative of another shot entering or passing over the presidential limo. Despite five random 3-frame episodes of significant blurring within Zapruder frames Z133 to Z211 which covers the interval most lone-gunman advocates argue a first shot was fired off target, we can see enough of the presidential entourage and spectators to easily conclude there were no auditory reflex or alarm reactions to shot noise.

Summary of motion-picture evidence as to the source of the three shots (Chapter 8)

Camera jiggles in the Zapruder film - Due to the involuntary auditory reflex reaction, it is a certainty that there is discernible blurring on certain Zapruder film images resulting from flinches caused by the loud reports of the shots fired during the assassination. Given the above and assuming a sniper fired three shots from the TSBD sniper's nest using the rifle that was recovered at the scene, the jiggle pattern present on the Zapruder film images coupled with the photographic evidence of human-reflex reactions to the sounds or the effects of the shots supports the following conclusions relating to the three shots.

The Z221 Shot - A bullet hit the president and governor within frame Z223 that was fired from the TSBD sniper's nest at Z220.5 plus or minus a Z frame. Amidst overt human-reflex and alarm reactions to a shot, there is pronounced horizontally oriented blurring at Z227 or equivalent in the two films for which jiggle analysis was conducted (Zapruder and Dorman). With the limo about 180 feet away from the rifle, the shock wave would have entered the pergola to the east of Zapruder. At 260 feet away, Zapruder would have heard the boom of the muzzle blast within frame Z225, Wiegman at 125 feet within Z223 and Dorman at 36 feet within Z221.

The Z310 Shot - A bullet hit the president within frame Z313 that was fired from the TSBD sniper's nest at Z309.5 plus or minus a Z frame. Amidst overt human-reflex-and-alarm reactions to a shot, there is pronounced horizontally oriented blurring commencing at Z318 or equivalent in all six films for which jiggle analysis was conducted (Zapruder, Bronson, Nix, Muchmore, Wiegman, and Dorman). Assuming a 60-degree M wave and a speed of 1,125 feet, the shock wave would have reached Zapruder within frame Z313. At 260 feet away, Zapruder would have heard the boom of the muzzle blast within frame Z314 and Muchmore at 220 feet within Z313.

The Z328 Shot - A bullet hit the president within frame Z330 that was fired from the TSBD sniper's nest at Z327.5 plus or minus a Z frame. Amidst overt human-reflex-and-alarm reactions to a shot, there is pronounced horizontally oriented blurring at Z336 or equivalent in five of the six films for which jiggle analysis was conducted (Zapruder, Nix, Muchmore, Wiegman, and Dorman). Bronson took his finger off the shutter in reaction to the final shot. Assuming a 60-degree M wave and a speed of 1,125 feet, the shock wave would have reached Zapruder at frame Z331. At 260 feet away, Zapruder would have heard the boom of the muzzle blast within frame Z332 and Nix and Bronson at 345 feet within Z333.

The overlooked startle-reaction evidence in the other assassination sequences - Chapter 7 presents the results of a jiggle analysis I conducted using an entirely different and much more rigorous approach than prior researchers. Key to the analysis, I precisely synchronized Zapruder's 18.3 frames per second assassination footage with that of Muchmore (18.3), Nix (18.3), Bronson (12.0), Wiegman (32.0), and Dorman (16.0). This allowed me to not only provide definitive scientific proof of the shot timing and sequence but to mathematically confirm the location of the assassin.

For example, I was able to show that shot-induced signature blurring occurred predictably quicker in the assassination sequence recorded by Elsie Dorman who was located by far closest to the TSBD sniper's nest of all the motion-picture takers. She was perched behind a 4th floor TSBD window just 36 feet away from the sniper's nest and a similar distance from the passing supersonic bullets. Where Zapruder's shot-induced blurring occurred seven to eight frames after a shot, Ms. Dorman's blurred images predictably occurred in three Z-frame equivalents. As the final shot rang out at Z328, she captured six spectators lining the sidewalk on the south side of Elm simultaneously reacting to the sound commencing Z333 by turning their heads rapidly to the right. Two of them looked directly up toward the TSBD sniper's nest. Her signature blurring commenced at the equivalent of Z330 versus Zapruder's at Z336.

The observed signature blurring for all the filmmakers and all the shots occurred in the exact frame that was mathematically predicted based on the distance from the filmmaker to the TSBD sniper's nest, the speed of sound in air, and the assumed auditory reflex reaction latency period adjusted for their relative distances away from the assassin within the range of 0.11 to 0.19 second (2.0 to 3.5 Z frame equivalents).

Going beyond the camera jerks and jiggles, all the distinguishable shot-related reflex reactions that are captured on film among spectators and members of the presidential entourage are all also in sync with all shots coming from the TSBD sniper's nest applying the normal human-auditory reflex-reaction time of 0.14 to 0.16 seconds (Kosinsky, 2008). The further away the reacting person is from the sniper's nest, the more Z frames or Z-frame equivalents there are between the shot and the shot-induced reaction. For example, the key Dave Wiegman film images for the Z310 shot reveal that the spectators lining the street directly in front of the TSBD and almost directly under the bullet's path, commenced signature reflex reactions two Z-frame equivalents before Wiegman's conspicuous startle-induced blurring commences. Although Wiegman was only 115 to 125 feet away from the sniper's nest as the last two shots rang out, the sound not only reached these spectators faster, but precipitated a reflex reaction in the exact time mathematically predicted taking into account the speed of the bullets, the speed of sound in air and the distances involved.

Summary of evidence as to minimum-firing time (Chapter 9)

MC-rifle firing-test results - The collective test-firing data available via the web establishes that the minimum firing time for the weapon is about 2.3 seconds per shot using the telescopic sights to aim, about 1.2 second using the iron sights, and 0.8 second to rapid fire while simply maintaining aim. Thus, Oswald could indeed have operated the bolt and rapid-fired his third shot at the president during the 1 second interval between Z310 and Z328. My trajectory analysis for the Z328 shot, reveals the bullet had an excellent chance of hitting the president again at Z330 provided Oswald did not appreciably change the rifle's aim in operating the bolt and pulling the trigger other than an inadvertent small rise in the vertical plane. He had a sling and a couple of boxes stacked in front of him to help steady his aim.

Oswald's marksmanship and bolt-operating proficiency - According to military records, Oswald, an ex-Marine, was an average-to-below-average marksman by military standards and by all indications was out of practice, except with respect to operating the bolt. As such, for the three-shot scenario in question where there is an interval of 5 seconds between the first two shots as the president was moving away from the sniper's position at distances of 180 and 260 feet, Oswald would still be expected to have easily hit his target with the carefully-aimed Z221 shot and the carefully aimed Z310 shot. According to expert testimony, he only needed to be an average out-of-practice marksman.

Given the fact that it is known that he practiced operating the bolt of the rifle for hours on end within six months of the shooting and likely thereafter, Oswald would be expected to be proficient in getting shots off very quickly if he had a mind to. He used the rifle's full sling and stacked boxes of books for arm support to maintain his Z313 aim in firing the rapid-fire final shot just 1 second after Z313.

Why a rushed final shot? - The fact that Oswald got the final shot off as quickly as he did without changing his aim is telling me that he did so deliberately. It was done so fast with such a degree of precision that he had to have been practicing and refining this particular skill. I have concluded he was simply putting it on display.

Key corroborating evidence as to the source of the shots (Chapter 10)

A credible ear/eyewitness (Howard Brennan) watching the motorcade from the street corner opposite the sniper's nest apprised Dallas police within minutes of the shooting that the noise of the first or second shot had drawn his attention to the sniper's nest in time for him to look up and observe a young man fitting Oswald's description firing a rifle from the window as the final shot rang out. There is photographic evidence confirming this witness was located exactly where he said he was at the time of the assassination.

A credible TSBD employee (Norman) who was watching the president pass by from the fifth-floor window located directly below the sniper's nest immediately told two companions and later FBI investigators and Warren Commission members that as the president was being assassinated he heard a sniper operating a bolt-action rifle fire three shots from the window directly above him and even heard the ejected cartridges hitting the floor. During an on-location interview, WC investigators confirmed that he would have easily heard these noises due to open gaps in the floorboards. He further recalled sticking his head out the window and looking up toward the sniper's nest in reaction. His two credible companions (Williams and Jarman) confirmed his observations and reactions. There is photographic evidence that these three fifth-floor witnesses were positioned exactly where they said they were as the shots rang out. Several witnesses (Couch and Jackson), who reported seeing the barrel of a rifle protruding from the sniper's nest, also reported seeing Norman with his head out the window looking up just after the third shot was fired.

There was a credible witness (Elizabeth Cabell, the mayor's wife) who happened to be sitting in the rear seat of an open-topped convertible that was fast approaching the southeast corner of the TSBD building as the first shot rang out at Z221. She reportedly looked up and saw the barrel of a gun projecting from the sniper's nest in the president's direction and smelled gunpowder. There is photographic evidence that this witness was exactly where she said she was at the time of the first shot.

There were two other credible media witnesses (Couch and Jackson) that happened to be sitting in the rear seat of an open-topped convertible that was fast approaching the southeast corner of the TSBD building about 5 seconds later as the last two shots rang out. They both reportedly looked up and saw the barrel of a rifle projecting from the sniper's nest in the president's direction. There is photographic evidence that these two witnesses were exactly where they said they were at the time of the head shots.

Introduction and Summary

There was a motorcycle patrolman (Baker) riding off the right-rear fender of this same open-topped convertible. We have TV-news footage that shows him entering the TSBD on the run within 20 seconds of the last shot to support his testimony that he believed the three shots had emanated from the roof.

The police crime-lab investigators took a number of photos within an hour of the shooting that document the discovery of the assassin's lair, his rifle and three spent shells lying on the floor directly behind the sixth-floor southeast-corner window.

There is sufficient ballistics evidence to link the three spent shells and bullet and bullet fragments that were recovered by the FBI to the rifle found at the scene.

Summary of key witness testimony on where the president was located on Elm as the first shot rang out (Chapter 11)

Key stationary witnesses to the first shot - There are twenty-four key ear/eyewitnesses in this group including: ten lining the curb on the north side of Elm corresponding to where the president passed by between frames Z190 to Z215 of the Zapruder film; five along the curb on the north side of Elm from Z215 to Z250; five on either side of Elm from Z250 to Z310; and four well-positioned spectators to the south of Elm that were taking pictures about the time the first shot rang out.

For the twenty four in this group, all the testimony except in one case is consistent with the first shot striking the president at Z223 and is summarized as follows: (1) testimony supports hearing a first shot Z150 to Z200 = 0; (2) testimony supports hearing a first shot at Z200 to Z215 = 1 (Berry); (3) testimony supports hearing a first shot at Z215 to Z225 = 23; (4) testimony supports hearing a first shot after Z225 = 0; and (5) testimony supports seeing the president react as he did commencing Z226 to the first shot they heard, or they reported that they took a photo about the time they heard a first shot ring out with the photo showing the presidential limo was fast approaching or had just passed the Thornton Freeway sign = 15 of the 24.

Key motorcade witnesses to the first shot - There are seventeen of the presidential entourage in this group that provided unambiguous information as to either where the president was located as the first shot rang out or its effects: five in the presidential limo, eight of the ten in the presidential follow-up car and the four-man motorcycle escort.

For the seventeen in this group, all the testimony is consistent with the first shot striking the president at Z223 and is summarized as follows: (1) testimony supports hearing a first shot at about Z150 = 0; (2) testimony supports hearing a first shot at about Z221 or were aware it had struck the president from his reactions to it = 17; and (3) either reported seeing the president react to the first shot they heard which reaction we know occurred commencing Z226 in response to the Z221 shot or recalled turning their heads in response to the first shot which head turning we know occurred in response to the Z221 shot = 17 of the 17.

Summary of key witness testimony on where the president was located on Elm as the final two shots rang out (Chapter 12)

Nine key eyewitnesses to the Z330/331 cranial eruption - The following key witnesses were looking directly at the president's head from relatively close proximity at Z330/Z331 and individually and collectively testified in so many words that as the final shot rang out, they witnessed a cranial eruption when he was positioned as he appears at Zapruder frames Z330 to Z342 rather than Z313 through Z325: south-of-Elm *AP* photographer James Altgens; Motorcycle-Escort Officers Hargis and Chaney; Secret Service Agents George Hickey, Clint Hill, Paul Landis, William McIntyre and Emory Roberts; and Aide Kenneth O'Donnell.

Key stationary witnesses to the second and third shots - There are eighteen total in this group. Twelve are collectively considered key grassy knoll ear/eyewitnesses with locations corresponding to where the president passed by between frames Z250 to Z370 of the Zapruder film. This includes seven on the north side of Elm and five on the south. The preeminent most optimally located witnesses Brehm at Z280 south and Zapruder at Z313 north both timely reported they saw the president react to the Z221 first shot, saw his head split open at the time of the Z310 second, and then heard a final shot immediately thereafter (the Z328 shot). There are six other credible witnesses at locations further distant that had a clear view of the president at Z310 and timely testified to seeing the president hit by the Z310 shot.

For the eighteen in this stationary ear/eyewitness group, all the testimony is consistent or compatible with the Z221/310/328 shooting sequence and is summarized as follows: (1) testimony supports hearing just two shots while making it clear that the first shot wounded the president and recalled the final shot hit him in the head = 4 (Altgens, Decker, Bill Newman, Sitzman); (2) testimony supports hearing just two shots while making it clear that they were the final two shots and that they occurred when the president received his fatal head wounds - 1 (Burney); (3) testimony supports hearing two or three shots while making it clear that the first shot wounded the president and the last two were bunched near the cranial explosion = 2 (Mudd, Zapruder); (4) testimony supports hearing exactly three shots while making it clear that the first shot wounded the president and either the last two shots were bunched or they saw the president's head explode when they heard the second = 7 (Brehm, Betzner, J. Foster, Hudson, Summers, L. Willis, M. Willis); (5) testimony supports hearing exactly three shots while making it clear the first shot hit the president but with an impression that the second hit the governor and the last hit the president in the head = 1 (Gayle Newman); and (6) testimony supports hearing three shots or more with two ringing out very close to the time the president's head exploded at Z313 = 2 (Moorman and Hill).

Key motorcade witnesses to the second and third shots - The key motorcade witnesses are the nineteen in the presidential entourage which includes five in the presidential limo, ten in the presidential follow-up car and the four motorcycle escort police. For the nineteen in this motorcade ear/eyewitness group, all the testimony is consistent or compatible with the Z221/310/328 shooting sequence and is summarized as follows: (1) testimony supports hearing just two shots while making it clear that the first shot wounded the president and the final shot hit him in the head = 5 (Agent Hill, J. Kennedy, J. Connally, Hargis, and Landis); (2) testimony supports hearing exactly three shots while making it clear that the first shot wounded the president and the last two shots were bunched around the time of the cranial explosion = 10 (Greer, Kellerman, Martin, Chaney, Jackson, Kinney, Roberts, Ready, McIntyre, Hickey); (3) testimony supports hearing exactly three shots while making it clear the first shot hit the president but with an impression that the second hit the governor and the last hit the president in the head = 2 (N. Connally, Powers); (4) testimony supports hearing exactly three shots while making it clear that the first shot wounded the president but with an obvious false impression that the second shot was simultaneous with the first and that the third hit the president in the head = 1 (O'Donnell); and (5) testimony supports hearing exactly three shots while making it clear that the first shot rang out at about Z221 but with an obvious false impression that they "saw" the second hit the president in the back and that the last hit the president in the head = 1 (Agent Bennett). Kellerman, who was in the right front seat of the limo, was spot on in testifying that the last two bullets entered the limo as he was speaking into the radio mic which we can see him doing from about Z300 to Z330.

Introduction and Summary

Summary of findings on the fate of the Z328-third-shot: resolving the "lost bullet" mystery (Chapter 13)

If you plot the trajectory in the lateral plane of a bullet fired from the TSBD at Z328 that passed through the president's head at Z330 and exited the limo through the driver's window without deflection and then continued on about 90 feet to the south before striking ground, you will find a conspicuous gouge located on the top south corner of a storm-sewer catch basin that forms part of the curb on the south side of Elm. Continue on another 146 feet in the direction the tail end of the scar is pointing and you will arrive at the location where the FBI cut out a section of curb along the south side of Main Street, which had a small scar smeared with lead. View a certain high-resolution press photo taken by *Dallas Morning News* Photographer Tom Dillard within a minute of the assassination as he was approaching the triple underpass in leaving Dealey Plaza, and you can see what appears to be a fresh scar (bright spot) about 17 feet up along the right edge of the weathered gray concrete column separating Main and Commerce Streets. This is the column that slightly wounded south-of-Elm spectator James Tague was standing in front of. The base of the column is about 23 feet from the Main Street scar along the most likely line of deflection. See Figure 1.

For a concrete chip from a bullet strike at the white spot in Dillard's photo to have hit Tague in the left cheek, it had to have arrived at a 65-degree descending angle with Tague standing about 8 feet away from the base of the column. Tague was standing about 8 feet away from the base of the column and the scratch on his left check descends downward toward the front of his face at a 65-degree angle. I am pointing to what appears to be a bullet hole about 6 feet to the right of the scar on the column. It is about 17 feet above Main Street in the concrete span extending above it. Via Google Earth, there are other suspicious scars and gouges in the general area suggesting the bullet may have arrived in pieces.

Thus, we have concrete ballistics evidence of a Z328 final shot. Though government investigators and experts and most assassination researchers are aware of the gouge on the catch basin cover on the south curb of Elm and the scar on the south curb of Main, nobody ever realized their true significance. In the larger scar on the catch basin, we see a double impression of the intact bullet fired from Oswald's rifle: the first time with the nose pointing in the direction of the TSBD sniper's nest allowing for impact-related toppling, and the second time with the nose pointing in the direction of its departure. The gouge on the catch basin cover is telling us the bullet measured approximately 0.6 by 3 cm and arrived nose first and in intact condition.

Summary of findings on wound locations (Chapter 14)

In conducting their respective investigations of the wound locations, the teams of experts retained by the Clark Panel, Rockefeller Commission and HSCA were all operating without knowledge of key wound-location evidence - These experts were completely unaware that the Zapruder, Nix, and Muchmore assassination sequences collectively reveal that the president's head jumps 3 inches downward and forward at Z330/Z331 in the midst of a substantial cranial eruption that was seen by nine eyewitnesses. Were they provided this critical information, they would surely have come to the same conclusions I have reached on the head-wound locations.

The president's Z223 wound locations to the base of the neck - The entrance point is as described by the HSCA forensic panel. It is 1.8 inches right of the midline of the back just above the transverse process of the seventh cervical vertebra. The exit point is as described by the Parkland doctors and depicted in autopsy view 5. It involves the right wall of the trachea and is located about a quarter-inch to the right of the midline of the neck just below the Adam's Apple. The HSCA report erroneously shows the wound as being a quarter-inch to the left of the midline.

The governor's Z223 wound locations to his right torso and left thigh - These wound locations are as described by Connally himself during his April 21, 1964, WC testimony. His surgeon Doctor Shaw provided a clinical description of the bullet's path through the chest during his April 21, 1964, testimony to the WC that primarily describes the damage the bullet did to the fifth rib and lung when it entered the right side of the chest. During his testimony, the governor removed his shirt to allow the WC members to observe the entrance and exit locations as Shaw pointed to them. The entrance was at the base of the rear inner side of the right shoulder about 4.75 inches below the line of the shoulders. It was about 8 inches to the right of the midline of the back and about a half-inch inside and a half-inch above the apex of the crease of the armpit (7HSCA143). It was about 3 inches from the side of the right arm when held tight against the side of the body assuming a total shoulder width of 11 inches. The exit point was about an inch below and about 1.5 inches inside of the right nipple and about 3.5 inches from the midline of the chest.

In attempting to defend the single bullet theory, government experts took great liberties in placing the governor's wounds on illustrations of his body. For example in arguing a non-existent bullet exit location directly below the governor's right nipple, government experts and their supporters have been pointing to the locations of the holes in the front side of the governor's suit jacket and dress shirt rather than the medical record.

The president's Z313 head-wound locations - The Z313 inshoot is as depicted in the autopsy face-sheet, except that the direction of the slanting is reversed. It is in the right occipital bone, 1.1 inches from the midline, 1.4 inches above the EOP and 5.5 inches below the vertex. The Z313 outshoot is as depicted and described in the HSCA report. It is about 4 inches above the right temple in parietal bone just inside its margin with frontal bone, 2.2 inches from the midline, and 1.5 inch below the vertex. In portions of the report, however, the HSCA experts claim the wound location is a few inches above the right eye in frontal bone near a conspicuous v-shaped notch. The Z313 inshoot is visible in autopsy views 6 and 7 and the AP and lateral X-rays. The outshoot cannot be seen in the autopsy photos and x-rays. Misunderstood autopsy view 2 shows the general area and does not depict a v-shaped notch in its vicinity. The HSCA inadvertently puts the Z313 inshoot wound 0.8 inches from the midline and 4 inches from the EOP.

The governor's Z313 wrist-wound locations - The inshoot and outshoot locations to the right forearm and wrist are as described by the Parkland doctors and depicted on their sketches. The inshoot was a transverse glancing wound on the inner top side of the right forearm starting about 2 inches above the main crease. The outshoot was for just a tiny fragment of the bullet and was on the bottom side of the wrist about a half-inch above and parallel to the main crease.

The president's Z330 head-wound locations - The Z330 inshoot was just above where inadvertently described by the HSCA forensic panel as the Z313 inshoot. It was along the rear margin of the greater scalp/skull defects in parietal bone, 0.8 inches from the midline, 4.3 inches above the EOP, and 1.5 inches below the vertex. As with the Z313 inshoot, the Z330 inshoot is visible in autopsy views 6 and 7. Using the lateral X-ray and autopsy view 7, I have tentatively identified the Z330 outshoot in parietal bone 0.4 inches from the midline, 0.3 inches below the vertex, and 2.4 inches forward of the Z330 inshoot. I conclude that both the inshoot and outshoot are visible in the lateral X-ray and that the inshoot is also visible in the AP X-ray. I conclude that autopsy view 7 has a bone fragment in view that was lifted off the cowlick area in reflecting the scalp that contains a semi-circular portion of the beveled exit defect along its forward margin.

Introduction and Summary

The single bullet theory is correct except with respect to the description of the locations of the wounds to the governor's torso and the notion that it deflected and struck the governor's right forearm and wrist - I found overwhelming evidence that a damaged bullet exiting about 4 inches above the president's right temple caused the glancing wound to the back of the governor's right forearm before ending up in the front seat with a mangled piece of the governor's flesh attached to it (CE-567). For example, the Zapruder film images show the governor's right wrist jumping at least an inch forward and away from him between Z312 and Z314.

The locations of the wounds to the base of the president's neck and the governor's chest and left thigh confirm that the Z221 shot came from the TSBD sniper's nest and did not appreciably deflect in the vertical or lateral planes - A simple trajectory analysis revealed that as of Z223 all of these wounds lay along the path of a shot fired from the TSBD sniper's nest at Z221 at a descending angle of 20.5 degrees and a right to left angle of 8 degrees. There was no significant vertical or lateral deflection and no possibility of the bullet striking the top of the governor's right forearm given the position his right shirt cuff is at as of Z222.

The locations of the president's head wounds and governor's forearm and wrist wounds confirm that the Z310 shot came from the TSBD sniper's nest - A simple two dimensional trajectory analysis revealed that as of Z312/Z313 all of the wounds lay along the path of a shot fired from the TSBD sniper's nest at Z310 at a right to left angle of about 6 degrees. The analysis further shows that the bullet started off at a descending angle of 15.6 degrees and then deflected downward an additional 7 degrees upon entering the president's head. After exiting the right side of the head at about a 23 degree descending angle, the somewhat damaged bullet struck the back of the governor's forearm and then deflected forward and upward and hit the chrome trim above the rearview mirror. The 7-degree downward deflection is based on the orientation of the Z313 inshoot and outshoot locations in the president's skull. With the president's head oriented as it appears at Z312, the 6.5 by 15 mm gash in the scalp where the bullet entered at the back of the head is aligned with the exit wound and the TSBD sniper's nest.

The locations of the president's head wounds and the location and orientation of the bullet strike on the catch-basin cover located at about Z400 on the south side of Elm confirm that the Z328-shot bullet came from the TSBD sniper's nest - A lateral trajectory analysis revealed that as of Z330 the head wounds and the gouge in the top of the catch basin lay along the path of a shot fired from the TSBD sniper's nest at Z328 at the exact same right to left angle as the Z310 shot. The trajectory lines are superimposed and show that the bullet exited the limo through the open driver's-side window or vent. A vertical trajectory analysis revealed the shot followed almost the same trajectory as the Z310 shot and in exiting the limo deflected upward in passing through the president's skull just barely enough to pass over the head of the hunched-down Nellie Connally.

The medical experts retained by three government commissions collectively fell victims to optical illusions in interpreting the autopsy photos referred to as view numbers 2, 6 and 7 and overlooked or misinterpreted the key anatomical features of view 7 - Autopsy views 6 and 7 clearly show the 6.5 mm by 15 mm Z313 inshoot wound in the rear of the president's head before and after the scalp was reflected. These two photos as well as the AP and lateral X-rays all serve to confirm that the Z313 inshoot wound in the president's head was in occipital bone, 1.1 inch to the right of the midline and 1.4 inches above the EOP. The experts were primarily relying on the X-rays to identify the Z313 inshoot wound location and would not have made this mistake if they were aware a final shot hit the president in the head at Z330 and visibly disrupted the cowlick area. They also misinterpreted autopsy view 2, a side view of the president's head, in identifying a non-existent v-shaped notch near a non-existent semi-circular portion of an exit defect in frontal bone.

The so-called 6.5 mm bullet fragment that is conspicuous in the AP X-rays but not the lateral, is from the nose of the Z310 bullet and was recovered during the autopsy just behind and a little above the right eye - This semi-circular fragment that was incorrectly measured at about 6.5 mm in diameter, left a separate track through the tissues of the right side of the brain that was substantially below the main bullet track. The Rydberg side-view drawing of the wounds to the president's head shows the fragment and the trail it left. The X-rays show that it struck the front of the skull just above the right eye and fractured the roof and floor of the spherical orbit bone as well as the right cheekbone.

The so-called 6.5-mm fragment was photographed by the FBI upon its receipt at the crime lab prior to any testing when it was still intact. I was able to establish via photo recreation that the image of the intact fragment in the FBI photo closely matches what is seen in the AP view assuming we are looking at the flip side with the right amount of rotation. From its shape and size (about 5.3 cm in diameter taking into account magnification), it is readily identifiable as a portion of the tip of bullet's nose.

Summary of findings on who did it and why (Chapter 15)

Given my findings on exactly what happened and applying all the proof that has been previously assembled that Oswald acted alone, I have concluded that there was no conspiracy or cover-up. The opportunity presented itself to Oswald by chance just days before the assassination. The evidence shows that Oswald drew up his very simple shooting and escape plan on Thursday, November 21, and carried it out on Friday, November 22, improvising as the day went along.

Oswald had clear-cut political motives. In March 1963, he purchased a high-powered rifle with a scope and a revolver for the express purpose of assassinating political figures. Acting completely on his own, he attempted to assassinate retired Major General Edwin Walker in April 1963 because he considered him a right-wing Fascist and a threat to would-be Marxist revolutionary leaders like himself. He barely missed his mark. Oswald left behind a Marxist manifesto and a set of photographs fully explaining his motives. He considered himself a working-class hero.

In his final interview, Oswald admitted that he was on one of the upper floors of the TSBD during the shooting finishing up some unspecified task. He admitted he was on his way down to the first floor from this unspecified upper floor when he was stopped for questioning by a Dallas police officer (Baker) who was heading upstairs to look for the assassin.

Summary tables

Tables 1 through 4 which follow summarize the signature jolts, cranial eruptions and reflex and alarm reactions that can be found in the six films that were recorded as three shots rang out. Except as indicated, the start of the reaction is considered accurate to plus or minus one Z frame (0.055 second) from mid frame for reflex reactions and two frames (0.11 second) for alarm reactions.

Tables 5 through 7 which follow summarize the reflex and alarm reactions that can be found in the Zapruder, Dorman and Wiegman films with the objective of scientifically identifying the assassin's location. The data provides hard scientific proof that the three shots were fired from the TSBD at Z220.5, Z309.5 and Z327.5 plus or minus a Z frame. Most of the human-reflex-reaction times in the fifth column of Tables 5, 6 and 7 are within the normal range of 0.14 to 0.16 second reported by Kosinski in 2008.

Introduction and Summary

Table 1
Signature two-frame jolts and cranial eruptions due to a bullet striking the president or governor or a bullet shock wave passing under and striking a camera at Mach 1 speed
1. Z221/D371: a bullet shock wave passed below and struck Ms. Dorman's camera as it was generating a loud cracking sound creating a single frame of blurred images (D film);
2. Z223/Z224: the governor's right shoulder was driven downward and forward to a discernible degree (Z film);
3. Z313: a bullet shock wave passed under and struck the left side of Zapruder's camera as it was generating a loud cracking sound creating blurred images in two frames (Z film);
4. Z313/314: the governor's right wrist jumped an inch forward and away from him (Z film);
5. Z313/314: the president's head was driven downward and forward about an inch amidst a conspicuous near vertical cranial eruption of blood and brain matter that rose up over the president's head a few feet and slightly forward (Z/M/N/B films). Because it was near vertical and not very high, the Z313 cranial eruption did not appear to create significant fallout of brain matter outside of the rear seat area with most of it landing on the president by Z319;
6. Z330/331: the president's head was driven downward and forward about 3 inches in the midst of head-and-shoulder level jettisons of brain matter with the sprays hitting Ms. Connally in the back of her head and driving it downward and forward between Z330 and Z331. Brain matter rained down within the limo and on the lid of the trunk from Z332 to Z337 (Z/M/N films) and engulfed Hargis from about Z335 to Z337 (M film) as well as Agent Hill (N film);
7. Z331: a bullet shock wave passed under and struck the left side of Zapruder's camera as it was generating a loud cracking sound creating blurred images in two frames (Z film).

Table 2
Observable first shot reflex and alarm reactions for the Zapruder and Dorman films
Z221/D371-shot reflex reactions: distinguishable blurred film images and spontaneous movements commencing 2.5 +/- 1 Z-frame equivalents after the sound reaches the person reacting
1. Z223/D373: startled filmmaker Elsie Dorman on the 4th floor of the TSBD began jerking her camera down and up creating four frames with blurred images (D film);
2. Z225: wounded President Kennedy and Governor Connally began grimacing (Z film);
3. Z226 startled President Kennedy began darting his head to the left and jerking his arms up (Z film);
4. Z226: startled Governor Connally began darting his head to the left and jerking his right arm up and commencing Z230 attempted to take a concerted look back over his left shoulder (Z film);
5. Z226: startled Jackie Kennedy commenced a quick glance to her left (Z film);

6. Z226: startled Agents Greer and Kellerman commenced quick glances to their right (Z film);

7. Z226: two south-of-Elm spectators that were looking at the president and clapping when he passed by them at about Z215 stopped clapping and began darting their heads toward the TSBD (Z film);

8. Z226: startled Nellie Connally began darting her head to the right and commencing Z230 took a concerted look back over her right shoulder toward the president (Z film);

9. Z226: startled Motorcycle-Officers Hargis and Martin began darting their heads slightly to the right and commencing Z230 took concerted looks to the right toward the president (Z film);

10. Z226: startled Agents Hill and McIntyre who were respectively looking forward/right and straight forward from the Queen Mary's left running board began stiffening and darting their heads left/right (Hill) and slightly right (McIntyre) and commencing Z230 Hill began taking a concerted look hard right (Z film);

11. Z227: startled grassy knoll filmmaker Zapruder jiggled his camera creating a single frame with blurred images (Z film).

Z221/D371-shot alarm reactions: deliberate movements or actions 7.5 +/- 2 Z-frame equivalents after the sound reaches the person reacting

1. Z227/D376: alarmed filmmaker Elsie Dorman took her finger off the shutter button (D film);

2. Z230: alarmed Motorcycle-Officer Chaney who disappeared from Zapruder's view at Z207 presumably began turning his head to the left in looking toward the president (the look toward the president was complete as of the Z253 Altgens photo);

3. Z230: alarmed Agent Ready on the Queen Mary's right running board; Agent Landis on the right running board, and Agent Hickey in the left rear seat who collectively disappeared from Zapruder's view at Z208 presumably began turning their heads to look back toward the TSBD (the head turns are complete as of the Altgens Z253 photo).

Introduction and Summary

Table 3
Observable second shot reflex and alarm reactions for the Zapruder, Dorman, Wiegman, Muchmore, Nix and Bronson films
Z310/D394/W073/M39/N020/B10-shot reflex reactions: distinguishable blurred film images and spontaneous movements commencing 2.5 +/- 1 Z-frame equivalents after the sound reaches the person reacting
1. Z313/W077: a group of over 20 startled spectators either standing on or near the sidewalk where it begins on the north side of Elm in front of the TSBD or lining the curb to their west collectively flinched, darting their heads to the left or right within three Z frame equivalents and one ducked to her left (W film);
2. Z313/D396: startled 4th-floor-TSBD-filmmaker Dorman jerked her camera creating two frames of heavily blurred images followed by five frames of slightly blurred images (D film);
3. Z315/D398: four startled south-of-Elm spectators standing in front of the reflecting pool began concurrently darting their heads to the right toward the sniper's nest and three others darted their heads to the left (D film);
4. Z315/W080: startled cameraman Dave Wiegman in the front seat of camera car 1 began abruptly stopping his pan to the left creating four frames of heavily blurred images and four frames of slightly blurred images (W film);
5. Z316: mortally wounded President Kennedy began jerking his right arm up in front of his chest as his head began snapping back in whiplash fashion due to Ms. Kennedy spontaneously shoving him away from her (Z film);
6. Z316: startled Jackie Kennedy began spontaneously shoving her husband away by extending both of her arms in the process of recoiling (Z film);
7. Z316: wounded Governor Connally started darting his head to the left and by Z321 was frantically lunging toward the front of the limo to get his head down (Z/M/N films);
8. Z316: startled Nellie Connally began leaning back/recoiling and by Z321 was ducking toward the front of the limo to get her head down (Z/M/N films);
9. Z316: startled Agent Greer behind the wheel of the presidential limo began darting his head to the left and by Z321 began ducking his head down toward the steering wheel (Z/M/N films);
10. Z316: startled Agent Kellerman in the right-front seat of the presidential limo began darting his head to the left and by Z321 began ducking it down toward the dash (Z/M/N films);
11. Z316/M45/N026: startled Motorcycle-Officers Martin, Chaney and Jackson commenced a collective left/right/left darting of their heads and Hargis stiffened and darted his head up and to the right (N film for all, M film for Martin, and Z and N films for Hargis);
12. Z316/M45: startled south-of-Elm spectator Mary Moorman Jean Hill began raising their right shoulders and rotating/recoiling slightly to the left (M film);
13. Z316/N26: startled south-of-Elm grass-infield-spectator Toni Foster a.k.a. the Running Woman who was trotting toward the limo began raising her right hand, turning to her left and leaning back (Z and N films);
14. Z316/M45: startled Agent Hill began sprinting toward the limo at full speed (M and B films);

15. Z316/N26: startled north-of-Elm spectators Bill and Gayle Newman began turning to their left and leaning back in recoiling (N film);

16. Z316/M45: startled grassy knoll spectators Red Shirt Man, Emmett Hudson and Flying Tackle Man who were standing on the pergola steps began darting their heads slightly to the left (M film);

17. Z317/M46: startled north-peristyle-filmmaker Muchmore jiggled her camera causing a single frame of blurred images (M film);

18. Z318: startled grassy knoll-filmmaker Zapruder jiggled his camera causing two frames of blurred images (Z film);

19. Z319/N29: startled south-of-Main-filmmakers Nix and Bronson jiggled their cameras creating single frames of blurred images (N and B films).

Z310/D394/W073/M39/N020/B10 shot alarm reactions: deliberate movements or actions commencing 7.5 +/- 2 Z-frame equivalents after the sound reaches the person reacting

1. Z318/W084: the alarmed female TSBD employee standing on the sidewalk on the north side of Elm in front of the TSBD who had ducked to her left began walking or running toward the TSBD (W film);

2. Z320/D402: alarmed 4th-floor-TSBD-filmmaker Dorman began filming spectator reactions on the south side of Elm rather than filming the motorcade (D film);

3. Z320/D402: a young girl in a blue dress began approaching one of the five spectators in front of the reflecting pool on the south side of Elm who had turned their heads presumably trying to attract his attention (D film);

4. Z320/D402: an alarmed woman in a blue dress standing in front of the reflecting pool on the south side of Elm began running to the west (D film);

5. Z320/W087: alarmed cameraman Dave Wiegman in the front seat of camera car 1 began reversing his panning direction as if trying to capture on film either the source of the noise or the crowd's reaction (W film);

6. Z321/N50: alarmed Jackie Kennedy began straightening up in her seat and inspecting the damage to her husband's head and began spontaneously flipping her right hand up behind her husband's head commencing Z324 when she lost contact with his left shoulder (Z and N films);

7. Z321/N031: alarmed north-of-Elm-spectator Bill Newman began turning to his left and crouching (N film);

8. Z316/M45: alarmed grassy knoll spectator Red Shirt Man began crouching and raising his arms and the nearby Flying Tackle Man began lifting his left foot (M film);

9. Z321/N31/B17: alarmed south-of-Elm grass-infield-spectator Toni Foster a.k.a. the Running Woman who was trotting toward the limo began abruptly stopping (Z/N/B films);

10. Z321/M50/N031: alarmed Motorcycle-Officers Hargis, Martin and Chaney began looking out to the right through Z325 and then commencing Z326 began darting their heads to the left and were looking directly at the president by Z330 with Hargis obstructing Martin's view (M and N films and Z for Hargis).

Introduction and Summary

Table 4
Observable Z328 third shot reflex and alarm reactions for the Zapruder, Dorman, Wiegman, Muchmore, Nix and Bronson films
Z328/D409/W098/M57/N038/B22-shot reflex reactions: distinguishable blurred film images and spontaneous movements commencing 2.5 +/- 1 Z-frame equivalents after the sound reaches the person reacting
1. Z330/D411: startled 4th-floor-TSBD-filmmaker Dorman jerked her camera creating two frames of heavily blurred images followed by three frames of slightly blurred images (D film);
2. Z330/W100: the entire line of about 20 spectators standing in view along the north side of Elm in front of the TSBD entrance collectively flinched, darting their heads to the left or right within three Z frame equivalents with two looking hard over their left shoulders and several jerking their arms (W film);
3. Z332/W103/04: startled cameraman Dave Wiegman in the front seat of camera car 1 jerked his camera up and down creating three frames of heavily blurred images followed by three frames of lightly blurred images in abruptly ending his rapid pan to the right (W film);
4. Z332/D413: six startled south-of-Elm spectators standing in front of the reflecting pool began concurrently darting their heads to the right with at least two of them looking up toward the TSBD sniper's nest (D film);
5. Z333: startled Jackie Kennedy began cringing and leaning right in recoiling and jerking her right forearm up behind the president's head (Z/N/B films);
6. Z333/M62/N43: startled Nellie Connally began darting her head to the right and leaning back as she was showered with brain matter and by Z338 was diving down toward the center of the limo (Z/M/N films);
7. Z333/M62/N43: startled Agent Greer behind the wheel of the presidential limo began leaning/turning/ducking slightly to his right and cringing (Z/M/N films);
8 Z333/M62: startled Agent Kellerman started turning/ducking his head to the left and by Z338 was diving down toward the center of the limo (Z and M films);
9. Z333/M62/N43: unconscious Governor Connally began dropping down left-shoulder first onto his wife's lap (Z/M/N films);
10. Z333/M62/N43: startled Motorcycle-Officer Hargis began darting his head left then right and flexing his wrists as he looked at the president (Z/M/N films);
11. Z333/M62/N43: startled Motorcycle-Officers Martin, Chaney and Jackson began darting their heads to the right (M and N films) and Martin and Jackson began flexing their left wrist (Z/N for Martin, N for Jackson);
12. Z333/M62: startled Agent McIntyre on the Queen Mary's left running board started ducking and turning his head to the right (in progress as of M65/Z236 of M film);
13. Z333/M62: startled Agent Sam Kinney behind the wheel of the Queen Mary who was already turned slightly to the right began darting his head further to the right (M/N films);
14. Z333/N43 startled Agent Ready on the Queen Mary's right running board started ducking and turning his head slightly to the left (N film);

15. Z333/N43: startled south-of Elm-picture-taker Richard Bothun began turning to his left and leaning back as part of a rubbery kneed recoil (Z and N films);

16. Z333/M62: startled south-of-Elm spectator Mary Moorman began darting her head to her right and Jean Hill began raising her shoulders, rotating slightly right and jerking her right arm up (M film);

17. Z333/N043: the startled Running Woman started turning to her right and leaning back/recoiling (N film);

18. Z333: a startled-unidentified-south-of-Elm grass-infield spectator who was trotting toward the presidential limo began dropping his arms and commencing Z339 began stopping dead in his tracks (Z film);

19. Z333/M62: startled grassy knoll spectators Red Shirt Man, Emmett Hudson and Flying Tackle Man began darting their heads to their left and Flying Tackle Man began running up the pergola steps (M film);

20. Z333/N43: startled north-of-Elm-spectator Bill Newman began turning to his left and ducking (N film).

21. Z334-37: startled filmmakers Muchmore and Zapruder jiggled their cameras creating a single frame of blurred images at Z334 and Z336 respectively, and Nix abruptly dipped his camera at Z337.

Z328/D409/W098/M57/N038/B22-shot alarm reactions: deliberate movements or actions commencing 7.5 +/- 2 Z-frame equivalents after the sound reaches the person reacting

1. Z337/W110: the spectator standing on the north side of Elm in front of the TSBD entrance that had looked hard over his left shoulder began to turn and run (W film);

2. Z337/W110: alarmed north-of-Elm spectator Roy Truly standing along the edge of the street in front of the TSBD entrance began turning his head to the right toward the sniper's nest (W film);

3. Z337/M66/B26: alarmed south of Elm filmmakers Muchmore and Bronson stopped filming (M and B films);

4. Z338/W112 alarmed cameraman Dave Wiegman in the front seat of camera car 1 began reversing his panning direction as if trying to capture on film either the source of the noise or the crowd's reaction (W film);

5. Z338/D419: an alarmed male spectator wearing a business suit and light-colored overcoat standing at the southwest corner of Houston and Elm began turning his head to the right and tilting it back and looking up toward the TSBD sniper's nest (D film);

6. 338/D419: an alarmed woman standing on the southwest corner of Houston and Elm began turning her head hard to the left and setting off on a run (in progress as of frame D424/Z345 of the D film);

7. Z339/N49: alarmed Jackie Kennedy began rising in her seat and climbing on the trunk (Z and N films);

8. Z339/N49: alarmed Motorcycle-Officer Margin began turning his head hard right and Hargis began stopping his cycle and turning his head hard right partly in response to being struck by brain matter (Z and N films).-Officers Chaney and Jackson began stopping their cycles and turning their heads back over their right shoulders (N film);

9. Z339/N49: alarmed Agent Ready on the Queen Mary's right running board commenced squatting down into a ready-to-jump position (N film);

10. Z339: alarmed south-of-Elm grass-infield-spectator Malcolm Summers started dropping to the ground (in progress as of Z345 of Z film).

Table 5

First shot jiggle analysis for the Zapruder and Dorman assassination sequences and the Bronson Z227 photo of the limo under fire confirms it was fired from the TSBD sniper's nest at Z221/D371 (muzzle blast noise in all cases except Bronson)

Filmmaker and the frame the shot was fired	Distance of filmmaker to rifle (feet)	Speed of sound (feet per second)	Sound travel time (seconds and frames)	Assumed reflex reaction time tolerance for range 0.11 to 0.19 sec (frames)	Predicted time from shot to blurred frame (frames)	Predicted blurred frame for shot fired at Z220.1 to Z221.0	Observed blurred frame # as recorded on film	Difference between estimated and actual reflex reaction time (frames)
Zapruder at Z220.5	260	1,125	260/1,125=0.23 = 4.2	2.5 to 3.5 (0.14-0.19 sec)	4.2+2.5 = 6.7	220.1+6.7 =226.8 = Z227	**Z227**	0
Dorman at W371/Z220.5	36	1,125	36/1,125=0.03 = 0.5	2.0 to 2.7 (0.11-0.15 sec)	0.5+2.2 = 2.7	220.5+2.7 = 223.2 = Z224/D373	**Z224**/D373	0
Bronson Z227 photo for Z220.5 shot	Bullet speed = 2000 feet/second; distance to president = 140 feet; distance from president to Bronson = 247 feet: [140/2,000=0.07], [247/1,125=0.22], [0.07+0.22=0.29] and [0.29x18.3=5.3]			Not applicable	5.3 = 6	220.5+6 = Z226.5=Z227	Z227	0

Conclusions: Dorman's signature blurring for the Z221 shot comes four Z frames (~0.2 second) before Zapruder's because she is the equivalent of four Z-frames (~0.2 second) closer to the sniper's nest taking into account the distances involved, the speed of the bullet, the speed of sound and the level of noise. The result of the analysis for the Bronson Z227 photo confirms that blurring was the result of shock waves passing under and striking the camera.

Table 6

Second shot jiggle analysis for the Zapruder, Dorman, Wiegman, Muchmore, Nix and Bronson assassination sequences confirm it was fired from the TSBD sniper's nest at Z310/W073/D394/M39/N20/B10 (muzzle blast noise in all cases except Bronson)

Filmmaker and the frame the shot was fired	Distance of filmmaker to rifle (feet)	Speed of sound (feet per second)	Sound travel time (seconds and frames)	Assumed reflex reaction time tolerance for range 0.11 to 0.19 sec (frames)	Predicted time from shot to blurred frame (frames)	Predicted blurred frame for shot fired mid frame Z310 = Z309.5	Observed blurred frame as recorded on film	Difference between estimated and actual reflex reaction time (frames)
Zapruder at Z309.5	260	1,125	260/1,125=0.23 = 4.2	2.7 to 3.5 (0.15-0.19 sec)	4.2+3.5 = 7.7	309.5+7.7 = Z317.2 = Z318	**Z318**	0
Wiegman at W073/Z309.5	125	1,125	125/1,125=0.11 = 2.0	2.5 to 2.7 (0.14-0.16 sec)	2+2.6 = 4.6	309.5+4.6 = 314.1 = Z315/W080	**Z315**/W080	0
Dorman at D394/Z309.5	36	1,125	36/1,125=0.03 = 0.5	2.0 to 2.7 (0.11-0.15 sec)	0.5+2.5 = 3	309.5+2.7 = 312.2 = Z313/D396	**Z313**/D396	0

Muchmore at M39/Z309.5	220	1,125	220/1,125=0.20 = 3.7	2.4 to 2.7 (0.14-0.16 sec)	3.7+3.0 = 6.7	309.5+7.2 = 316.2 = Z317/M47	**Z317**/M46	0
Nix at N20/Z309.5	340	1,125	340/1,125=0.3 = 5.5	2.7 to 3.5 (0.15-0.19 sec)	5.5+3.2 = 8.7	309.5+8.7 = 318.2 = Z319/N029	**Z319**/N029	0
Bronson at B10/Z309.5	Bullet speed = 2,000 feet/second; distance to president = 140 feet; distance from president to Bronson = 247 feet: [140/2,000=0.07], [247/1,125=0.22], [0.07+0.22=0.29] and [0.29x18.3=5.3]			2.7 to 3.5 (0.15-0.19 sec)	5.3+3.5 = 8.8	309.5+8.8 = 318.3 = Z319/B16	**Z319**/B16	0

Conclusions: Dorman's signature blurring for the Z310 shot comes five Z frames (~0.3 second) before Zapruder's and two (~0.1 second) before Wiegman's because she is the equivalent of five Z-frames (~0.3 second) closer to the TSBD sniper's nest than Zapruder and the equivalent of two Z frames (~0.1 second) closer than Wiegman taking into account the distances involved, the speed of the bullet, the speed of sound, and the level of noise. Similarly, Wiegman is the equivalent of three Z frames (0.16 second) closer to the sniper's nest than Zapruder. Assuming the reaction time was 2.0 to 3.5 Z-frame equivalents (0.11-0.19 second) as assumed above, the results confirm the bullet was fired at Z309.5 plus or minus a Z frame equivalent.

Table 7

Third shot jiggle analysis for the Zapruder, Dorman, Wiegman, Muchmore, and Nix assassination sequences confirms it was fired from the TSBD sniper's nest at Z328/W098/D409/M57/N038/B22 (muzzle blast noise in all cases)

Filmmaker and the frame the shot was fired	Distance of filmmaker to rifle (feet)	Speed of sound (feet per second)	Sound travel time (seconds and frames)	Assumed reflex reaction time tolerance for range 0.11 to 0.19 sec (frames)	Predicted time from shot to blurred frame (frames)	Predicted blurred frame for shot fired at mid frame Z328= Z327.5	Observed blurred frame as recorded on film	Difference between estimated and actual reflex reaction time (frames)
Zapruder at Z327.5	260	1,125	260/1,125=0.23 = 4.2	2.5 to 3.5 (0.15-0.19 sec)	4.2+3.4 = 7.6	327.4+7.6 = 335.1 = Z336	**Z336**	0
Wiegman at W098/Z327.5	115	1,125	115/1,125=0.10 = 1.8	2.5 to 2.7 (0.14-0.16 sec)	1.8+2.5 = 4.3	327.5+4.3 = 331.8 = Z332/W103-04	**Z332**/W103-04	0
Dorman at D409/Z327.5	36	1,125	36/1,125=0.03 = 0.5	2.0 to 2.7 (0.11-0.15 sec)	0.5+2.0 = 2.5	327.5+2.5= 330 = Z330/D411	**Z330**/D411	0
Muchmore at M57/Z327.5	220	1,125	220/1,125=0.19 = 3.5	2.5 to 2.7 (0.14-0.16 sec)	3.5+2.5 = 6.0	327.5+6.0 = 333.5 = Z334/M63	**Z334**/M63	0
Nix at N038/Z327.5	340	1,125	340/1,125=0.3 = 5.5	2.7 to 3.5 (0.15-0.19 sec)	5.5+3.2=8.7	327.5+8.7 = 336.2 Z337/N047	**Z337**/N047 (faint)	0

Conclusions: Dorman's signature blurring for the Z328 shot comes six Z frames (~0.3 second) before Zapruder's and two (~0.1 second) before Wiegman's because she is the equivalent of six Z-frames (~0.3 second) closer to the TSBD sniper's nest than Zapruder and the equivalent of two Z frames (~0.1 second) closer than Wiegman taking into account the distances involved, the speed of the bullet, the speed of sound, and the level of noise. Similarly, Wiegman is the equivalent of four Z frames (0.16 second) closer to the sniper's nest than Zapruder. Assuming the reaction time was 2.0 to 3.5 Z-frame equivalents (0.11-0.19 second) as assumed above, the results confirm the bullet was fired at Z327.5 plus or minus a Z frame equivalent.

Introduction and Summary

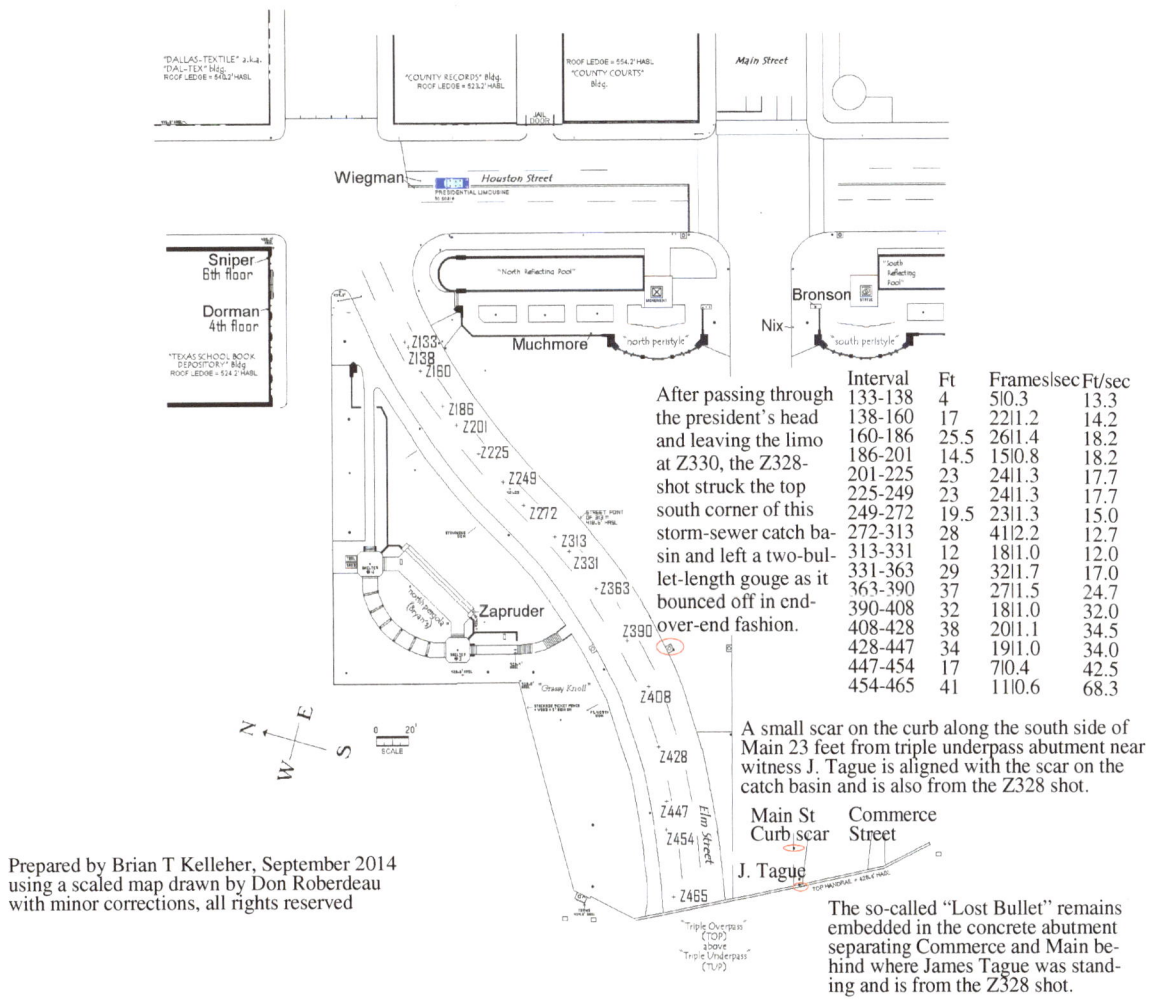

Interval	Ft	Frames|sec	Ft/sec
133-138	4	5|0.3	13.3
138-160	17	22|1.2	14.2
160-186	25.5	26|1.4	18.2
186-201	14.5	15|0.8	18.2
201-225	23	24|1.3	17.7
225-249	23	24|1.3	17.7
249-272	19.5	23|1.3	15.0
272-313	28	41|2.2	12.7
313-331	12	18|1.0	12.0
331-363	29	32|1.7	17.0
363-390	37	27|1.5	24.7
390-408	32	18|1.0	32.0
408-428	38	20|1.1	34.5
428-447	34	19|1.0	34.0
447-454	17	7|0.4	42.5
454-465	41	11|0.6	68.3

After passing through the president's head and leaving the limo at Z330, the Z328-shot struck the top south corner of this storm-sewer catch basin and left a two-bullet-length gouge as it bounced off in end-over-end fashion.

A small scar on the curb along the south side of Main 23 feet from triple underpass abutment near witness J. Tague is aligned with the scar on the catch basin and is also from the Z328 shot.

The so-called "Lost Bullet" remains embedded in the concrete abutment separating Commerce and Main behind where James Tague was standing and is from the Z328 shot.

Prepared by Brian T Kelleher, September 2014 using a scaled map drawn by Don Roberdeau with minor corrections, all rights reserved

Figure 1

Dealey Plaza scaled drawing: presidential limo's path on Elm showing the president's location and speed at key Z frames, the six key filmmakers Zapruder, Nix, Muchmore, Bronson, Dorman and Wiegman, and the points of impact for the missing Z328 bullet - The scaled base map that I used for this illustration was prepared by assassination researcher Don Roberdeau whose web site is found at droberdeau.blogspot.com. As far as I can tell, Roberdeau's is the most accurate scaled drawing that is currently available to assassination researchers. There are scaling problems with a widely used surveyor's drawing published by the HSCA. I revised and adapted the Roberdeau drawing for my purposes by converting to primarily black and white, deleting certain extraneous features and all Roberdeau commentary. I did my own sightline analyses for all Z-frame and filmmaker and witness locations. In addition to Z sightlines, I used Willis sightlines for Z133, Z138 and Z201; Croft for Z160; Betzner for Z186; and Nix for Z313, Z331, Z363 and Z390. I had to adjust the locations of certain landmarks that I used for sightlines as follow: added 1 foot to east and west walls of the TSBD; added some length to the north end of the Stemmons sign, moved the lamp post near the Newmans several feet to the east; moved the tree near the Thornton sign to the northwest; moved the traffic light pole on the NW corner of Houston and Elm to the south. I do not agree with Roberdeau on certain witness locations or certain Elm Street Z frame locations including Z133.

Figure 2
Dealey Plaza from the air October 1, 1967 - Charles Rotkin/CORBIS, via David Von Pein's blog site "The Kennedy Gallery."

Chapter 2

The Zapruder Assassination Sequence

In the following manner at approximately 2:30 p.m. Dallas time, broadcast live on local TV, the American public first learned of the 58-year-old Russian immigrant and self-made businessman and his extraordinary 26.5-second film of the assassination of their president. See Figure 4.

A gentleman just walked into our studio that I am meeting for the first time as well as you. This is WFAA-TV in Dallas, Texas. May I have your name, please, sir?

My name is Abraham Zapruder.

Zapruder?

Zapruder! And would you tell us your story, please sir?

Zapruder, yes sir.

As I got out about a half-hour early to get a good spot to shoot some pictures, and I finally spotted one of those concrete blocks near the park, near the underpass, and I got up there. There was another girl from my office [Marilyn Sitzman], she was behind me. And I was filming as the president was coming down [Elm] from Houston Street [after] making his turn. It was about halfway down there, I heard a shot, and he slumped to the side like this (indicating). Then I heard another shot, or two, I couldn't say whether it was one or two, and I saw his head practically open up (indicating), all blood and everything, and I kept on shooting. That's about all. I'm just sick. . . . I can't . . . . it was a terrible thing.

I think that pretty well expresses the entire feeling of the whole world. You have the film in your camera? Well . . .

Yes, I brought it to the studio.

We'll try to get that processed as soon as possible. Recording of live TV interview by Jay Watson WFAA TV, at about 2:30 p.m., 11/22/63, "The Story Behind the Story," Belo Interactive, 2003, DVD, track 14.

If one had known in advance that President Kennedy was going to be assassinated in front of Bryan's Pergola at the north end of Dealey Plaza while traveling west on Elm Street in an open-topped limo, and wanted to film the event to record it for posterity, they could not have chosen a better location than the one Zapruder inadvertently selected to make his home movie. His perch, located on a 4-foot-high concrete pedestal located at the west end of the pergola and at the crest of the soon to be infamous grassy knoll, was about 70 feet due north of the center of Elm. He was 240 feet east of the intersection of Houston and Elm and 170 feet from the point he began filming the presidential limo. The perch gave him an unobstructed elevated view of the president in the right-rear seat of his limo as it proceeded slowly down Elm toward his rendezvous with an assassin's bullets and ever closer to Zapruder's camera's eye. See Figure 3.

Zapruder, situated 260 feet from the TSBD sniper's nest including the vertical and lateral components of the distance, was about 105 feet away from the motorcade when the president was struck in the upper back and about 70 feet away when his head exploded.

Had Oswald lived to stand trial for his actions, Zapruder presumably would have been the first witness called by the prosecution. Similarly, his testimony would have set the stage for what follows in this book regarding both shot timing and effects. In this first chapter, we will examine the key evidence provided by Zapruder in his testimony and film images.

What follows is not a rehash of any other interpretation of the Zapruder film. As explained in the introduction, the reader will be looking at the film through the dispassionate eyes of a neutral court consultant whose task is to systematically examine scientific evidence and provide contentious parties and their experts an objective and unbiased opinion of what the evidence is showing. As we examine the images together, I will be pointing out quite a bit of subtle but powerful photographic evidence in the film that government experts and independent researchers alike have overlooked. Hopefully, the validity of this bold statement will become apparent to the reader as we go along.

Zapruder is considered one of the key stationary eyewitnesses to the assassination and more of his testimony is covered in Chapter 11 and 12.

Tables 8 through 11 and Figures 5 through 10 follow and relate to the ensuing discussions.

The camera and the filming speed

I provide here the complete text of Zapruder's December 1963 FBI interview including detailed information on his camera and film.

FBI interview, 12/4/63 - *Abraham Zapruder, 3909 Marquette Street, Dallas, TX advised that on November 22, 1963, he was standing in the park area north of Elm Street and just west of the intersection of Elm and Houston Streets. He had taken this position in order to take 8-mm movie film of the president and presidential motorcade as it passed by him. He stated he had with him a Bell and Howell 8-mm zoom-lens camera, which was either a 1962 or 1963 model. He advised he had loaded this camera previously with a 25-foot roll of 16-mm film, which in effect affords 50 feet of 8-mm film. He had shot the first 25 feet earlier and had reversed the roll and shot a few feet on November 22, 1963, at the park area of some girls [Hester and Sitzman] who work in his office, prior to the arrival of the presidential motorcade. He stated his camera was fully wound, was set manually on maximum zoom lens. The camera was set to take normal-speed movie film or 24 frames per second [actually 16 frames per second]. The control buttons for the zoom lens were not touched once he started taking photographs of the presidential motorcade.*

Zapruder stated that he first picked up the motorcade as it made the turn onto Elm Street from Houston Street. The motorcade then passed behind a street-directional sign and from that point until it disappeared from sight to his right, or the west, he was taking pictures of the president's car. He stated he started taking pictures prior to the first shot being fired and continued taking pictures until the motorcade disappeared to his right. Zapruder advised he could not recall but having heard only two shots, and, also stated that he knew from watching through his viewfinder that the president had been hit. He stated he took the exposed film immediately to the Jamieson Film Company on Bryant Street, Dallas, and stayed with the film through its entire processing. He had the original print and three copies made. The film was in color. The original is on 16-mm film and according to Mr. Zapruder is much clearer than those appearing on 8-mm film. He subsequently turned over two copies to the United States Secret Service and sold the original and one copy to Life Magazine. FBI interview in full, 12/4/63 (WR CD 7).

2: The Zapruder Assassination Sequence

The 8-mm camera Zapruder used to film the assassination was a top-of-the line Bell & Howell Director Series Model 414 with fully automatic exposure control and a zoom lens. He purchased it in May 1963. The camera featured a built-in electric eye, a spring-tension indicator, and three shutter-speed settings: "animation" (one frame at a time); "run" (nominal 16 frames per second; and "slow motion" (42 frames per second). The fully wound camera had a run time of 73 seconds. When he filmed the assassination, Zapruder had the camera set on "run" and maximum zoom.

The day of the assassination the camera was loaded with Kodachrome II Safety film that was well suited for outdoor use. The first 25 feet was already exposed.

Despite the fact that the camera was set to run at a nominal 16 frames per second, the FBI reported the camera was running at 18.3 frames per second when they tested it fully wound. On this basis, the Warren Commission (WC) and most researchers since have taken it as a given that the camera speed was 18.3 frames per second.

History has shown that the FBI's investigative work on the assassination, in general, is not to be trusted blindly especially with respect to the opinions of their experts. *CBS* had a highly qualified expert look at the issue of Zapruder's camera speed in the course of making their 1966 documentary "Should We Now Believe the Warren Report?" The expert, Charles Wycoff of Cambridge, Massachusetts, tested nine brand-new Bell & Howell cameras from the same production line as Zapruder's. By statistical analysis of the results, he concluded a fully wound camera would most likely run at 17 frames per second plus or minus two frames. There is more to it, however.

> ***CBS News*** *- But Mr. Wycoff found something far more interesting. Whatever the speed of the camera, its' optimal [fully wound] speed was likely to be greater than its speed under ordinary operating conditions. Wound to less than its full tension, permitted to accumulate dirt or scraps of film in its movement, the speed invariably fell . . . he concluded that the camera was in all likelihood running slower than its rated speed of 18.3 frames per second. . . . It is CBS News view that the film was probably passing through the camera at the rate of about 16.5 frames per second.* White, 1968, page 39.

As discussed in the ensuing chapter, in syncing the Zapruder assassination sequence with the uncut raw Wiegman film images that *NBC* broadcast the day of the assassination, I have confirmed that the Zapruder camera was indeed recording in real time at 18.3 frames per second. This is consistent with the fact that Zapruder reported that the camera was fully wound when he filmed the assassination and confirms that the FBI conducted sufficient testing to establish the average speed.

The film and camera timelines

Shortly following the assassination, Zapruder brought the film to the attention of the secret service at which point it was developed and first observed. Soon after, Zapruder sold it to *Life Magazine*, who published some of the images in print for the first time.

The saga of the Zapruder film is a story unto its own. It is currently in possession of the Sixth Floor Museum at Dealey Plaza.

First interview and testimony

Dismounting the pedestal on the west end of the pergola after the shooting, Zapruder and Sitzman entered and spent a few minutes in the concrete shelter behind them. They were quickly joined there by Zapruder's employee Beatrice Hester and her husband Charles who had been watching the procession from the east end of the pergola. Shortly thereafter, Zapruder walked back to the corner of Houston and Elm and stood in front of the Dal Tex Building anguishly crying out to no one in particular, "they killed him, they killed him." He soon encountered *Dallas Morning News* reporter Harry McCormick who had just been dropped off in front of the TSBD after departing the Trade Mart, where the president was supposed to have had lunch and given a speech. Zapruder, who had apparently attracted his attention with his cries, told McCormick that he had the shooting on film and needed to speak to the authorities. McCormick was well acquainted with Forrest Sorrels head of the local branch of the secret service and took off to find him. Zapruder went up to his offices. McCormick arrived with Sorrels at approximately 1:45 p.m.

In the meantime, *Dallas Times Herald* reporter Darwin Payne encountered Sitzman and Hester in the vicinity of the TSBD after arriving on foot from his newsroom six blocks away. During the course of interviewing them, he learned of Zapruder and his film and with their assistance managed to gain entrance to his office. Using Zapruder's phone, Payne transmitted his hand-written notes of his interviews with Sitzman and Zapruder to the newsroom within 20 to 30 minutes of the assassination. The notes were recorded by hand on what is called "tear sheets" that were preserved in newsroom archives. David Wrone provides a summary of these events citing Payne's 6th Floor Museum Oral History interview in 1993 and McCormick's account in his 2003 *The Zapruder Film, Reframing JFK's Assassination*, pp. 16-19.

As we start the evaluation, be aware that during this very first interview, Zapruder recalled three shots with the first two hitting the president and that a rapid-fire final shot rang out just before Ms. Kennedy crawled on the trunk. These notes were found in *Dallas Times Herald* archives and are now held by the Dealey Plaza Sixth Floor Museum along with oral interviews of the two reporters and Sitzman and Payne's notebook.

> **Darwin Payne** - *Abraham Zapruder Pres. Jennifer Juniors corner Elm and Houston. M. heard three shots. After first one president slumped over [from Z245 to Z312] and grabbed stomac . . . hit in stomach [actually in his upper back/lower neck] . . . two more shots, looked like head opened up and everything came out . . . blood splattered everywhere . . . side of his face . . . looked like blobs out of his temple. . forehead. . . . Jackie first reached over to the president [from about Z255 to Z325] and after second shot [second of final two, the Z328 shot] . . . she crawled over to back of car [commencing about Z339] . . . . Darwin Payne Dallas Times Herald reporter telephoned notes tear sheets, November 22, 1963, Sixth Floor Museum and interviews by Payne by the Sixth Floor Museum Oral History Program, 1996.*

The images

Figure 3 shows Zapruder's field of vision and the witnesses in view. The home movie of the motorcade as published on commercially available copies runs 26.5 seconds and is comprised of 486 frames (18.3 frames per second). It has two sequences.

The first sequence (Z001 to Z132) runs 7.2 seconds/132 frames and captures the motorcade's lead motorcycles making the left turn off Houston onto Elm. The presidential limo was still on Houston at the time, almost a block behind the lead motorcycles and out of view.

The second sequence (Z133 to Z486), which commenced about 15 to 20 seconds after the first ended, captures the assassination. It runs 19.3 seconds over 354 frames. Picking up the presidential limo in front of the TSBD about 60 feet west of the intersection, Zapruder tracks it as it travels west down Elm about 400 feet and then disappears within the triple underpass. The president is in view center frame during the critical points of the movie except for a brief 1-second/18-frame interval from Z208 to Z224 when he disappeared behind the Stemmons Freeway sign.

2: The Zapruder Assassination Sequence

The following observations and analyses were made by viewing the *MPI Media Group* 1998 DVD "Image of an Assassination," on a plasma TV at normal speed, slow motion, ultra-slow speed, and in frame-by-frame fashion. The DVD includes four versions of the film including close-up, full screen, medium screen, and wide screen. All four versions are missing four frames (Z208-11) the originals of which were damaged by *Life* during processing. The video was reportedly made by taking high-quality zoom photographs of each individual frame on the original 16-mm color film including the area between the sprocket holes, making high-resolution scans of the prints to create digital images, and then photo-editing and aligning the digital images using image-enhancing computer software. The wide-screen version shows the area between the sprocket holes for the first time in a motion sequence.

Pre-first-shot movements

President Kennedy - The president in his sitting position in the right-rear seat of the limo is centered in Zapruder's camera eye. From Z133 until he briefly disappears behind the Stemmons sign at about Z210, we see him tucked into the corner of his seat in a slightly slouched position. His left arm is drawn across his body with his left hand resting atop the car door. His upper-right arm and elbow, when not waving or saluting, are resting on the top of the right side of the car.

From Z133 to Z154, he is looking at the crowd on the south (left) side of Elm with his head turning to the left. From Z155 to Z160, he spins his head to look forward right. While some experts interpret this rapid head turn as a reaction to gunfire, it very clearly is not. The Zapruder film shows us that Kennedy turned to his right at this point because he noticed the line of spectators had ended. Why would he continue looking to his left with nobody there? And why is there no response to the alleged shot by any of the secret service agents and the motorcycle police escort who were there to protect the presidential entourage?

From Z160 to Z184 the president is looking forward-right interacting with the spectators lining the north side of Elm. From Z185 to Z193 he turns his head hard right in the direction of the Woodward group on the north side of Elm and breaks into a broad smile. The two-second interval Z165 to Z201 corresponds to the point Nellie Connally reported that she looked back at the president while exclaiming: "Mr. President, you can't say that Dallas doesn't love you." From Z194 to Z201, the president turns his head to the left and is ostensibly looking at Ms. Connally until he disappears from view behind the Stemmons sign at about Z207. The one-second interval from Z202 to Z220 corresponds to the period he reportedly replied with his last words in life which according to Ms. Kennedy's WC testimony were: "Yes, you certainly can't." There is nothing in his movements to suggest he heard a shot ring out or received a bullet during this interval.

The president gives two semi-salutes before disappearing behind the sign at Z208 which, along with his dazzling smile, was his signature mode of interacting with the crowd. The first salute is to the spectators on his left and is in progress at Z133 at which time he has his right hand to his right forehead and then lowers it onto his left hand by Z145. His final salute is to the spectators on his right and commences at Z170. It starts as a quick wave and smile at a line of spectators on the north side of Elm (Woodward group). From Z190 to Z198 his hand is in front of his forehead in salute fashion. From Z199 until it disappears from view behind the Stemmons sign at Z207 he is lowering his arm.

John Connally - *He was watching the crowds, waving at them steadily with a stiff forearm, his right hand moving only a few inches out from his face and back. It was a small movement and curiously formal, but, I thought, quite effective.* John Connally, Governor of Texas, "Why Kennedy Went to Texas, Life, November 24, 1967, p. 104.

Jackie Kennedy - Ms. Kennedy is in the rear seat to the left of her husband. When she comes into view from Z133 to Z169 she is facing left and turning her head to the left, interacting with the crowd on the south side of Elm. As the line of spectators ends, she turns quickly to her right between about Z170 and Z174. From Z175 until she disappears from view behind the Stemmons sign at Z217, she appears to be looking toward Ms. Connally correlating with her recollection of the interval when Ms. Connally commented on the president's warm reception in Dallas and her husband responded with his last words in life. There is nothing in her movements to suggest she heard a shot ring out during this interval.

Nellie Connally - Ms. Connally is in the left jump seat next to her husband and in front of Ms. Kennedy. When she comes into blurry view at about Z140, she is turning her head from forward-left to forward-right and as of Z164 is looking out the right-front windshield. From Z165 through Z179 she looks back over her right shoulder toward the president and continues looking directly at him until her head disappears into shadows by about Z200. This interval correlates with when she recalled seeing him smiling broadly while interacting with the spectators with his arm raised and exclaimed: "Mr. President, you can't say that Dallas does not love you." There is nothing in her movements to suggest Ms. Connally heard a shot ring out during this interval.

While Jackie Kennedy's WC testimony supports Ms. Connally's recollection of speaking to the president immediately before he was shot, the governor insisted that his wife's comments came earlier while the limo was still on Houston. Looking at the collective photographic evidence for Dealey Plaza, there is continuous footage showing Ms. Connally from the time the presidential limo began its right turn off Main onto Houston to the point she briefly disappeared behind the Stemmons sign. The interval Z165 to Z200 is the only time she looked back toward the president. The severely wounded governor's recollections are untrustworthy.

Governor Connally - The governor is in the right jump seat just in front of and slightly inboard of the president. When he comes into view at Z133 through Z159, the governor is sitting upright and leaning slightly back in the approximate center of the right jump seat looking stoically to the right with his shoulders/upper torso rotated to the right. From Z160 to Z164 he takes a quick glance to the left and then abruptly turns back between Z165 and Z169. From Z170, until he briefly disappears behind the Stemmons sign at Z208, he is again looking stoically to the right with his shoulders/upper torso rotated to the right. While the HSCA experts and most lone-gunman advocates interpret his abrupt turn to the right commencing at Z165 to be a reaction to a shot fired at Z151, it clearly is not. The Zapruder film shows that as the governor looked to his left at this point, there was not a single spectator in his view on the south side of Elm. Why would he continue looking to the left with nobody there? And why no response to the alleged shot by any of the secret service agents and the motorcycle-police escort who were there to protect the presidential entourage? In truth, there is nothing in his movements to suggest he heard a shot ring out or received a bullet during this interval.

Agent Greer - The driver, Secret Service Agent William Greer, commencing Z133 appears to be looking to the right front until he disappears behind the Stemmons sign at about Z205. There is nothing in his movements to suggest he heard a shot ring out during this interval.

Agent Kellerman - Agent Roy Kellerman, who was in charge of presidential security, is in the right-front seat. He is obstructed from Zapruder's view by the front-windshield trim until about Z180 and then is in just partial view until he disappears behind the Stemmons sign at about Z200. During this interval he appears to be looking forward-right to forward. There is nothing in his movements to suggest he heard a shot ring out during this interval.

Presidential follow-up car occupants and motorcycle escort - Nine of the ten agents/aides in the follow-up car and three of the four motorcycle officers flanking it are in view from Z133 to about Z215 when most disappear behind the Stemmons sign. The two motorcycle officers to the left of the car and the two agents riding on the left running board remain in view until about Z250. All collective and individual movements of the security forces in the presidential follow-up car, and presidential police escort through Z224 appear to be normal and predictable interactions with spectators or each other. There is nothing in their individual and collective movements to suggest anyone heard a shot ring out during this interval. The head and body movements of Secret Agent George Hickey in the left-rear seat of the presidential follow-up car are discussed below in connection with Phil Willis and his daughter Rosemary.

Spectators - All movements of the spectators lining Elm through Z225 appear to be normal and predictable interactions with the motorcade or each other including those of 10-year-old Rosemary Willis who HSCA experts concluded was responding to gunfire from approximately Z160 to Z190. During this interval she can be seen running along the sidewalk on the south side of Elm keeping pace with the presidential limo and then suddenly coming to a stop while looking back over her right shoulder toward the Queen Mary.

The Zapruder film images show that Rosemary stopped running and looked to her right-rear primarily because her 14-year old sister Linda was yelling or whistling at her from that general direction. As discussed in Chapter 4, the Dorman film shows both sisters running down the sidewalk chasing the limo, with Linda stopping at a point behind her father who is standing in the gutter of the street taking his Z138 picture of the president as the limo passes by him. From about Z135 to Z155, the careful observer will note that Linda, who is wearing a blue dress, has her hands to her mouth either in megaphone fashion or is using her fingers to whistle. Linda has lowered her hands by Z160. The Zapruder film also suggests that Agent Hickey from his position in the elevated left-rear seat of the presidential follow-up car was admonishing Rosemary to stop running. He is leaning over and looking in her direction from Z175 to Z185. Looking at the collective movements of Agent Hickey and Phil Willis from Z140 to Z165, it appears that Hickey had shooed her father back onto the sidewalk just before instructing Rosemary to stop running.

There is nothing in the individual or collective movements of the spectators to suggest any of them heard a shot ring out during this interval.

Reactions to the Z221 shot

President Kennedy - As he emerges from behind the Stemmons sign at Z224-25, the president is just beginning to react to a shot that struck him when he was behind the sign. As the president's arms come into view at Z224-25, his left hand is still on or near the top of the door and his right hand is lifted just above the left as if he were completing his aforementioned salute-type wave in similar fashion to the way he completed his prior salute at about Z145. As his face comes into view at Z225, he is grimacing and looking forward and slightly to the right. From Z225 to Z245 he splays his elbows, jerks both arms up in front of his face, and straightens up in his seat in an overt reflex reaction. By all appearances the bullet struck him at Z223 and his reflex arm jerk reaction begins at Z226 concurrent with the governor's.

Governor Connally - As he emerges from behind the Stemmons sign at Z222, the governor is still looking out into the crowd to the right with a little more rightward shoulder rotation than when his torso was last in view at Z196. Commencing with frame Z224, we see the governor reacting dramatically to a shot that appears to have struck him at Z223 from the sudden jolt of his right shoulder and arm which made his shirt cuff lower and disappear from view between Z222 and Z223. From Z226 to Z229, we see him grimace heavily, drop his right shoulder, spin slightly to the left into an approximately straight-ahead position in the seat, and jerk his right arm, with hat in hand, up in front of his face in an overt reflex reaction. This involuntary right-arm movement is concurrent with the president's involuntary upward arm movements, making it obvious that the governor was hit in the right side of his chest by the same bullet that passed through the base of the president's neck. In testifying to the WC that these movements were part of his attempt to look back over his right shoulder out of concern for the president, the governor appears to be rationalizing rather than remembering. From Z230 to about Z339, the alarmed governor appears to be making a failed attempt to look back at the president over his left shoulder. While looking back over his left shoulder, from Z235 to Z239 he grimaces heavily and puffs his cheeks out. This is consistent with his WC testimony where he states that he became acutely aware of his chest wound while attempting to look back over his left shoulder.

Jackie Kennedy - When she comes into camera view at Z221, Ms. Kennedy whose face is obstructed from view by the governor through Z229 is looking out toward the spectators on the north side of Elm, presumably the Chisms or Mudd. Commencing at Z226 she darts her head to her left toward the governor in an overt reflex reaction which is complete by Z229. Commencing at Z230 she re-focuses her attention on the spectators. In her WC testimony, she recalled that she thought the first shot was a motorcycle backfiring and paid it no heed.

Nellie Connally - When she comes back into reasonably clear view from behind the Stemmons sign and other obstructions at about Z223, Ms. Connally is looking straight ahead. Commencing at Z226 she darts her head to the right and by Z230 begins to look back over her right shoulder. She is looking at her husband by Z240.

Agent Greer - When he reappears from behind the Stemmons sign at about Z215, the only thing we can see of Greer is the white of his collared shirt within the V-shaped lapel area of his suit coat. By its orientation, we can see him dart his head to the right commencing at Z226. He is still looking forward, however, and continues to do so until he briefly disappears from view about Z265 behind a lamppost and the windshield trim.

Agent Kellerman - Commencing at Z226, Kellerman who was still looking to the right front when he emerges from behind the sign at Z219, darts his head to his right in an overt reflex reaction that is complete by Z229. Commencing at Z245, Kellerman begins to look back toward the president over his left shoulder. He is turned in his seat looking back at the president by about Z270.

Presidential follow-up-car occupants and motorcycle escort - The four members in view of the trained professionals in the motorcade vehicles immediately following the presidential limo all dart their heads to the right or left commencing Z226. This includes motorcycle Officer Hargis and Martin (both right) riding off the left rear fender and Secret Service Agents Hill (left/right) and McIntyre (right) who were on the Queen Mary's left running board. The reactions are complete by Z228.

One would expect these individuals who were there to protect the presidential party to react in unison to hearing the loud crack of a possible rifle shot. Indeed, many of these protective personnel testified that they immediately reacted to the sound of the first shot by turning their heads to either look back over their shoulder or at the president. The collective photographic record bears this out. We see a simultaneous turning of heads in alarm toward the perceived source of the sound or toward the presidential limo among the four-man motorcycle escort and most occupants of the presidential follow-up car. The timing of this collective turn is very important and powerful first-shot-timing evidence. The Zapruder film and/or the Altgens Z253 photo confirm this deliberate head movement for the following protective personnel who recalled it: Motorcycle Officers Chaney, Hargis, and Martin; Secret Service Agents John Ready and Paul Landis standing on the right (passenger's side) running board of the presidential follow-up car; Agents Clint Hill and William McIntyre standing on the left (driver's side) running board; and Agent George Hickey sitting on the left side of the elevated rear bench-type seat. See Figures 3 and 5.

2: The Zapruder Assassination Sequence

We can establish from the Zapruder film that the collective turn we see in the Altgens Z253 photo commenced at about Z230 for all the above security personnel who remain in Zapruder's view long enough to see it, including officers Hargis and Martin and agents Hill and McIntyre. They were all looking either to their left or pretty much straight ahead from Z133 to Z207 and were looking hard into the presidential limo or points east of it by Z253. Note that these collective head movements are concurrent with Nellie Connally's head turn and were preceded in each case by a auditory reflex reaction between Z225 and Z228.

The rest of the head-turners, including Officer Chaney and Agents Hickey, Ready and Landis are out of Zapruder's view after Z207, but they had clearly not started their respective head turns by then. From the collective photographic evidence, we know that their respective head turns commenced sometime between Z208 and Z253 and presumably about halfway between, at about Z230, consistent with the others.

Spectators - There is a group of five spectators standing near the edge of the curb on the north side of Elm that are visible in the Zapruder film from Z133 through Z207, four of who gave testimony that the first shot they heard rang out when the president was almost directly in front of them: Karen Westbrook, June Dishong, Gloria Calvary, and Karen Hicks. They are standing at about Z220 to Z225 when the president passed by. No other Elm Street witnesses made this claim.

After Z208 there are no spectators in view on the north side of Elm, initially because they are obstructed from view by the Stemmons Freeway sign, and then because Zapruder is filming above their heads. The only exception is that we get a glimpse of the back of F. Lee Mudd's head and raised right arm from Z227 to Z240. During this interval he witnessed the president and governor reacting to the first shot from close range consistent with what he reported in his testimony. His position at the curb was Z250 as the president passed him.

Commencing at Z208, there are no spectators in view on the south side of Elm until Z219 when two African American men come into view, one of who is wearing a cook's apron. Their position was about Z215 when the president passed by. From the point they come into view they are looking directly at the president and are enthusiastically clapping their hands. Commencing Z226, they both stop clapping and dart their heads to their right. By Z230 they are looking toward the TSBD and continue to until they disappear from view to camera left at about Z253. Unfortunately, these key ear/eyewitnesses have never come forward.

First-shot testimony for these and other key stationary ear/eyewitnesses is covered in Chapter 11.

Movements between the Z221 and Z310 shots

President Kennedy - From about Z245 to Z290, the president is slumping forward/left into his wife's arms while slowly lowering his arms. He remains in the same vulnerable position from about Z290 to the fatal head shot which by all appearances struck him at Z313. Assuming he did indeed receive a bullet in the back at Z223, there is nothing in his movements to indicate that he heard or received another bullet between the time he was struck at Z223 and again at Z313.

Governor Connally - From Z240 to Z270 the stricken governor is turning his head hard right over his right shoulder attempting to look back at the president with his mouth forming the words, "Oh, no, no, no." He appears to be looking over his right shoulder toward the president from Z271 to Z279. Corresponding to the time at which Kellerman, according to his testimony, is ordering Greer to get moving and out of the line of fire, from Z280 to Z294 the governor turns away from the president and with his back to the left side of the limo, visibly relaxes and leans back toward his wife until the rear of his head is on her right shoulder. From Z295 to Z307 he is leaning back against his wife looking straight ahead toward the right side of the limo and his mouth is forming/shouting the words, "Oh my God." From Z308 to Z312 while he continues to shout, he turns his head to the left in the direction of Kellerman who has just picked up and started speaking into the radio mike. At Z313, Connally is face-to-face with Agent Greer who has just looked over his right shoulder as if to listen to what he was saying. Their faces are within about 3 feet of each other.

Jackie Kennedy - Commencing Z238, Ms. Kennedy is raising her right hand to wave at the spectators and is doing so as of Z247 when the stricken president who has been slumping in her direction makes contact with her waving right arm. As she begins to look toward her husband and gather him into her arms, her attention is drawn by the shouting governor. From about Z252 to Z289 she is looking quizzically at the governor. Between Z290 and Z293 she diverts her attention back to her husband who has slumped into her arms at this point. From Z294 to Z298 she bends forward and lowers her head to look at his face. She is looking toward his neck at the time his head explodes at Z313. Her movements are consistent with her testimony that she did not realize that anyone had been shot until her husband's head exploded. There is nothing in her movements to indicate that she heard another shot between the two that struck the president at Z223 and Z313.

Nellie Connally - From about Z240 to Z249, Ms. Connally is looking toward the rear of her husband's head and/or the president and still holding her large bouquet of yellow roses up against her chest. From Z250 to Z269 she is looking away from her husband and toward the president as he is slumping to his left. From Z270 to Z279 she takes a quick look at Kellerman who is just then looking back toward the president. From Z280 to Z285 she takes a quick glance at the governor. From Z286 to Z289 she takes a final look at the president. From Z290 to Z300 she is looking at the rear of her husband's head as he is leaning back toward her. From Z301 to Z313 with her husband leaning his head on her right shoulder, she is lowering her head toward the left side of his face as if to listen to him as he is shouting, "Oh my God . . ." From her movements, it appears that Ms. Connally was trying to figure out what was going on during this 5-second interval and did not yet realize her husband had been shot. There is nothing in her movements to indicate that she heard another shot between the two that struck the president at Z223 and Z313.

Agent Kellerman - From Z245 to Z269, Kellerman is turning in his seat to look over his left shoulder. From Z270 to Z279, he is looking back at the silent, slumping president. From Z280 to Z289, he turns back to the front, speaking to Greer as he turns, correlating with his WC testimony as to when he recalled saying, "Lets get out of here, were hit." Between Z290 and Z299, he reaches down and grabs a radio microphone. From Z300 to Z313, he is beginning to speak into the mike and is starting to look back at the shouting governor. There is nothing in his movements to indicate that he heard another shot between the two that struck the president at Z223 and Z313.

Agent Greer - Greer is looking forward from Z240 until he disappears from view behind a lamppost and windshield trim about Z265. When he emerges back into view right-shoulder first at about Z270 to Z279, he seems to be turned slightly in his seat looking toward Kellerman. From Z280 to Z289, Greer is looking in the direction of the then leftward-slumping governor while Kellerman is speaking to him. He turns forward between Z290 and Z294 and is looking forward from Z295 to Z299. At Z300 to Z304, he looks hard over his right shoulder into the rear seat apparently in response to the governor's shouting. He is looking directly into the shouting governor's face from a distance of about 3 feet from Z305 until the president's head explodes at Z313. There is nothing in his movements to indicate that he heard another shot between the two that struck the president at Z223 and Z313.

Presidential follow-up car occupants - The occupants of the presidential follow-up car and two of the four policemen of the motorcycle escort are all out of view by Z250. Most of them are out of view by Z215.

2: The Zapruder Assassination Sequence

Motorcycle Officers Hargis and Martin - When Hargis and Martin disappeared from view at Z276, they were still looking in alarm towards the presidential limo. When Hargis re-appears at the far left side of the frame at Z307, he is looking further to his right out over the knoll. There is nothing in the collective movements of Hargis and Martin to indicate that they heard another shot between the two that struck the president at Z223 and Z313.

Spectators - None of the spectators in Zapruder's view during this interval show any signs of a reaction to hearing a shot between the two that struck the president at Z223 and Z313. They include Charles Brehm, the Babushka Lady, Jean Hill and Mary Moorman all on the south side of Elm. It is apparent at Z292 to Z295, that the Babushka Lady is watching the president using a pair of chrome-rimmed (opera) binoculars.

Reactions to the Z310 shot

President Kennedy - From Z310 to Z312 the president is leaning against Ms. Kennedy and does not move. Just as the president's head explodes at Z313, there is a slight downward/slightly forward movement that occurs during Z313 revealing that the bullet struck the head from behind at Z313 driving the left side of his head into his wife's right cheek and right shoulder. The film images at Z313/314 are heavily blurred from up and down/left to right camera movement. From Z316 to Z319, the president's right arm jerks up to about shoulder level in an overt involuntary reflex reaction to the head-shot and then falls limply to his side from Z320 to Z325. The president's controversial rearward head-snap in the aftermath of the fatal head shot occurs between Z316 and Z325. As explained below, the head snap, was clearly the result of a spontaneous auditory reflex reaction by his wife (shove by her right forearm in the process of recoiling). If the whiplash were the result of an involuntary reflex action by the president instead, Ms. Kennedy's arm would not have moved. In any event, as a result of this whiplash-type movement, we can see loose pieces of reflected scalp in motion on the right side of the president's head. In the aftermath of the whiplash-type movement, the president slumps forward/left onto his wife's chest from Z327 to Z329. There is no disruption of the cowlick area or crown of the head at this point. Although the jettison of brain matter is conspicuous, because it was near vertical and just a few feet high, the Z313 cranial eruption did not appear to create significant fallout outside of the rear seat area with most of it landing on the president by Z319.

Governor Connally - We observe reflex-type reactions to the head-shot noise in the frantic movements of the governor and his wife in the jump seats. From Z316 to Z319, the shouting governor who is leaning back against his wife in the left jump seat with his shoulders parallel to the side of the limo, darts his head left and spins his shoulder to his right. Commencing Z320, he lunges forward through Z324 at which point he slams his head hard against a metal bar on the top of the back of the front seat. From Z325 to Z332 he is visibly losing consciousness. With his head jolted to the left by the impact, his chin slumps toward his chest as he crumples/collapses left-shoulder first to the left onto the ducking Ms. Connally's right side pinning her up against the inside of the car door. He was acting exactly as if he had been shot dead by the Z310 shot.

Nellie Connally - Concurrent with her husband's lunge forward, from Z316 to Z325 Ms. Connally recoils back against the side of the limo and then leans forward in ducking her head down toward the front of the limo. By Z329 her unconscious husband has slumped his left shoulder against her right side and she is pinned up against the inside of the door with her arms in front of her and her head tilted down. Commencing Z290, the president was completely out of her field of vision.

Agent Greer - Greer is still looking back at the governor through Z315. From Z316 to Z320, Greer darts his head to the left in spinning forward and commencing Z321 ducks his head forward until he is hunkering down over the steering wheel. As of Z330, Greer is still hunkered down severely hunching his shoulders.

Agent Kellerman - Kellerman is talking into the radio mike from Z300 to Z315 as the president's head explodes. In reaction, he darts his head to the left commencing Z316 and commencing Z321 ducks forward to get his head down. As of Z332 he is hunkered down to the maximum extent possible with his head by appearances pressing against the dash. He is ostensibly still talking into the mike.

Jackie Kennedy - From Z310 to Z320, Ms. Kennedy hardly moves her head and is looking downward. From Z316 to Z320, however, even though her head is nearly stationary, we see an overt reflex-type reaction to the Z313 shot in her right-arm movement. As of Z315 Ms. Kennedy right arm was fully bent at the elbow and the back of her right hand and forearm was in contact with the left side of her husband's upper chest and shoulder. Commencing Z316 she starts extending both arms in recoiling, pushing her husband away in the process. This causes his head to snap back in whiplash fashion. From Z321 to Z329, Ms. Kennedy straightens back up into her original sitting position while inspecting the damage to her husband's head as it falls forward-left onto her right shoulder from Z325 to Z329 after she lost right-arm contact with his chest.

Motorcycle Officer Hargis - The only member of the group of fourteen protective personnel who is still in view at Z313 is Hargis riding off the left-rear fender of the presidential limo. He had disappeared at Z276 with his head turned right. He is still looking out to the right when he reappears at Z307 as a result of the limo slowing when Greer looked back into the rear seat as mentioned above. Between Z315 and Z317 he stiffens and darts his head slightly to the right and upward. Frames Z318 and Z319 are heavily blurred. By Z321 he is looking out to the right toward a group of spectators on the pergola stairs (see Chapters 5 and 6 in connection with Red Shirt Man and Flying Tackle Man). Though obviously alarmed by the shot noise, he seems oblivious to the Z313 cranial explosion. Commencing Z326 he darts his head to the left and is looking directly at the president as of Z330 his attention apparently drawn either by the roar of the engine as Greer stomped on the accelerator pedal and/or the governor's loud shouting.

Agent Clint Hill - From his forward position on the right-side running board of the Queen Mary, Hill had disappeared from Zapruder's view at about Z250 while looking at the president with a very concerned expression. He reappears at about Z330, chasing the limo on foot. The Bronson film reveals that Hill hit the street running at Z300 and commenced an all out sprint at Z316 in reaction to the sound of the Z313 head shot (Chapters 5, 6, 7). Hill is just about to grab the limo's left-rear handhold with his left hand at Z337.

Spectators - A woman who has been trotting toward the limo since coming into view at Z296 begins turning to her left and leaning back (recoiling) commencing Z316 and then stops dead in her tracks commencing Z321 in an overt response to witnessing/hearing the Z313 head shot. Originally labeled the "Running Woman," she is generally believed to be one Toni Foster who came forward with her story of hearing four-shots in 1996.

Reactions to a third shot among other unmistakable visual evidence

President Kennedy - From Z325 to Z329, the president slumps to the left and as of Z330 is leaning the left side of his shattered head up against Ms. Kennedy's right shoulder as she gathers him into her arms. From Z331 to Z332 the president's already shattered head jolts downward and forward about 3 inches into his wife's right cheek and shoulder amidst a head-and-shoulder level cranial eruption that is hard to see due to rapid camera movement. As was the case with the first cranial explosion at Z313/314, the film images during the second explosion at Z331/332 are heavily blurred. What we can discern, however, is blood and brain matter jettisoned from the open area of the cranium raining down on Nellie Connally's head from Z331 to Z337. Even more telling is that from Z332 to Z335 we can clearly see whitish brain fluids landing on the lid of the trunk in the area directly behind the president's head, creating a substantial puddle. This is also evident

2: The Zapruder Assassination Sequence

in the Muchmore and Nix films. From Z336 to Z342 we then see the puddled fluid spreading out over the middle and rear of the trunk. As of Z332, we also see that the scalp of the president's cowlick area is heavily disrupted. Based on when the head movement started and as verified by the Muchmore and Nix films, the bullet entered the limo at the very end of Z330.

From Z333 to Z338, the dying president is slumped to the left with his left shoulder and the left side of his head propped up against the middle of Ms. Kennedy's chest. As Ms. Kennedy begins to rise from her seat commencing Z339, the president starts his final collapse onto the rear seat left-shoulder first. We can no longer see the top of his head during this interval. Commencing Z340, all we can see of the president is his right shoulder and upper arm and some of the right side of his shattered head.

The Zapruder film images reveal that the Z330/331 cranial eruption occurred in direct view of Agent Clint Hill (within 10 feet), Motorcycle Officer Bobby Hargis (within 15 feet) and *AP* Photographer James Altgens (within 35 feet). They are looking right at him at Z330 and were not looking at him at Z313. I will point out here that all three of these key witnesses testified that the final shot drove the president down to his left in the midst of a cranial eruption and that none of them mentioned a rearward head snap. Altgens in particular, described what we see from Z326 to Z340 to a T. See Chapter 13.

Jackie Kennedy - By Z326, in the aftermath of the rearward head snap, Ms. Kennedy has leaned back into to her original sitting position, rotated her shoulders parallel to the left side of the car and is facing the president. Commencing Z327 through Z330, she gathers her stricken husband into her arms as he slumps toward her, left-shoulder first with the left side of his head settling on her right shoulder. Between Z330 and Z331, it is evident that the force of a bullet hitting the top right side of the president's head has slammed the left side of his head into Ms. Kennedy's right shoulder and right cheek; her head and shoulders rise as her upper torso is driven backwards toward the left side of the limo. Ms. Kennedy's upper body movement and the president's concurrent head movement are also visible in the Nix film amidst a more conspicuous cranial eruption that starts at the very end of N040/Z330. From Z333 to Z338, the horrified Ms. Kennedy cringes and recoils back and to her right putting herself into position to rise from her seat. Her eyes are wide open and her mouth is agape. Significantly, commencing at Z333 through Z338, we see rapid right-forearm movement over seven frames that mimics to a considerable degree the movement we observed between Z316 and Z320. This time, however, Ms. Kennedy's bent right arm is already behind her husband's head with her right hand resting on his right shoulder. The rearward right-forearm jerk had no effect on the stricken president. By Z370, Ms. Kennedy has both hands on the trunk. As was the case with the Z313 jolt, the spontaneous right-arm movement might have been partially or fully related to the president's head slamming into her face.

Nellie Connally - As of Z330, Ms. Connally is hunkered down on the far-left side of the jump seat with her unconscious husband slumped back against her. She is pinned up against the inside of the door, still cradling in her arms a large bouquet of yellow roses. Remarkably, as the president's head jolts forward between Z330 and Z332, Ms. Connally is struck on the back of her head at Z331 with such force by a spray of whitish brain matter that her own head jolts downward from Z331 to Z332 ringed by a halo of brain matter that bounced off it (the Nix film confirms the jolt and the halo). From Z333 to Z336, concurrent with Ms. Kennedy's recoil, Ms. Connally darts her head to the right and leans back allowing her limp husband to collapse left-shoulder first onto her lap. During this interval the careful observer can see bloody brain matter descending on her. From Z338 to Z350, concurrent with Ms. Kennedy's flight from the rear seat, Ms. Connally lets go of her flowers and drops her right shoulder down onto the seat with her head behind her husband's lower back and her left arm extending protectively over his right side. By Z355, she is buried under a heap of tumbling flowers.

Governor Connally - From Z328 to Z332, the limp governor is slumped backward onto his wife's right side with his chin on his chest and his shoulders crumpling toward his knees. From Z333 to Z340, the governor collapses left-shoulder first down onto his wife's lap into the area she has just cleared by leaning back and to the right. He remains motionless in his wife's arms and lap from Z345 to Z369, presumably in an unconscious state. From Z338 to about Z350 we can see a bloody stain section of the back of his coat under and just inside his right armpit.

Agents Greer and Kellerman - From Z333 to Z337, Greer who is already hunkered down, leans/ducks/turns slightly to the right and cringes. Kellerman, whose movements are easier to see in the Muchmore film, ducks down to his left from Z333 to Z337 and by Z338 is diving for the center of the seat. He rises back up to his original hunkered down position from Z346 to Z355.

Motorcycle Officer Hargis and Agent Hill - Commencing at Z333, Hargis who was looking at the president as his head exploded darts his head a short distance to the left and then back to the right and flexes both wrists. He is looking back at the president by Z335. He is obstructed from view by Agent Hill from Z337 to Z338. When he comes back into view at Z339, Hargis is turning his head hard right and is rapidly slowing to a stop as he disappears from view to camera left at Z343. The careful observer will discern brain matter descending on the lid of the trunk from Z332 to Z337. Hargis appears to have slowed and stopped in response to being struck in the face by brain matter. He has become fully aware that the president has been shot in the head and turns his immediate attention to finding the assassin.

Richard Bothun - Between Z333 and Z336, South-of-Elm picture-taker Richard Bothun who came into view to camera right at Z330 about 10-feet back from the curb darts his head slightly to his left and leans back exhibiting a classic weak-kneed recoil. This recoil can also be seen in the Nix film. Unfortunately, this key ear-eyewitness never came forward to describe what he heard and saw.

James Altgens - As he enters Zapruder's view with camera-to-eye at Z339 through Z350, the *A.P.* photographer is in the midst of a classic, weak-kneed, stumbling backward recoil that is concurrent with Ms. Kennedy's rise from her seat. According to Altgens' testimony, he was so shocked by the sound and effects of the final shot that he was not able to operate his camera's shutter as the stricken president passed by him.

Unidentified spectator - An unidentified male spectator who entered Zapruder's view at about Z325 standing perhaps 30 feet from the curb, is walking quickly toward the presidential limo at a point the president would have passed at about Z350. Commencing Z333 he begins dropping his arms and just before he disappears from view at about Z350, he is in the midst of stopping dead in his tracks and recoiling commencing Z339 concurrent with Ms. Kennedy's rise from her seat. Unfortunately, this key ear-eyewitness never came forward to describe what he heard and saw.

Malcolm Summers - The 39-year old Korean-War veteran was standing on the grass infield near the curb on the south side of Elm at the point the president passed at about Z350. He is in Zapruder's camera view from Z345 to Z363. As he begins coming into Zapruder's view right-arm first at Z344, he is in the midst of dropping to the ground.

Conclusions

Zapruder's shot-sequence testimony - Within 15 to 30 minutes of the assassination Zapruder told a news reporter with notebook and pen in hand that he heard a third and final shot clustered with the Z313 head shot that rang out just before Jackie Kennedy rose up in her seat and crawled on the trunk. This is considered to be Zapruder's most relevant testimony as to the timing and effects of the third shot.

2: The Zapruder Assassination Sequence

Signature jolts and cranial eruptions due to the transfer of a bullet's momentum - Zapruder's film images are telling us that whenever a bullet struck the president or governor from the rear, it produced a signature jolt as it transferred a portion of its momentum to the stricken area. The jolts occur in just the Z frame of impact and the next frame thereafter and are identifiable in the following frames: Z223-24 with the governor's right shoulder jolting downward and forward; Z313/Z314 with the president's head and the governor's right wrist jolting downward and forward amidst a conspicuous high-trajectory cranial eruption; Z330/Z331 with the president's head jolting forward amidst a less-conspicuous, lower-trajectory cranial eruption that jettisoned brain matter forward with such force that the leading edge of the spray drove Ms. Connally's head downward and forward when it reached her at Z331.

Signature reflex and alarm reactions to the bullet shock-wave noise generated in the limo - The Zapruder film images are telling us that as the three bullets entered the limo at mid Z223, early Z313 and late Z330, the shock waves that arrived with them produced at least one and sometimes two signature patterns of reactions amongst all the limo occupants and security forces in view and all the spectators in view as well.

Reflex reactions - With respect to presidential limo occupants, these are spontaneous reactions commencing 2.5 Z frames (0.14 second) plus or minus a frame (0.06 second) after the bullet's arrival in the limo and include grimacing, flinching, cringing, and rapid head and arm movements. With respect to spectators or motorcade participants, these are spontaneous reactions commencing 2.5 Z frames plus or minus a frame after shot-related sound waves reach them and consist primarily of a dart of the head in the perceived direction of the noise. With respect to Zapruder and the rest of the assassination filmmakers, this is a flinch or camera jerk that created signature blurring of the film images 2.5 frames plus or minus a frame after the noise reached their ears. The reactions are typically complete within 3 Z frames (0.15 seconds), but five frames after they commence, reflex reactions commonly morph into alarm reactions. See Figures 5 through 9.

Alarm reactions - With respect to presidential limo occupants, these are conscious reactions commencing 7.5 Z frames (0.4 second) plus or minus two frames (0.11 second) after the bullet's arrival in the limo and include head turning, fleeing and stopping. With respect to spectators or motorcade participants, these are reactions commencing 7.5 Z frames plus or minus two frames after the first shot-related sound waves reach them. Neurologically speaking, whenever an alarm reaction occurs, it commences as a reflex reaction, but not all reflex reactions morph into alarm reactions.

Shot timing and sequence - Assuming the three shots that caused the jolts to wounded body parts came from the TSBD sniper's nest and were traveling at an average speed of 1,900 to 2,000 feet per second, they had to have been fired within Z frames Z221, Z310 and Z328. See Chapter 8 and Figures 5 through 8.

Negative visual evidence of any more than three shots - There is nothing to point to anywhere else in the film where there are concurrent movements or reactions among multiple motorcade participants, spectators, and in particular presidential security that are in any way indicative of another shot entering or passing over the presidential limo. There are no such reactions from Z133 to Z207.

The vindication of Nellie Connally - The Zapruder film images are telling us that the governor was struck by the same two bullets that hit the president at Z223 and Z313 and that he briefly lost consciousness at Z326 just before the final shot rang out consistent with what he stated in his testimony. This explains why he recalled hearing only one of the two rapid-fire final shots. Moreover, the images reveal that while the limo was under fire, Ms. Connally felt certain that her husband had been shot near dead by the Z310 second shot and that the president was hit in the head by just the third for the following reasons: (1) she could not see the president from Z290 through about Z335; (2) her husband reacted exactly as if he had been shot dead by just the Z310 shot; (3) she was showered with brain matter at the exact same time she heard the Z328 shot enter the limo and hit the president. The Z film images corroborate her testimony that she felt the impact.

The president's controversial rearward head snap in the immediate aftermath of the Z310 head shot was the sole result of a reflex reaction by Jackie Kennedy to the shot noise and/or the president's head slamming into her right cheek and shoulder - The Zapruder film images show Jackie Kennedy reacting in similar fashion to the loud cracks of the shots that entered the limo at early Z313 and late Z330. In both instances, in the process of recoiling over a period of five Z frames, she jerks her right forearm to the rear commencing three Z frames after the bullet arrived. The proof that Ms. Kennedy's spontaneous right-arm movement caused the president's head to snap back commencing Z316 is as follows: (1) from Z316 to Z320 her right forearm moves upward and to the rear at the exact same speed the president's upper body moves back (they are in contact); (2) her right hand flips up behind the president's head the moment her lower forearm loses contact with the top of his left shoulder; and (3) the president's upper body stops moving back the moment Ms. Kennedy's lower forearm loses contact with the top of his left shoulder. If the whiplash-type head movement was caused by any other force, Ms. Kennedy's right arm would have either dropped down onto her lap commencing Z316, or stayed put. I note that scientists from Itek Optical Solutions independently arrived at the same conclusion when they analyzed the Zapruder film in 1976.

The Babushka Lady is not holding a camera - From what I see in frames Z292 to Z295, Ms. Burrows is holding up to her eyes a shiny pair of gold-colored opera binoculars. See intro to Chapter 5.

Table 8
Signature two-frame jolts and cranial eruptions due to a bullet striking the president or governor and transferring momentum to the wounded area or a bullet shock wave passing under and striking a camera at Mach 1 speed
1. Z223/Z224: the governor's right shoulder is driven downward and forward (Z/M/N films);
2. Z313/314: a bullet shock wave passed under and struck the left side of Zapruder's camera as it was generating a loud cracking sound creating blurred images in two frames (Z film);
3. Z313/314: the governor's right wrist jumps at least an inch forward and away from him (Z film);
4. Z313/314: the president's head is driven downward and forward about an inch amidst a conspicuous cranial eruption of blood and brain matter (Z/M/N/B films). Because it was near vertical and just a few feet high, the Z313 cranial eruption did not appear to create significant fallout outside of the rear seat area with most of it landing on the president by Z319;
5. Z330/331:the president's head was driven downward and forward about 3 inches in the midst of head-and-shoulder level jettisons of brain matter with a spray hitting Ms. Connally in the back of her head and driving it downward and forward between Z331 and Z332. Brain matter rains down within the limo and on the lid of the trunk from Z332 to Z337 (Z/M/N films and reaches Hargis from Z335 to Z338 (M/N films) and Agent Hill as well (N film);
6. Z331: a bullet shock wave passed under and struck the left side of Zapruder's camera as it was generating a loud cracking sound creating blurred images in two frames (Z film).

2: The Zapruder Assassination Sequence

Table 9
Observable first shot reflex and alarm reactions for the Zapruder film
Z221-shot reflex reactions: distinguishable blurred film images and spontaneous movements commencing 2.5 +/- 1 Z-frame equivalents after the sound reaches the person reacting
1. Z225: wounded President Kennedy and Governor Connally began grimacing (Z film);
2. Z226: startled President Kennedy began darting his head to the left and jerking his arms up (Z film);
3. Z226: startled Governor Connally began darting his head to the left and jerking his right arm up and commencing Z230 attempted to take a concerted look back over his left shoulder (Z film);
4. Z226: startled Jackie Kennedy commenced a quick glance to her left (Z film);
5. Z226: startled Agents Greer and Kellerman commenced quick glances to their right (Z film);
6. Z226: two south-of-Elm spectators that were looking at the president and clapping when he passed by them at about Z215, stopped clapping and began darting their heads toward the TSBD (Z film);
7. Z226: startled Nellie Connally began darting her head to the right and commencing Z230 took a concerted look back over her right shoulder toward the president (Z film);
8. Z226: startled Motorcycle-Officers Hargis and Martin began darting their heads to the right and commencing Z230 took concerted looks toward the president (Z film);
9. Z226: startled Agents Hill and McIntyre who were respectively looking forward/right and straight forward from the Queen Mary's left running board began stiffening and darting their heads left/right (Hill) and slightly right (McIntyre) and commencing Z230 Hill began taking a concerted look hard right (Z film);
10. Z227: startled grassy knoll filmmaker Zapruder jiggled his camera creating a single frame with blurred images (Z film).
Z221-shot alarm reactions: deliberate movements or actions commencing 7.5 +/- 2 Z-frame equivalents after the sound reaches the person reacting
1. Z230: alarmed Motorcycle-Officer Chaney who disappeared from Zapruder's view at Z207 presumably began turning his head to the left in looking toward the president (the look toward the president was complete as of the Z253 Altgens photo);
2. Z230: alarmed Agent Ready on the Queen Mary's right running board; Agent Landis on the right running board, and Agent Hickey in the left rear seat who collectively disappeared from Zapruder's view at Z208 presumably began turning their heads to look back toward the TSBD (the head turns are complete as of the Altgens Z253 photo).

Table 10
Observable second shot reflex and alarm reactions for the Zapruder film
Z310-shot reflex reactions: distinguishable blurred film images and spontaneous movements commencing 2.5 +/- 1 Z-frame equivalents after the sound reaches the person reacting
1. Z316: mortally wounded President Kennedy began jerking his right arm up in front of his chest as his head began snapping back in whiplash fashion due to Ms. Kennedy spontaneously shoving him away from her (Z film);
2. Z316: startled Jackie Kennedy began spontaneously shoving her husband away by extending both of her arms in the process of recoiling (Z film);
3. Z316: wounded Governor Connally began darting his head to the left and by Z321 was frantically lunging toward the front of the limo to get his head down (Z/M/N films);
4. Z316: startled Nellie Connally began leaning back/recoiling and by Z321 was ducking down toward the front of the limo to get her head down (Z/M/N films);
5. Z316: startled Agent Greer behind the wheel of the presidential limo began darting his head to the left and by Z321 was ducking his head down toward the steering wheel (Z/M/N films);
6. Z316: startled Agent Kellerman in the right-front seat of the presidential limo began darting his head to the left and by Z321 was ducking it down toward the dash (Z/M/N films);
7. Z316/317: startled Motorcycle Officer Hargis started darting his head slightly to the right and slightly upward and then continued looking out over the knoll as if oblivious to the Z313 cranial explosion (Z/M/N films);
8. Z316/317: startled south-of-Elm grass-infield-spectator Toni Foster a.k.a. the Running Woman who was trotting toward the limo began turning to the left and leaning back/recoiling (Z film);
9. Z318: startled-grassy knoll filmmaker Zapruder jiggled his camera causing two frames of blurred images (Z film).
Z310-shot alarm reactions: deliberate movements or actions commencing 7.5 +/- 2 Z-frame equivalents after the sound reaches the filmmaker or person reacting
1. Z321: alarmed Jackie Kennedy started straightening up in her seat and inspecting the damage to her husband's head (Z/N/B films);
2. Z321: alarmed south-of-Elm grass-infield-spectator Toni Foster a.k.a. the Running Woman who was trotting toward the limo began stopping dead in her tracks (Z/N/B films);
3. Z321: alarmed Motorcycle-Officer Hargis began turning his head to the right and was looking out to the right from Z321 to Z325. He then darted his head to the left commencing Z326 and was looking toward the president by Z330 (Z/N/M films).

2: The Zapruder Assassination Sequence

Table 11
Observable third shot reflex and alarm reactions for the Zapruder film
Z328-shot reflex reactions: distinguishable blurred film images and spontaneous movements including grimacing, flinching, cringing, ducking, and very rapid arm or head movements commencing 2.5 +/- 1 Z-frame equivalents after the sound reaches Zapruder or the person reacting
1. Z333: started Jackie Kennedy began cringing and recoiling while jerking her right forearm up behind the president's head commencing Z333 (Z and N films);
2. Z333: startled Nellie Connally began turning/ducking her head to the right and leaning back as she was showered with brain matter and was diving down toward the center of the limo by Z338 (Z/M/N films);
3. Z333: startled Agent Greer behind the wheel of the presidential limo began leaning/turning/ducking slightly to his right and cringing (Z/M/N films);
4. Z333: startled Agent Kellerman in the presidential limo's right-front seat started turning/ducking his head to the left and was diving down toward the center of the limo by Z338 (Z/M/N films);
5. Z333: unconscious Governor Connally began dropping down left-shoulder first onto his wife's lap (Z/M/N films);
6. Z333: startled Motorcycle-Officer Martin began flexing his right wrist concurrent with Hargis (M /Z films);
7. Z333: startled Motorcycle-Officer Hargis began darting his head to the left then right while looking toward the president and flexing his wrists (Z/M/N films);
8. Z333: startled south-of-Elm picture-taker Richard Bothun began darting his head to his left and leaning back in recoiling (Z and N films);
9. Z333: a startled-unidentified-south-of-Elm grass-infield spectator who was trotting toward the presidential limo began dropping his arms and commencing Z339 began stopping dead in his tracks (Z film);
10. Z336: startled grassy knoll-filmmaker Zapruder jiggled his camera creating a single frame with blurred images (Z film).
Z328-shot alarm reactions: deliberate movements or actions including head turns toward the president or sound source, stopping, and flight commencing 7.5 +/- 2 Z-frame equivalents after the sound reaches Zapruder or person reacting
1. Z339: alarmed Jackie Kennedy began rising in her seat and climbing on the trunk (Z and N films);
2. Z339: alarmed Motorcycle-Officer Hargis began turning his head to the right and stopping his cycle partly in response to being struck by brain matter (Z and N films);
3. Z339: alarmed south-of-Elm grass-infield *AP* photographer James Altgens continued a classic week-kneed recoil that presumably started as a reflex reaction at Z333 (Z film);
4. Z339: alarmed south-of-Elm grass-infield-spectator Malcolm Summers started dropping to the ground (in progress as of Z345 of Z film).

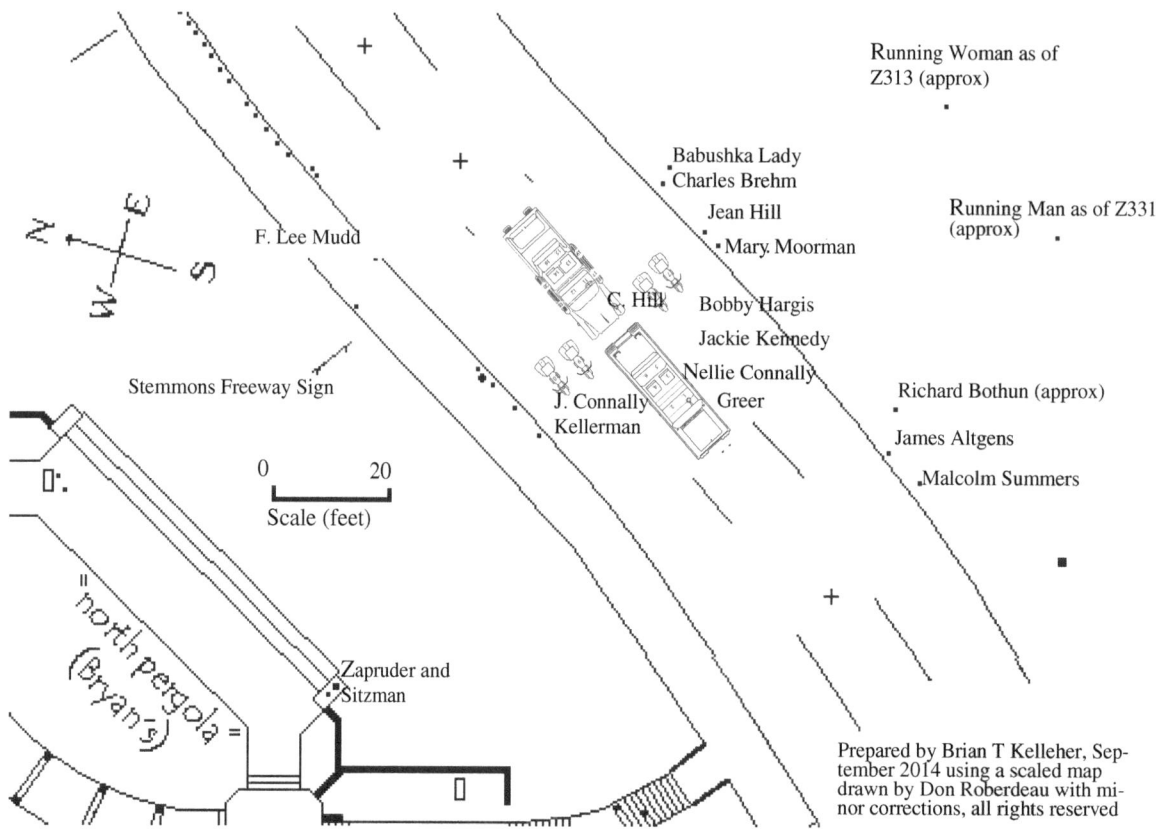

Figure 3

Zapruder's field of vision from Z225 to Z350 - The presidential limo, Queen Mary, and motorcycle escort are positioned and shown approximately to scale as they were as of Z313. The spectators shown are the only ones in Zapruder's view during this interval in the area depicted. Note that as of Z313, Altgens' view of the president's head was completely obstructed by the Connallys and Ms. Kennedy. The limo/Queen Mary drawing is from Trask, 1994, p. 63.

National Archives via Wikipedia

Figure 4

Abraham Zapruder's live interview by Jay Watson, *WFAA TV*, 2:30 P.M. Dallas time, November 22, 1963 and his camera - Watson, who was program director witnessed the assassination from the east side of Houston Street in the company of TV-personality Jerry Hanes, Mr. Peppermint. Still out of breath from racing five blocks back to his office with the Newman family in tow, Watson broke the news to local TV viewers at 12:45 interrupting a show on the latest women's fashions (WFAA TV Collection/Sixth Floor Museum at Dealey Plaza, www.JFK.org).

2: The Zapruder Assassination Sequence

Figure 5

Signature jolts and reflex reactions for the Z221 first shot: Z frames Z222-Z224 and Z228: - <u>Right shoulder jolt</u> - Between Z222 and Z223, the governor's right shoulder jolts downward and forward causing his right shirt cuff to disappear from view. <u>Reflex reactions</u> - From frame Z225 to Z330, we see the president and governor just beginning to react in unison to the effects of a bullet that passed through both their bodies at Z223. Between Z224 and Z228 Ms. Kennedy glances left and Agents Greer and Kellerman to the right. Agents McIntyre and Hill, Motorcycle Officers Martin and Hargis, and the two spectators on the south side of Elm all dart their heads to the right. The reflex reactions commence within frame Z226 and are complete by Z228. These are cropped images that I photo edited to increase brightness and contrast (Zapruder Family Collection/The Sixth Floor Museum at Dealey Plaza http://www.jfk.org).

The Complete Unraveling of the JFK Assassination

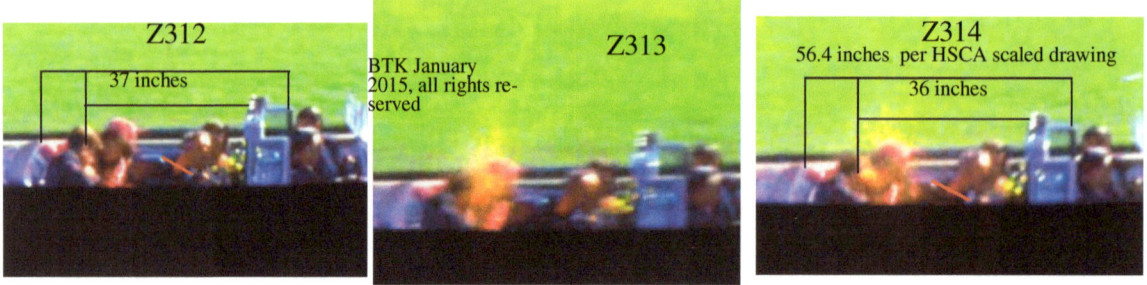

The conspicuous Z313 cranial explosion just before the start of reflex reactions for all limo occupants. The bullet's impact drove the president's head about an inch downward and forward from Z312 to Z314 and drove the governor's right wrist an inch or two forward and to the right also causing it to flex.

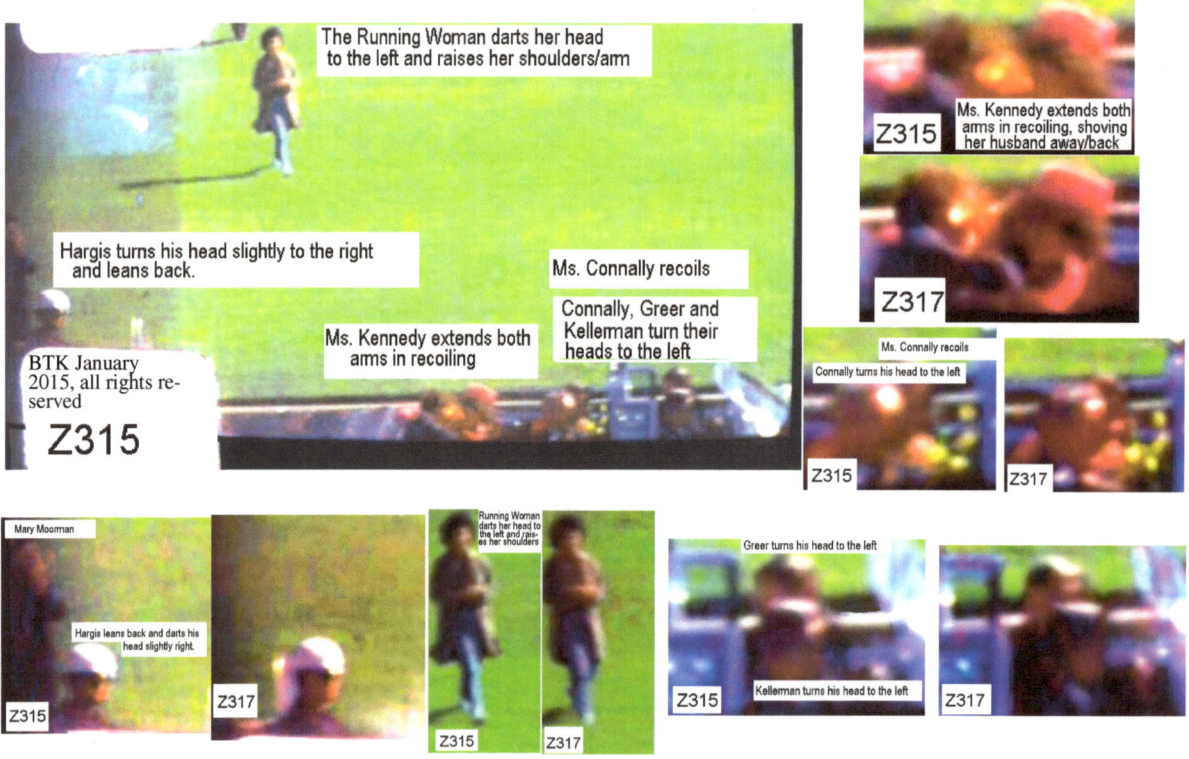

Figure 6

Signature jolts, cranial eruptions and reflex reactions for the Z310 second shot: Z frames Z312-Z315 and Z317 - <u>Signature jolts</u> - From Z312 to Z314, we see the president's head jolting downward and forward an inch amidst a cranial eruption. We also see the governor's right wrist jumping forward and flexing. <u>Reflex reactions</u> - From frame Z315 to Z317, everyone in view exhibits discernible reflex reactions. Within the limo, the president is jerking his right arm upward. Ms. Kennedy is extending both arms as she recoils away from the president and is shoving the president away from her causing his head and upper body to snap back. The governor and Agent Greer are turning their heads to the left and ducking. Ms. Connally is recoiling/leaning back. Agent Kellerman is turning his head to the right and ducking. Outside the limo Officer Hargis is turning his head to the right and tilting it back. The Running woman is darting her head to the left and raising her right arm and shoulders. In the midst of these human-reflex reactions, Zapruder jiggled his camera resulting in two frames of blurred images at Z318/319. The reflex reactions commence within frame Z316 and are complete by Z318. These are cropped images that I photo edited to increase brightness and contrast (Zapruder Family Collection/The Sixth Floor Museum at Dealey Plaza http://www.jfk.org).

2: The Zapruder Assassination Sequence

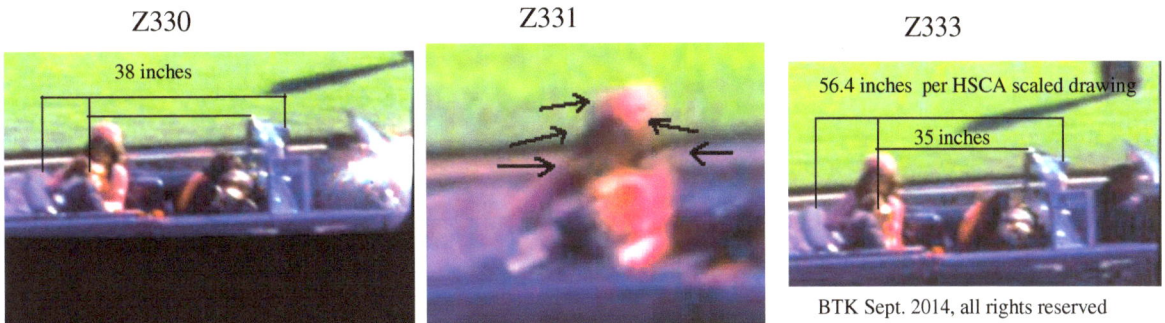

Another cranial eruption at Z330/331 just before the start of reflex reactions for all limo occupants. The bullet's impact at the end of frame Z330 drove the president's head about 3 inches downward and forward from Z330 to Z332 with most of the movement at Z331. The black arrows show a jettison from the cowlick area that correlates with what we see in the Muchmore and Nix film images. The jettison is just barely starting at Z330 and is difficult to see at Z331 and Z332 due to the blurring caused by bullet shock waves passing under Zapruder's camera.

Figure 7

Signature jolts and cranial eruptions for the Z328 third shot: Z frames Z330, Z331, Z332, and Z333 - Between Z330 and Z332 we see the president's head jolting downward and forward about 3 inches in the midst of another cranial eruption with most of the movement at Z331. Based on when the movement started, the impact occurred at the very end of Z330. The president's head slammed into Ms. Kennedy's right shoulder and right cheek at Z331 with enough force to drive her upper body backward and upward a few inches. A forward jettison of brain matter hit the back of Ms. Connally's head at Z331 with enough force to drive it forward and downward. As of Z332, brain fluids are landing on the lid of the trunk in the area directly behind the president's head (see red arrows and also Figure 8). These are cropped images that I photo edited to increase brightness and contrast (Zapruder Family Collection/The Sixth Floor Museum at Dealey Plaza http://www.jfk.org).

The Complete Unraveling of the JFK Assassination

Z334 Hargis with Agent Hill coming into view

Z330 from *Life*, 2013 - just before reflex reactions commence and just before brain matter appears on the trunk and Ms. Connally's head.

Z335 Hargis and Hill engulfed in a cloud of brain matter in Muchmore film and per testimony

Z334 from *Life*, 2013 - reflex reactions in progress as blood and brain matter rain down on Ms. Connally and the lid of the trunk

Z337 Hargis and Hill engulfed in a cloud of brain matter in Muchmore film and per testimony

Z337 from *Life*, 2013 - reflex reactions morph into alarm reactions as brain matter stops raining down about this time but continues to spread out over the trunk

Z340 - alarm reactions just starting for Ms. Kennedy, Ms. Connally and Officer Hargis who have been struck by sprays of brain matter. We see a large blood stain directly under the location of the bullet wound in the base of the governor's right shoulder and the president's disrupted cowlick area

Figure 8

Reflex and alarm reactions for the Z328 third shot and visible brain matter fallout: Z frames Z330-Z335, Z337 and Z340 - <u>Fallout</u> - As of Z334, brain matter is raining down on Ms. Connally. Fluids landed on the trunk from Z332 to Z337 and began flowing/spreading rearward. <u>Reflex reactions</u> - From Z334 though Z337, Ms. Kennedy is in the process of recoiling and jerking her right forearm up behind the president's head. Ms. Connally is turning her head to the right. Agent Kellerman, Hargis and Bothun are turning their heads to the left. Agent Greer is cringing and leaning to the right. <u>Alarm reactions</u> - As of Z340 a horrified Hargis is in the process of turning his head hard right and slowing to a stop, Jackie is rising out of her seat and Ms. Connally and Kellerman are diving for the center of the limo. These are cropped images that I photo edited to increase brightness and contrast (Zapruder Family Collection/The Sixth Floor Museum at Dealey Plaza http://www.jfk.org).

2: The Zapruder Assassination Sequence

Figure 9
Zooming in on the reflex reactions for the Z328 shot: Zapruder frames Z333 and Z335. The reflex reactions commence in frame Z333 and are complete by Z335.

Figure 10
The presidential limo traveling west on Main minutes before the assassination - Walt Cisco, *Dallas Morning News*/Bettmann/CORBIS via Wikimedia.

Chapter 3

The Wiegman Assassination Sequence

Along with Bronson, Muchmore, Nix and Zapruder, there were two additional movie makers in Dealey Plaza who had their cameras running during the interval when the final two shots were ringing out. In both instances, however, the presidential limo was not in camera view at the time. Despite this limitation, the images they captured during this interval contain critically important visual evidence in connection with shot timing and shooter location that has been completely overlooked by government and independent investigators. The Dave Wiegman assassination sequence is covered here, and Elsie Dorman's in the next chapter. The Wiegman film turned out to be key once I discovered evidence of his exact camera recording speed (32.0 frames per second) in preparing the fifth edition of this soft-cover book.

In a nutshell, given the documented high amplitude of the shot noise, the visual shot identifiers in the Zapruder and Wiegman films prove irrefutably that the second shot was fired from the TSBD sniper's nest within frame Z310 plus or minus a Z frame given the following: (1) Wiegman, who was about 125 feet away from the assassin, jerked his camera commencing the equivalent of Z315 which is three Z-frame equivalents before Zapruder who was about 260 feet away jerked his at Z318. (2) The spectators lining the street directly in front of the TSBD all jerked their heads or arms commencing at the equivalent of Z313 which is three Z-frame equivalents before the occupants of the presidential limo reacted commencing at Z316, five before Zapruder reacted at Z318 and two before Wiegman reacted at the equivalent of Z315. (3) All of these reaction times are mathematically predictable from the available scientific data (see Chapter 8).

The visual shot identifiers in these same two films similarly prove that the third shot was fired from the TSBD sniper's nest exactly 1 second later within frame Z328 (Z327.5). Since we know Zapruder was recording at 18.3 frames per second, add 18 Z frames or Z-frame equivalents to the Z-film-image counts provided above and the film images confirm that the spectators in front of the TSBD started reacting the equivalent of Z330 [312.5+18=330], Wiegman at the equivalent of Z332 [314.5+18=332], the occupants of the limo at Z333 [315.5+18=333] and Zapruder at Z336 [317.5+18=336].

Camera car 1

Camera car 1, a yellow 1964 Chevy Impala convertible, was jam packed with five media representatives and their equipment. *NBC TV* White-House Cameraman Dave Wiegman and his sound man John Hoefen were in the front seat with the driver, a Texas Ranger. From left to right in the rear seat were *CBS TV* cameraman Tom Craven, White House cameraman Tom Atkins, and White House Press Pool Electrician Cleve Ryan. The information in this chapter on the occupants of camera car 1 and the car itself is culled from Trask's 1994, *Pictures of the Pain*, Chapter 15.

As camera car 1 traveled north down Houston approaching the TSBD, *NBC's* 37-year old Wiegman was sitting on the right side of the open-topped Chevy with his feet on the right-front seat cushion. Wearing his trademark dark Fedora hat, Wiegman and his fellow cameramen are visible in a pre-assassination photo taken by spectator Jay Skaggs just as their car turned onto Houston. Wiegman is holding his 16-mm Bell & Howell FILMO movie camera in his left hand. When he took the photo, Skaggs was standing on the curb near the northeast corner of Houston and Main. Home-movie-maker Mark Bell is visible in the background at the south end of the colonnade with his camera at his eye aimed north. This clue in conjunction with the Hughes-film images puts the timing of the photo at a point in which the presidential limo was still making the turn onto Elm roughly 4 seconds before Zapruder started filming it at Z133 and 11 seconds before Wiegman started his assassination sequence at Z259. See Figure 11.

The yellow convertible is visible in the top of frames Z211 to Z237 of the Zapruder film, at which point it is passing by the southwest corner of the County Records Building. These film images tell us that, as the first shot rang out at Z221, Wiegman's position in camera car 1 was about 55 feet from the point that it began its hard left turn onto Elm and that the car was traveling about 14 feet per second in the straightaway.

> **Tom Atkins, camera car 1** - *We came to the end of the street [Main] and made the right-hand turn, and were going directly at the depository [TSBD]. Just as we turned [about 5 seconds before they started to turn left onto Elm], I remember looking at my watch, and it was 12:30, and just as I looked at my watch I heard an explosion [the Z221 shot]. The thought ran through my mind, "Oh brother, somebody lit a cherry bomb; I bet the secret service are jumping out of their britches." And then immediately following [actually 5 seconds after] there were two more quick explosions [the Z310 and Z328 shots], and my stomach just went into a knot. The explosions were very loud, like they were right in front of me. . . . You know when kids play cowboys and Indians and they go Bam Bam Bam! The last two shots clustered together.* Richard Trask interview, 3/18/89, cited in Trask, 1994, p. 371.

Also under the impression that someone had tossed a cherry bomb, Wiegman raised his camera to his eye about 2 seconds after the first explosion and began filming with his camera pointed at the crowd lining the north side of Elm in front of the TSBD.

About 10 seconds into the sequence and 7 seconds after the Z313 cranial explosion, camera car 1 came to a stop with Wiegman's position in his car about 20 feet shy of the president's position in his limo at the point Zapruder started filming him at Z133. The car had stopped directly in front of Elsie Dorman just after she had completed her final sequence at D494 (Z425). The driver stopped because the three cars in front of them had stopped commencing with the VP follow-up car. We know this because the uncut Wiegman film's frame W330 shows the VP follow-up car stopped opposite the grassy knoll with its brake lights on and left-rear door wide open. Secret Service Agent Lem Johns reportedly exited the car just as the second shot sounded. The car departed before Johns returned as a result of which he reportedly jumped aboard camera car 1.

Within a few seconds and oblivious to the fact that the president had just been assassinated, Wiegman jumped out of the right side of the car with his camera still running. He hit the ground running and sprinted about 75 feet west down the street to a point near the sidewalk that correlates with the position the president passed at about Z185. His camera was swinging wildly. He briefly paused about 10-feet shy of the first lamppost, and then ran about 25-feet west along the street gutter cutting over onto the sidewalk at about Z205. He continued on another 25-feet down the sidewalk and veered up the knoll at a point at about Z230 approximately 25-feet east of the Stemmons Freeway sign. He then ran about 55-feet straight up the knoll to a point on the pergola front steps. After taking some footage of the Hesters who were sprawled on the ground, he bolted about 55-feet back down and across the knoll to a point near the edge of the sidewalk at about Z290 just east of where the Newmans were lying on the ground. After taking some brief footage of the Newmans, he walked out onto the sidewalk and filmed his car as it approached him from a point at the curb right beside the second lamppost. His Dealey Plaza footage ended with some final glimpses of action along the eastern side of the knoll, capturing north-of-Elm witness Cheryl McKinnon lying on the ground, the Chisms heading back down the knoll, and the so-called Umbrella Man sitting at the edge of the sidewalk. His actions were mimicked to some extent by Tom Atkins and then Tom Craven. All three cameramen then piled back into camera car 1 as it proceeded slowly down Elm. Once all were back aboard, the driver sped to the Trade Mart where they learned the presidential entourage was on the way to Parkland Hospital. They had departed Dealey Plaza within about a minute of the assassination. See Figure 11 showing Wiegman's track on foot.

Interviews and testimony

It was not until 26 years after the event that Wiegman was asked to put his memories of his filming on the record. In a telephone interview in March 1989 he told assassination researcher Richard Trask that the shots were evenly spaced and that he hit the ground running between the second and third shots. His film images, however, refute his distant recollections.

> **Dave Wiegman, NBC TV, camera car 1** - *We were in the straightaway heading down to what I now know as the book depository, and I heard the first report and I thought like everybody that it was a good-size firecracker, a cherry bomb. Then when I heard the second one, the adrenaline really started pumping because there was a reaction in the motorcade [presumably referring to Agent Johns' sudden departure from the vice-presidential follow-up car three cars ahead]. . . . I keenly remember right after the incident that my feet were on the ground during one of the reports [his film images refute this]. I don't think I was fast enough to react to the second, but I think on the third one I was running . . . . when the third went off, I really thought I felt the compression on my face. . . . As far as I can remember I heard three shots. I know that they were three shots. The report was the same on the first one as it was on the third one; equidistant apart like a metronome. The only pathetic thing was the sound was like in a gymnasium where you don't know where it's coming from.*
> Richard Trask interview, 3/18/89, cited in Trask, 1994, p. 372 and 387.

Film timeline

Upon their arrival at Parkland Hospital, Wiegman handed his 100-foot-long roll of exposed film to his sound man John Hoefin. After providing the telephone interview with *NBC* headquarters in New York that is cited below, Hoefin was instructed to deliver the film to *NBC* affiliate *WBAP TV* whose studio was located about 30-miles away. He managed to hitch a ride, arriving there by 2:00 p.m. Dallas time. We have his eyewitness report that was broadcast live on *NBC TV* at about 2:00 p.m. Dallas time:

> **John Hoefin, NBC TV, camera car 1** - *As we turned down [actually approached] this moderate curve here, there was a loud shot. . . Then it was immediately followed by two or three more. Everybody sort of ducked and there were people falling on the ground. We did not know who was shot.* Recording of live NBC TV News coverage broadcast from New York approximately 2:00 Dallas time, 11/22/63, "The Kennedy Assassination-Part I," Mad Phat Enterprises, Inc., VHS video tape, 2002.

Via a live feed to New York, *WBAP-TV* newsman Charles Murphy introduced the 2 minutes and 45 seconds of historic footage to anchorman Bill Ryan and a national TV audience at approximately 4:05 p.m. eastern time.

> **Charles Murphy, WBAP-TV newsman** - *Here now are late unedited, unscreened films of the shooting scene in Dallas. This is the scene near the Stemmons Freeway in front, no, this is front of the city hall in Downtown, Dallas, a mile east of the shooting. Heavy crowds lined the downtown streets to view the presidential party.*

As in all the Texas stops, there were many teenagers attracted there by the first lady and the president. This is Main Street. Is this moving west? This is moving west toward the fatal moment. The motorcade is traveling about 20 to 25 miles per hour slowly westward down Main Street in the heart of Dallas, the time about 12:20 during the noon hour, heavy crowds from downtown offices lining the route. That looks like the School Depository Building on the right; I'm not sure. This, this is the scene of confusion. Something has happened here: the cameraman running toward the scene for the presidential car ahead of him. We caught just a blurry glance at the old school depository building from which the sniper fired the shot. This is the reaction from the crowd. All is confusion at the scene: here, a woman shelters herself; now, racing toward the hospital . . .
Recording of live NBC TV News coverage broadcast from New York approximately 2:20 Dallas time, 11/22/63, "The Kennedy Assassination-Part I," Mad Phat Enterprises, Inc., VHS video tape, 2002.

After cutting all but 13 seconds of the original including a little bit of the Dealey Plaza footage, *NBC* used the Wiegman footage extensively during the first three days of its assassination coverage. Soon after, it sold a copy of the edited footage and its broadcast rights to *Hearst Newsreel*.

In 1967, *NBC* donated all its tapes of the Kennedy era to the Kennedy Library (TNN 255-4). *NBC* is presumably still in possession of the original exposed film if it exists.

Available versions and Wiegman's original and re-recorded camera speed

Wiegman's complete footage covering the president's arrival in Dallas, the motorcade, and the assassination's aftermath includes more than twenty sequences, just three of which were taken in Dealey Plaza.

It was not until July 2016 when I took the trouble to do a manual frame count for the unedited/uncut version of Wiegman's Dealey Plaza footage, that I made the monumental discovery that it runs at 30.0 frames per second and was recorded by Wiegman at 32.0 frames per second. The three Dealey Plaza sequences comprise 1,091 frames that run for 36.4 seconds at 30 frames per second. The extremely important first sequence runs 27.2 seconds and has 816 frames. It starts 2 seconds after the first shot was fired and documents the auditory reflex reactions of the spectators lining Elm Street in front of the TSBD as the second and third shots were fired. The second sequence runs about 4.2 seconds and has 126 frames. The third runs 5.0 seconds and has 149 frames. The first two sequences are separated by an approximately 4-second-long camera stop and the last two by an approximately 1-second-long interruption. The entire recording is of poor resolution.

I call the discovery of Wiegman's camera speed monumental because it confirms the forensic value of using visual shot identifiers to establish beyond a reasonable doubt that two shots were fired from the TSBD sniper's nest at Z309.5 and Z327.5, plus or minus a Z frame (0.06 seconds). To defend this claim, I need only point out that in my earlier editions of this book, I was able to establish the precise re-recorded speed of Wiegman's camera at 25.6 frames per second using the onset of Wiegman's overt reflex reaction to the Z310 shot noise.

Here is how this happened. Because of the poor resolution of the raw footage on the *NBC-TV* broadcast, I was compelled from the start to use the widely distributed higher quality version of the Wiegman Dealey Plaza footage I found on Robert Grodin's DVD *JFK Assassination Films: A Case for Conspiracy* published in 2003 by *Delta Entertainment Corporation*, Los Angeles, CA. Though Grodin's version has much better image quality than what I could find of the raw footage, the first sequence is missing the first 7.5 frames as well about a second and a half of additional footage in the middle where Wiegman is running west down Elm with his camera swinging wildly; there are two splices.

Like other unwary assassination researchers, because the Grodin version runs at 24 frames per second, I assumed that Wiegman recorded his film at something close to 24 frames per second which according to what I have read is considered standard for that era. I should have known better. It is now plainly obvious to me that either Grodin or someone before him had re-recorded at 24 frames per second the raw footage that *NBC* had broadcast at 30 frames per second. This explains why I was encountering 25 percent duplicate frames conducting my frame-by-frame analysis of his enhanced version. I now understand that to convert the non-duplicate Grodin-version frame numbers to the actual broadcast speed of 30 frames per second, one has to use a 1.25 multiplier: [30/24=1.25]. Alternatively, one can establish a re-recorded Wiegman film speed of 25.6 frames per second by using a 1.25 divider: (32/1.25=25.6).

Since the universal standard for TV news has long been 24 frames per second and the Grodin version runs at 24 frames per second, it has been generally assumed that Wiegman was recording his news footage at this speed. This assumption was oblivious to the fact that the unedited version runs at 30 frames per second in slightly slowed motion consistent with the common practice of over-cranking when taking motion pictures from a moving vehicle. The over-cranking provides a much more stable and appealing product. According to manufacturer information, the FILMO camera that Wiegman was using had multiple camera-speed settings to choose from including 12, 16, 18, 24, 32, and 64. The speed could also be adjusted manually within these settings by simply turning a knob. We now know he had the camera set to record at 32 frames per second.

Zapruder-film correlation for the original and re-recorded camera speeds

Knowing the uncut version's precise camera recording speed was 32.0 frames per second, we can sync the Wiegman film with the Zapruder film to the nearest Z frame using Wiegman-frame W330. This frame has the presidential limo in distant view accelerating toward the underpass with the staff of the flag mounted on its right-front fender just about even with the second-to-last street-light tower on the north side of Elm. Via sightlines, frame W330=Z447 (see Figure 11). Thus, assuming the camera was recording at exactly 32.0 frames per second, Wiegman started filming at W001=Z259: [330/32=10.31] and [10.31x18.3=188.7] and [258+189=447].

We can confirm this start time using visual shot identifiers. Turning our attention to the raw Wiegman-film images, there is a conspicuous seven-frame interval of blurred images commencing 3.09 seconds into the sequence at W099, just before Wiegman reversed his right-to-left panning direction [099/32=3.09]. As discussed later on, I was able to confirm that this blurring is shot related because it comes two Z-frame equivalents after overt telltale human-reflex reactions commence among the spectators that were in view at the time. As shown later, if we reasonably assume that the shot that caused the blurring and spectator reactions was fired from the TSBD sniper's nest within frame Z310, allowing two Z frames for sound travel and three for Wiegman's human reflex reaction it follows that W099=Z315: [310+5=315]. This confirms that Wiegman started his first Dealey Plaza sequence at W001=Z259 plus or minus a frame: [3.09x18.3=56.5] and [258+57=315].

We can further verify the Z259 start time by conducting a sightline analysis that takes advantage of the fact that, between Z211 and Z237, Zapruder had inadvertently filmed camera car 1 moving down Houston Street within a few seconds of when Wiegman started filming his first Dealey Plaza sequence. At Z228, Wiegman's camera position has just moved behind the trunk of a tree from Zapruder's perspective at which point camera car 1 is moving about 13.9 feet per second. We know this because the Z film shows it traversing its own length of 17.5 feet in 23 Z frames (Z213 to Z236) which is 1.26 seconds: [23/18.3=1.26] and [17.5/1.26 = 13.9]. At Z228, Wiegman's camera's position in the front seat of the car is about 55 feet from the stop line at the south side of the intersection of Houston and Elm. From Wiegman's sightlines to various points on the front side of the TSBD we can establish that at frame W008 he was 28 feet closer to the same stop line. Thus, providing the driver maintained his speed at 13.9 feet per second throughout, the car would have covered the 28 feet distance in 2.0 seconds: [28/13.9=2.0]. This is 37 Z frames: [2.0x18.3=36.6). Thus, W008=Z264: [227+37=264]. This would put the start of the Wiegman sequence at W001=Z257: [264-8=257].

Figures 11 and 12 show the sightlines that were used to sync the W film to the Z assassination sequence including those used to document the exact positions of filmmaker Tina Towner and north-of-Elm spectators Stetson-Hat Man and O.V. Campbell.

In view of the above correlations, in conducting the following visual shot identifier analysis, I assumed W001=Z259 with 100 percent confidence in the results.

Despite the fact I would have much preferred to use the uncut version at 32 frames per second for the following analysis, I was compelled to use the Grodin DVD version because I needed the best resolution possible to discern and illustrate reflex reactions. Thus, to allow for use of the Grodin version that is in sync with the Z, N and M films, I divided Wiegman's 32 frames per second recording speed by 1.25 to arrive at a re-recorded Wiegman recording speed of 25.6 frames per second: [32/1.25=25.6].

The first 150 frames/6 seconds based on a re-recorded camera speed of 25.6 frames per second

From the triangulated sightlines (Figure 12) we can tell that Wiegman started filming at W001 (Z259) when his position in the car was about 30 feet from the stop line that marks the start of the intersection of Houston and Elm.

As the sequence opens, Wiegman has all but the east and west ends of the first floor of the TSBD in view and the spectators lining the street in front of it including near center frame Vice President O.V. Campbell, Oswald's boss Roy Truly, and a tall man in a light-colored suit and Stetson hat. The press-pool car and the rear two-thirds of the mayor's car are in camera view just ahead. The mayor's car has almost completed the left-hand turn and the press pool car is about halfway through it. The right-rear corner of the mayor's car disappears from view to camera left by W035 (Z283).

The sightlines further show that the driver slows down to about 7 feet per second as he approaches the intersection and starts cutting the wheel to the left at about W070 (Z308). At this point, Wiegman's camera position is about 10 feet shy of the stop line. During these first few seconds, Wiegman is panning his camera slowly to the left, presumably trying to record the crowd's reaction to the first explosion and/or its source. There is nothing in the movements of the camera or the spectators, however, to suggest any reactions to loud explosions during this interval. See Figure 12.

By W073 (Z310), the car is just about to start the left turn. As the assassin fires his second shot, Wiegman is about 110 feet southeast of the base of the TSBD at a point 125 feet southeast of the sniper's nest. With the car turning left, Wiegman is holding the camera steady giving the impression of a slow pan to the left. The northwest corner of the TSBD is in view to camera right in the background as well as the front of the small building it adjoins with its garage door wide open. To camera left there is a blurry line of spectators in view lining the edge of the sidewalk going west down Elm.

Wiegman's reflex reaction to the blast of the Z310 shot is evident in seven frames of conspicuous blurring from W080 to W086. Commencing at W087, with the camera back under control and the car turning left, he pans upward and to the right to the line of spectators at the curb as if looking for the source of or a reaction to the noise.

During the critical interval W073 through W079, there are approximately twenty spectators in reasonably clear view allowing us to closely scrutinize their reflex reactions to the Z310/W073 shot noise. This includes a group of nine TSBD employees comprised of one man in a dark suit and hat and eight women to his immediate left (camera right) that are clustered together at the edge of where the sidewalk begins on the north side of Elm. From Wiegman's vantage point they are directly in front of a traffic-light pole and just to camera right of the southwest corner of the TSBD building. To camera left of the man in the dark suit, there are another nine or ten women in view standing in single file along the edge of the sidewalk. From Zapruder's vantage point they are behind the press-pool car and in front of a route-direction sign and the trunk of the big oak tree that the assassin was shooting over.

The careful observer will discern classic concurrent reflex reactions (rapid head turns primarily up and to the left) between W076 (Z312) and W078 (Z314) for everyone in view. The head turning is so rapid and pronounced in frame W077 (Z313) that it results in localized blurring which is why I am tagging it as the start time despite the fact that some of the arm jerking and head darting starts in the prior frame. A short-stature woman who is standing in the street at the very edge of the sidewalk along with darting her head to her left jerks her right hand to her ear. Some of the reflex reactions morph into alarm reactions. Commencing W085 (Z319), a woman standing behind the man in the hat starts running toward the TSBD and another woman standing at the curb to his immediate right begins looking back over her right shoulder.

From W093 through W102 (Z324.5-331), Wiegman pans rapidly to his right filming the same line of spectators he shot just a few seconds before as if he is continuing to look for the source of or a reaction to the second-shot noise. When TSBD Vice President O.V. Campbell comes into camera view commencing W097 (Z327) he seems to be talking to some women to his immediate right. According to WC testimony given by TSBD female employees standing in this particular area, one of the women Campbell was addressing was TSBD clerical supervisor Geraldean Reid.

Geraldean (Mrs. R.A.) Reid, north side of Elm in front of TSBD entrance, 51-year-old TSBD employee with fellow-employees Arnold, Campbell, Drago, Holt, Jacobs, Johnson, Nelson, Rackley/Baker, Richey, Simmons, Truly, et al. *I heard three shots. And I turned to Mr. Campbell and I said, "Oh, my goodness, I am afraid those came from our building," because it seemed like they came just so directly over my head, and then I looked up at the windows, and saw three colored boys up there . . . WC testimony, 3/25/64.*

The sightlines show that by W098 (Z328), as the third shot rang out, camera car 1 had traveled another 10 feet into the turn and was about 100 feet southwest of the base of the TSBD and 115 feet from the sniper's nest. Wiegman's reactions to the loud blast of the final shot are evident from W103 to W109 (Z332-36) during which time he brings his rapid pan to the right to an abrupt halt directly in front of the TSBD entrance. The first three of these frames W103 to W105 (Z332-33) contain overt signature up and down blurring.

As was the case for the Z310/W073 shot, Wiegman's signature blurring is coming two Z frame equivalents after all the spectators in blurry view exhibit signature reflex reactions to the W098/Z328) shot noise. This includes the entire group of nine TSBD employees mentioned above and another ten standing in single file to their left directly in front of the TSBD entrance. Due to the left to right blurring from the rapid pan, these movements, which commence at W102/Z331, are easiest to see among those in the right half of the frames including from camera left-to-right O.V. Campbell, a young Latin man, and Roy Truly. The young man in particular takes a dramatic hard look back over his left shoulder at the same time Campbell and Truly dart their heads to their left. As the images clear during the transition period W110-11 (Z337), we see two women spectators with their hands covering their mouths in "oh my goodness!" fashion. We also see that Roy Truly has turned his head slightly to the right and looks further to his right between W110 and W128 (Z337-50) at which point he disappears from blurry view.

From W112 to W117 (Z338-42), Wiegman pans upward and to camera left. In the blurry images we see the same young man that had dramatically turned his head starting off in the direction of the TSBD commencing W110 (Z337) concurrent with Roy Truly looking further to the right. The Couch film reveals he changed his mind. It shows him at about the same location 20 seconds or so later at which point Roy Truly is heading toward the TSBD entrance having noticed Motorcycle Officer Baker heading that way on the run. Stetson Hat Man is looking up toward the sniper's nest. See Figure 51.

Commencing W118 (Z342), Wiegman pans quickly left picking up the same spectators lining the north side of Elm that he has already filmed twice. We see two women on the run, one of whom is presumably the woman in the group of eleven TSBD employees who set off running toward the TSBD at W085 (Z319). Commencing at W140 (Z358), we encounter an additional eight-frame interval of heavily blurred images with the camera swinging to the left (west down Elm). Wiegman's rapid pan to the left stops with a few clear frames commencing at W149 (Z365) providing a glimpse of a group of women lining the curb just down the street from a concrete pillar. Some of them are craning their necks to look west down Elm and one has moved out into the street gutter and is looking west down Elm.

At this point, camera car 1 is opposite the north end of the reflecting pool with its wheels still turned hard to the left. Clearly, Wiegman is still in the car as it was straightening out and heading down Elm at a crawl before coming to a stop. This is about 5 seconds before the car came to a full stop and still about 6 seconds before he jumps out.

Expected timing of reflex and alarm reactions in the Wiegman film assuming the shots were fired from the TSBD sniper's nest and a re-recorded camera speed of 25.6 frames per second

The time for shot noise to reach Wiegman from the sniper's nest would be 0.10 to 0.11 second - Taking into account both the vertical and lateral components of the distance, when the last two shots rang out Wiegman was approximately 125 feet and 115 feet respectively southeast of the sniper's nest and the paths of the bullets at their closest points. With sonic waves traveling though air at 1,125 feet per second, the loud noise from the Z310 and Z328 muzzle blasts would reach Wiegman's ears in 0.10 to 0.11 second: [115/1,125=0.10] and [125/1,125=0.11]. Wiegman was not in the path of bullet shock waves for shots fired at the president from the TSBD.

If the shots were fired from the TSBD sniper's nest, Wiegman's signature blurring would come five Z-frame equivalents after the shots - Given the expected loud level of the shot noise at this relatively close distance, we would expect to see substantial involuntary movement within 0.14 second of the arrival of the sound which is three Z frames [0.14x18.3=2.6]. This is based on a published literature review of auditory response time giving 0.14 to 0.16 as the normal range (Kosinsky, 2008). Adding the time of travel of the sound waves to the anticipated reflex-response time, we would expect to see blurring associated with Wiegman jerking his camera within 0.24 to 0.25 second of the shots [0.10+0.14=0.24] and [0.11+0.14=0.25]. This is five Z frames after a shot [0.24x18.3=4.4] and [0.25x18.3= 4.6].

3: The Wiegman Assassination Sequence

If the shots were fired from the TSBD sniper's nest, Wiegman's alarm reactions would come ten Z-frame equivalents after the shots - The Zapruder film images tell us to look for alarm reactions about eight Z-frame equivalents after the noise reaches the filmmakers' ears. Thus, allowing for 0.11 second (two Z frames) sound-travel time we would expect to see Wiegman's alarm movements commencing ten Z-frames after the shots [8+ 2=10] plus or minus a few frames.

The time for shot noise to reach the crowd on the north side of Elm from the sniper's nest would be 0.05 second - The spectators in Wiegman's view at Z310 (W073) were within about 70 feet of the base of the TSBD building and about 92 feet from the rifle via a hypotenuse calculator. They were in a position where they would hear the muzzle blast in 0.08 second which is 1.5 Z frames [92/1,125=0.08] and [0.08x18.3=1.46]. More significantly, they were within about 50 feet of the bullets' paths meaning they were fully exposed to the sharp crack of the bullet shock wave after it traveled a mere 30 feet. With the bullet traveling at 2,100 feet per second and sonic waves traveling though air at 1,125 feet per second, the shock waves from a shot fired from the sniper's nest would reach the spectators' ears within 0.05 seconds [50/1,125=0.04] and [30/2,100=0.014] and [0.04+0.014=0.05], which is within one Z frame [0.05x18.3=0.7).

If the shots were fired from the TSBD sniper's nest, spectator reflex reactions would come three Z-frame equivalents after the shots - Given the expected very loud level of the shot noise at this relatively close distance, we would expect to see spectator involuntary movement within 0.12 second of the arrival of the noise which is two Z frames [0.12x18.3=2.2]. This is based on a published literature review of auditory response time giving 0.14 to 0.16 as the normal range for lesser noise levels. Adding the time-of travel of the sound waves to the anticipated reflex-response time, we would expect to see spectator reflex reactions within 0.16 second of the shots [0.05+0.12=0.17]. This is three Z frames after a shot [0.17x18.3= 3.1].

If the shots were fired from the TSBD sniper's nest, spectator alarm reactions would come nine Z-frame equivalents after the shots - The Zapruder film images tell us to look for alarm reactions about eight Z-frame equivalents after the noise reaches the spectators ears. Thus, allowing 0.05 second (one Z frame) for sound travel time [0.05 x 18.3 = 0.91], we expect to see spectator-alarm movements commencing nine Z-frames from the shots [8+1=9] plus or minus a few frames.

Distinguishable reactions to the Z310/W073 shot based on a re-recorded camera speed of 25.6 frames per second

Overview - Wiegman's reflex reaction to the Z310 shot is an abrupt stop in his right to left pan. Wiegman's alarm reaction is the reversal of his panning direction commencing at W087.

Wiegman's signature blurring for the Z310/W073 shot commences at W080 (Z315), which is five Z-frame equivalents after the shot as predicted - Commencing at W080 there are seven frames of blurred images resulting from Wiegman abruptly stopping his pan to the left. The first four have very heavy blurring.

Spectator reflex reactions to the Z309.5/W073 shot commence at W077 (Z313), which is three Z-frame equivalents after the shot as predicted - Between W076 (Z312) and W078 (Z314) the entire group of spectators in Wiegman's view as of W076 (Z312) have exhibited discernible reflex reactions comprised primarily of rapid head movements up and to the left. Referring to Figures 13 and 14, the most conspicuous include the following by W078 (Z314): spectators A2, B2, B3, B4, B5 and C1 have conspicuously darted their heads to their left, spectator B2 has ducked to her left, and spectator C1 has jerked her right hand to her ear.

Wiegman's own alarm reaction to the Z310/W073 shot commences at W087 (Z320), which is ten Z-frame equivalents after the shot as predicted - Commencing at W087 (Z320), Wiegman pans up through W092 (Z324) and then quickly to the right in reversing his panning direction as if looking for a reaction to the explosion or its source among the spectators in front of him.

Spectator alarm reactions to the Z310/W073 shot commence at W085 (Z319), which is nine Z-frame equivalents after the shot as predicted - Commencing at W085 (Z319), the woman that ducked starts running toward the TSBD and another woman to her right begins looking back over her right shoulder.

Distinguishable reactions to the Z328/W098 shot based on a re-recorded camera speed of 25.6 frames per second

Overview - Wiegman's reactions to the Z328 shot are a mirror image of his reactions to the Z310 shot. His reflex reaction is an abrupt stop in his left-to-right pan commencing W103 (Z332). His alarm reaction is the reversal of his panning direction commencing W112 (Z337). See Figures 15 and 16.

Wiegman's signature blurring for the Z327.5/W098 shot commences at W103/104 (Z331), which is five Z-frame equivalents after the shot as predicted - Commencing at W103/104 (Z331) and continuing through W110 (Z336) Wiegman abruptly stopped his pan to the right. The camera jolts up and down creating heavy up and down vertical blurring at W103-05 (Z331-32).

Spectator reflex reactions to the Z327.5/W098 shot commence W101 (Z330), which is three Z-frame equivalents after the shot as predicted - Commencing at W101 (Z330), a woman and a young Latin man commence dramatic hard looks back over their left shoulders at the same time everyone else begins darting their heads primarily to the left. Campbell and one of the women jerk their arms. As the images clear during the transition period W110/111, (Z337) we also see two women spectators with their hands covering their mouths in "oh my goodness!" fashion who appear overtly startled one of them being the woman that jerked her arm up. Truly and Stetson Hat Man are looking slightly to their right.

Wiegman's own alarm reaction to the Z328/W098 shot commences at W112 (Z338), which is ten Z-frame equivalents after the shot as predicted - Commencing at W112 (Z338), Wiegman reverses his panning direction. After coming to a stop at W110-11, (Z337), he pans up from W112 through W117 (Z338-42) as if looking for a reaction to the explosion or its source among the spectators in front of him, and then hard left commencing W118 (Z342).

Spectator alarm reactions to the Z328/W098 shot commence at W110 (Z336), which is nine Z-frame equivalents after the shot as predicted - The same startled spectator that had looked hard left commencing at W101 (Z330) starts walking or running away commencing at W110 (Z337) concurrent with Roy Truly looking further to his right. Everyone in view from W110 to W118 (Z337-42) and beyond looks alarmed and is no longer watching the motorcade.

3: The Wiegman Assassination Sequence

Table 12
Observable second shot reflex and alarm reactions for the Wiegman film
Z310/W073-shot reflex reactions: distinguishable blurred film images and spontaneous movements commencing 2.5 +/- 1 Z-frame equivalents after the sound reaches the person reacting
1. Z313/W077: a group of over 20 startled spectators either standing on or near the sidewalk where it begins on the north side of Elm in front of the TSBD or lining the curb to their west began darting their heads primarily up and to the left and one ducked to her left (W film);
2. Z315/W080: startled cameraman Dave Wiegman jerked his camera in abruptly stopping his pan to the left creating four frames of heavily blurred images and three frames of slightly blurred images (W film).
Z310/W073 shot alarm reactions: deliberate movements or actions commencing 7.5 +/- 2 Z-frame equivalents after the sound reaches the filmmaker or person reacting
1. Z318/W084: the alarmed female TSBD employee standing on the sidewalk on the north side of Elm in front of the TSBD who had ducked to her left began walking or running toward the TSBD (W film);
2. Z320/W087: alarmed cameraman Dave Wiegman in the front seat of camera car 1 began reversing his panning direction as if trying to capture on film either the source of the noise or the crowd's reaction (W film).

Table 13
Observable third shot reflex and alarm reactions for the Wiegman film
Z328/W098-shot reflex reactions: distinguishable blurred film images and spontaneous movements commencing 2.5 +/- 1 Z-frame equivalents after the sound reaches the person reacting
1. Z330/W101: the entire line of about 20 spectators standing in blurry view along the north side of Elm in front of the TSBD entrance began darting their heads primarily to the left with two looking hard over their left shoulders and two including O.V. Campbell jerking their arms (W film);
2. Z332/W103/4: startled cameraman Dave Wiegman in the front seat of camera car 1 jerked his camera up and down creating 3 frames of heavily blurred images followed by three frames of lightly blurred images in abruptly ending his rapid pan to the right (W film).
Z328/W098-shot alarm reactions: deliberate movements or actions commencing 7.5 +/- 2 Z-frame equivalents after the sound reaches the filmmaker or person reacting
1. Z337/W110: the alarmed spectator standing on the north side of Elm in front of the TSBD entrance that had looked hard over his left shoulder began to turn and run (W film);
2. Z337/W110: alarmed north-of-Elm-spectator Roy Truly standing along the edge of the street in front of the TSBD entrance began looking further to the right (W film);
3. Z338/W112 alarmed cameraman Dave Wiegman in the front seat of camera car 1 began reversing his panning direction as if trying to capture on film either the source of the noise or the crowd's reaction (W film).

Table 14						
Scientific evidence that the second shot came from the TSBD at Z310/W073						
Synchronization of Zapruder film images at 18.3 frames per second with the re-recorded Wiegman assassination sequence at 25.6 frames per second						
Filmmaker location and camera recording speed (frames per second)	Calculation of time for bullet shock-wave to reach person at 60 degree Mach angle (seconds) (see Chapter 8)	Calculation of time for muzzle-blast noise to reach person from sniper's nest (seconds)	Calculation of minimum time for muzzle-blast or shock wave to reach person (Z frames)	Observed start signature jiggle blurring and human-reflex reactions (frame number as of end of frame)	Calculated reflex-reaction times: the range assumes shot fired at Z309.1 to Z310.0 with reactions commencing early to late in the first frame impacted by the sound. The estimated actual is based on Kosinski
Zapruder on concrete pedestal at grassy knoll's Bryan's pergola ca Z313; camera speed = 18.3 frames per second	See Chapter 8	Zapruder: Z to sniper = 260 ft; sound-travel time to Z: 260/1,125 = 0.23 second	Zapruder: minimum-sound-travel time to Z: 0.23 x 18.3= 4.2 Z frames	Zapruder: Z318 (signature blurring from flinch)	Zapruder's reflex-reaction time: 318-309.1=8.9-4.2=4.7; 317.1-310=7.1-4.2=2.9; Estimated actual: 3
	Limo occupants: bullet to sniper = 260 ft; bullet to person = 5 ft; sound-travel time to person: 260/1,900=0.14 + 5/1,125 = 0.004 = 0.14 second	Limo occupants: person to sniper = 265 ft; sound-travel time to person: 265/1,125 = 0.24 second	Limo occupants: Minimum-sound-travel time to persons: 0.14 x 18.3 = 2.6 Z frames	Limo occupants: Z316 (cringing, ducking and diving)	Limo occupants reflex-reaction time: 316-309.1=6.9-2.6=4.3 315.1-310=5.1-2.6=2.5; Estimated actual: 3
Wiegman in camera car 1 just starting left turn at intersection of Houston and Elm; camera speed = 25.6 frames per second (re-recorded)	Not applicable	Wiegman: W to sniper = 125 ft; sound-travel time to W: 125/1,125]= 0.11 second	Wiegman: minimum-sound-travel time to W: 0.11 x 18.3 = 2.0 Z frames	Wiegman: Z315/W080 (signature blurring caused by abruptly stopping the pan to the left)	Wiegman reflex-reaction time: 315-309.1=5.9-2.0=3.9; 314.1-310=4.1-2=2.1; Estimated actual: 2.5
	Crowd in front of TSBD: bullet to sniper =50 ft; bullet to person = 30 ft; sound-travel time to person: 50/2,100 + 30/1,125 = 0.05 second	Crowd: person to sniper = 70 ft; sound-travel time to person: 70/1,125 = 0.06 second	Crowd: minimum-sound-travel time to persons: 0.05 x 18.3 = 0.9 Z frame	Crowd: Z313/W077 (cringing, head turning and arm movements by multiple spectators)	Crowd reflex-reaction time: 313-309.1=3.9-0.9=3; 312.1-310=2.1-0.9=1.2; Estimated actual: 2.5
Conclusions: Wiegman's s signature blurring for the Z310 shot comes three Z frames (~0.15 seconds) before Zapruder's because he is the equivalent of three Z-frames closer to the sniper's nest taking into account the distances involved, the speed of the bullet, the speed of sound, and the level of noise. Similarly, the crowd reactions that W picked up come two to three Z frame equivalents (~0.1 to 0.15 seconds) before his signature blurring for the exact same reasons.						

3: The Wiegman Assassination Sequence

Table 15
Scientific evidence that the third shot came from the TSBD at Z328/W098
Synchronization of Zapruder film images at 18.3 frames per second with the re-recorded Wiegman assassination sequence at 25.6 frames per second

Filmmaker location and camera recording speed (frames per second)	Calculation of time for bullet shock-wave to reach person at 60 degree Mach angle (seconds) (see Chapter 8)	Calculation of time for muzzle-blast noise to reach person from sniper's nest (seconds)	Calculation of minimum time for muzzle-blast or shock wave to reach person (Z frames)	Observed start signature jiggle blurring and human-reflex reactions (frame number as of end of frame)	Calculated reflex-reaction times: the range assumes shot fired at Z327.1 to Z328.0 with reactions commencing early to late in the first frame impacted by the sound. The estimated actual is based on Kosinski
Zapruder on concrete pedestal at grassy knoll's Bryan's pergola ca Z313; camera speed = 18.3 frames per second	See Chapter 8	Zapruder: Z to sniper = 260 ft; sound-travel time to Z: 260/1,125 = 0.23 second	Zapruder: minimum-sound-travel time to Z: 0.23 x 18.3= 4.2 Z frames	Zapruder: Z336 assuming mid frame (signature blurring from flinch)	Zapruder's reflex-reaction time: 336-327.1=8.9-4.2=4.7; 335.1-328=7.1-4.2=2.9; Estimated actual: 3
	Limo occupants: bullet to sniper = 260 ft; bullet to person = 5 ft; sound-travel time to person: 272/1,900=0.14 + 5/1,125 = 0.004 = 0.14 second	Limo occupants: person to sniper = 265 ft; sound-travel time to person: 265/1,125 = 0.24 second	Limo occupants: Minimum-sound-travel time to persons: 0.14 x 18.3 = 2.6 Z frames	Limo occupants: Z333 (cringing, ducking and diving)	Limo occupants reflex-reaction time: 333-327.1=5.9-2.6=3.3; 332.1-328=4.1-2.6=1.5; Estimated actual: 3
Wiegman in camera car 1 just starting left turn at intersection of Houston and Elm; camera speed = 25.6 frames per second	Not applicable	Wiegman: W to sniper = 115 ft; sound-travel time to W: 115/1,125]= 0.10 second	Wiegman: minimum-sound-travel time to W: 0.10 x 18.3 = 1.8 Z frames	Wiegman: Z332/W103-04 (signature blurring caused by abruptly stopping the pan to the right)	Wiegman reflex-reaction time: 332-327.1=4.9-1.8=3.1; 331.1-328=3.1-1.8=1.3; Estimated actual: 2.5
	Crowd in front of TSBD: bullet to sniper =50 ft; bullet to person = 30 ft; sound-travel time to person: 50/2,100 + 30/1,125 = 0.05 second	Crowd: person to sniper = 70 ft; sound-travel time to person: 70/1,125 = 0.06 second	Crowd: minimum-sound-travel time to persons: 0.05 x 18.3 = 0.9 Z frame	Crowd: Z330/W101 (head turning by five spectators)	Crowd reflex-reaction time: 330-327.1=2.9-0.9=2.0 329.1-328=1.1-0.9=0.2; Estimated actual: 2
Conclusions: Wiegman's signature blurring for the Z328 shot comes four Z frames (~0.22 seconds) before Zapruder's because he is the equivalent of four Z-frames closer to the sniper's nest taking into account the distances involved, the speed of the bullet, the speed of sound, and the level of noise. Similarly, the crowd reactions that W picked up come two to three Z frame equivalents (~0.1 to 0.15 seconds) before his signature blurring for the exact same reasons. Wiegman and the spectators lining the north side of Elm in front of the TSBD reacted a frame faster than mathematically predicted for the Z328 shot.					

The Complete Unraveling of the JFK Assassination

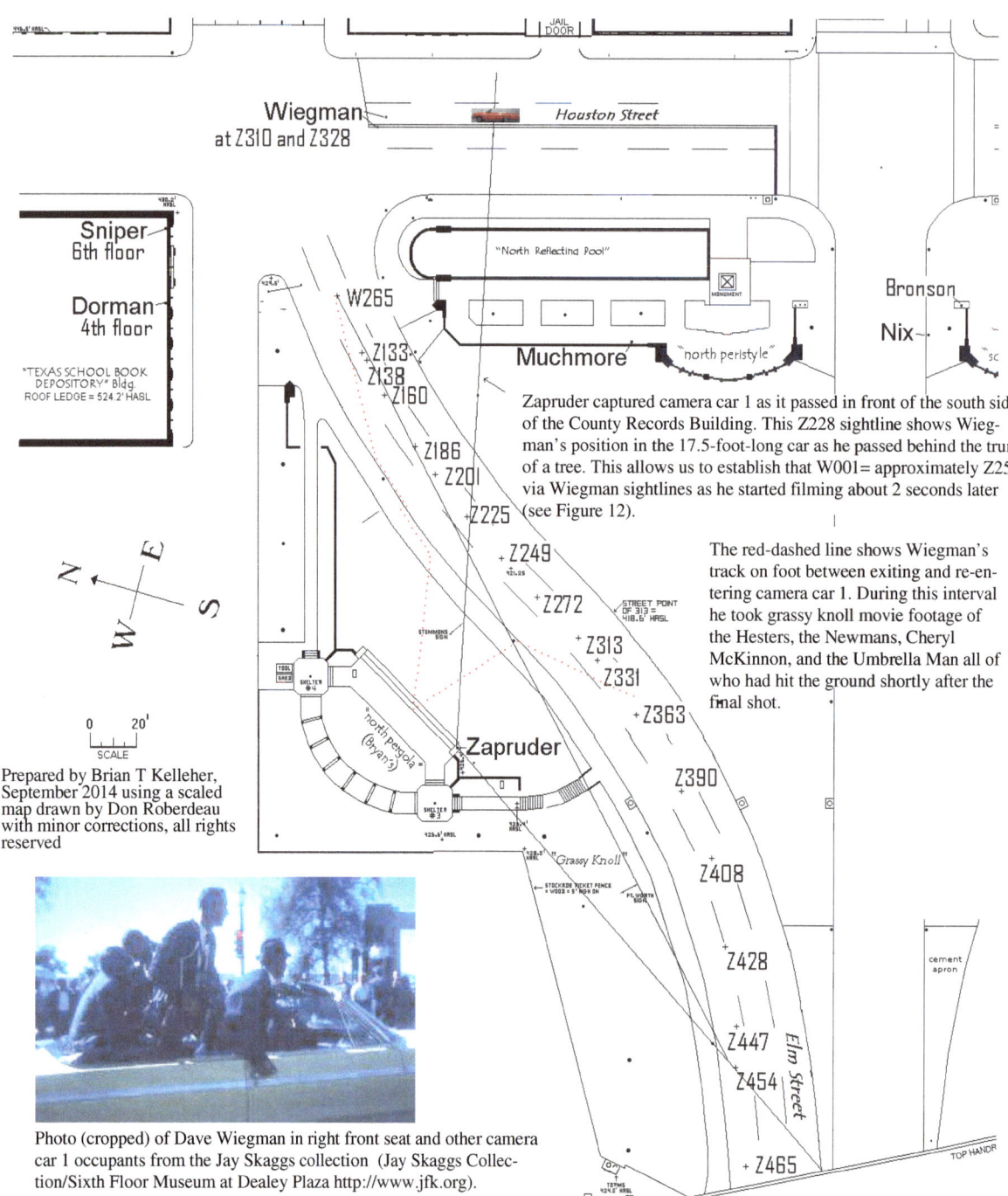

Photo (cropped) of Dave Wiegman in right front seat and other camera car 1 occupants from the Jay Skaggs collection (Jay Skaggs Collection/Sixth Floor Museum at Dealey Plaza http://www.jfk.org).

Figure 11

Syncing the Wiegman and Zapruder films: W265/330=Z447 - Just before he jumped out of the car, Wiegman filmed the action ahead of him on Elm and captured the presidential limo about 30 feet before it entered the triple underpass. It is passing the lead car to its left. I used several lampposts on the north side of Elm and part of the bridge abutment to plot these sightlines for Zapruder at Z228 and Z447 and Wiegman at W265/330. For frame Z228 I show Zapruder's sightline through a tree trunk for Wiegman's position 9 feet from the rear of the 17.5-foot-long camera car 1.

3: The Wiegman Assassination Sequence

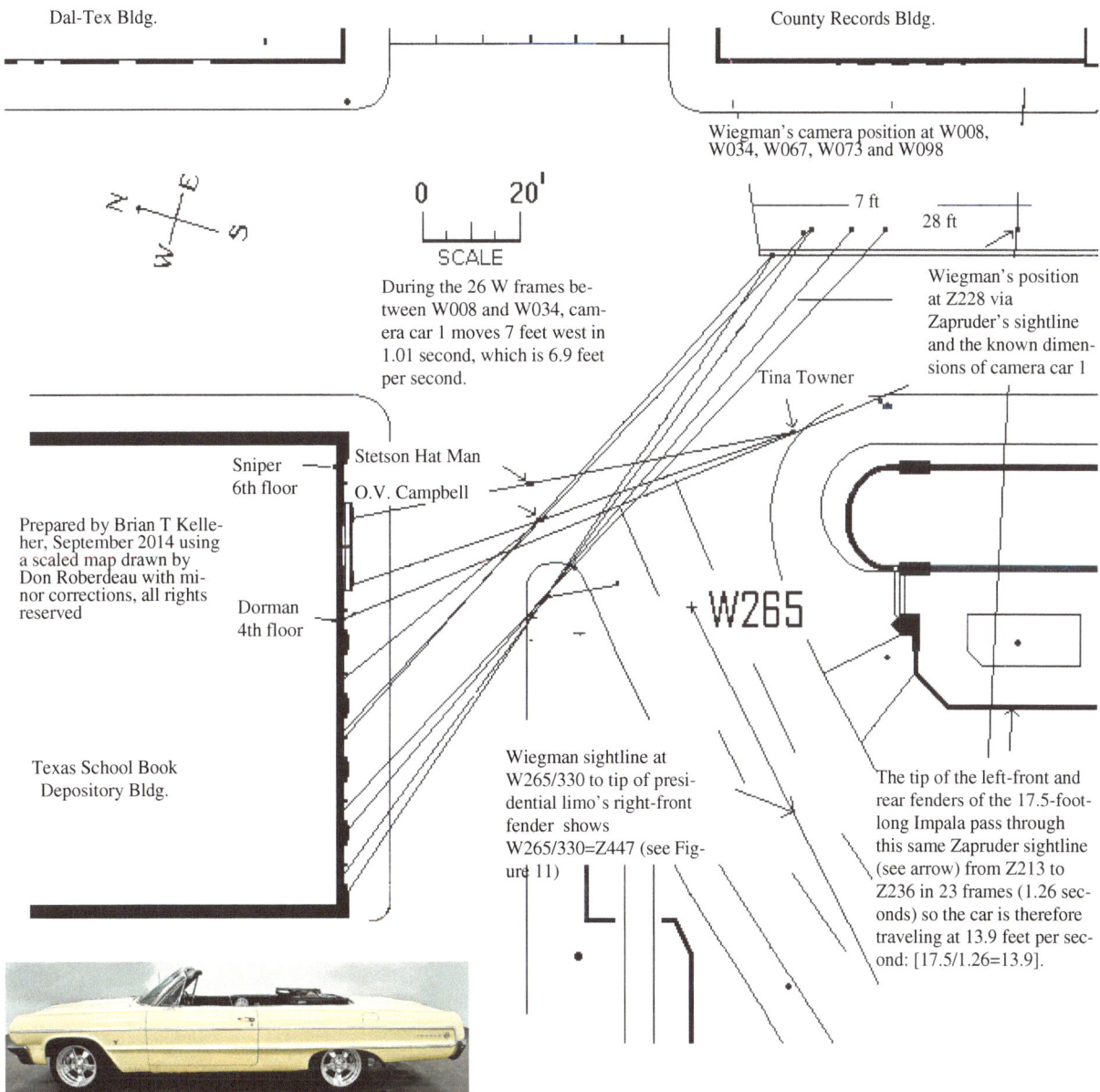

Figure 12

Syncing the Wiegman and Zapruder films: W001=Z259 - Here I used Wiegman and Zapruder sightlines to plot Wiegman's camera position as camera car 1 traveled north on Houston and approached the intersection of Houston and Elm. As indicated above, between Z228 and W008, camera car 1 traveled 28 feet and, at the onset, was traveling at 13.9 feet per second. Assuming the driver maintained this speed over the entire 28 feet, this amounts to 2.0 seconds which is 37 Z frames: [28/13.9=2.0] and [2.0x18.3=36.6]. Thus W001=Z256: [227+37=264] and [264-8=256]. I arrived at W001=Z259 using the onset of signature blurring and human-reflex reactions to the noise of the Z310 shot. Wiegman's camera was recording at 32 frames per second (25.6 for re-recorded versions) and Zapruder's at 18.3. The 1964 Chevy Impala convertible was 17.5 feet long. As indicated, as of W073 (Z310 shot), Wiegman was 110 feet from the base of the TSBD at a point directly below the sniper's nest and 125 feet from the sniper's nest itself 60-feet above. As of W098 (Z328 shot), Wiegman was 100 feet and 115 feet respectively from these same points.

Group A: 1, 2, 3
Group B 1 2, 3/4, 5/6
Group C 1, 2, 3

W075/Z312 - just before the start of reflex reactions that are most obvious for A2, B1, B2, B3, C1, C2

All approximately 20 spectators in Wiegman's camera view between W075 and W077 (Z311-313), including 6 more to camera left, concurrently dart their heads mostly to the left within the same tenth of a second interval of time due to the human auditory reflex reaction to the extremely loud blast of the Z310 shot. Wiegman's camera jerk commences at W080/Z315.

W079/Z314 - reflex reactions that commenced at W077/Z313 are complete within 2 tenths of a second (3 Z frames)

Brian T. Kelleher September. 2014, all rights reserved

Figure 13

Reflex reactions for the Z310 shot: Wiegman frames W075 and W079 (Z312/Z314) - Group A is the three women standing on the edge of the sidewalk in front of the route-direction sign that are leaning forward and looking west down Elm. Group B is the one man and five women standing on the edge of the sidewalk where it begins who are looking toward the press-pool car or camera car 1. Group C is the three women standing on the street directly in front of Group B looking in various directions. Within the 0.11-second interval between W077 and W079 (Z313-314), just after the bullet fired at W073 passed over their heads, all twelve exhibit rapid head movements (flinches) that are most conspicuous for head-turners A2 (left), A3 (right), B1 (tilt back), B2 (left/down), B3 (left), C1 (left) and C2 (left). C1 also raised her right arm. Wiegman's signature blurring commences at frame W080 (Z315) three Z-frame equivalents after the spectators start turning their heads at W077 (Z313) confirming the spectators were closer to the assassin than he was. These are cropped images that I photo edited to increase brightness and contrast (Dave Wiegman, Kennedy Library via *NBC*).

3: The Wiegman Assassination Sequence

W084/Z318 - reflex reaction morph into alarm reactions for A3's head and B2's feet

W089/Z322 - alarm reactions in progress for A3's head and B2's feet

Figure 14
Alarm reactions for the Z310 shot: Wiegman frames W084 and W089 (Z318/Z322) - Group A is the three women standing on the edge of the sidewalk in front of the route-direction sign that are leaning forward looking west down Elm. Group B is the one man and five women standing on the edge of the sidewalk where it begins looking toward the press-pool car. Group C is the five women standing on the street directly in front of Group B looking in various directions. Between W084 and W089 (Z318-322), Spectator A2 is starting to turn her head back to the right and B3, B4, C1 and C2 are looking further to their left than they were at W079/Z318. Spectator B2 has disappeared from view except for her feet. Spectator A3 is in the midst of taking a hard look over her right shoulder. Spectator B2 is walking or running toward the TSBD. Spectator C1 has become engaged in conversation with a woman six spectators to her left who is near O.V. Campbell and has her left hand at her ear. Wiegman has reversed his panning direction. These are cropped images that I photo edited to increase brightness and contrast (Dave Wiegman, Kennedy Library

All these female TSBD employees concurrently dart their heads left or right between W100/Z330 and W103/Z331.5 but the heavy blurring makes it difficult to see

1, 2, 3, 4, 5 6, 7/8, 9/10

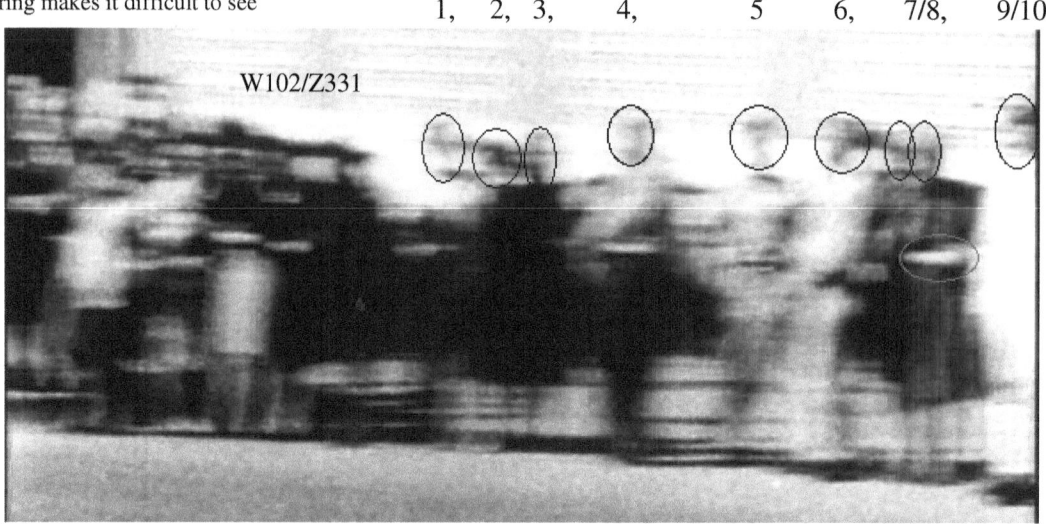

W102/Z331 - All approximately 20 spectators in Wiegman's camera view between W101 and W103 (Z330-332) concurrently dart their heads mostly to the left within the same 0.1 second interval of time due to the human auditory reflex reaction to the extremely loud blast of the Z328 shot [2/18.3=0.11]. Wiegman's camera jerk commenced within frame W103/Z331.5 proving he was located two Z frame equivalents further away from the sniper (see pages 64-65)

1, 2, 3, 4, 5, 6, 7/8, 9/10

BTK Sept. 2014, all rights reserved

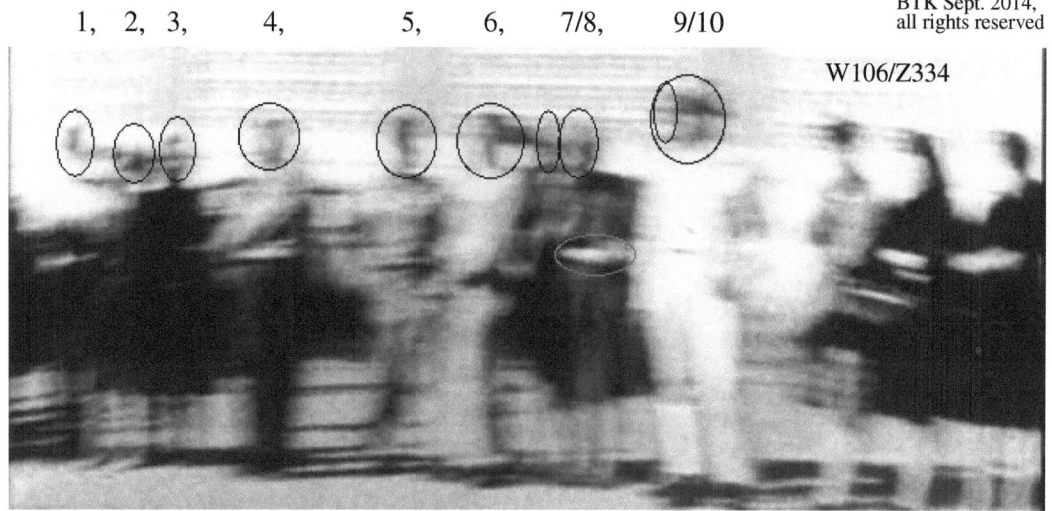

W106/Z334 - reflex reactions that commenced within W101 are complete see 1 thru 6 and 10, head, 8 left

Figure 15

Reflex reactions for the Z328 shot: Wiegman frames W102 and W106 (Z331/Z334) - Spectator 4 is identified as O.V. Campbell, 6 as Roy Truly and 10 as Stetson Hat Man. Within the 0.14-second interval between W101 and W103 (Z330-331.5), Spectators 1 and 5 dart and then turn their heads hard left over their left shoulders and 8 jerks her arm. All the rest dart their heads to the left or right. Some of these subtle movements become more apparent in clear frames W110/111 (see Figure 16). Wiegman's own reflex reaction/camera jerk commences at W103/104 two Z-frame equivalents after the spectators start turning their heads at W101(Z330) confirming the spectators were closer to the assassin than he was. Campbell jerks his left arm up between W100 (Z329.5) and W101 (Z330) (not shown). These are cropped images that I photo edited to increase brightness and contrast (Dave Wiegman, Kennedy Library via *NBC*).

3: The Wiegman Assassination Sequence

W111/Z338 - reflex reactions complete, alarm reactions in progress for 2 and 3

W125/Z347 - alarm reactions continue for 2 and 3

Figure 16
Alarm reactions for the Z328 shot: Wiegman frames W111 and W125 (Z337/Z347) - At they enter camera view at about W110/Z337), two women on either side of Stetson Hat Man have their hands to their mouth in "oh my goodness" fashion. By W125/Z347, Turning Man (2) has turned around and is walking or running away. Roy Truly (3) has turned his head further to the right and is leaning further back. O.V. Campbell (1) is engaged in conversation with the women to his right some of whom have turned around to face him. Wiegman has reversed his panning direction. These are cropped images that I photo edited to increase brightness and contrast (Dave Wiegman, Kennedy Library via *NBC*).

Figure 17
Photograph (cropped) of the Kennedys' arrival at Love Field taken by White House Photographer Cecil Stoughton, with *NBC* cameraman Dave Wiegman in the background wearing his trademark black Fedora hat
- Cecil Stoughton, John F. Kennedy Library, via David Von Pein's blog "The Kennedy Gallery."

Chapter 4
The Dorman Assassination Sequences

The Dorman film is the second of the two motion pictures that have sequences that were filmed as the shots rang out, but without the presidential limo in camera view. As with Wiegman's, the evidentiary value of Dorman's two assassination sequences with respect to establishing the source and sequence of the shots has been completely overlooked. This will be the first proper systematic analysis of the film's images as they relate to shot timing that has been published to date.

The published version of the Dorman film includes five sequences, the first three of which are comprised of pre-assassination footage. The final two sequences that are covered here have a total of 159 frames, run 9.9 seconds, and are separated by a 3.6-second-long camera stop. They cover in part the interval Z182 to Z425. Fortunately, in recording her last two sequences Ms. Dorman had the camera running as all three shots rang out. As a result, the images by correlation and comparison with the Z film images provide scientific/photographic proof that all three shots were fired from the TSBD sniper's nest at Z221/310/328.

In a nutshell, given the documented high amplitude of the shot noise, the visual shot identifiers in the Zapruder and Dorman films prove irrefutably that the second shot was fired from the TSBD sniper's nest at Z309.5 plus or minus a Z frame given the following. (1) Dorman, who was about 36 feet away from the assassin, jerked her camera commencing the equivalent of Z313 which is five Z-frame equivalents before Zapruder who was about 260 feet away jerked his. (2) The spectators lining Elm Street across the street from the TSBD at about 115 feet away from the sniper's nest all jerked their heads or arms commencing at the equivalent of Z315 which is one Z-frame equivalent before the occupants of the presidential limo reacted commencing at Z316, three before Zapruder reacted at Z318 and two after Dorman reacted at the equivalent of Z313. (3) All of these reaction times are mathematically predictable from the available scientific data (see Chapter 8).

The visual shot identifiers in these same two films similarly prove that the third shot was fired from the TSBD sniper's nest exactly 1 second later within frame Z328 (say Z327.5). Since we know Zapruder was recording at 18.3 frames per second, add 18 Z frames or Z-frame equivalents to the Z-film-image counts provided above and the film images confirm that the spectators across the street from the TSBD started reacting the equivalent of Z332 [314.5+18=332], Dorman at the equivalent of Z330 [312.5+18=330], the occupants of the limo at Z333 [315.5+18=333] and Zapruder at Z336 [317.5+18=336].

Tables 16 through 21 and Figures 18 through 23 follow and relate to the ensuing discussions.

Inside the TSBD

Fifty-seven year old Elsie Dorman, a Scott-Foresman and Company mail supervisor, was watching the motorcade from the fourth floor of the TSBD. She was accompanied at the third set of double windows from the east side by fellow-workers Dorothy Garner, Sandra Styles and 23-year-old Victoria Adams.

Along with being unfamiliar with the camera's operation, Ms. Dorman by all indications was not very skilled in aiming the camera or holding it still. There is a great deal of pronounced blurring and rapid camera movement, some of which represents reactions to gunfire and most of which does not.

Interviews and testimony

Here is what Ms. Dorman told the FBI when they discovered she had made a home movie of the motorcade from a point near the TSBD sniper's nest using her husband's seven-year old Kodak Brownie 8-mm movie camera:

Elsie Dorman, fourth floor window, TSBD with Victoria Adams and others - *I was using my husband's camera and was not too familiar with its operation. As the motorcade turned onto Houston Street from Main Street, I started taking photographs. I was seated on the floor with the camera in the window. The window was raised. I continued taking photographs but as the motorcade [president's car] turned from Houston Street to Elm Street, I became excited [stopped using her viewfinder] and did not get any more photographs [of the president because she was aiming too high]. I was at this window attempting to photograph the motorcade [the vice-president's car, VP-follow-up car, mayor's car, press-pool car, and camera car 1 as they passed below her] when I heard a noise like gunshots.* FBI interview, 3/20/64 (WRv.22Hp.644).

Victoria Adams who was seated right beside Dorman had this to say to the WC during her April 1964 deposition about what she and her co-workers heard and saw that day.

Victoria Adams, fourth floor window, TSBD with Elsie Dorman - *I watched the motorcade come down Main as it turned from Main onto Houston and watched it proceed around the corner on Elm. And apparently someone called to the late president, because he and his wife both turned abruptly and faced the building, so we got a very good view of both of them [the president and his wife who were both facing south rotated their heads quickly to the north toward the TSBD commencing Z155 and Z165 respectively]... And from our vantage point we were able to see what the president's wife was wearing, the roses in the car, and things that would attract a woman's attention. Then we heard—then we were obstructed from the view [commencing at some point after Z170 by the big Oak tree]. And we heard a shot, and it was a pause, and then a second shot, and then a third shot. It sounded like a firecracker or a canon at a football game. It seemed as if it came from right below rather than left above, possibly because of the report.* WC deposition, 4/7/64 (WRv.6Hp.388).

Film and camera timelines and available versions

Presumably, the FBI viewed Ms. Dorman's poor-quality film during the course of her March 1964 interview and decided that it was of no value to the WC's investigation. Ms. Dorman and her film were first introduced to the public in November 1967 when *Life Magazine* published a picture of her and three frames of her movie in a feature story titled "Last Seconds of the Motorcade: Together with Unpublished Pictures of Nine Bystanders." In the preface to the story, *Life*'s managing editor explained that they had just discovered Ms. Dorman's movie that summer and were told that she had been keeping it in a closet and had never shown it to anyone.

4: The Dorman Assassination Sequences

Ms. Dorman retired from Scott-Foresman in 1971 and her son John took possession of the film and camera when Ms. Dorman passed away in 1983. He donated both to the Sixth Floor Museum in 1995.

The Dorman film has appeared in various TV specials on the assassination and is included in several commercially available videos. The museum made a valuable contribution to the assassination research community by preparing an optically enhanced digital version of the film that includes the images between the sprocket holes. This digital version is included in *Discovery Channel's* "Death at Dealey Plaza," which originally aired in June 2004 and is now available on DVD. I used this version to a considerable extent in conducting the following analysis. I also used the version contained in Robert Grodin's DVD *JFK Assassination Films: A Case for Conspiracy* published in 2003 by *Delta Entertainment Corporation*, Los Angeles, CA.

Camera recording speed

The published version of the Dorman film runs at 16.5 frames per second. By counting frames in the Muchmore's and Dorman's pre-assassination footage, I was able to determined that Ms. Dorman's camera was actually recording at very close to 16.0 frames per second. In the Dorman-film's first pre-assassination sequence, it takes 28 frames for the flashing running lights to complete the first two observable complete on-off cycles: six-frames per cycle for the left and eight for the right. In the Muchmore-film's fifth sequence it takes 32 frames: seven frames per cycle for the left and nine for the right. Knowing Muchmore's camera was recording at 18.3 frames per second, the ratio of the frame counts tell us that Dorman's camera was running at about 16 frames per second: [28/32 = 0.875] and [0.875 x 18.3 = 16.01].

In Dorman's fifth sequence, the careful observer will find the onset of unmistakable signature reflex reactions to the loud blasts of the last two shots 16 frames apart at D398 (Z315) and D413 (Z332). This confirms that the camera was recording at 16 frames per second.

Zapruder-film correlation

Fourth-sequence correlation: D337 to D376 (Z182-227) - We can establish the start time of the 40-frame fourth sequence via the movements of picture-taker Hugh Betzner that commence a half second after he took his well-known Z186 photo. From eleven to sixteen D frames into Dorman's fourth sequence, we see Betzner lowering his camera from his face to the level of his stomach between D347 through D352 (Z194-199) at which point he starts to rewind. In the Zapruder film we see him doing this between Z194 through Z199. According to his testimony and confirmed by the Zapruder and Dorman film images, Betzner finished rewinding his camera and set off down Elm just as the first shot sounded. Applying a D352=Z199 correlation and assuming camera speeds of 16.0 frames per second for Dorman and 18.3 frames per second for Zapruder, the third sequence begins 1 second before Z200 which is 18 Z frames. Thus, D337=Z182: [181+18=182]. Since the sequence has 40 D frames and covers 2.5 seconds, it runs for the equivalent of 46 Z frames: [40/16=2.5] and [2.5x18.3=45.8]. Thus, D376=Z227: [181+46=227]. See Figure 19.

Fifth-sequence correlation: D377 to D494 (Z291-425)

As with the Wiegman film, we can use the onset of signature blurring from Ms. Dorman's camera jerks in response to the sound of the Z310 shot to precisely sync the Zapruder film with the fifth sequence. The telltale blurring commences twenty frames into the sequence at D396, which is confirmed by telltale reflex reactions among all the spectators in view commencing two frames later at D398. Reasonably assuming the shot came from the TSBD sixth floor sniper's nest just 36 feet away, D396=Z313. This allows 0.03 second for sound travel time and 0.12 seconds for human reflex-reaction time, which is three Z frames: [36/1,125=0.03] and [0.03+0.12=0.15] and [0.15x18.3=2.7]. Thus, Dorman began her fifth sequence at D377=Z291: [20/16=1.25] and [1.25x18.3=22.9] and [314-23=291].

We can confirm the sync of the Dorman fifth sequence to within a few frames of the Zapruder film via sightline analysis using the Wiegman-film images. The opening frame of Dorman's 118-frame fifth sequence (D377) shows the mayor's car at a point it is passing by the northwest end of the reflecting pool. Accordingly, we used Wiegman's frame W034 showing the rear of the mayor's car passing in front of the northeast end of the reflecting pool to estimate the start time and synchronize the D film with the W and Z films. In so doing, we used sightlines to plot on the same scaled drawing, the mayor's car's position on Elm, first at D377, and then at W034. In so doing, we determined that the rear end of the car at W034 was a mere 8-feet short of its position at D377. According to manufacturer' specifications, the 1963 comet is 16.2 feet long and the tip of the open rear window is 7 feet from the rear end of the car. See Figure 18.

Following Dale Myers' lead, we used Dorman sightlines to determine the speed the mayor's car was traveling between D377 and D391 using the top of the raised left-rear window (Myers, p. 101). The top of the window moved 13.7 feet in 14 frames, which at 16 frames per second is 0.875 seconds [14/16=0.875]. This means the car was traveling 15.66 feet per second [13.7/0.875=15.66]. Thus, using the speed the car was traveling, it took 0.51 second for the car to travel the 8-foot distance between W034 and D077 [8/15.66=0.51]. Knowing Wiegman's camera was re-recorded at 25.6 frames per second, this equates to 13 W frames [0.51x25.6=13.0]. Thus, D377=W046 [13+33=46]. From Chapter 3, W046=Z291 confirming the start of the Dorman fifth sequence is within Z291.

Given the above, assuming a camera speed of 16.0 frames per second and knowing that W046=Z291 (see Chapter 3), the 118-frame 7.38-second-long Dorman fifth sequence begins at the equivalent of Z291 and ends at the equivalent of Z426: [7.38x18.3=135] and [290+135=425]. Thus, D377=Z291=W045 all at mid frame.

Fourth-sequence images: D337 to D376 (Z182-227)

The Dorman film's fourth sequence has 40 frames. Assuming a camera speed of 16.0 frames per second it runs 2.5 seconds. As explained above, it correlates with Z182 to Z227 ending 0.44-second after the first shot was fired at Z221/D371 as a result of Ms. Dorman's alarm reaction to the shot noise.

As the sequence opens, Dorman has the camera aimed across the street and to her right toward the north end of the peristyle. At roughly three-quarter of a second intervals, she pans right to left, then left to right, and then right to left again, going back and forth over the area between the northwest end of the reflecting pool and the area in front of the north end of the peristyle. She apparently thought she was filming the vice-president's bluish-gray 1964 Lincoln convertible, and its secret service follow-up car, an ivory colored 1963 Mercury sedan, but she was aiming too high.

During her first pan left, Ms. Dorman is moving the camera erratically suggesting that she was readjusting her position. In the enhanced version that includes the images between the sprocket holes, just before she begins panning back to the right we get a ten-frame glimpse from D347 to D357 (Z194-205) of amateur-photographer Hugh Betzner who is standing on the sidewalk in front of the northwest end of the reflecting pool. The images capture Betzner as he lowers his camera first from his face to his upper chest and then to his waist and begins rewinding within a second after taking his well-known Z186 photo.

4: The Dorman Assassination Sequences

As Ms. Dorman pans back to the right, we get a glimpse of 14-year old Linda Willis from about D360 to D370 (Z209-220). Linda is running west along the sidewalk presumably to rejoin her little sister Rosemary who is standing just west of the edge of the grass infield. During her third sequence, Ms. Dorman captured the sisters racing around the corner of Houston and Elm as they passed by Hugh Betzner as he was taking a photo of the presidential limo rounding the corner. Linda, who has her father's early 1960s-vintage Argus camera case strapped around her neck, stopped in front of the northwest corner of the reflecting pool at a point not far from where Betzner would soon be taking his Z186 picture. Rosemary kept running. Betzner is no longer in sight indicating that to keep the president in view he dashed further west along Elm immediately after completing his Z186 rewind.

At a point 35 to 36 frames into the sequence between frames D371 and D372 (Z221/Z222), there is a conspicuous downward camera jolt resulting from bullet shock waves striking and/or passing under the camera.

Ms. Dorman's final-pan left ends at D376 (Z227) amid a four-frame interval of down and up camera movement. During this interval D373 to D376 (Z224-227), we catch a glimpse of the extreme left-rear of the vice-president's car and the front two-thirds of the vice-presidential-follow-up car.

Fifth-sequence images: D377 to D494 (Z291-425)

The important final sequence has 118 frames. Assuming a camera speed of 16.0 frames per second, it is 7.4 seconds long and, as explained above, correlates with the critical Zapruder film interval Z291 to Z425. Through synchronization with the Zapruder and Wiegman film images, we can differentiate Ms. Dorman's startle reactions to the second and third shots and also discern telltale head movements among a significant number of spectators.

As the final sequence begins, we get a fleeting glimpse of the upper-left side of the mayor's car as it moves by Ms. Dorman. All we can see of the 1963 white Mercury convertible is the front windshield and driver's-side raised-rear window along with the very tops of the heads of the driver and Mayor Cabell's wife Elizabeth. Just three seconds before, Ms. Cabell had looked up at the sniper's nest after the Z221 shot and saw a rifle barrel extending out in the president's direction. As the vehicle passes her, Ms. Dorman pans right following it down Elm for about a half second. She then reverses direction and pans slowly left with the apparent intention of filming the press-pool car. Once again, however, she is aiming too high and for the most part captures the spectators on the southwest corner of Houston and Elm.

At a point 20 frames into the final sequence commencing D396 (Z313), there is a two-frame interval of heavily blurred images followed by another five frames of lighter blurring that make it somewhat difficult to see the telltale head movements associated with the sound of the Z310 shot. The careful observer, however, will easily discern concurrent rapid head turns for seven spectators in the interval between the 22nd and 23rd frames D398 and D399 (Z315-16). From camera right to left, the head turners include: a man in a dark suit; a lady with a yellow scarf; a young boy in the street gutter; a lady in a blue dress behind him; a dark-skinned young man wearing a pale-red, short-sleeved shirt; a young man in a white shirt with an open jacket; and a young girl standing directly behind him with just her face in view. The man in the suit, the young man and and the girl behind him dart their heads to the left. The rest dart their heads to their right in the direction of the TSBD sniper's nest.

In terms of alarm reactions, commencing at D402 (Z320), the young girl in a blue dress standing behind the young man with an open jacket, starts walking toward his left side and continues so until they both disappear from view at D414 (Z333). More telling, a woman in a blue dress standing behind the same young man, begins running west down Elm commencing at D402 (Z320) through disappearing from view at D413 (Z332): an overt flight response to the Z310 shot.

At a point 35 frames into the sequence, at D411 and D412 (Z330-31), there is another two-frame interval of very heavily blurred images caused by Ms. Dorman's reaction to the final shot. This blurring is followed by several frames of lighter blurring that makes it somewhat difficult to see the very telling rapid head movements that occur between D413 and D417 (Z332-37) among the six spectators in view. These head turners include the three members of the Towner family, a man in a business suit to the right (east) of Jim Towner, a man wearing overalls to his left, and a gray haired woman to Tina's left. They all concurrently turn their heads to their right and at least two end up looking up toward the TSBD sniper's nest. The man in the business suit continues looking up at the sniper's nest through D426 (Z347) at which point he turns his head down and to his left before disappearing from view at D430 (Z352). In conjunction with all the other evidence, these concurrent head turns provide hard photographic proof that the final shot was fired at Z328 (D409) from the TSBD sniper's nest.

As Ms. Dorman continues panning left, another business man in a light-colored overcoat standing at the edge of the curb near the corner whose head comes into view at D418 (Z338), is turning it to the right and tilting it back to look up at the sniper's nest. Six frames later, a woman comes into view behind him who is in the midst of taking a hard look over her left shoulder. She presumably commenced her head turn at D418 (Z338) and is on the move by the time she disappears from view at D450 (Z375).

As the film ends, Ms. Dorman has panned far enough left to capture two white Mercury convertibles and a motorcycle officer traveling down Houston as they fast approach the intersection. These were the second and third dignitary cars and Motorcycle Officer Hollis McLain who was riding off the left-rear fender of camera car 3. The left side of the second dignitary car is just briefly in view from D478 to D482 (Z407-11). As it disappears, it is just starting the left turn onto Elm. The third dignitary car is in view from D485 (Z417) until the film ends at D494 (Z425). McLain comes into view at D466 (Z393) and remains in view until the film ends. This is about 6.1 seconds after the head shot and about 4 seconds before the motorcade came to a brief stop commencing with the VP-follow-up car.

Expected timing of reflex and alarm reactions in the Dorman film assuming the shots were fired from the TSBD sniper's nest

The time for shot noise to reach Ms. Dorman from the sniper's nest would be 0.03 second - The sniper's nest is about 20 feet above the fourth floor and Ms. Dorman was located about 30 feet to its west as the three shots rang out. For muzzle blast noise, this amounts to 36 feet using a hypotenuse calculator: [36/1,125=0.03]. Using my protractor and a right-angle calculator and assuming the shock waves were traveling at the speed of sound, I found they were reaching her in about the same 0.03 second. Thus, the combined muzzle-blast and bullet shock wave was arriving in about 0.03 second at very loud levels.

If the shots were fired from the TSBD sniper's nest, Ms. Dorman's signature blurring would come three Z-frame equivalents after the shots - Given the expected very loud level of the shot noise at this close distance, we would expect to see Ms. Dorman's involuntary movement within 0.12 second of the arrival of the sound which is 2.2 Z frames [0.12x18.3 =2.2]. This is based on a published literature review of auditory response time giving 0.14 to 0.16 as the normal range for lower-level shot noise (Kosinsky, 2008). Adding the time of travel of the sound waves to the anticipated reflex-response time, we would expect to see blurring associated with Ms. Dorman jerking her camera within 0.15 seconds of the shots [0.03+0.12=0.15]. This is three Z frame equivalents after a shot [0.15x18.3=2.7].

If the shots were fired from the TSBD sniper's nest, Ms. Dorman's alarm reactions would come nine Z-frame equivalents after the shots plus or minus two frames - The Zapruder film images tell us to look for alarm reactions about eight Z-frame-equivalents after the noise reaches the filmmakers' ears. Thus, allowing for 0.03 second (0.5 Z frame) sound travel time [0.03x18.3=0.55] we would expect to see Ms. Dorman's alarm movements commencing nine Z frame equivalents from the shots [0.55+8=8.5].

The time for shot noise to reach the crowd on the south side of Elm from the sniper's nest would be 0.1 second - The spectators Ms. Dorman was filming on the south side of Elm were located about 90 feet away from the base of the TSBD. Using a hypotenuse calculator, this amounts to 115 feet from the sniper's nest which is 60 feet above the base of the building. Thus the muzzle-blast noise was reaching them at relatively high levels in about 0.1 second [115/1,125=0.1]. In addition, the crowd was heavily exposed to the bullet shock-waves from a distance of about 85 feet after the bullet had traveled about 30 feet with the sound waves reaching them in about the same 0.1 second as the muzzle blast: [30/2,100=0.014] and [85/1,125)=.076] and [0.076+0.014= 0.09]

If the shots were fired from the TSBD sniper's nest, spectator reflex reactions would come five Z-frame equivalents after the shots - Given the expected loud level of the shot noise at this relatively close distance, we would expect to see spectator involuntary movement within 0.15 second of the arrival of the noise which is three Z frames [0.15x18.3=2.7]. This is based on a published literature review of auditory response time giving 0.14 to 0.16 as the normal range and the three Z-frame-response times for reactions within the presidential limo to the sound of the Z310 shot. Adding the time of travel of the sound waves to the anticipated reflex time, we would expect to see spectator reflex reactions within 0.25 seconds of the shots [0.1+0.15=0.25]. This is five Z frames after a shot [0.25x18.3=4.6].

If the shots were fired from the TSBD sniper's nest, spectator alarm reactions would come ten Z-frame equivalents after the shots plus or minus two frames - The Zapruder film images tell us to look for alarm reactions about eight Z-frame equivalents after the noise reaches the spectators' ears. Thus, allowing 0.1 second which is two Z frames for sound travel time [0.1x18.3=1.8], we expect spectator alarm movements commencing ten Z frames from the shots [2+8=10].

Distinguishable reactions to the Z221/D371 shot in the Dorman fourth sequence

Overview - Dorman's reflex reaction is an abrupt downward jerk and loss of control of her camera as she was panning left producing four heavily blurred frames. Dorman's alarm reaction is lifting her finger off the shutter button. See Figure 19.

Dorman's signature blurring for the Z221/D371 shot commences at D373 (Z224), which is three Z-frame equivalents after the shot as predicted - Commencing at D373 (Z224) Ms. Dorman jerked her camera up and down creating four frames of blurred images before she took her finger off the shutter.

Spectator reflex reactions to the Z221/D371 shot, which were expected to commence at D375 (Z226) are not conspicuous - The spectators are out of view in the first three of the last four frames.

Dorman's own alarm reaction to the Z221/D371 shot commences at D376 (Z227), which is seven Z-frame equivalents after the shot as predicted - The alarmed Ms. Dorman released the shutter button at D376/Z227. The sequence ends eight Z-frames equivalents after the Z221 shot before the onset of anticipated spectator reactions.

Distinguishable reactions to the Z310/D394 shot in the Dorman fifth sequence

Overview - Dorman's reflex reaction is an abrupt jerk of her camera to her left as she was panning left producing two frames of heavily blurred frames and five frames of lighter blurred images that captured seven spectators turning their heads, four toward the TSBD. Dorman's alarm reaction is the continuation of her panning to her left but she is now purposefully filming the spectators on the south side of Elm rather than the motorcade. See Figures 20 and 21.

Dorman's signature blurring for the Z310/D394 shot commences at D396 (Z313), which is three Z-frame equivalents after the shot as predicted - Following two frames of very heavy blurring at D396 and D397 (Z313-14), there is five frames of lighter blurring concurrent with telltale head movements among six of the spectators.

Spectator reflex reactions to the Z310/D394 shot commence at D398 (Z315), which is five Z-frame equivalents after the shot as predicted - Commencing D398 (Z315) through D400 (Z317.5), Ms. Dorman's blurred images captured concurrent hard looks to the right toward the TSBD for four spectators standing directly across the street from her perch including: a lady with a yellow scarf; a young boy in the street gutter; a lady in a blue dress behind him; and a dark-skinned young man at the curb wearing a pale-red, short-sleeved shirt. Three others darted their heads to the left: A man in a suit, a young man in an open jacket and white shirt, and a young girl behind him with just her face in view. See Figure 20.

Dorman's own alarm reaction to the Z310/D394 shot commences at D402 (Z320), which is ten Z-frame equivalents after the shot as predicted - Commencing D400 (Z317.5), Ms. Dorman appears to be purposefully filming the reactions of the spectators on the north side of Elm rather than the motorcade. This is evidenced by her continuing to pan left opposite the direction the cars were traveling, where before she was panning back and forth as each car passed by.

Spectator alarm reactions to the Z310/D394 shot commence at D402 (Z320), which is ten Z-frame-equivalents after the shot as predicted - Commencing D402 (Z320) a woman and a young girl both wearing blue dresses who were standing directly behind the young man with an open jacket from Ms. Dorman's vantage point got on the move. The woman broke into a dead run heading west down Elm and the young girl moved forward apparently trying to gain the young man's attention. See Figure 21.

Distinguishable reactions to the Z328/D409 shot in the Dorman fifth sequence

Overview - Dorman's reflex reaction is an abrupt jerk of her camera to her left as she was panning left producing two frames of heavily blurred images followed by three frames of lighter blurred images that captured six spectators with sudden head turns toward the TSBD with two starting to look up toward the sniper's nest in alarm. Dorman's alarm reaction is her continuing to film spectators on the south side of Elm rather than the motorcade. See Figures 22 and 23.

Dorman's signature blurring for the Z327.5/D409 shot commences at D411 (Z330), which is three Z-frame equivalents after the shot as predicted - Following two frames of very heavy blurring at D411 and D412 (Z330-11), there are three frames of lighter blurring concurrent with telltale head movements among six of the spectators.

Spectator reflex reactions to the Z327.5/D409 shot commence at D413 (Z332), which is five Z-frame equivalents after the shot as predicted - Commencing D413 (Z332) through D415 (Z335), Ms. Dorman's blurred images captured concurrent head turns to the right or left by all six spectators in view including the three members of the Towner family (movie-maker Tina and her mother and father picture-taker James), a woman with gray hair to the left of Tina, a man wearing overalls to the left of James, and a man in a suit standing to the right of James. See Figure 22.

Dorman's own alarm reaction to the Z328/D409 shot which was expected to commence at D417 (Z337), which is nine Z-frame equivalents after the shot is not conspicuous - There are no conspicuous alarm reactions nine frames after the shot was fired for Ms. Dorman other than the fact that for a short period she continued to focus her attention on the spectators rather than the motorcade.

Spectator alarm reactions to the Z328/D409 shot commence at D416 (Z336), which is eight Z-frame equivalents after the shot as predicted - Commencing D416/Z336, at least two of the five head turners mentioned above including James Towner and the man in the suit began looking in the direction of the TSBD sniper's nest. Towner completed his quick glance up by D419 (Z339). The man in the suit continued looking up through about D426 (Z347) at which point he turned his head down and to his left. As Dorman pans further to camera left, another man in a business suit and light-colored overcoat comes into view at D418 (Z338) who is just starting to turn his head to the right and tilt it back to look up toward the sniper's nest. As Ms. Dorman continues panning left a woman standing directly behind him that came into view at D424 (Z345) was in the midst of taking a hard look over her left shoulder and was just beginning to run as she disappeared from view. The man continues looking up through about D440 (Z363) at which point he turns his head down and to his left. See Figure 23.

Also relevant

Pearce Allman, curb, south side of Elm - One of the men wearing a business suit that Ms. Dorman's fourth sequence captured standing on the sidewalk was *WFAA Radio*'s production manager who had these distant recollections.

> **Pearce Allman, curb near southwest corner of Houston and Elm,** *WFAA Radio* - *So we walked over, ended up standing on the corner, directly opposite the school book depository building . . . And the first shot, that loud explosion; it wasn't a sharp, flat crack sound at all . . . then bam, the second one. And you realized indeed that it was shooting, then the third shot. My memory was so vivid that during the interview with the secret service the next day [interview report not found], they asked me to recall the time sequence, and I came out with 6-½ seconds [6 seconds in reality]. But on the second shot [more likely the third based on the reactions of other spectators in his area], I glanced up, my gaze stopped one floor below [the sixth floor sniper's nest] on the depository building. I saw the three guys looking out the windows, looking up. . . .* Transcript of Joe Nick Patoski's interview, 11/22/98, published on Texas Monthly web site.

Motorcycle Officer McLain's position - The Dorman-film images solidly refute speculation raised by the HSCA acoustics panel that McLain was fast approaching the intersection of Houston and Elm with a stuck microphone when a hypothetical first-shot miss rang out ca Z160. As indicated above, the Dorman-film's final sequence shows McLain just entering the intersection of Houston and Elm at D466 (Z393) about 4.5 seconds after the fatal head shot. Assuming he was traveling at the same speed as the president's car (14 feet per second) on the straightaway, the Dorman film tells us that at Z160 McLain was 174 feet up the street having just turned right off Main onto Houston. The Robert Hughes' film tells us the same thing.

Table 16
Observable first shot reflex and alarm reactions for the Dorman Film
Z221/D371-shot reflex reactions: distinguishable blurred film images and spontaneous movements commencing 2.5 +/- 1 Z-frame equivalents after the sound reaches the person reacting
1. Z223/D374: startled 4th-floor-TSBD-filmmaker Dorman began jerking her camera down and up creating four frames of rapid camera movement and blurred images. This comes one D/Z frame after substantial downward movement of the camera due to bullet shock waves striking or passing under the camera (D film).
Z221-shot alarm reactions: deliberate movements or actions commencing 7.5 +/- 2 Z-frame equivalents after the sound reaches the filmmaker or person reacting
1. Z227/D376: alarmed 4th-floor-TSBD-filmmaker Elsie Dorman abruptly stopped filming (D film).

Table 17
Observable second shot reflex and alarm reactions for the Dorman film
Z310/D394-shot reflex reactions: distinguishable blurred film images and spontaneous movements commencing 2.5 +/- 1 Z-frame equivalents after the sound reaches the filmmaker or the person reacting
1. Z313/D396: startled 4th-floor-TSBD-filmmaker Dorman jerked her camera creating two frames of heavily blurred images followed by five frames of lightly blurred images;
2. Z315/D398: four startled south-of-Elm spectators standing in front of the reflecting pool began concurrently darting their heads to the right toward the sniper's nest and three others darted their heads to the left (D film).
Z310/D394 shot alarm reactions: deliberate movements or actions commencing 7.5 +/- 2 Z-frame equivalents after the sound reaches the filmmaker or person reacting
1. Z320/D402: alarmed 4th-floor-TSBD-filmmaker Dorman began filming spectator reactions on the south side of Elm rather than the motorcade (D film);
2. Z320/D402: a woman and a young girl both wearing blue dresses who were standing directly behind a young man with an open jacket got on the move. The woman broke into a dead run heading west down Elm and the young girl moved forward apparently trying to gain the young man's attention (D film).

4: The Dorman Assassination Sequences

Table 18
Observable third shot reflex and alarm reactions for the Dorman film
Z328/D409-shot reflex reactions: distinguishable blurred film images and spontaneous movements commencing 2.5 +/- 1 Z-frame equivalents after the sound reaches the person reacting
1. Z330/D411: startled 4th-floor-TSBD-filmmaker Dorman jerked her camera creating two frames of heavily blurred images followed by three frames of lightly blurred images;
2. Z332/D413: six startled south-of-Elm spectators standing in front of the reflecting pool began concurrently darting their heads to the right with a least two of them looking up toward the TSBD sniper's nest (D film).
Z328/D409-shot alarm reactions: deliberate movements or actions commencing 7.5 +/- 2 Z-frame equivalents after the sound reaches the person reacting
1. Z336/D416: picture taker James Towner and an alarmed male spectator wearing a business suit and light-colored overcoat standing at the southwest corner of Houston and Elm began turning their heads and looking up toward the TSBD sniper's nest (D film);
2. 338/D419: an alarmed woman standing on the southwest corner of Houston and Elm began turning her head hard to the left and setting off (in progress as of frame D424/Z345 of the D film).

Table 19					
Scientific evidence that the first shot came from the TSBD at Z221/D371					
Synchronization of Zapruder film images at 18.3 frames per second with the Dorman assassination sequence at 16 frames per second					
Filmmaker location and camera recording speed (frame per second)	Calculation of time for bullet shock-wave to reach person at 60 degree Mach angle (seconds) (see Chapter 8)	Calculation of time for muzzle-blast noise to reach person from sniper's nest (seconds)	Calculation of minimum time for muzzle-blast or shock wave to reach person (Z frames)	Observed start signature jiggle blurring and human-reflex reactions (frame number as of end of frame)	Calculated reflex-reaction times: the range assumes shot fired at Z220.1 to Z221.0 with reactions commencing early to late in the first frame impacted by the sound. The estimated actual is based on Kosinski
Zapruder on concrete pedestal at grassy knoll's Bryan's pergola as of Z221; camera recording speed = 18.3 frames per second	Not applicable	Zapruder: Z to sniper = 260 ft; sound-travel-time to Z: 260/1,125=0.23 sec	Zapruder: 0.23 x18.3= 4.2 Z frames	Zapruder: Z227-(signature-blurring from flinch)	Zapruder's reflex-reaction time: 227-220.1=6.9-4.2=2.7; 226.1-221=5.1-4.2=0.9; Estimated actual: 2.7
	Limo occupants: bullet to sniper = 180 ft; bullet to person = 5 ft; sound-travel time to person: 180/1,900=.0095+ 5/1,125] = 0.1 sec	Limo occupants: person to sniper=190 ft; sound-travel-time to persons: 180/1,125= 0.16 sec	Limo occupants: minimum-sound-travel time to persons: 0.1x 18.3=1.8 Z frames	Limo occupants: Z226 (rapid head turns and arm jerking)	Limo occupants reflex-reaction time: 226-220.1=5.9-1.8=4.1; 225.1-221=4.1-1.8=2.3; Estimated actual: 3
Dorman at 4th floor TSBD third window from SE corner; camera recording speed = 16 frames per second	Dorman: bullet to sniper =13 ft; bullet to D: 27 ft; sound-travel time to D: 13/2,100+ 27/1,125 = 0.03 second	Dorman: D to sniper = 36 ft; sound-travel time to D: 36/1,125= 0.03 second	Dorman: minimum-sound- travel time to D: 0.03 x 18.3= 0.5 Z frames	Dorman: Z223/D373 (signature-blurring from camera jerk)	Dorman reflex-reaction time: reflex-reaction time: 223-220.1=2.9-0.5=2.4; 222.1-221=1.1-0.5=0.6; Estimated actual: 2.2
	Crowd: person to sniper =115 ft; sound-travel time to person: 115/1,125 = 0.1 second	Crowd: person to sniper =115 ft; sound-travel time to person: 115/1,125 = 0.1 second	Crowd: minimum-sound-travel time to persons: 0.1 x 18.3= 1.8 Z frames	Crowd: not discernible because the spectators are out of view for three-of-the-four blurred frames	
Conclusions: Dorman's signature blurring for the Z220 shot comes four Z frames (~0.2 second) before Zapruder's because she is the equivalent of four Z-frames closer to the sniper's nest taking into account the distances involved, the speed of the bullet, the speed of sound and the level of noise.					

4: The Dorman Assassination Sequences

Table 20
Scientific evidence that the second shot came from the TSBD at Z310/D393
Synchronization of Zapruder film images at 18.3 frames per second with the Dorman assassination sequence at 16 frames per second

Filmmaker location and camera recording speed (frames per second)	Calculation of time for bullet shock-wave to reach person at 60 degree Mach angle (seconds) (see Chapter 8)	Calculation of time for muzzle-blast noise to reach person from sniper's nest (seconds)	Calculation of minimum time for muzzle-blast or shock wave to reach person (Z frames)	Observed start signature jiggle blurring and human-reflex reactions (frame number as of end of frame)	Calculated reflex-reaction times: the range assumes shot fired at Z309.1 to Z310.0 with reactions commencing early to late in the first frame impacted by the sound. The estimated actual is based on Kosinski
Zapruder on concrete pedestal at grassy knoll's Bryan's pergola as of Z313; camera speed = 18.3 frames per second	Zapruder: See Chapter 8	Zapruder: Z to sniper = 260 ft; sound-travel time to Z: 260/1,125 = 0.23 sec	Zapruder: minimum-sound-travel time to Z: 0.23 x 18.3 = 4.2 Z frames	Zapruder: Z318 (signature blurring from flinch)	Zapruder's reflex-reaction time: 318-309.1=8.9-4.2=4.7; 317.1-310=7.1-4.2=2.9; Estimated actual: 3.5
	Limo occupants: bullet to sniper = 260 ft; bullet to person = 5 ft; sound-travel time to person: 260/1,900 + 5/1,125 = 0.14 sec	Limo occupants: person to sniper = 265 ft; sound-travel time to person: [265/1,125] = 0.24 sec	Limo occupants: Minimum-sound-travel time to persons: [0.15 x 18.3] = 2.7 Z frames	Limo occupants: Z316 (cringing, ducking and diving)	Limo occupants reflex-reaction time: 316-309.1=6.9-2.7=4.2; 315.1-310=5.1-2.7=2.4; Estimated actual: 3
Dorman at 4th floor TSBD third window from SE corner; camera speed = 16 frames per second	Dorman: bullet to sniper = 13 ft; bullet to D = 27 ft; shock-wave travel time to D: 13/2,100 + 27/1,125 = 0.03 second	Dorman: D to sniper = 36 ft; sound-travel time to D: 36/1,125 = 0.03 second	Dorman: minimum-sound-travel time to D: 0.03 x 18.3 = 0.5 Z frames	Dorman: Z313/D396 (signature blurring from camera jerk)	Dorman reflex-reaction time: 313-309.1=3.9-0.5=3.4; 312.1-310=2.1-0.5=1.6; Estimated actual: 2.5
	Crowd: person to sniper = 115 ft; sound-travel time to person: 115/1,125 = 0.1 second	Crowd: person to sniper = 115 ft; sound-travel time to person: 115/1,125 = 0.1 second	Crowd: minimum-sound-travel time to persons: 0.1 x 18.3 = 1.8 Z frames	Crowd: Z315/D398 (head turning by at least four spectators)	Crowd reflex-reaction time: 315-309.1=5.9-1.8=4.1; 314.1-310=4.1-1.8=2.3; Estimated actual: 3

Conclusions: Dorman's signature blurring for the Z310 shot comes five Z frames (~0.3 second) before Zapruder's because she is the equivalent of five Z-frames closer to the sniper's nest taking into account the distances involved, the speed of the bullet, the speed of sound, and the level of noise. Similarly, the crowd reactions that Dorman picked up come two Z-frame equivalents (~0.1 second) after her signature blurring for the same reasons.

Table 21

Scientific evidence that the third shot came from the TSBD at Z328/D409

Synchronization of Zapruder film images at 18.3 frames per second with the Dorman assassination sequence at 16 frames per second

Filmmaker location and camera recording speed (frames per second)	Calculation of time for bullet shock-wave to reach person at 60 degree Mach angle (seconds) (see Chapter 8)	Calculation of time for muzzle-blast noise to reach person from sniper's nest (seconds)	Calculation of minimum time for muzzle-blast or shock wave to reach person (Z frames)	Observed start signature jiggle blurring and human-reflex reactions (frame number as of end of frame)	Calculated reflex-reaction times: the range assumes shot fired at Z327.1 to Z328.0 with reactions commencing early to late in the first frame impacted by the sound. The estimated actual is based on Kosinski
Zapruder on concrete pedestal at grassy knoll's Bryan's pergola as of Z328; camera speed = 18.3 frames per second	See Chapter 8	Zapruder: Z to sniper = 260 ft; sound-travel time to Z: 260/1,125 = 0.23 second	Zapruder: minimum-sound-travel time to Z: 0.23 x 18.3 = 4.2 Z frames	Zapruder: Z336 (signature blurring from flinch)	Zapruder's reflex-reaction time: 336-327.1=8.9-4.2=4.7; 335.1-328=7.1-4.2=2.9; Estimated actual: 3.5
	Limo occupants: bullet to sniper = 270 ft; bullet to person = 5 ft; sound-travel time to person: 270/1,900 + 5/1,125 = 0.15 second	Limo occupants: person to sniper = 275 ft; sound-travel time to person: 275/1,125 = 0.24 second	Limo occupants: minimum-sound-travel time to persons: 0.15 x 18.3 = 2.7 Z frames	Limo occupants: Z333 (cringing, ducking, diving and head turning)	Limo occupants reflex-reaction time: 333-327.1=5.9-2.7=4.2; 332.1-328=4.1-2.7=1.4; Estimated actual: 3
Dorman at 4th floor TSBD third window from SE corner; camera speed = 16 frames per second	Dorman: bullet to sniper = 13 ft; bullet to D = 27 ft; sound-travel time to D: 13/2,100 + 27/1,125 = 0.03 sec	Dorman: D to sniper = 36 ft; sound-travel time to D:36/1,125 = 0.03 sec	Dorman: minimum-sound- travel time to D: 0.03 x 18.3 = 0.5 Z frames	Dorman: Z330/D411 (signature blurring from camera jerk)	Dorman reflex-reaction time: 330-327.1=2.9-0.5=2.4; 329.1-328=1.1-0.5=0.6; Estimated actual: 2
	Crowd: person to sniper = 115 ft; sound-travel time to person: 115/1,125 = 0.1 second	Crowd: person to sniper = 115 ft; sound-travel time to person: 115/1,125 = 0.1 second	Crowd: minimum-sound-travel time to persons: 0.1 x18.3 = 1.8 Z frames	Crowd: Z332/D413 (head turning or arm jerks by six spectators)	Crowd reflex-reaction time: 332-327.1=4.9-1.8=3.1; 331.1-328=3.1-1.8=1.3; Estimated actual: 2.5

Conclusions: Dorman's signature blurring for the Z328 shot comes six Z frames (~0.3 seconds) before Zapruder's because she is the equivalent of six Z-frames closer to the sniper's nest taking into account the distances involved, the speed of the bullet, the speed of sound, and the level of noise. Similarly, the crowd reactions that Dorman picked up come two Z-frame equivalents (~0.11 second) after her signature blurring for the same reasons. Dorman and the spectators lining the south side of Elm in front of the TSBD reacted a frame faster than mathematically predicted for the Z328 shot.

4: The Dorman Assassination Sequences

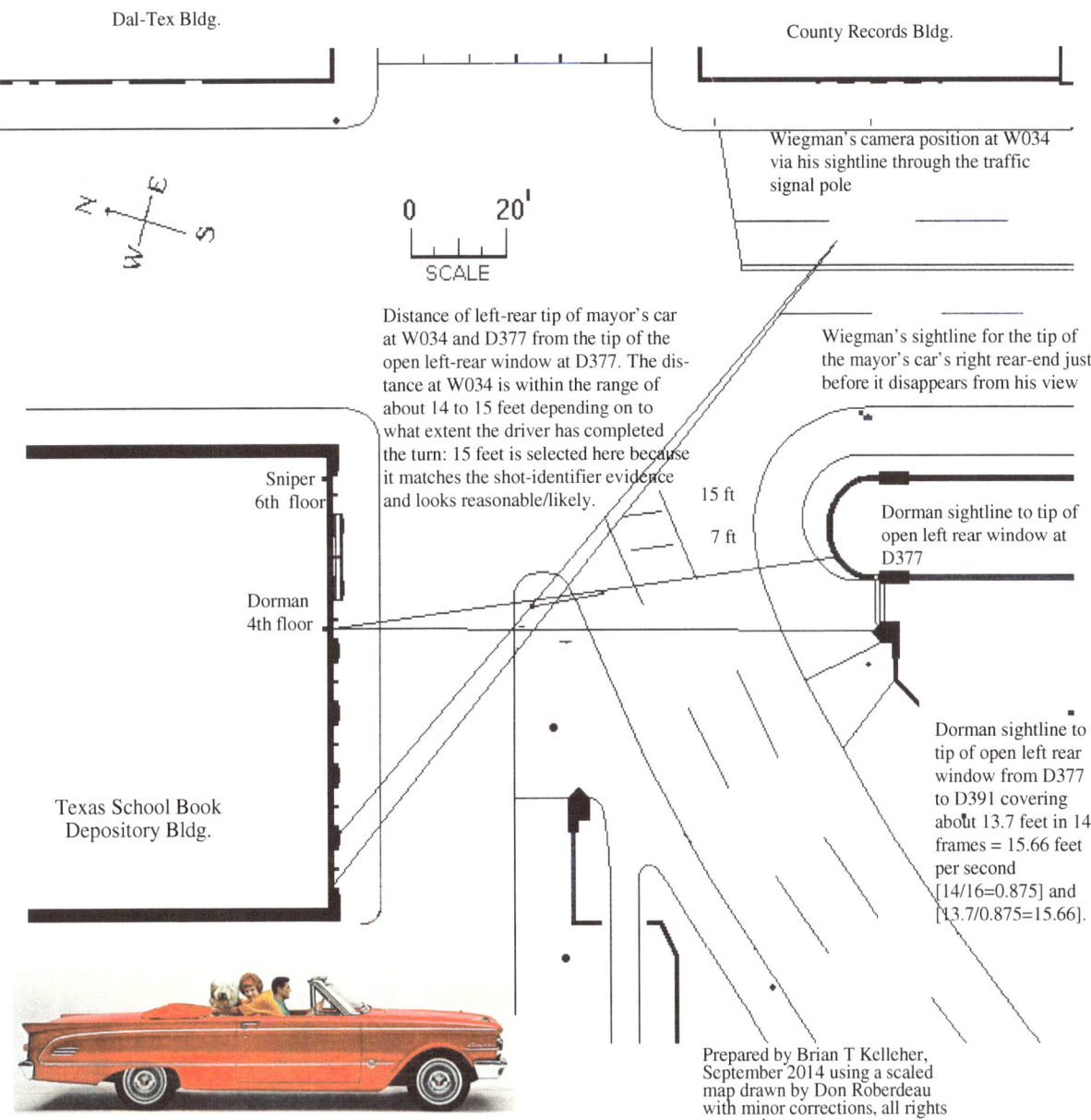

Figure 18

Syncing the Dorman and Wiegman films: D377=W046=Z291 - Here I used Wiegman and Dorman sightlines to plot the position of the tail end of the mayor's car as it completes the left turn from Houston onto Elm. As indicated, between W034 which is the last frame that the right-rear end of the mayor's car was in Wiegman's view and D377 when Dorman's fifth sequence begins, the mayor's car moves 8 feet southwest in 0.5 seconds (13 W frames) at an average speed of 15.66 feet per second [8/15.66=0.51] and [0.51x25.6=13.0]. Thus D377=W044 [33+13=46] according to the sightlines. This start time is confirmed by the onset of signature reflex reactions to the noise of the Z310 shot. Dorman's camera was recording at 16 frames per second and Wiegman's at 25.6 frames per second. The mayor's 1963 Mercury Comet convertible was 16.2-feet-long and the tip of the open left-rear window was 7 feet from the rear of the tip of the left rear end of the car.

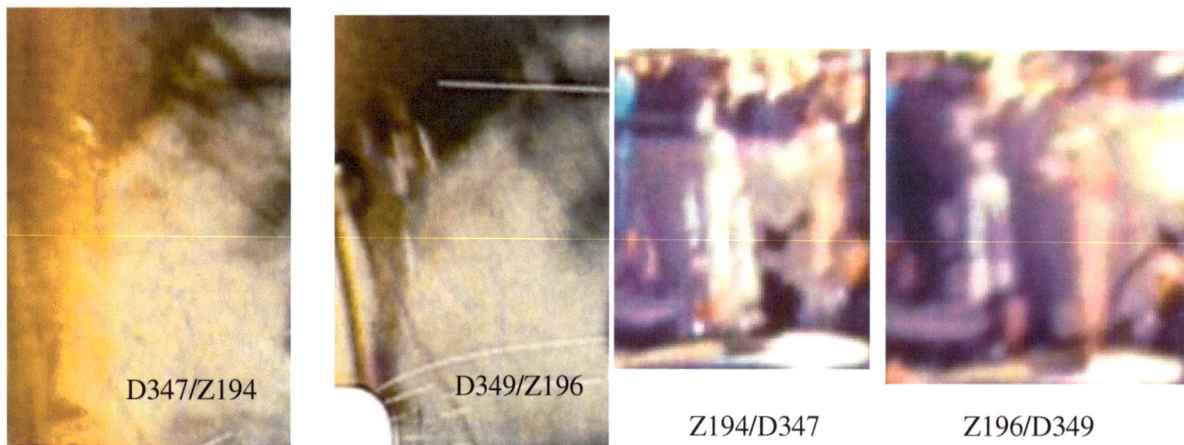

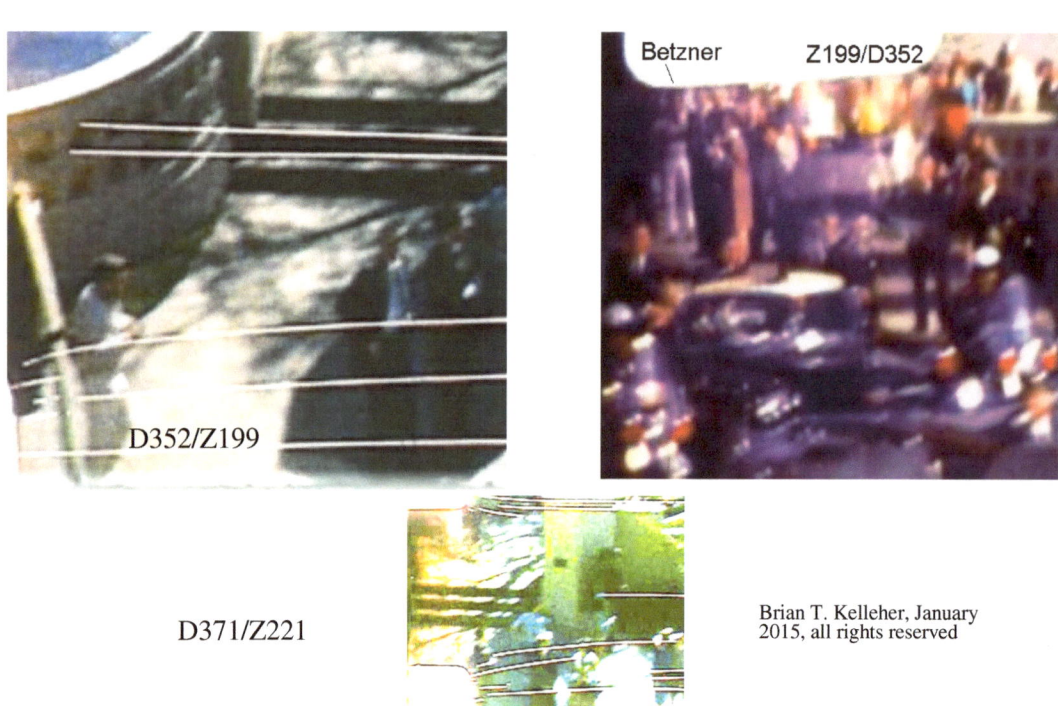

Figure 19

Syncing Dorman's fourth sequence to the Zapruder film (D337=Z182) - As shown above, from D347 to D349 (Z194-196) Dorman captured picture-taker Hugh Betzner as he was lowering his camera from eye level to upper-chest level just after taking his Z186 picture of the presidential limo heading west on Elm. By D352, Betzner had lowered the camera to stomach level and had begun to rewind it. As shown, Zapruder captured these same movements from Z194 to Z199. In lightened frame D371/Z221, we see Linda Willis running west on Elm toward her sister Rosemary and/or her father Phil who are out of view to camera right. As of Z221, their dad had just taken his famous Z201 photo of the presidential limo and is visible with camera to eye in cropped frame Z199 above. These are cropped images that I photo edited to increase brightness and contrast (Elsie Dorman Collection and Zapruder Family Collection/The Sixth Floor Museum at Dealey Plaza http://www.jfk.org).

4: The Dorman Assassination Sequences

D395/Z312 - just before the start of Dorman's signature blurring and reflex reactions for 1 through 6

Figure 20
Reflex reactions for the Z310 shot: Dorman frames D395 and D399 (Z312 and Z316) - Within the 0.14-second interval between frames D398/Z315 and D400/Z317.5, Spectators 1 through 5 concurrently dart their heads to their right and Spectator 6 and a young girl behind him dart their heads to the left. The woman in a blue dress behind Spectator 1 also appears as if she just turned her head to the right. Some of the spectators in view in the background appear to be ducking. Ms. Dorman's camera jerk to the left created very heavy blurring at D396, 397 398 (Z313-315) followed by five frames of lighter blurring including that seen above at D399/Z316. These are cropped images that I photo edited to increase brightness and contrast (Elsie Dorman Collection/The Sixth Floor Museum at Dealey Plaza http://www.jfk.org).

Figure 21

Alarm reactions for the Z310 shot: Dorman frames D405 and D409 (Z323/Z328) - Spectators 1, 2 and 4 are the Towner family including picture-taker James (1), his movie-making daughter Tina (4), and his wife (2). Between D405 (Z323) and D410 (Z329), Mr. Towner's wife (2) approaches him from the rear. Spectator 6 turns and is starting to run west. She is attracting the attention of Spectator 5. Commencing at D402/Z320, Spectator 9 is walking toward Spectator 8 who seems to be turning to look back at her. The businessman that entered into view at camera left will soon be exhibiting a very telling reflex reaction to the sound of the final shot. These are cropped images that I photo edited to increase brightness and contrast (Elsie Dorman Collection/The Sixth Floor Museum at Dealey Plaza http://www.jfk.org).

4: The Dorman Assassination Sequences

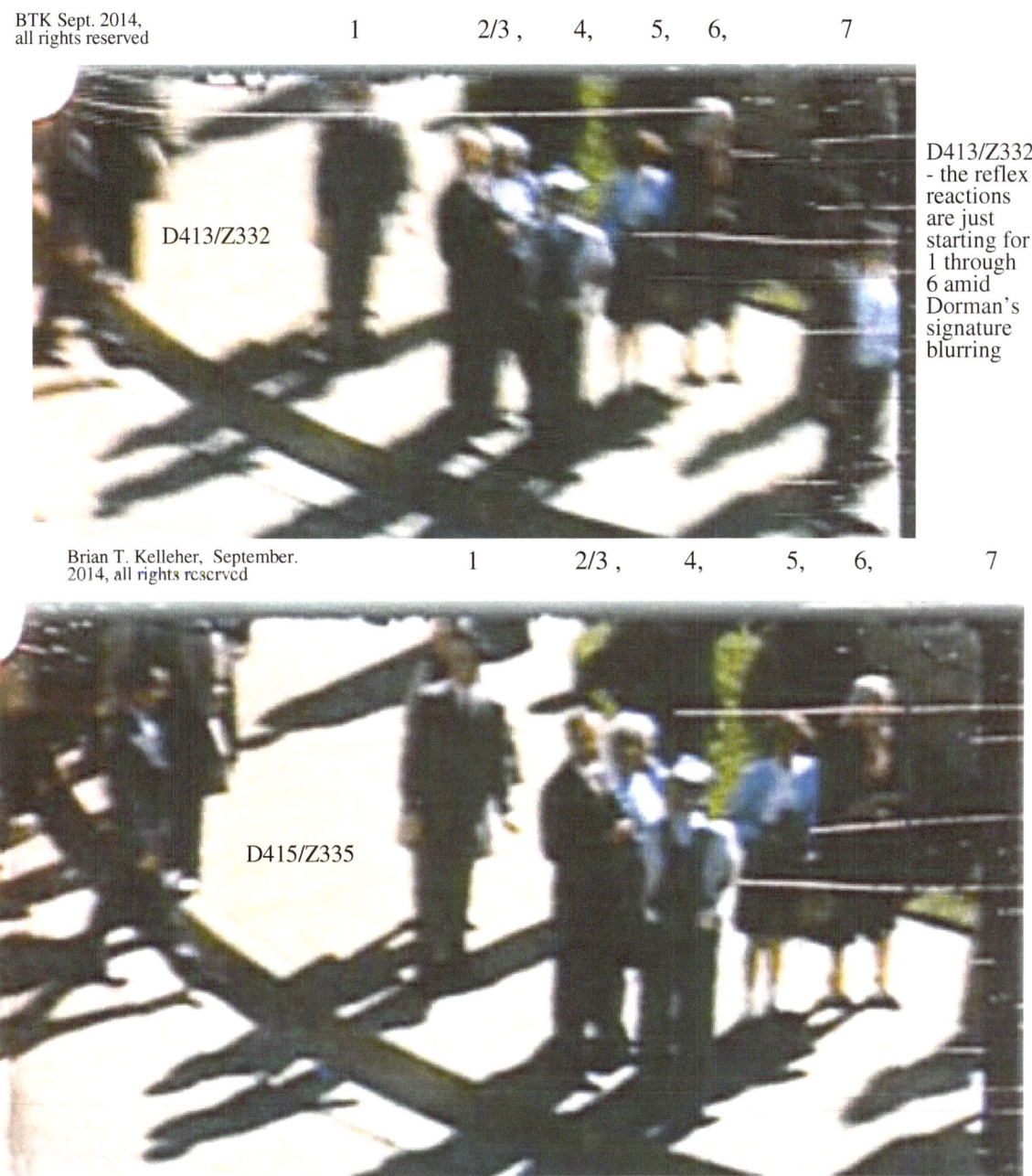

D415/Z335 - reflex reactions in progress for 1 through 6. The reactions are essentially flinches and are complete within three Z frames, sometimes morphing into alarm reactions a few frames later.

Figure 22

Reflex reactions for the Z328 shot: Dorman Frames D413 and D415 (Z332/Z335) - As of Z413/Z332, Spectator 6 is looking back at Spectator 7 who has started running west and is almost out of view by D415. Within the 0.2-second interval between frames D413/Z332 and D415/Z335, Spectator 6 turns her head to the left and then darts it back around to the right. Spectators 1 through 5 (2, 3 and 5 are the Towners) also dart their heads to the right. Dorman's right to left startle-induced camera jerk caused very heavy blurring at D411-412 (Z330-31) and then three frames of lighter blurring including that you see above for D413/Z332. These are cropped images that I photo edited to increase brightness and contrast (Elsie Dorman Collection/The Sixth Floor Museum at Dealey Plaza

1, 2 just coming into view

D417/Z337 - just starting alarm reactions for 1 and 2 who are just coming into view

D420/Z341 - alarm reactions in progress for 1 and 2   D426/Z348 - alarm reactions in progress for 1 and 2

Figure 23

Alarm reaction for the Z328/D409 shot: Dorman frames D417, D420 and D426 (Z/337Z340/Z347) - Commencing at D416/Z336, James Towner and the man in the suit to his right begin looking up toward the TSBD sniper's nest. The man in the suit continues to look up toward the sniper's nest through D426 (Z347). To his right, another man in a suit and light-colored overcoat comes into view who is turning his head to the right and tilting it back to look up toward the sniper's nest. A woman in view behind him has turned and looked hard to her left and is about to take off running. These are cropped images that I photo edited to increase brightness and contrast (Elsie Dorman Collection/The Sixth Floor Museum at Dealey Plaza http://www.jfk.org).

Chapter 5

The Muchmore Assassination Sequence

Besides Zapruder, there were three individuals (Bronson, Muchmore, and Nix) in Dealey Plaza making home movies who captured the presidential limo from the south side of Elm at the moment of the head shot. The Bronson assassination sequence is not of sufficient clarity/resolution to be of much use, but as you are about to see, the Muchmore and Nix assassination sequences provide dramatic visual evidence on final-shot timing and effects that has been completely overlooked by both government investigators and independent researchers.

Main value - The conclusions reached from my rigorous systematic evaluation of reflex and alarm movements in the Zapruder film's assassination sequence is that three bullets reached the presidential limo within frames Z223, Z313, and Z330. The Muchmore assassination sequence, as is the case with Nix assassination sequence, confirms two conspicuous downward and forward jolts to the president's head, the first at Z313/Z314 and the second at Z330/Z331. In particular, due to the bullet's impact high on the right rear of the head at the end of Z330, we can actually see that the president's head has rotated to the left a little as of Z331 as it is driven downward and forward about 3 inches. At Z331 there are discernible upward, forward and rearward sprays of brain matter from the cowlick area that are initially easiest to see in the digital Nix film. The Muchmore images confirm that a portion of the rearward spray landed on the lid of the trunk directly behind the president's head from Z332 to Z337 and further reveal that bloody brain matter reached Motorcycle Officer Hargis from about Z335 to Z337. In addition to the above, the Muchmore film is of particular value in confirming a third-shot entering the limo at Z330 via auditory reflex reactions for an additional nine individuals. The reactions all start and end at the exact same frames (Z333 and Z335). The initial jettisons at Z331 are easier to see when the contrast and brightness are increased using photo editing software.

Babushka Lady's identification - As a side note, I have concluded that the so called "Babushka Lady," who we get a good look at in the Muchmore film, was using opera binoculars, not taking motion pictures. From what I see in Zapruder frames Z292 to Z295, I have identified her as one of six Postal Annex workers interviewed by Gerald Posner for his book *Case Closed*, three of whom he reports were using binoculars. Posner relayed that Francine Burrows was wearing a tan coat, which is a match, that the wounded president passed within about 25 feet of her, which is a match, and that she barely got their in time, which is match given what we see in the Nix film images. According to her March 2010 obituary, she was an opera enthusiast. Posner erroneously identified her as the Running Woman who was later identified as one Toni Foster (interview with Gerald Posner, 3/6/92, *Case Closed*, 1993, pp. 260-61).

Tables 22 through 24 and Figures 24 through 28 follow and relate to the ensuing discussions.

The Justin McCarty women

On November 22, 1963, The Justin McCarty Dress Manufacturing Company was located four blocks south of Houston and Main. Marie Muchmore, a 54-year-old Dallas native, was one of six Justin McCarty co-workers who walked to Dealey Plaza just before noon that day to watch the motorcade. She took along her year-old Keystone K-7 zoom-lens 8-mm home-movie camera loaded with color film. Like Zapruder's, her camera speed was set at 16 frames per second. Much of the information on Muchmore is culled from Trask's, 1994 *Pictures of the Pain*, Chapter 7.

The Muchmore group first positioned itself on the curb on the west side of Houston Street across from the County Criminal Court House. From this location, Marie took about 30 seconds of pre-assassination footage including a 16-second sequence of the presidential and vice-presidential entourages turning right off Main and traveling north on Houston.

To watch the presidential limo travel west on Elm, the group ran about 80 feet to the west and into the confines of Dealey Plaza's north peristyle. Muchmore was now behind a waist-high wall at the northern end of an elliptical colonnade. She was about 210 feet from the TSBD sniper's nest and 110 feet from the spot on Elm where the president's head exploded at Z313. In between, was an open area of lawn (north infield) with relatively few mostly scattered spectators.

As Muchmore was getting ready to take her final footage of the presidential limo, she heard a loud explosion. About 3 seconds later she resumed filming at a point where the president was about halfway to the triple underpass and approximately between her position and Zapruder's position on the north side of Elm. By the time she finished her final sequence a little over 3 seconds later, she heard two more loud explosions that severely frightened her and sent her running for cover.

In the aftermath of the shooting, Ms. Muchmore reportedly quickly departed the scene and returned to her office some four blocks away. Soon thereafter she departed to Oklahoma to spend the Thanksgiving Holiday with family who apparently convinced her to contact the local FBI in connection with witnessing the assassination.

Interviews and testimony

Ms. Muchmore was interviewed twice by the FBI, the first time in December 1963 before the agency was aware that she had filmed the assassination, the second time in February 1964 after *UPI* had published the three frames from her assassination sequence. The first interview took place in Oklahoma.

Marie Muchmore, behind wall within northern end of peristyle - *As the parade passed by there she heard the first shot, but from where they were standing could not observe where the shot came from. She said she panicked after this shot [actually after the last two shots] and ran back to the office, later becoming deathly sick over the incident when learning of the president's death . . .* FBI interview, 12/4/63 (WRCD7).

Mrs. Muchmore stated that after the car turned onto Elm Street from Houston Street, she heard a loud noise which she at first thought was a firecracker, but then with the crowd of people running in all directions and hearing two further noises sounding like gunfire, she advised that she began to run [she appears to have stopped filming in response to the sound of the Z328 shot] to find a place to hide. She related that she panicked and does not recall the setting on the camera or what she did after learning that the noise was gunshots. FBI interview, 2/18/64 (WRCD735).

Ms. Muchmore like Zapruder shunned interviews by assassination researchers. She passed away in April 1990.

5: The Muchmore Assassination Sequence

The film and camera timelines and available versions

The Monday after the assassination, Ms. Muchmore showed up with her yet undeveloped film at the *United Press International (UPI)* offices in Dallas unsure of its content, quality, and value. By the time she left, *UPI* had acquired the unprocessed footage at risk for $1,000. She reportedly declined their offer to allow *UPI* staff to view the film before making a potentially higher or lower offer, or no offer.

UPI immediately had the film processed by Kodak in Dallas and then transported it the same day by air to their New York City headquarters. The next day *UPI* affiliate *WNEW-TV* aired the film for the first time. Three frames (M14/Z285, M38/Z309, and M54/Z325) showing the presidential limo just before and just after the head shot were enlarged, photo-enhanced, and reproduced in color in the widely distributed *UPI-American Heritage* souvenir hardcover book *Four Days*, published in January 1964.

The FBI contacted *UPI* in February 1964 shortly after *Four Days* was published and obtained an exact copy of the film that reportedly had a 66-frame sequence of the presidential limo on Elm. The FBI loaned its copy of the film to the Warren Commission (WC) which included three frames (M19/Z290, M42/Z313, and M55/Z326) in the Warren Report that are significantly wider than the cropped copies available today.

Muchmore provided the camera to the FBI in February 1964. When the FBI tested the camera, it was fully wound and reportedly running at about 18.5 frames per second. They used the Muchmore, Zapruder, and Nix cameras in May 1964 in staging a recreation of the assassination at the request of the WC. The FBI returned the camera to Muchmore in early June 1964. Much of the above information is culled from Trask's 1994, *Pictures of the Pain*, Chapter 7.

In late 2002 *Associated Press Television News*, the video arm of *Associated Press*, acquired the film from *UPI*. They promptly prepared a cropped digital copy allegedly from the original and contracted with *Metro Broadcast* in London to have it optically enhanced using Archangel™ technology developed by broadcast equipment designers Snell & Wilcox. The optically enhanced digital reproduction was displayed at a convention in January 2003 for the National Association of Television Program Executives. The release was timed to promote licensing agreements with program makers that might consider using the Muchmore film in productions commemorating the 40th anniversary of the assassination. The Archangel™ technology digitally stabilizes and restores film images by removing dirt, scratches, tape tear, film weave and other imperfections *(Associated Press*, Press Release November 21, 2002, J F Kennedy Assassination: http://aptm.com/aptn/web site).

In conducting my analysis, I initially used the version of the Nix film found on Robert Grodin's DVD *JFK Assassination Films: A Case for Conspiracy* published in 2003 by *Delta Entertainment Corporation*, Los Angeles, CA. To a lesser extent, I also used the version of the Muchmore film found on the DVD "Death in Dealey Plaza" published in 2003 by *Discovery Channel*.

Zapruder-film correlation and camera recording speed

As mentioned above, the FBI tested the camera in February 1964 and found it recorded at 18.5 feet per second when fully wound. The Muchmore film's 66-frame assassination sequence captured the Z313 cranial explosion at frame M42 (Z313) and Agent Hill first grabbing the rear hand rail of the presidential limo at M66 which occurs at Z337. Since there are 24 frames in each case, it is evident that Muchmore's camera was running at about the same speed as Zapruder's. On this basis, we will assume that Muchmore's camera was running very close to 18.3 frames per second. As such, her assassination sequence correlates with Zapruder frames Z272 to Z337 (M01-66).

The assassination sequence

Figure 24 shows Muchmore's field of vision and the witnesses in view. The assassination sequence begins at M01 (Z272) with thirteen blurry frames showing approximately the front half of the presidential limo on the far right. The camera is aimed toward the masonry wall extending off the western end of the pergola and Zapruder is just out of view to camera right. The limo is in full camera view by M12 (Z283) at approximately the point Ms. Muchmore begins panning left following it down Elm.

When Jackie Kennedy first comes into view at M03 (Z274) she is upright in her seat with her back to the camera. From M21 to M27 (Z292-98) she leans forward and down as if to look into her husband's face during which time she is partially obstructed from view behind north of Elm spectators Brehm and the Babushka Lady. She remains in this leaning-forward position from the time she returns to view at M28 (Z299) until she disappears from view behind Motorcycle Officers Hargis and Martin at about M57 (Z328).

When the president comes into view at M04 (Z275) he is slumping to his left and largely hidden from view behind Ms. Kennedy who appears to have her right arm around his shoulders. After Ms. Kennedy bends forward, all we can see of the president is the left-rear quarter of the top of his head and the top and back of his right shoulder. He is obstructed from view at several points by south-of-Elm spectators or the white helmets of Motorcycle Officers Hargis and Martin, first from M24 to M28 (Z295-99) and again from M48 to M57 (Z319-28).

Due to the resolution limits of the film at the distance involved, the explosive effects of the head shots (jettison of blood and brain tissue at M42 (Z313) and M59/M60 (Z330/331) are barely visible. Nevertheless, the images are clear enough to confirm the telltale downward and forward movement of the president's head at M42/M43 (Z313-314). We get a good view of the president's head jolting forward in response to the Z328 shot at M59/60 (Z330/331). We can actually see the leftward rotation resulting from the bullet's impact high on the right side. We see a cloud of bloody brain matter reaching Motorcycle Officer Hargis from about Z335 to Z337.

Secret Service Agent Clint Hill of the presidential follow-up car comes into camera view at M44 (Z315). From M45/Z316 until the film ends, he is chasing after the limo at full speed and has just reached the left-rear hand hold with his left hand and placed his right foot on the left-rear running board as the film ends at M66 (Z337). The Bronson film shows Agent Hill jumped off the front of the left running board at B03/Z300.

The following spectators are in view on the north side of Elm: Gayle Newman from M01 to M10 (Z272-81); her husband Bill from M01 to M15 (Z272-86); and Emmett Hudson and two unidentified spectators standing near him on the concrete steps leading to the west side of the pergola from about M32 to M66 (Z303-37).

On the south side of Elm we see: Charles Brehm from M01 to M39 (Z272-310); the Babushka Lady from M05 to M49 (Z275-329); Jean Hill from M19 to M66 (Z290-337); and Mary Moorman from M26 to M66 (Z297-337).

The front portion of the presidential follow-up car comes into view toward the end of the film allowing us to observe the reactions of several occupants. This includes Secret Service Agent Sam Kinney who is driving and Agent William McIntyre on the left-side running board. They appear only in the last three frames M64 to M66 (Z335-37).

Due to the presidential limo slowing down, three of the president's four-man police-escort enter into view from camera right during the second half of the assassination sequence. Officers Hargis and Martin on the driver's side are in clear view from about M30 (Z301) until the film ends. Officer Chaney on the inside position on the passenger side is in view from M49 (Z320) until the film ends.

Signature jolting, cranial eruption and reflex reactions to the Z310 (M39) shot

As discussed in Chapter 2, the Zapruder film images indicated forward and downward movement of the president's head amidst a large cranial eruption at Z313/Z314 (M42/43). This was followed by overt reflex reactions among the presidential entourage and spectators commencing the equivalent of three Z frames thereafter which is Z316 (M45). See Figure 25.

Confirmation of the same head movements and reflex reactions that we see in the Zapruder film commencing at M42 (Z313) - The Muchmore film confirms the president's head moves downward and forward at M42/43 (Z313/314) amidst a near vertical cranial eruption. To the extent the presidential-limo occupants are in view, the Muchmore film confirms the following second-shot-related reflex movements from M45 to M47 (Z316-18) that we see in the Zapruder film: President Kennedy's head snapping back; Governor Connally turning his head to the left and ducking forward; Nellie Connally recoiling; Agent Kellerman turning his head to the left; and Motorcycle Officer Hargis darting his head slightly to the right. Ms. Kennedy and Agent Greer are largely obstructed from view.

Additional reflex reactions seen in the Muchmore film commencing at M45 (Z316) - Muchmore's film images allow us to add eight more to the list of those that exhibit signature reflex reactions to the head-shot noise that start and end between the equivalent of Z316 and Z318.

Secret Service Agent Clint Hill - Muchmore captures Agent Hill commencing an all-out sprint at M45/Z316. He is chasing after the presidential limo.

Emmett Hudson, Red Shirt Man and Flying Tackle Man (Hudson group) - All three north-of-Elm spectators standing halfway up the concrete stairway leading to the west end of Bryan's Pergola simultaneously dart their heads slightly to the left between M45/Z316 and M47/Z318.

Motorcycle Officer Martin - When Hargis and Martin disappeared from Zapruder's camera view at Z276 they were both looking to the right in alarm into the limo. From the point they come into view at M30/Z301 they are still looking out to right but now toward the Hudson Group on the knoll. Between M45 and M48 (Z316-19), Martin darts his head first down to the left, then up to right and then back to the left.

Mary Moorman, Jean Hill and the Babushka Lady - These south-of-Elm witnesses exhibit classic reflex reactions between M44 and M45 (Z315-316). Moorman/Hill raise their right shoulders and rotate/recoil slightly to the left. Babushka Lady rotates/recoils to the right. The images need to be lightened to see Ms. Moorman's movements.

Alarm reactions to the Z310 (M39) shot

The Zapruder film images indicated overt alarm reactions among the presidential entourage and spectators commencing the equivalent of eight Z frames after Z313 (M42) which is Z321 (M50). The Muchmore film confirms that Officer Hargis looked out toward the Hudson Group commencing Z321 and then darted his head to the left and was looking at the president as of M59 (Z330). Commencing Z321 Ms. Kennedy is obstructed from view and the Running Woman is out of Muchmore's view to camera right during this interval.

Additional alarm reactions seen in the Muchmore film commencing at M50 (Z321) - Her film images allow us to add four more to the list of those that exhibit signature alarm reactions to the head-shot noise.

<u>Motorcycle Officers Martin and Chaney</u> - Commencing M50/Z321 Martin, who was already looking right, turns his head further right. From the point his head enters into view at M50 (Z321) through M54 (Z325), Chaney, who is riding off the right-rear fender of the presidential limo, is turning his head to his right toward the Hudson Group. Between M55 and M58 (Z326-29) Chaney, Martin and Hargis have all darted their heads to the left and are looking directly at the president when the Z328 shot struck him in the head at M59 (Z330). Hargis was obstructing Chaney's view. I presume their eyes were drawn suddenly back to the limo by the roar of its engine as Greer floored the accelerator pedal and/or the governor shouting.

<u>Red Shirt Man and Flying Tackle Man</u> - Standing on the steps leading up to the pergola just in front of Dealey Plaza Groundskeeper Emmett Hudson, there is an unidentified man wearing a red-plaid shirt who begins raising his arms and crouching at M50 (Z321). Standing beside Hudson, there is a dark-skinned man (Flying-Tackle Man) that is lifting his left leg commencing M50 (Z321). His instincts are telling him to run.

Signature jolting, cranial eruption and reflex reactions to the Z328 (M57) shot

As discussed in Chapter 2, The Zapruder film images indicate forward and downward movement amidst a lower-trajectory cranial eruption of the president's head at Z330/Z331 (M59/60) with a rearward spray of brain matter landing on the trunk from Z331 to Z337. They also indicated secondary jolts at Z331/332 to Ms. Kennedy's right shoulder from the force of her husband's head striking it and Ms. Connally's head from the force of an initial spray of brain matter striking the top rear. This was followed by overt reflex reactions among the presidential entourage and spectators commencing the equivalent of three Z frames thereafter which is Z333 (M62). See Figures 26, 27 and 28.

Confirmation of the same head movements, cranial eruptions and reflex reactions that we see in the Zapruder film commencing at M59 (Z330) and M62/Z333 - The Muchmore film confirms that the president's head not only jolts downward and forward at M59/60/61 (Z330/331/332) but also rotates slightly to the left due to the impact high on the right rear. There are discernible upward, forward and rearward sprays of whitish fluids from the cowlick area at M60 (Z331) consistent with what we see in the Zapruder and Nix films. The careful observe can discern considerable brain matter raining down within the limo from M62 to M66 (Z332 to Z337). The careful observer can also discern a whitish substance landing on the lid of the trunk from M62 to M66 (Z332 to Z337) and reaching officer Hargis from about M64 to M66 (Z335 to Z337). The back of Ms. Kennedy's head is out of view behind Hargis and Martin as of M57/Z328. The back of Ms. Connally's head is effectively out of view commencing M53/Z324 when it becomes superimposed on the rear of Agent Kellerman's head. The top left side of the governor's ducking head disappears from view at M57/Z328.

The images confirm the following reflex movements commencing at M62 (Z333): Agent Greer leaning/turning/ducking slightly to the right; Agent Kellerman ducking his head down toward the center of the limo; and Ms. Connally turning her shoulders to the right toward the center of the limo. Although Motorcycle Hargis is largely blocked from view by Officer Martin, we can barely discern his left/right head movements commencing M62 (Z333).

Additional reflex reactions seen in the Muchmore film commencing at M62 (Z333) - If there was indeed a third-shot that entered the limo at Z330 (M59), the Muchmore film images should have picked up

5: The Muchmore Assassination Sequence

additional reflex reactions commencing M62 to M63 (Z333 to Z334) among others that were not within Zapruder's camera view. Such is the case. The Muchmore film allows us to add the following nine to those showing overt reflex reactions to the Z328 third-shot that start and end between the equivalent of Z333 and Z335 M62/64).

Motorcycle Officers Martin and Chaney - As of M61/Z332, Martin is still looking at the back of Officer Hargis' head. Between M62 and M66 (Z333-37), he darts his head upward to his right. From M59 through M62 (Z330-33), Chaney is looking directly at the president. Between M62 and M65 (Z333-36), he makes an abrupt and very telling about-face. By M66 (Z337) as the sequence ends, he is looking hard right rear as his classic reflex reaction morphs into an alarm action.

Emmett Hudson, Red Shirt Man and Flying Tackle Man - All three north-of-Elm spectators standing halfway up the concrete stairway leading to the west end of Bryan's Pergola exhibit classic auditory reflex reactions between M62/Z333 and M64/Z335. They concurrently dart their heads slightly to the left, Red Shirt Man does a little jig, and Running Man jerks his right arm up and down.

Mary Moorman and Jean Hill - Between M62/Z333 and M64/Z335, Moorman darts her head to her right and Jean Hill raises her shoulders, rotates slightly right and jerks her right arm up in a classic recoil.

Agents Sam Kinney and William McIntyre - Commencing M61/Z332, Kinney, the driver of the presidential follow-up car comes into view on the extreme-right side of the frames with his head turned right. From M62/Z333 to M64/Z335, he darts his head further right. Agent McIntyre on the left-side running board of the Queen Mary comes into partial view on the extreme right side of the frames. McIntyre is already somewhat hunched over as he comes into view at M65 (Z336) and has ducked his head considerably forward and downward and has turned his head to the right in alarm as the sequence ends at M66 (Z337). Alarm reactions to shot noise always start as reflex reactions. In the Nix film images we see him continue to duck down. The un-cropped original would be helpful here.

Note that all these spontaneous reactions occurred at the exact time Secret Service Agent Hill, who was chasing the limo, and Agents Greer and Kellerman in the front seat of the limo reportedly heard the final shot ring out consistent with the testimony of most of the presidential entourage and key Grassy Knoll witnesses. Agent Hill and Motorcycle Officers Hargis and Chaney, who we see looking right at the president as of Z330, all testified to seeing the president's head driven downward and forward amidst a cranial eruption as the final shot rang out. Hargis testified that the bullet's impact turned the president's head to the left and that brain matter hit him in the face (see Chapter 12).

Table 22
Signature two-frame jolts and cranial eruptions due to a bullet striking the president or governor and transferring momentum to the wounded area
1. Z313/314/M42-43: the president's head is driven downward and forward in the midst of a conspicuous cranial eruption that jettisons blood and brain matter upward and forward a few feet above the president's head (Z/M/N films);
2. Z331/332/M60-61: the president's head is driven downward and forward in the midst of head-and-shoulder level jettisons of brain matter. Brain matter rains down within the limo and on the lid of the trunk from Z332 to Z337(Z/M/N) and engulfs Officer Hargis from about Z335 thru Z337 (M film).

Table 23

Observable second shot reflex and alarm reactions for the Muchmore film

Z310-shot reflex reactions: distinguishable blurred film images and spontaneous movements commencing 2.5 +/- 1 Z-frame equivalents after the sound reaches the person reacting

1. Z316/M45: mortally wounded President Kennedy's head began snapping back in whiplash fashion due to Ms. Kennedy spontaneously shoving him away from her (Z/M/N films);

2. Z316/M45: wounded Governor Connally started turning his head to his left and by Z221 was lunging toward the front of the limo to get his head down (Z/M/N films);

3. Z316/M45: startled Nellie Connally began leaning back/recoiling and by Z321 was ducking toward the front of the limo to get her head down (Z film);

4. Z316/M45: startled Agent Kellerman in the right-front seat of the presidential limo began leaning forward and ducking his head down toward the dash (Z and M films);

5. Z316/M45: startled Agent Hill began running toward the back of the limo at full speed (M and B films);

6. Z316/M45: startled Motorcycle Officer Hargis began darting his head up and to the right (Z/M/N films);

7. Z316/M45: startled Motorcycle Officer Martin began darting his head left/right/left (M and N films);

8. Z316/M45: startled south-of-Elm spectators Mary Moorman and Jean Hill raise their right shoulders and rotate/recoil slightly to the left (M film);

9. Z316/M45: startled north-of-Elm spectators on the pergola stairs Red Shirt Man, Emmett Hudson and Flying Tackle Man began darting their heads slightly to the left (M film);

10. Z317/M46: startled-north-peristyle-filmmaker Muchmore jiggled her camera causing a single frame of blurred images (M film).

Z310-shot alarm reactions: deliberate movements or actions commencing 7.5 +/- 2 Z-frame equivalents after the sound reaches the person reacting

1. Z321/M50: alarmed grassy-knoll-spectator Red Shirt Man who was standing on the pergola steps began crouching and raising his arms and the nearby Flying Tackle Man began lifting his left leg (M film);

2. Z321/M50: alarmed Motorcycle-Officers Hargis, Martin and Chaney began looking out to the right through Z325 and then commencing Z326 began darting their heads to the left and were looking directly at the president by Z330 with Hargis obstructing Martin's view (M and N films).

5: The Muchmore Assassination Sequence

Table 24
Observable third shot reflex and alarm reactions for the Muchmore film
Z328-shot reflex reactions: distinguishable blurred film images and spontaneous movements commencing 2.5 +/- 1 Z-frame equivalents after the sound reaches the person reacting
1. Z333/M62: startled Nellie Connally began turning/ducking her head to the right and leaning back as she was showered with brain matter (Z/N films);
2. Z333/M62: startled Agent Greer behind the wheel of the presidential limo began leaning/ducking to the right and turning his head slightly to the right (Z/M/N films);
3. Z333/M62: startled Agent Kellerman in the presidential limo's right-front seat began turning/ducking his head to the left (Z and M films);
4. Z333/M62: startled Motorcycle-Officer Martin darted his head left and down and then up and to the right (M and N films);
5. Z333/M62: startled Motorcycle-Officer Hargis began darting his head left as he looked at the president (Z/M/N films);
6. Z333/M62: startled Motorcycle-Officer Chaney began darting his head hard right (M and N films);
7. Z333/M62: startled Agent McIntyre on the Queen Mary's left running board started ducking and turning his head to the right (in progress as of M65/Z236 of M film);
8. Z333/M62: startled Agent Sam Kinney behind the wheel of the Queen Mary began turning his head hard to the right (M film);
9. Z333/M62: startled south-of-Elm spectator Mary Moorman began darting her head to her right and Jean Hill began raising her shoulders, rotating slightly right and jerking her right arm up (M film);
10. Z333/M62: startled grassy knoll spectators Red Shirt Man, Emmett Hudson and Flying Tackle Man began darting their heads to their left and Flying Tackle Man began running up the pergola stairs (M film);
11. Z334/M63: startled north-peristyle filmmaker Muchmore jiggled her camera creating a single frame of blurred images (M film).
Z328-shot alarm reactions: deliberate movements or actions commencing 7.5 +/- 2 Z-frame equivalents after the sound reaches the person reacting
1. Z337/M66: alarmed north-peristyle-filmmaker Muchmore stopped filming (M film).
2. Z337/M66: alarmed Motorcycle Officer Chaney began looking hard over his right shoulder toward the TSBD (M and N films).

The Complete Unraveling of the JFK Assassination

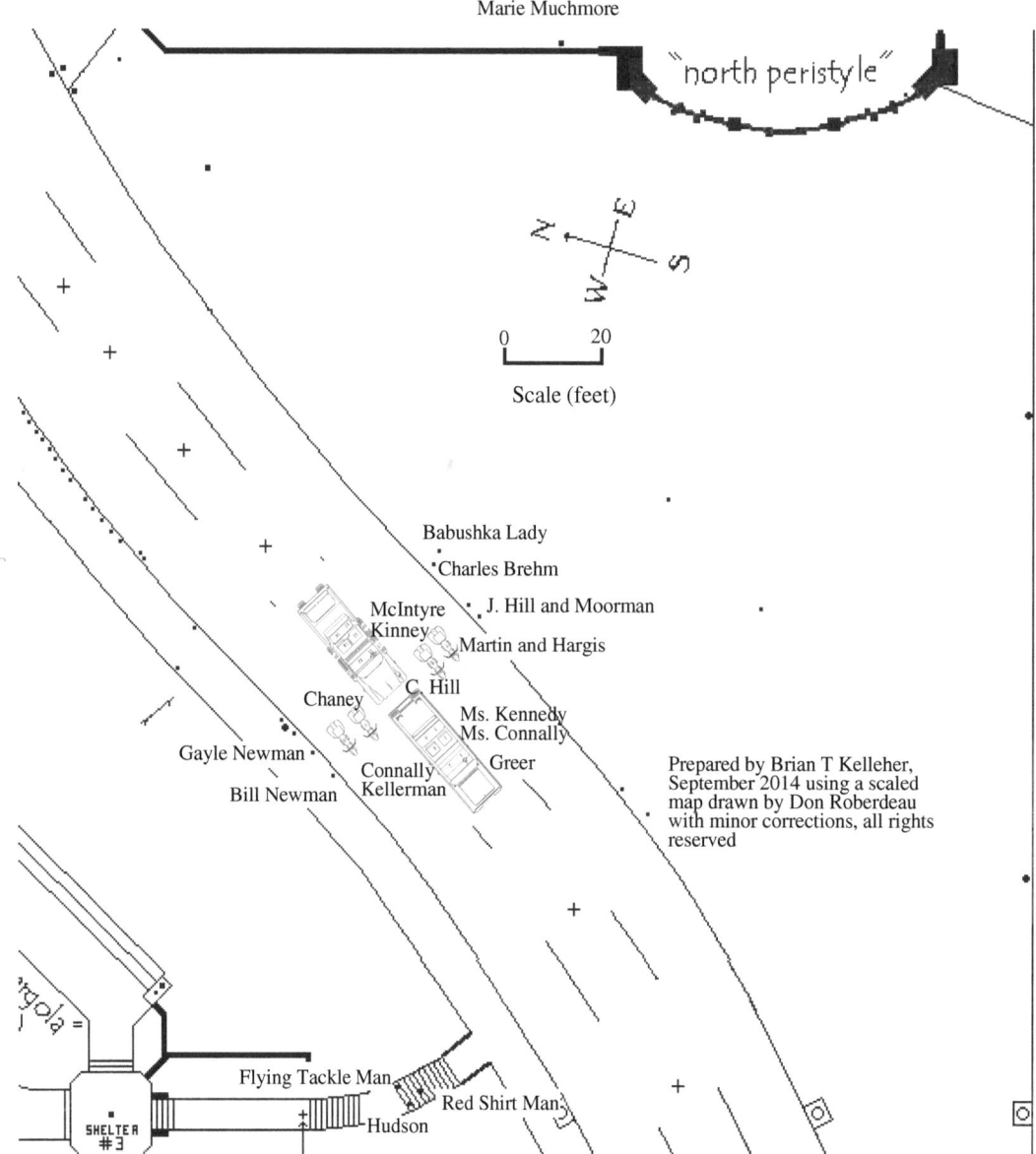

Figure 24

Muchmore's field of vision from Z272 to Z337 - The presidential limo, Queen Mary and motorcycles are approximately positioned to scale as of their locations at Z313. All the Queen Mary occupants are out of Muchmore's view to camera right during the sequence except Agent Hill who was chasing after the limo, the driver Agent Kinney and Agent McIntyre on the left running board. Three of the four motorcycle officers are in view (all but Jackson). The spectators shown are the only ones in Muchmore's view during this interval. The Limo/Queen Mary drawing is from Trask, 1994, p. 63.

5: The Muchmore Assassination Sequence

Table 24
Observable third shot reflex and alarm reactions for the Muchmore film
Z328-shot reflex reactions: distinguishable blurred film images and spontaneous movements commencing 2.5 +/- 1 Z-frame equivalents after the sound reaches the person reacting
1. Z333/M62: startled Nellie Connally began turning/ducking her head to the right and leaning back as she was showered with brain matter (Z/N films);
2. Z333/M62: startled Agent Greer behind the wheel of the presidential limo began leaning/ducking to the right and turning his head slightly to the right (Z/M/N films);
3. Z333/M62: startled Agent Kellerman in the presidential limo's right-front seat began turning/ducking his head to the left (Z and M films);
4. Z333/M62: startled Motorcycle-Officer Martin darted his head left and down and then up and to the right (M and N films);
5. Z333/M62: startled Motorcycle-Officer Hargis began darting his head left as he looked at the president (Z/M/N films);
6. Z333/M62: startled Motorcycle-Officer Chaney began darting his head hard right (M and N films);
7. Z333/M62: startled Agent McIntyre on the Queen Mary's left running board started ducking and turning his head to the right (in progress as of M65/Z236 of M film);
8. Z333/M62: startled Agent Sam Kinney behind the wheel of the Queen Mary began turning his head hard to the right (M film);
9. Z333/M62: startled south-of-Elm spectator Mary Moorman began darting her head to her right and Jean Hill began raising her shoulders, rotating slightly right and jerking her right arm up (M film);
10. Z333/M62: startled grassy knoll spectators Red Shirt Man, Emmett Hudson and Flying Tackle Man began darting their heads to their left and Flying Tackle Man began running up the pergola stairs (M film);
11. Z334/M63: startled north-peristyle filmmaker Muchmore jiggled her camera creating a single frame of blurred images (M film).
Z328-shot alarm reactions: deliberate movements or actions commencing 7.5 +/- 2 Z-frame equivalents after the sound reaches the person reacting
1. Z337/M66: alarmed north-peristyle-filmmaker Muchmore stopped filming (M film).
2. Z337/M66: alarmed Motorcycle Officer Chaney began looking hard over his right shoulder toward the TSBD (M and N films).

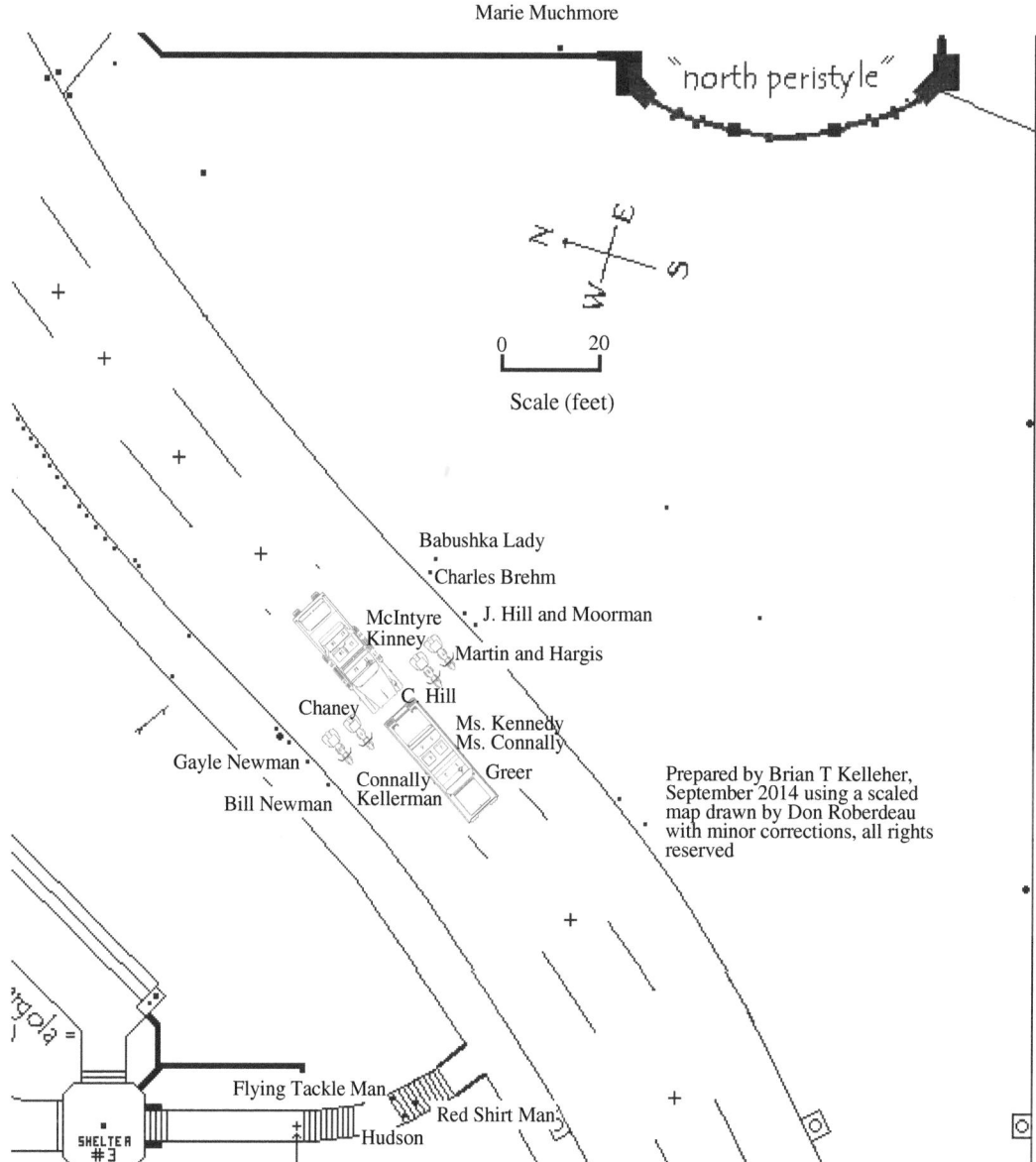

Figure 24

Muchmore's field of vision from Z272 to Z337 - The presidential limo, Queen Mary and motorcycles are approximately positioned to scale as of their locations at Z313. All the Queen Mary occupants are out of Muchmore's view to camera right during the sequence except Agent Hill who was chasing after the limo, the driver Agent Kinney and Agent McIntyre on the left running board. Three of the four motorcycle officers are in view (all but Jackson). The spectators shown are the only ones in Muchmore's view during this interval. The Limo/Queen Mary drawing is from Trask, 1994, p. 63.

5: The Muchmore Assassination Sequence

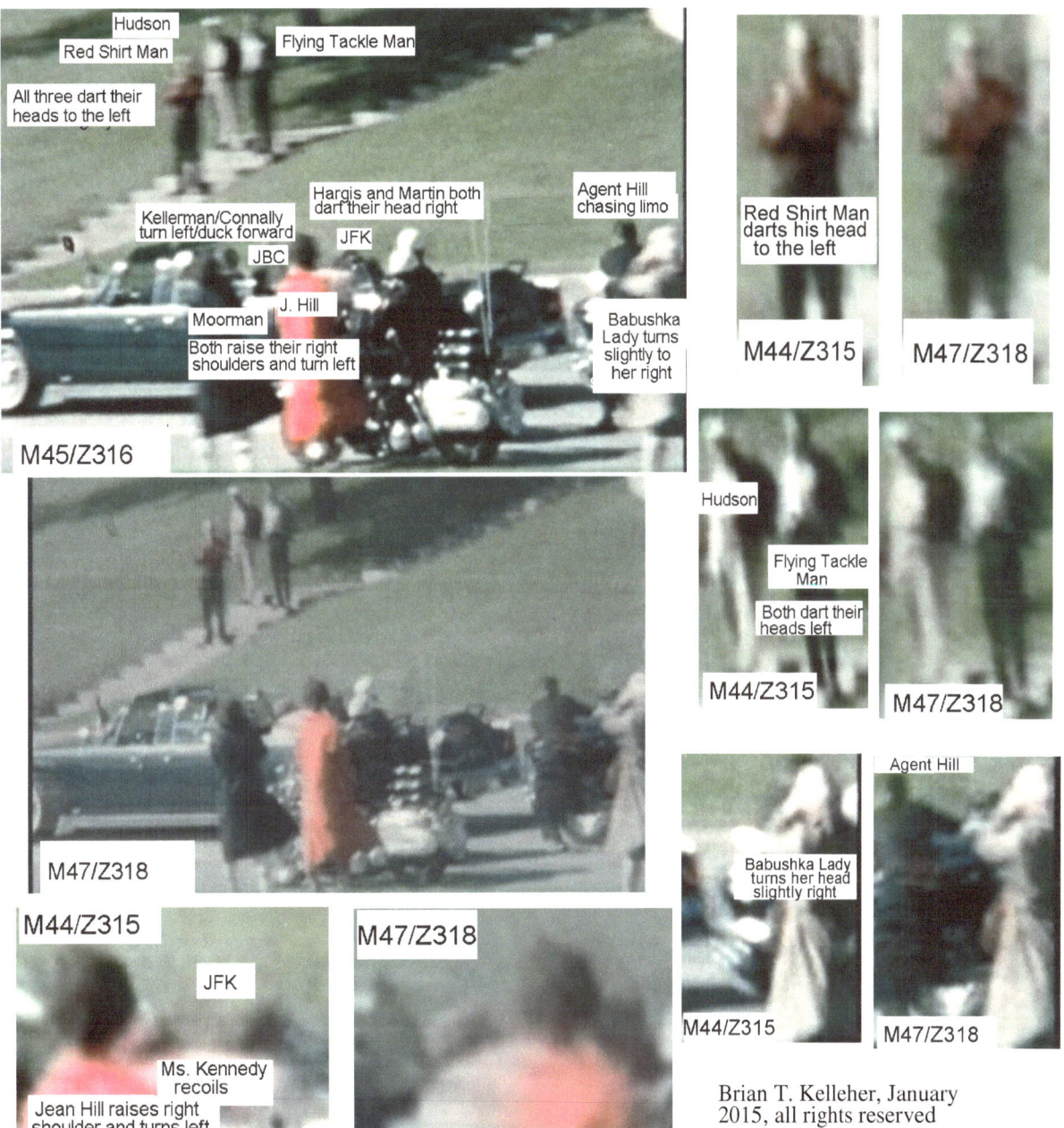

Figure 25
Reflex reactions for the Z310 second shot: Muchmore frames M44, M45, and M47 (Z315/Z316/Z318) - Everyone in sight is exhibiting a discernible reflex reaction. Within the limo, President Kennedy's head is snapping back due to his wife recoiling and pushing him away. Governor Connally and Agent Kellerman are turning their heads to the left and ducking forward. Nellie Connally and Agent Greer are completely obstructed from view. Outside the limo, Police Motorcycle Officers Martin and Hargis simultaneously dart their heads to the right as Agent Hill starts running at full speed toward the limo. Mary Moorman and Jean Hill raise their right shoulders and recoil/rotate to the left. The Babushka Lady turns her head slightly to the right and leans back. Red Shirt Man, Emmett Hudson and Flying Tackle Man dart their heads slightly to the left. These are cropped images that I photo edited to increase brightness and contrast (Marie Muchmore/*Associated Press TV News*).

The Complete Unraveling of the JFK Assassination

BTK Sept. 2014, all rights reserved

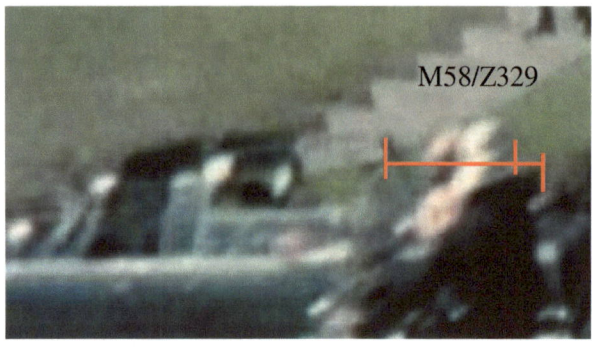

Between M58 (Z329) and M60 (Z331) the president's head is driven downward and forward about 3 inches as it rotates amidst discernible upward, forward and rearward jettisons of whitish fluids from the cowlick area.

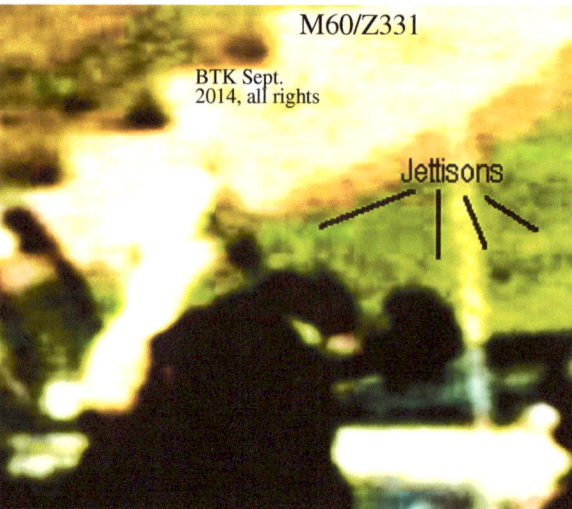

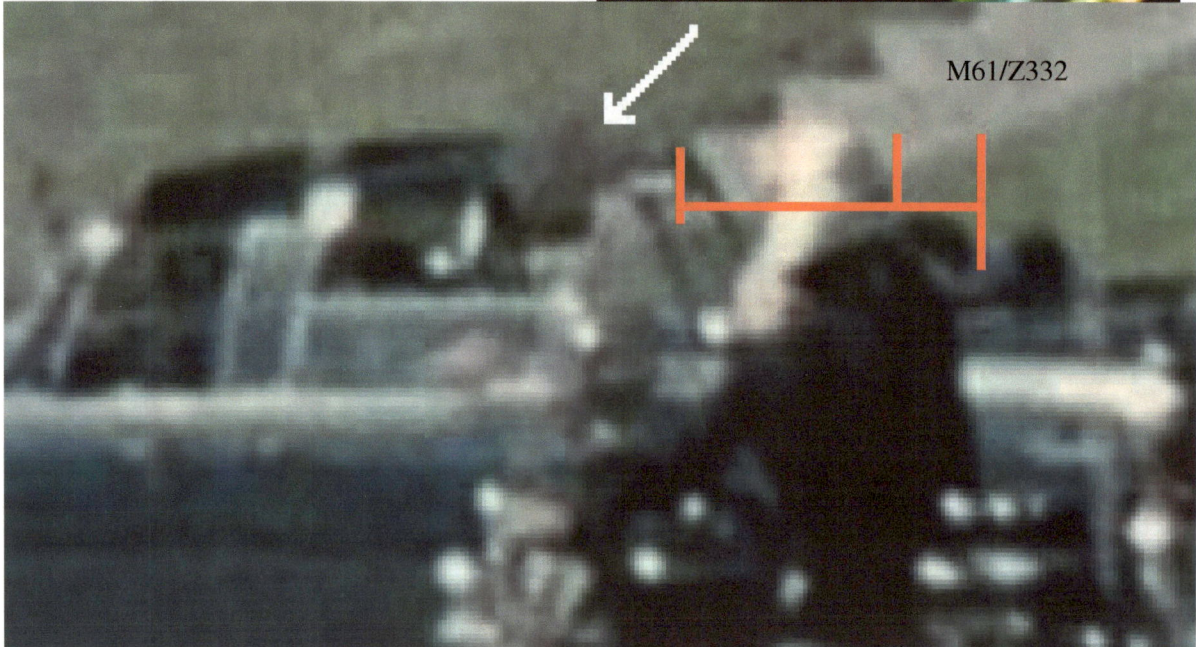

Brian T. Kelleher, September 2014, all rights reserved

M61/Z332 - The white arrow points to what appears to be a cloud of bloody brain matter moving toward Motorcycle Officer Hargis. It reached him from M64 through M66 (Z335-37).

Figure 26

Signature jolts and cranial eruptions for the Z328 third shot: Muchmore frames M58, M60, and M61 (Z329/Z331/Z332) - Consistent with the Zapruder and Nix films, the Muchmore film images show the bullet struck the cowlick area late in the equivalent of frame Z330. From M59 to M61 (Z330 to Z332), we see the president's head driven forward about 3 inches amidst a cranial eruption that jettisons brain matter towards the Connallys and Motorcycle Officer Hargis. As of M61/Z332, there is some brain matter on what we can see of the lid of the trunk. These are cropped images that I photo edited to increase brightness and contrast (Marie Muchmore/*Associated Press TV News*).

5: The Muchmore Assassination Sequence

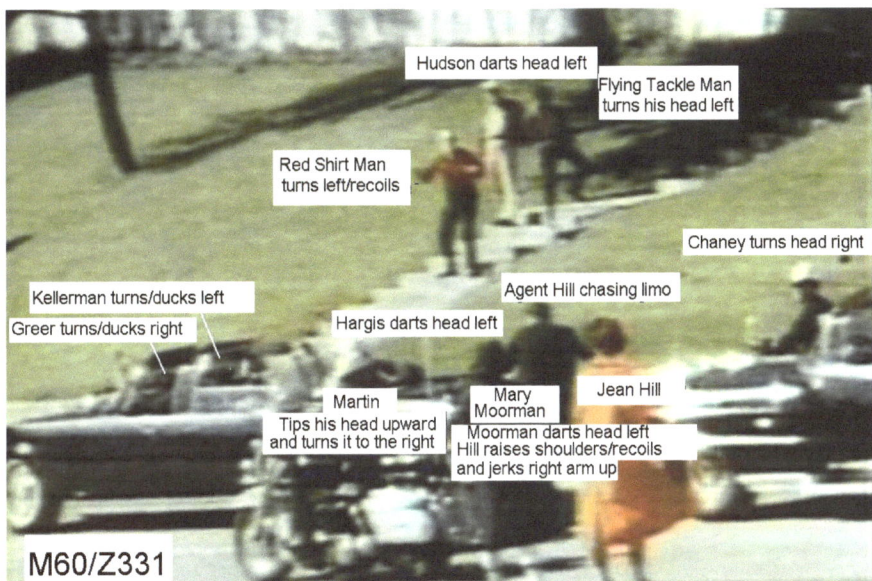

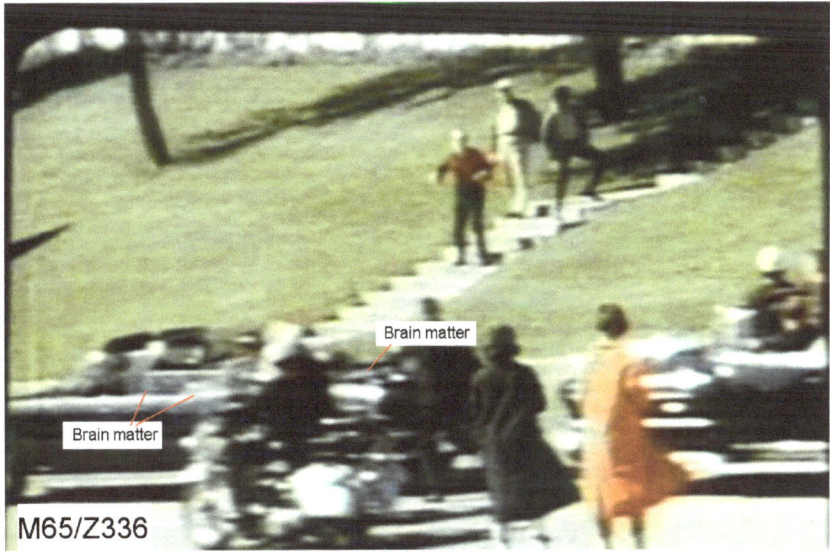

Figure 27

Reflex reactions for the Z328 third shot and visible brain matter fallout: Muchmore frames M60, M61, M64 and M65 (Z331/Z332/Z335/336) - <u>Fallout</u> - The whitish brain matter that is visible on Ms. Connally and the lid of the trunk at M65, began to appear at M61/Z332 with most landing at M62/Z333 through M64/Z336. As of M65/66 (Z336/337) it reaches Motorcycle Officer Hargis. <u>Reflex reactions</u> - Everyone in sight exhibits discernible reflex reactions. Within the limo, commencing M62/Z333 Ms. Connally and Agent Kellerman are turning their heads and ducking toward the middle of the limo. Greer is turning and leaning/ducking slightly to his right. Ms. Kennedy is largely obstructed from view. Outside the limo, commencing M63/Z334 the three police officers in view simultaneously dart their heads, Hargis to the left, Martin and Chaney up and to the right. Mary Moorman darts her head to the right. Jean Hill raises her shoulders, recoils slightly right and jerks her right arm up. Red Shirt Man, Emmett Hudson and Flying Tackle Man dart their heads slightly left. Red Shirt Man does a jig and Flying Tackle Man jerks his right arm up and down. These are cropped images that I photo edited to increase brightness and contrast (Marie Muchmore/*Associated Press TV News*).

Figure 28
Zooming in on the reflex reactions for the Z328 shot: Muchmore frames M61 and M64 (Z332 and Z335)

Chapter 6

The Nix Assassination Sequence

Native Texan 52-year-old Orville Nix, who stood six foot 6 inches tall, was working as an air conditioning engineer for the United States General Services Administration on November 22, 1963. At that time, the Dallas offices of the USGSA were located on Commerce Street, about seven blocks east of Dealey Plaza. As he exited the office that day en route to Dealey Plaza to see the president, Nix was carrying a Keystone Auto-Zoom Model K810 8-mm camera.

This was a more expensive Keystone K series camera than the one that Marie Muchmore had used, but designed to run at the same speed. As with Zapruder and Muchmore, it is apparent that Nix had his camera fully wound when he started shooting with the camera speed set at 16 frames per second. Unfortunately, the camera was loaded with a Type-A tungsten film designed for indoor use.

Main value - The Nix assassination sequence is considered by most including me to be the second most important film of the assassination behind Zapruder's. Like Muchmore's fourth film sequence, it provides some critically important information on second and third shot timing and effects that has been completely overlooked by government investigators and private researchers alike. The Nix film images confirm two conspicuous downward and forward jolts to the president's head, the first at Z313/Z314 and the second at Z330/Z331. The Nix film images provide critically important confirmation of both forward and rearward shoulder-level jettisons of brain matter at Z330/331 with the initial forward spray knocking Ms. Connally's head downward and forward at Z331 and then engulfing her by Z335. The images also pick up whitish brain matter landing on the lid of the trunk from Z331 to Z335 and a cloud reaching Motorcycle Officer Hargis and Agent Hill from about Z335 to Z338. The initial jettisons at Z330/331 are easier to see when the contrast and brightness are increased using photo editing software.

To see visual proof of a bullet entering the presidential limo at Z330/N040, find the digital version on YouTube and using ultra-slow motion go back and forth between Nix frames N039 and N046 (Z329 and Z336) taking note of the forward head jolt and cloud of brain matter that immediately engulfs Nellie Connally's head (just as she repeatedly testified) followed commencing N043/Z333 by the concurrent subtle to dramatic head turning/ducking/diving/recoiling of everyone in view.

Tables 25 through 27 and Figures 29 through 33 follow and relate to the ensuing discussions.

The three sequences

Upon his arrival at the plaza, Nix took up a position among a horde of spectators curled across Houston Street where Dallas police had barricaded its intersection with Main Street to allow the motorcade to pass. He was standing in approximately the middle of west-bound Main where it intersects the west side of Houston about 40 feet south of the Muchmore group. From this location through the surrounding crowd, he took 170 frames (9.3) seconds of pre-assassination footage of the presidential limo, its follow-up car, and the vice-presidential limo traveling north on Houston.

To get some additional action of the presidential limo traveling on Elm, Nix made his way to his southwest and took up a position at the south curb of Main about 50 feet west of an imaginary line dividing Main and Houston. He was about 340 feet due south of the TSBD sniper's nest and 200 feet east of the spot on Elm where the president's head exploded at Z313 and directly opposite Zapruder. As the presidential limo traveled west on Elm it was out of Nix's view behind the north peristyle until it reached a point about halfway to the underpass. He raised his camera to his eye and resumed filming as the presidential limo entered his viewfinder. In between was the western end of Dealey Plaza's north infield with the grassy knoll just beyond. He ended up with 122 frames (6.7 seconds) of assassination footage that covers the interval Z291 to Z412.

Nix's third and final Dealey-Plaza' sequence has 147 frames (8 seconds) of grassy knoll' post-assassination footage.

Interviews and testimony

Nix provided the following information during a December 1963 meeting with the FBI and a follow-up meeting in January 1964 at which time he agreed to turn over his camera for "experimental purposes."

Orville Nix, south curb of Main, at about Z313 - *Nix then moved west on Main Street and the film picks up the motorcade subsequent to the firing of the first two shots [actually 3.8 seconds after the Z221 first shot and 1.2 seconds before the Z310 second shot]. Nix believed the film depicts the third shot hitting President Kennedy and the sequence of events immediately after. FBI interview, 12/1/63 (WRv.24Hp.539).*

After the car got by, he then proceeded to a point about 20-feet west of Houston Street on the south side of Main Street and made the later series [the assassination sequence] across the open area, which was in view of his position, using the zoom lens completely open. As to whether or not the camera was wound tightly, he pointed out that he could not recall specifically, but his experience had been that it would only run at a slower speed when the spring was almost run down. Mr. Nix advised that the FBI was welcome to use the camera for experimental purposes and that he would be available as a witness if needed. FBI interview, 1/29/64 (WRv.24Hp.539).

Correlating Nix's FBI testimony to the Zapruder film images, he heard the first shot at a point where he could not see the president and paid it no heed. He heard the second and third shots as he was filming and because of the considerable distance involved, he did not notice the cranial explosion or the president's subsequent movements. As such, his testimony is of interest in relation to the number of shots, but not with respect to shot timing and effects.

In the December 1963 testimony, it was most likely the FBI interviewer Joe Abernathy who concluded that the film picked up the motorcade after the first two shots rather than Nix. At the time of the interview, the FBI was just about to issue a December 9, 1963, report in which it erroneously concluded that the first shot hit Kennedy at about Z190 and that the second hit Connally at about Z233.

There is some Orville Nix testimony that the amateur movie-maker did indeed recall hearing the last two shots ring out while he was filming the assassination sequence, but it comes from his son Orville. When Orville Jr. was interviewed on location by the *Discovery Channel* in its 2003 documentary "JFK: Murder in Dealey Plaza," he reported that his father stopped walking down Main and started filming the limo on Elm in response to hearing the first shot ring out.

6: The Nix Assassination Sequence

In early 1967, *CBS News* invited Nix among other eyewitnesses to come to Dealey Plaza and be interviewed on location as part of their documentary "Should We Now Believe the Warren Report?" The program was aired over four days in June 1967. The network ended up airing just this snippet of the Nix interview where he responds to being asked how many shots he heard and in what kind of sequence: "I would say-Bang-Bang-Bang" (CBS News Inquiry: "Should We Now Believe the Warren Report?": Part I, Broadcast June 25, 1967).

The film and camera timelines and available versions

Shortly after Nix had the film developed, on December 1, 1963, he voluntarily turned it over to the Dallas FBI who promptly made a copy and returned it to him three days later. The WC included six frames from the FBI's copy of the film in the Warren Report. Nix provided the camera to the FBI again in February 1964. The FBI found it fully wound and running at about 18.5 frames per second. They used the Nix, Zapruder, and Muchmore cameras in May 1964 in staging a recreation of the assassination at the request of the WC. The FBI returned the camera to Nix in June 1964. He apparently sold it to a private collector at some point before he died in February 1972, victim of a heart attack.

United Press International (*UPI*) acquired the film from the Texan in December 1963 for $5,000, a good dinner, and a hat. In the widely distributed *UPI-American Heritage* souvenir hardcover book *Four Days*, published in January 1964, *UPI* reproduced photo-enhanced color prints of two frames N079 (Z369) and N121 (Z410) with dramatic views of Secret Service Agent Hill and Ms. Kennedy mounting the trunk of the presidential limo. Under a licensing agreement with *UPI*, *United Artists* first released the film's assassination sequence to public view in an October 1964 documentary titled "Four Days in November."

Following well-publicized claims in the late 1960s and early 1970s by several conspiracy advocates that the Nix film shows one-or-more grassy knoll shooters, *UPI* retained some of the country's top photographic experts to enhance the film images and assess the validity of the claims. *UPI* loaned the film to the HSCA in 1978 for use by their experts in evaluating these claims.

After agreeing to return the original exposed film to the family in 1991, *UPI* was unable to locate it and it is currently considered lost. In lieu of the original, *UPI* turned over to the family all of its copies of the film as well as the color and black-and-white prints it had produced. Upon request, the FBI gave its copy of the film to the Nix family in 1992. Nix's daughter Gayle has recently authored an interesting book on the subject: Orville Nix, *The Missing JFK Assassination Film*, 2014.

The Sixth Floor Museum at Dealey Plaza is currently in possession of the original Nix camera, which it acquired from a private collector. The museum is also in possession of copies and prints of the film, which they acquired from the Nix family. This includes the items given to the family by *UPI* and the FBI.

The three Nix sequences total 434 frames and about 24 seconds. Most of the publicly available versions of the film are in slightly slowed motion (16 frames per second). Due to the fact that Nix was using indoor rather than outdoor film, the images are darker and grainier than they would otherwise have been.

I initially used the version of the Nix film found on Robert Grodin's DVD *JFK Assassination Films: A Case for Conspiracy* published in 2003 by *Delta Entertainment Corporation*, Los Angeles, CA. This has a projection speed of 16 frames per second and is in slightly slowed motion. It has some useful close-ups. I also used the digital version published on YouTube. Much of the information on Nix including the information at the end of this chapter is culled from Trask's, 1994 *Pictures of the Pain*, Chapter 6.

Zapruder film correlation and camera recording speed

Nix's 122-frame assassination sequence captured the Z313 cranial explosion at frame N023 (Z313) and Agent Hill getting both feet on the left-rear running board at N092 (Z382). In both cases there are 69 frames between the correlation points. Thus, assuming 18.3 frames per second for the Zapruder film, Nix's camera was also running at about 18.3 frames per second. On this basis, his assassination sequence correlates with Zapruder frames Z291 to Z412 (N001-122), which covers almost the same interval as the Dorman fifth sequence (Z291 to Z425).

The assassination sequence

Figure 29 shows the witnesses in Nix's field of vision as of Z313. As Nix was waiting for the presidential limo to clear the peristyle, he heard a loud explosion. About 3.5-seconds later he resumed filming as it entered his view. Exactly 2.3 seconds later he heard another explosion but let the camera roll for another 5 seconds. He had his camera tilted slightly to the right of horizontal making it appear that the limo was traveling slightly uphill when it was actually traveling slightly downhill.

As the second sequence begins at N001 (Z291), the front third of the presidential limo is in view in the right side of the frame with Zapruder in the background at the top of the frame. The Running Woman (Toni Foster) and Mary Moorman are in view from the rear on the south side of Elm and Bill Newman is facing the camera on the north side. South-of-Elm spectator Jean Hill is just out of view to camera right.

From N003 through N028 (Z293-318), Nix has the camera pointed toward Zapruder and the Newman family (Bill, Gayle and their two small children) allowing the limo to come into full view before he starts panning left commencing N029 (Z319) in following it down the street.

Ms. Kennedy comes into view at N004 (Z294) and the president at N007 (Z297). The president is slumped to his left toward Ms. Kennedy who has her right arm around his shoulders and is cradling him. All we can see of the president until his head completely disappears from view at about N042 (Z332) is the upper-left-rear side of it. At the time she comes into clear view through N039 (Z329) Ms. Kennedy is bending forward and down as if to look into his face.

Due to the resolution limits at the distance involved, the explosive effects of the head shots (jettisons of blood and brain tissue are just barely visible in frames N023/N024 (Z313/14) and N040/N041 (Z330/331). Nevertheless, the images are clear enough to confirm the jettisons as well as the two telltale downward/forward jolts of the president's head, the first at N023/N024 (Z313-314) and the second at N040/N041 (Z330/331). As of N042 (Z332) the back of the president's head disappears from view behind Ms. Kennedy's black coat collar. We can see the secondary jolt to Ms. Kennedy's upper torso at N040/N041 (Z330/331). We can also see Ms. Connally's head being driven down at N041/N042 (Z331/332) by the force of a spray of brain matter and a cloud reaching Motorcycle Officer Hargis and Agent Hill from about N045 to N048 (Z335 to Z338).

The Nix assassination sequence captures the moment of the Z328 bullet's impact and the cranial eruption at the very end of frame N040 (Z330) where the Z film captures the start of the jolt at the beginning of Z330 (N040) and the jettison at Z331 (N041). With the bullet traveling 272 feet at an average speed of 1,900 feet per second, it was fired from the sniper's nest early in frame Z328: [272/2,900=1.43x18.3=2.6] and [329.9-2.6=327.3].

6: The Nix Assassination Sequence

In the immediate aftermath of the N040 (Z330) cranial eruption, we see Ms. Kennedy jerk her right forearm to the rear from N043 to N048 (Z333 to Z338) and commence her flight onto the trunk at N049 (Z339). By N080 (Z370) she is stretched across the trunk with both hands extending rearward toward Agent Hill.

Secret Service Agent Clint Hill has just leaped off the driver's side running board of the presidential follow-up car as he enters into camera view at N027 (Z317) at the extreme right side of the frame as does the front hood of the Queen Mary. Hill is chasing after the limo. He is just about to reach the left-rear hand hold with his left hand at N047 (Z337) and by N092 (Z382) has managed with considerable effort to get both feet on the left-rear running board.

Zapruder and Sitzman are in view from frames N001 to N057 (Z291-347). Other north-of-Elm spectators that are in view include: Gayle Newman from N003 to N031 (Z293-321); her husband Bill from N001 to N047 (Z291-337); and Dealey Plaza groundskeeper Emmett Hudson from N063 to N092 (Z353-82). Hudson is standing halfway up the concrete steps leading to the west side of the pergola directly in back of another man in a red-plaid shirt that has never been identified or come forward.

Notable south-of-Elm spectators that come in and out of Nix's view include: amateur-photographer Mary Moorman from N001 to N028 (Z291-318); Running Woman Toni Foster from N001 to N046 (Z291-336); amateur-photographer Richard Bothun from N042 to N085 (Z332-75); AP-photographer James Altgens from about N070 to N086 (Z360-76); Malcolm Summers from N066 to N094 (Z356-84); and Mr. and Mrs. Jack Franzen from about N083 to N114 (Z373-404).

Agent John Ready who is on the forward position on the Queen Mary's right-side running board comes into view at camera right at frame N039 (Z329) and Agent Kinney, the driver at N041 (Z331), allowing us to observe their reactions to the shots. This is also the case for the four-man police escort (Officers Chaney, Hargis, Martin, Jackson) flanking the front of the follow-up car who enter Nix's view at various times between N017 and N026 (Z307-316) and disappear to camera right at various times between N063 and N082 (Z353-72).

As the assassination sequence ends at N142 (Z432), the limo is accelerating toward the triple underpass with Clint Hill facing Ms. Kennedy on the trunk coaxing her back into the rear seat.

Signature jolting, cranial eruptions and reflex reactions to the Z310 (N020) shot

As discussed in Chapter 2, the Zapruder film images indicated forward and downward movement of the president's head amidst a cranial eruption at Z313/Z314 (N023/024). This was followed by overt reflex reactions among the presidential entourage and spectators commencing the equivalent of three Z frames thereafter which is Z316 (N026). See Figure 30.

Confirmation of the same head movement and reflex reactions that we see in the Zapruder film commencing at N023 (Z313) - The Nix film confirms that the president's head moves about an inch downward and forward amidst a cranial eruption at N023/024 (Z313/314). To the extent the presidential-limo occupants are in view, the Nix film confirms the same second-shot-related reflex movements commencing N026 (Z316) that we see in the Zapruder film: President Kennedy's head snapping back; Governor Connally turning his head left; Nellie Connally leaning back; Agent Greer turning his head left; Agent Kellerman ducking down over the dash; Motorcycle Officer Hargis darting his head slightly to the right; and Running

Woman turning to her left and recoiling. Ms. Kennedy has her back to Nix, but it is clear from what we see of her right-arm movements that she spontaneously shoved the president back toward the rear of his seat.

Additional reflex reactions seen in the Nix film commencing at N026 (Z316) - The Nix film images allow us to add five more to the list of those exhibiting reflex reactions to the sound of the N020/Z310 shot that start and end between the equivalent of Z316 and Z318 (N026 to N028)

Bill and Gayle Newman - Between N026/Z316 and N028/Z318 they both turn slightly to the left in recoiling and Gayle jerks her left arm up.

Motorcycle Officers Martin, Chaney and Jackson - Chaney and Jackson are looking straight ahead when they come into view to camera right at N017/Z307 and N019/Z309, respectively. Like Hargis, Martin is looking off to the right when he comes into view at N026/Z316. Between N026/Z315 and N028/Z319 all three dart their heads left/right/left. Chaney is obstructed from view at N028/Z318 and Martin at N025/Z315. Martin's movements are easier to see in the Muchmore film. Chaney was looking into the presidential limo when last seen in the Altgens' Z253 photo and Martin to the right when last seen at Z275.

Alarm reactions to the Z310 (N020) shot

The Zapruder film tells us to look for overt alarm reactions among the presidential entourage and spectators commencing the equivalent of eight Z frames after Z313 (N023), which is Z321 (N031).

Confirmation of the same alarm reactions that we see in the Zapruder film commencing at N031 (Z321) - The Nix film confirms the following alarm reaction commencing N031 (Z221): Toni Foster a.k.a. the Running Woman stopping dead in her tracks and Ms. Kennedy straightening up in her seat. We see Jackie Kennedy's gloved right hand flipping up behind the president's head from N034 to N038 (Z324-28).

Additional alarm reactions seen in the Nix film commencing at N031 (Z321) - The Nix film images confirm Hargis' movements and allow us to add three more to the list of those who exhibit signature alarm reactions to the head-shot noise commencing at Z321 (N031).

Motorcycle Officers Martin, Chaney and Jackson - As with Hargis, commencing N031/Z321 they all turn their heads to the right out over the knoll toward the Hudson Group. Also like Hargis, between N036 through N039 (Z326 to Z329), they concurrently dart their heads to the left and are looking into the presidential limo as the Z328 final shot rang out at Z330. Chaney's head movements during this period are easier to see in the Muchmore film. The Nix film confirms Chaney and Jackson's respective testimony that their eyes had been drawn to the president as the final shot rang out and that the bullet caused a cranial eruption and knocked the president forward and to his left. This leftward dart of the head is presumably related to Greer flooring the accelerator pedal and causing the engine to roar and/or the governor's shouting.

Bill Newman - From N031/Z221 to Z331, Mr. Newman turns slightly to his left and crouches.

Signature jolting, cranial eruptions and reflex reactions to the Z328 (N038) shot

As discussed in Chapter 2, The Zapruder film images indicate forward and downward movement amidst a lower-trajectory cranial eruption of the president's head at Z331 (N041) with rearward sprays of brain matter landing on the trunk at Z332 through Z337. They also indicated a secondary jolt to Ms. Kennedy's upper body at Z331/332 and to Ms. Connally's head commencing at Z331 from the force of the leading edge of the spray of brain matter. This was followed by overt reflex reactions among the presidential entourage and spectators commencing the equivalent of three Z frames thereafter which is Z333 (N043). See Figures 31 through 33.

Confirmation of the same head movement and reflex reactions that we see in the Zapruder film commencing at N040 (Z330) - The Nix film confirms the president's head begins to jolt forward about 3 inches at N040 (Z330) also causing movement of Ms. Kennedy's upper body. As of N042 (Z332), the president's head has completely disappeared behind Ms. Kennedy's black coat collar. There are discernible upward, forward and rearward jettisons of whitish fluids from the cowlick area with the leading edge of the sprays knocking Ms. Connally's head downward and forward commencing at N040/Z330. We see a cloud reaching Motorcycle Officer Hargis and agent Hill from N045 to N048 (Z335 to Z338). Whitish brain matter lands on the lid of the trunk commencing at N041 through about N047 (Z331 to Z337).

The Nix film images confirm the following reflex movements commencing N043/043 (Z333/334): Ms. Kennedy recoiling and jerking her right arm to the rear; Agent Greer ducking and turning his head slightly to the right; Nellie Connally ducking and turning her head to the right and leaning back as the governor collapses left-shoulder-first onto her lap; Motorcycle Officer Hargis darting his head left/right; and Richard Bothun turning to the left and leaning back in recoiling. Agent Kellerman is completely obstructed from view.

Additional reflex reactions seen in the Nix film commencing at N043/Z333 - If there was indeed a third-shot entering the limo at Z330 (N040), the Nix film images should have picked up additional reflex reactions among others not in Zapruder's view commencing N043 (Z333). Such is the case. The Nix film allows us to add the following seven to those exhibiting overt reflex reactions that start and end between the equivalent of Z333 and Z336 (N043-46).

Motorcycle Officer Martin -   From N043 to N045 (Z333-35) Martin darts his head left/right exhibiting a classic auditory reflex reaction and flexes his left wrist.

Motorcycle Officers Chaney and Jackson - From N043 to N046 (Z333-36), having just completed a collective glance left into the presidential limo, both officers simultaneously dart their heads to the right. Jackson flexes his left wrist. Like Hargis, commencing N047/Z337 they apply their brakes while taking a collective telltale hard look back over their right shoulders. Chaney and Hargis come to a complete stops by about N053 (Z343) and continues looking back over their right shoulders until they disappears from view to camera left at N062 (Z352). Jackson temporarily disappears from view behind Chaney at N048 (Z338) as he slows to a crawl. When he returns to view at N055 (Z345) he is in the midst of turning to look back toward the limo. He continues looking into the limo until he disappears from view to camera right at N065 (Z355).

Agent John Ready - Riding on the right-side running board of the presidential follow-up car, Ready comes into view at N039/Z329 at which point he is in a semi-crouched leaning-forward stance looking straight ahead. From N043 to N046 (Z334-36) he starts to duck and turns his head slightly to the left.

Agent Sam Kinney - During the five five frames of the Muchmore film, which is the equivalent of Z333-37 (N043-47), the Queen Mary's driver turned his head hard right. When he comes into Nix's view at N041 (Z331) he is looking slightly to the right through N043 and starts to turn hard right at N043/Z333. He disappears behind Running Woman from N045 through N046 (Z335-36). As he comes back into view at N047 through N048 (Z337-38) he is still looking right. From N049 to N052 (Z339-42), he turns his head left and is looking forward by N053 (Z343) and continues to do so until disappearing from view at N60 (Z350).

Bill Newman - In the version of the Nix film contained in *Discovery Channel's* "Death in Dealey Plaza," Mr. Newman is visible through N047/Z337. From N043 to N046 (Z333 to Z336) he ducks and spins to his left. As he disappears from view he appears to be reaching down to gather up his child.

Running Woman - From N044 (Z334) until she disappears from view at N056 (Z346) to camera right, the Running Woman is turning to her right and leaning back exhibiting a second recoil.

Alarm reactions to the Z328 (N038) shot

The Zapruder film indicated overt alarm reactions among the presidential entourage and spectators commencing the equivalent of eight Z frames after Z331 (N049), which is Z339 (N049).

Confirmation of the same alarm reactions that we see in the Zapruder film and Muchmore film commencing at N049 (Z339) - The Nix film images confirm the following alarm reactions commencing N049 (Z339): Jackie Kennedy rising from her seat and Motorcycle Officer Hargis turning his head hard right as he rapidly comes to a stop. Hargis seems to be watching Flying Tackle Man racing up the pergola steps. Malcolm Summers and the Running Man are just out of Nix's view to camera left during the alarm reaction interval. The images between the sprocket holes would be useful.

Additional alarm reactions seen in the Nix film commencing at N049 (Z339) - The Nix film allows us to add Secret Service Agent John Ready and Motorcycle officer Martin to the list of those exhibiting alarm reactions to the Z328 final shot. From Nix's vantage point, Ready's head is just behind those of Motorcycle Officers Chaney and Jackson. Commencing N048 (Z338) Ready squats and assumes a ready-to-jump crouched position and remains in this position until disappearing from camera right at N065 (Z355). Commencing N049/Z339, Martin turns his head hard right and continues looking hard right through N062 (Z352) at which point he looks forward until disappearing from view to camera left at N082 (Z372).

The Nix film's alleged "Station-Wagon Man"

In 1965, New York assassination researcher Jones Harris tentatively identified in Nix frames N001 to N073 a grassy knoll assassin that came to be known as the "Station Wagon Man." The buzz created by Harris finding prompted executives of *UPI* who had purchased the rights to the film in December 1963 to ask the Massachusetts firm ITEK Optical Solutions to evaluate the claim. After using various techniques to enhance the film images, in 1967 Itek issued a 55-page report with negative findings. In 1973-75, the California Institute of Technology Jet-Propulsion Lab used computer-image processing on 35-mm color transparencies made of the original frames and again found no evidence of a shooter. In 1978, the HSCA photographic panel with the assistance of the Los Alamos Scientific Lab and/or Aerospace Corporation used various enhancement techniques including frame averaging to evaluate the presence of a knoll gunman, again with negative findings. Putting aside the formal investigations and reports, the fact that the Station Wagon Man never moves after the head shot and is still there about 40 seconds after the shot in Nix's post-assassination film sequence provides definitive proof that the alleged assassin is an illusion.

The Nix film's alleged "Gunman in the Shadows" a.k.a. "Flying Tackle Man"

November 1991, in the aftermath of the release of the Oliver Stone movie *JFK*, assassination researcher/writer Robert Groden was interviewed on the TV talk show Geraldo along with Nix's granddaughter Gayle Nix Jackson. During the interview, Groden, who had served as a consultant to the HSCA

6: The Nix Assassination Sequence

photographic panel, displayed an enhanced reproduction of the Nix film's assassination sequence. Using extreme blowups, freeze frames, and repetitive-loop action covering the interval 2 to 3 seconds following the Z313 (N023) cranial explosion, Groden made a convincing argument that the Nix film shows a figure in motion behind the southern end of the masonry wall not far from where Zapruder was perched. This happens to be the same area where the so-called "Black Dog Man" can be seen in the Betzner Z186 and Willis Z201 photo. See Figures 54 and 55.

As noted above, this figure in motion is identifiable as frightened north-of-Elm spectator Flying Tackle Man, the hatless dark-skinned man that had been standing on the pergola steps next to Emmett Hudson. As he comes into fleeting view in the Nix film, we see Flying Tackle Man disappearing into the shadows behind the wall from N058 to N064 (Z348-54).

The Muchmore and Nix assassination sequences collectively reveal that Flying Tackle Man commenced his flight up the stairs at about Z334 (N044) in reaction to the third-shot noise and that Motorcycle Officer Hargis was watching him intently. After the final shot, Hargis racked his bike and chased after him on foot.

The frightened spectator's movements also caught the attention of Secret Service Agent Paul Landis who was on the right-side running board of the presidential follow-up car along with U.S. Senator Ralph Yarborough who was a passenger in the vice presidential limo. I give the senator credit for the moniker "Flying Tackle Man" that I applied in this book to this mysterious unidentified spectator.

Paul Landis, right-side running board, Queen Mary - *[After the shots rang out] The only person I recall seeing was a Negro male in light-green slacks and a beige-colored shirt running across a grassy section towards some concrete steps and what appeared to be a low stone wall. He was in a bent-over position, and I did not notice anything in his hands. . . . I was looking back and saw a motorcycle policeman [presumably Jackson or Chaney] stopping approximately where I saw the Negro male running.* Landis written statement, 11/27/63 (WRv.18Hp.759).

U.S. Senator Ralph Yarborough, vice presidential limo - *During that shooting my eyes were attracted to the right. I saw a movement and I saw a man jump about 10 feet like at the old time flying tackle in football and land against a wall. I thought to myself, "There's an infantryman who's either been shot at in combat or who's been trained thoroughly: the minute you hear firing, get under cover."* Interview by Nigel Turner in "The Men Who Killed Kennedy," 1988.

Table 25
Signature two-frame jolts and cranial eruptions due to a bullet striking the president or governor and transferring momentum to the wounded area
1. N023-24/Z313-14: the president's head is driven downward and forward about an inch in the midst of a conspicuous cranial eruption that jettisoned blood and brain matter up over the president's head and slightly forward. Because it was near vertical and not very high, the Z313 cranial eruption did not appear to create significant fallout outside of the rear seat area with most of it landing on the president by Z319 (Z/M/N films);
2. N040-41/Z330-31: the president's head is driven downward and forward about 3 inches in the midst of less conspicuous head-and-shoulder level jettisons of brain matter with spray hitting the back of Ms. Connally's head at Z330, landing on the lid of the trunk from Z331 to Z337 and reaching Motorcycle Officer Hargis and Agent Hill from Z335 to Z338 (Z/M/N films).

Table 26
Observable second shot reflex and alarm reactions for the Nix Film
Z310-shot reflex reactions: distinguishable blurred film images and spontaneous movements commencing 2.5 +/- 1 Z-frame equivalents after the sound reaches the person reacting
1. Z316/N026: wounded Governor Connally began turning and ducking his head to the left and by N031/Z321 was frantically lunging toward the front of the limo to get his head down (Z film);
2. Z316/N026: mortally wounded President Kennedy's head began snapping back in whiplash fashion due to Ms. Kennedy spontaneously shoving him away from her (Z/M/N films);
3. Z316/N026: startled Nellie Connally began recoiling and by N031/Z321 was ducking left toward the front of the limo to get her head down (Z/M/N films);
4. Z316/N026: startled Agent Greer behind the wheel of the presidential limo began turning to the left and by N031/Z331 was ducking his head down toward the steering wheel (Z/M/N films);
5. Z316/N026: startled Agent Kellerman in the right-front seat of the presidential limo began leaning forward and ducking his head down toward the dash board (Z/M/N films);
6. 316/N026: startled Motorcycle-Officers Martin, Chaney and Jackson commenced a collective left/right/left darting of their heads and Hargis stiffened and darted his head up and to the right (N film for all, M film for Martin and Z and N films for Hargis);
7. 316/N026: startled north-of-Elm-spectators Bill and Gayle Newman began turning slightly to their left and leaning back in recoiling and Gayle began jerking her left arm (N film);
8. Z316/N026: startled south-of-Elm grass-infield-spectator Toni Foster a.k.a. the Running Woman as she was trotting toward the limo began turning to her left and leaning back in recoiling and by N031/Z321 was stopping dead in her tracks (Z/N/B films);
8. Z319/N029: startled filmmaker Nix jiggled his camera creating a single frame of blurred images (N film).
Z310-shot alarm reactions: deliberate movements or actions commencing 7.5 +/- 2 Z-frame equivalents after the sound reaches the person reacting
1. Z321/N031: alarmed Jackie Kennedy began straightening up in her seat and inspecting the damage to her husband's head and began spontaneously flipping her right hand up behind her husband's head commencing N034/Z324 when she lost contact with his left shoulder (Z and N films);
2. Z321/N031: alarmed north-of-Elm-spectator Bill Newman began turning to his left and crouching (N film);
3. Z321/N031: alarmed Motorcycle-Officers Hargis, Martin, Chaney and Jackson began turning their heads to the right and were looking out toward the Hudson Group from Z321 to Z325. They then all darted their heads to the left and were looking directly at the president by Z330 with Hargis obstructing Martin's view (M and N films and Z film for Hargis).

6: The Nix Assassination Sequence

Table 27
Observable third shot reflex and alarm reactions for the Nix film
Z328-shot reflex reactions: distinguishable blurred film images and spontaneous movements commencing 2.5 +/- 1 Z-frame equivalents after the sound reaches the person reacting
1. Z333/N043: startled Jackie Kennedy began recoiling/leaning back (Z and N films);
2. Z333/N043: startled Agent Greer behind the wheel of the presidential limo began leaning/turning slightly to his right (Z/M/N films);
3. Z333/N043: startled Nellie Connally began turning her head to the right and leaning back as she was showered with brain matter and by N038/Z338 was diving down toward the center of the limo (Z/M/N films);
4. Z333/N043: unconscious Governor Connally began dropping down left shoulder first toward the left side of the limo onto his wife's lap (Z and N films);
5. Z333/N043: startled Motorcycle-Officer Hargis began darting his head left then right as he looked at the president (Z/M/N films),
6. Z333/N044: startled Motorcycle-Officers Martin, Chaney and Jackson began darting their heads to the right and Martin and Jackson started flexing their left wrist (M and N films and Z film for Martin's right wrist);
7. Z333/N043: startled Agent Ready on the Queen Mary's right running board started ducking and turning his head slightly to the left (N film);
8. Z333/N043: startled Agent Sam Kinney behind the wheel of the Queen Mary began looking hard right (M/N films) and Agent Ready began ducking and darting his head slightly to his left (in progress in N film);
9. Z333/N043: the startled Running Woman started turning to her left and recoiling again (N film);
10. Z333/N043: startled north-of-Elm-spectator Bill Newman began turning to his left and ducking (N film);
11. Z333/N043: startled south-of Elm-picture-taker Richard Bothun began turning to his left and leaning back as part of a rubbery kneed recoil (N film);
12. Z337/N047: Startled filmmaker Nix jiggled his camera creating a single frame with blurred images (N film).
Z328-shot alarm reactions: deliberate movements or actions commencing 7.5 +/- 2 Z-frame equivalents after the sound reaches the person reacting
1. Z339/N049: alarmed Motorcycle-Officers Hargis, Chaney and Jackson began stopping their cycles and all four motorcycle police commenced turning their heads hard right or hard right rear (N film);
2. Z339/N049: alarmed Jackie Kennedy began rising in her seat and climbing on the trunk (Z and N films);
3. Z339/N049: alarmed Agent Ready on the Queen Mary's right running board began squatting down into a ready-to-jump position (N film).

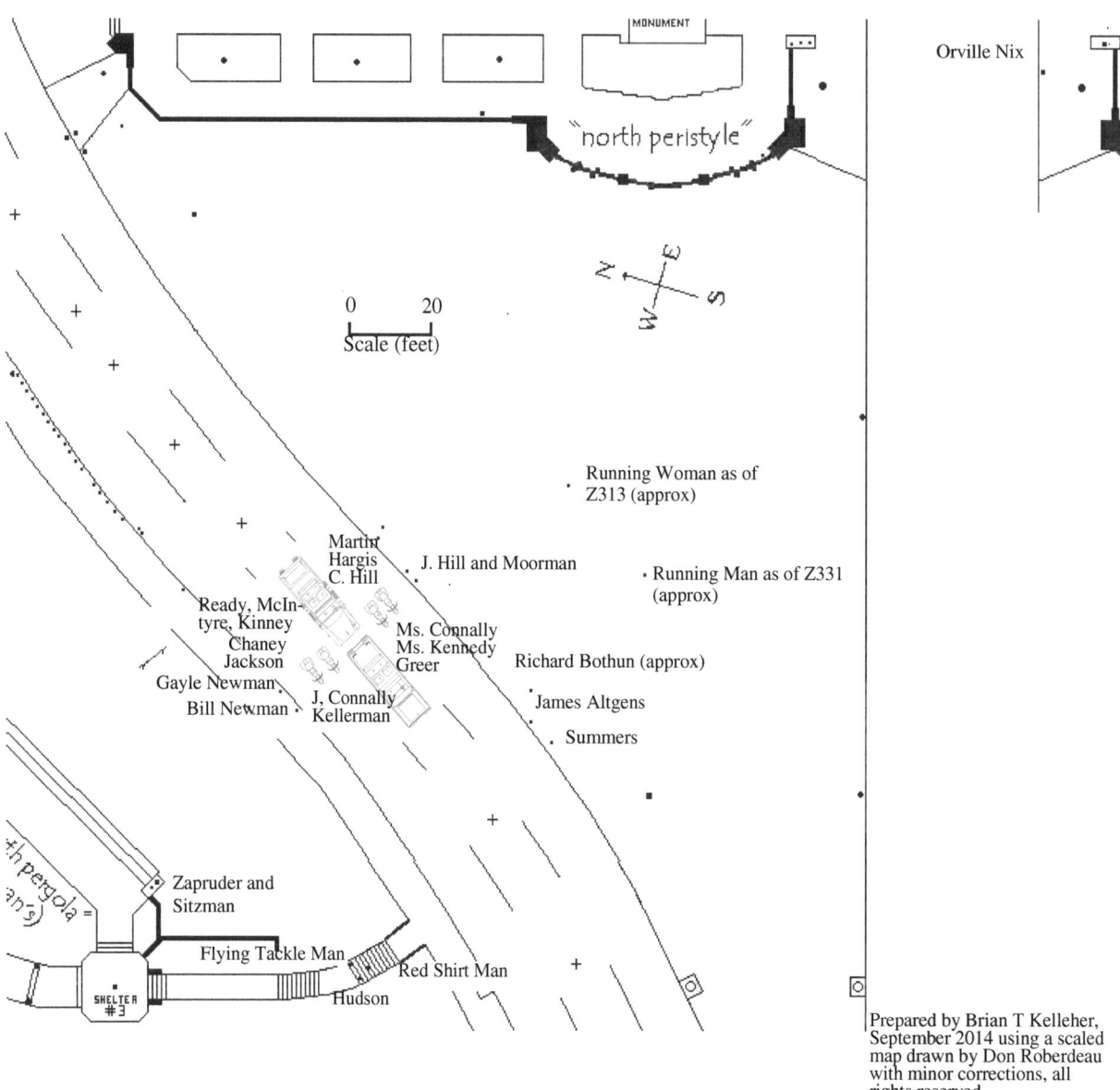

Figure 29

Nix's field of vision from Z291 to Z370 - The presidential limo, Queen Mary and motorcycles are approximately positioned to scale as of their locations at Z313. All the Queen Mary occupants were out of Nix's view to camera right as of Z313 except the driver Agent Kinney, Agent John Ready on the right running board and Agent Hill who was chasing after the limo. All four motorcycle officers are in periodic view. The spectators shown are the only ones in Nix's view during the interval Z290 through Z360. Everyone west of Zapruder was out of view to Nix camera left when the reflex and alarm reactions to the shots took place. In viewing Z frames Z310 through Z340, note that due to their altered seating positions, the Connallys and Ms. Kennedy were obstructing Altgens' view of the president's head at the time of the Z313 cranial explosion. The Limo/Queen Mary drawing is from Trask, 1994, p. 63.

6: The Nix Assassination Sequence

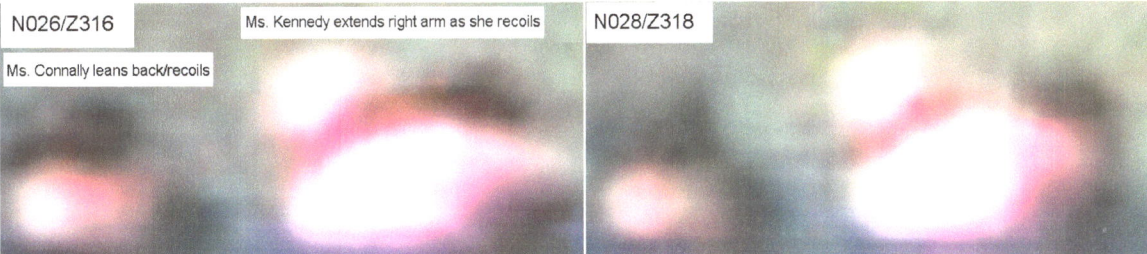

In these close ups we can clearly see that Ms. Kennedy has extended her right arm between Z316 and Z318 and is pushing the president away from her in spontaneously reacting to the sound and effects of the shot that hit her husband in the head at Z313. Ms. Kennedy and Ms. Connally are both overtly recoiling.

Figure 30
Reflex reactions for the Z310 second shot: Nix frames N026 and N028 (Z316/318) - In the 0.1-second interval between Z316 and Z318, all of those in view exhibit discernible signature head or body movements. Within the limo, Ms. Kennedy is recoiling and pushing her husband away from her with her right arm causing his head to snap back. Ms. Connally leans back/recoils. Her husband and Agent Greer turn/duck their heads left. Kellerman ducks forward. Outside the limo, all four motorcycle officers dart their heads to the right. Bill and Gayle Newman and the Running Woman lean back and turn slightly to their left in recoiling (Nix Family Collection/The Sixth Floor Museum at Dealey Plaza http://www.jfk.org).

The Complete Unraveling of the JFK Assassination

N039/Z329   BTK Sept. 2014, all right reserved   N040/Z330

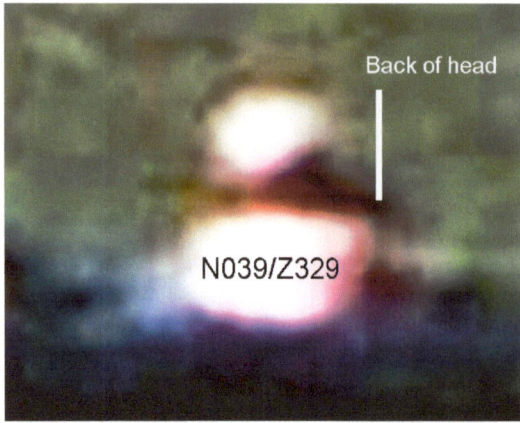 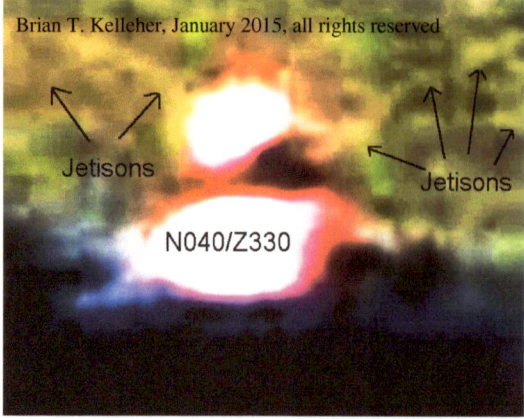

The president's head jolts downward and forward between N039 (Z329) and N041 (Z330/331) amidst barely perceptible sprays of whitish fluids forward and rearward of Ms. Kennedy's head. Note the elevated position of Ms. Kennedy's right shoulder at N040. This was caused by the president's jolted head striking her right-front shoulder and right cheek. I substantially increased contrast to make the jettisons more conspicuous.

N041/Z331 - In comparing frames N039/040/041 (Z329/330/331), the careful observer will note that the force of the bullet striking the president at N040 not only caused the president's head to jolt forward, but also caused movement of Ms. Kennedy's upper body. The careful observer will also note that Ms. Connally's head is driven downward and forward at N041/042 (Z331/Z332) (not shown).

Figure 31

Signature jolts and cranial eruptions for the Z328 third shot: Nix frames N039, N040, and N041 (Z329/Z330/Z331) - The Nix film captures the moment of the bullet's impact at the very end of frame N040 consistent with the Z film and Muchmore film. The Nix film, however, also captures the cranial eruption late in N040, which is why it provides the best view of the initial jettisons. Frames N040/41 (Z330-31) also capture the jolting movement to Ms. Kennedy's upper torso. Also significant, frames N040/42 (Z330-32) show Ms. Connally's head jolting downward and forward due to the leading edge of the spray of brain matter hitting the back of her head (not shown here). This is consistent with her steadfast testimony that she felt the brain matter hit her after her husband had collapsed his shoulders onto his knees as if shot dead by the second shot. These are cropped images that I photo edited to increase brightness and contrast (Nix Family Collection/The Sixth Floor Museum at Dealey Plaza http://www.jfk.org).

6: The Nix Assassination Sequence

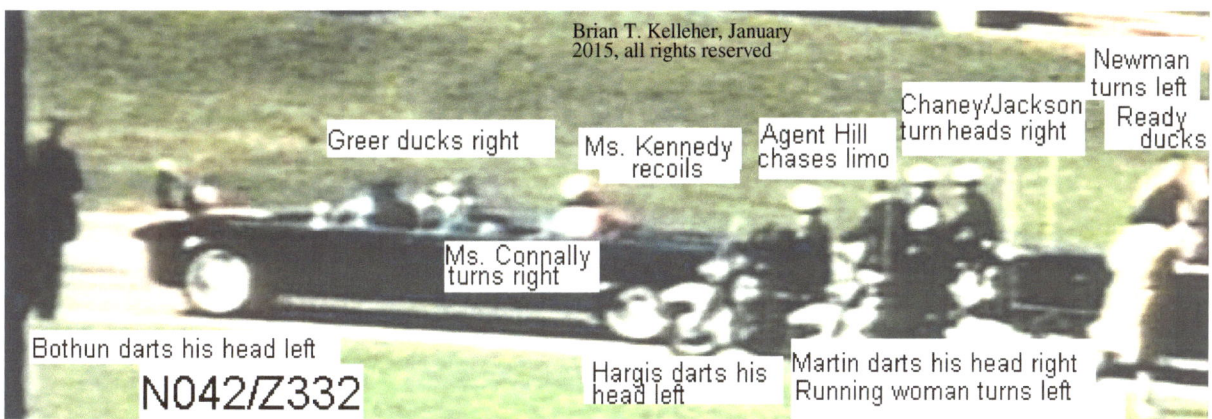

Figure 32
Reflex reactions for the Z328 third shot and brain matter fallout: Nix frames N042, N043 and N046 (Z332/333/336) - Fallout - There is discernible white matter on Ms. Connally's head and the lid of the trunk at N042 and N047, but it is by far most conspicuous at N043/Z333. Officer Hargis and Agent Hill are engulfed in a cloud from about N045 to N048 (Z335 to Z338) which is easiest to see in the digitally enhanced version of the film. Reflex reactions - In the 0.2-second interval between Z332 and Z336, there is discernible signature head or body movements for all of those in view. Within the limo commencing N043/Z333, Ms. Kennedy is recoiling and jerking her right arm. Ms. Connally and Agent Greer are turning their heads right and ducking or leaning. Kellerman is obstructed from view by Greer. Outside the limo, commencing N044/Z334 Hargis and Ready dart their heads to the left and the other three motorcycle officers to the right. Bill Newman, the Running Woman and Bothun lean back and turn slightly to the left in recoiling (Nix Family Collection/The Sixth Floor Museum at Dealey Plaza http://www.jfk.org).

The Complete Unraveling of the JFK Assassination

Figure 33
Zooming in on reflex reactions for the Z328 shot: Nix frames N042, N043, N045, N046 (Z332/333/335/336).

Chapter 7

The Bronson Assassination Sequence

The 45-year-old Charles Bronson was chief engineer of Varel Manufacturing, a drill-bit manufacturing firm in Dallas. He was not related to the well-known actor whose name he shared. Bronson was with his wife Frances near the southwest corner of Houston and Main perched on the concrete abutment at the north side of Dealey Plaza's south peristyle. They were approximately 350 feet south of the sniper's nest and 220 feet southeast of the spot on Elm where the president was located when his head exploded at Z313 (B12) (Figure 34). As of Z313, they were directly opposite Zapruder with their cameras aimed at each other.

When he arrived in Dealey Plaza, Bronson had a 50-mm single-frame camera and an 8-mm Keystone-Olympic K-35 movie camera both loaded with color film. He reportedly had purchased the movie camera at a local pawn shop just a week before.

By mistake, Bronson was filming that day in wide angle rather than zoom. This mistake ended up costing him at least $5,000 based on what Orville Nix was paid for his assassination sequence from approximately the same location.

As the motorcade arrived in Dealey Plaza, Bronson first took some obstructed footage of the presidential entourage as it went north on Houston.

He then switched to his regular camera as the presidential limo rounded the corner and proceeded down Elm. When it came back into his view after disappearing behind the north-peristyle colonnade at a point corresponding to Z227 plus or minus a few Z frames, he took a blurry off-center picture of the presidential limo that is discussed in Chapter 11. He reportedly jumped the gun in taking it due to his being startled by the sound of the first shot. My jiggle analysis in Chapter 8 predicts bullet shock waves for a shot fired at Z221 would hit his camera six frames later at Z227. This confirms that the heavy blurring in the picture was the result of bullet shock waves striking the camera. See Figure 35.

Bronson then switched back to his movie camera in time to take a 2.2-seconds 26-frame (12 frames per second) clip that provides a distant view of the head shot at frame B12. The presidential limo was approximately halfway to the triple underpass when he commenced filming.

Figures 34 through 36 follow and relate to the ensuing discussions.

Interviews and testimony

The Sunday after the assassination, Bronson wrote a letter to his sisters that included the following statements:

Charles Bronson - *As they were about halfway down to the underpass. And then it happened! My first impression was parade - celebration - fireworks, when I heard the first two shots ring out in rapid succession and a slight pause before the third shot rang out. My next thought was that crack-secret-service men had no doubt fired at someone who was about to cause real trouble. I remarked to Francis, "Is that fireworks or someone shooting?" As I said this I was looking through the viewfinder all the time. The parade was en route so I couldn't see any details. But right after my remark Francis [who was using binoculars] said, "President Kennedy is bent over and Jackie has her arm around him and Governor Connally is lying down." Then I looked and saw a few people lay flat on the ground just as the presidential car stopped for a split second and then take off. I told Frances, "Let's get out of here before we get caught in a crossfire!" And we did.* Cited in Trask, 1994, p.283.

In November 1985, Bronson returned to Dealey Plaza with assassination researcher/writer Richard Trask and recreated his filming positions. There he provided the following on-the-spot distant recollections concerning his Z227 photo and brief assassination sequence:

Charles Bronson - *I was waiting till the limousine got into full view at about right angles [to his camera's eye], but the shot rang out just before. I wasn't quite ready, but I had my finger on [the shutter button], and I had enough pressure on it so when the shot rang out . . . I instinctively jumped [flinched] and snapped it [the Z227 photo] at the same time, and that's the reason you will notice that the picture is a little blurred up and down. . . . then when the second and third shot rang out [as he was filming], that's when I decided they were rifle shots; and of course by that time people started running down there . . .* On-location interview by Richard Trask, 11/23/85 cited in Trask, 1994, p.283.

Available versions

I started with the version of the Bronson film found on Robert Groden's DVD "JFK Assassination Films: A Case for Conspiracy," published in 2003 by *Delta Entertainment Corporation*, Los Angeles, CA. This has a projection speed of 12 frames per second and is of poor quality. I found surprisingly good quality photo-enhanced excerpts including some cropped images in the introduction section of *Discovery Channel*'s 2003 DVD "Death and Dealey Plaza."

Zapruder film correlation and camera recording speed

Using a properly scaled drawing, as of Z313 the president is located along a sightline drawn between Bronson and Zapruder at frame B12. Bronson's assassination sequence captured Jackie Kennedy's Z324-28 right arm flip at B20-22. There are ten B frames [22-12=10] between the cranial explosion and the completion of the arm flip versus 15 Z frames [28-13 = 15]. Knowing Zapruder's camera was running at 18.3 frames per second, Bronson's was running at 12 frames per second: [10/15=0.66] and [0.66 x18.3 =12.1].

On this basis, Bronson's 26-frame assassination sequence starts 1.0 second before Z313, which equals eighteen Z frames: [12/12=1.0] and [1.0 x18.3=18.3]. Thus, the assassination sequence starts at Z296: [314-18=296].

Since the Bronson film has twenty-six frames, it lasts 2.2 seconds which is the equivalent of 40 Z frames: [26/12=2.17] and [2.17x18.3=39.65]. Thus, it runs through Z335: [295+40=335]. Thus, B01=Z296 and B26=Z335.

The assassination sequence

Figure 34 shows the witnesses in Bronson's field of vision as of Z227 through Z335.

7: The Bronson Assassination Sequence

It took Bronson about 3.8 seconds between Z227 and Z296 to lower his still camera from his eye, raise his movie camera back up and resume his filming. The camera was still set in wide-angle view and there is just a slight amount of panning to the left during the brief 2.2-second run time.

As the sequence opens, the presidential limo and its follow-up car and four-man police escort are in view. The president's car is in center frame with the front seat in line with Zapruder's position in front of the west side of the pergola. We would have a panoramic view of the entire grassy knoll except that the leaves and branches of a nearby tree are partially obstructing Bronson's view in the entire left half of the screen. We can still see the total length of the north pergola in approximately center screen. The north peristyle is just out of view to camera right.

Key spectators in view throughout the sequence from camera left to right on the north side of Elm include Zapruder and Sitzman, the Newman family, Umbrella Man, the Chism family, the Hesters, and part of the Calvary/Westbrook/Dishong group. Key spectators in view on the south side of Elm from camera left to right include Running Woman, Moorman and Hill, Charles Brehm and son, and the Babushka Lady. On the heels of Running Woman, there is a group of six spectators including four men and two women who have just arrived from the intersection of Main and Houston and are rushing north across the infield toward the presidential entourage. There is a man in white pants and a dark coat hustling north across Main Street.

Due to the wide-angle lens' low resolution and the slow recording speed we can barely make out the outlines of presidential limo and Queen Mary occupants. Ms. Kennedy is bending over her husband until the final two frames at which point she starts to straighten up in her seat commencing B25 (Z333/34).

As the sequence ends, the presidential limo is becoming obstructed from view behind the above-mentioned foliage. With some effort, we can discern that Agent Hill is chasing the limo on foot and that the Running Woman has stopped running. We can make out her recoil commencing B14 (Z316).

Reactions to the Z310 (B10) shot

Despite the film's low resolution, the jettison resulting from the Z313/B12 cranial explosion is discernible. Using blowups, it is evident that everyone in camera view exhibits an auditory reflex reaction between frames B14 and B16 (Z316 to Z319). The most conspicuous are as follows: the Newmans, Running Woman. Jean Hill and Charles Brehm and son recoil; the four motorcycle officers and the two closest spectators in view that are walking north toward Elm, Ms. Moorman, and Babushka Lady dart their heads to the left or right; Agents Ready and Landis and north of Elm Spectator Cheryl McKinnon duck forward and Agent Bennett leans back. I attribute up and down camera movement and blurred images from B16 to B18 (Z319 to Z322) and the blurry ending to the film commencing at B25/Z333 to a combination of bullet shock waves passing under and hitting his movie camera and the auditory reflex reaction. See Chapter 8.

Also of great value in the Bronson sequence is that it shows key witness Clint Hill jumping off the front of the Queen Mary's driver's side running board at B03/Z300 at which point he is largely obstructed from view by key south-of-Elm witness Charles Brehm. From B03 to B12 when he disappears from view behind Jean Hill's red coat for a frame, the careful observer can see Agent Hill's head moving forward just behind Motorcycle Officer Martin's white helmet. As further revealed and easier to see in the Muchmore and Nix films, commencing B14/Z316, Hill commences an all-out sprint in reaching the rear of the limo, getting his right foot on the left rear running board at Z337 just after the Bronson sequence ends. The timing of the sprint indicates that Hill was reacting to the sound of the Z310 shot in frantically picking up his pace.

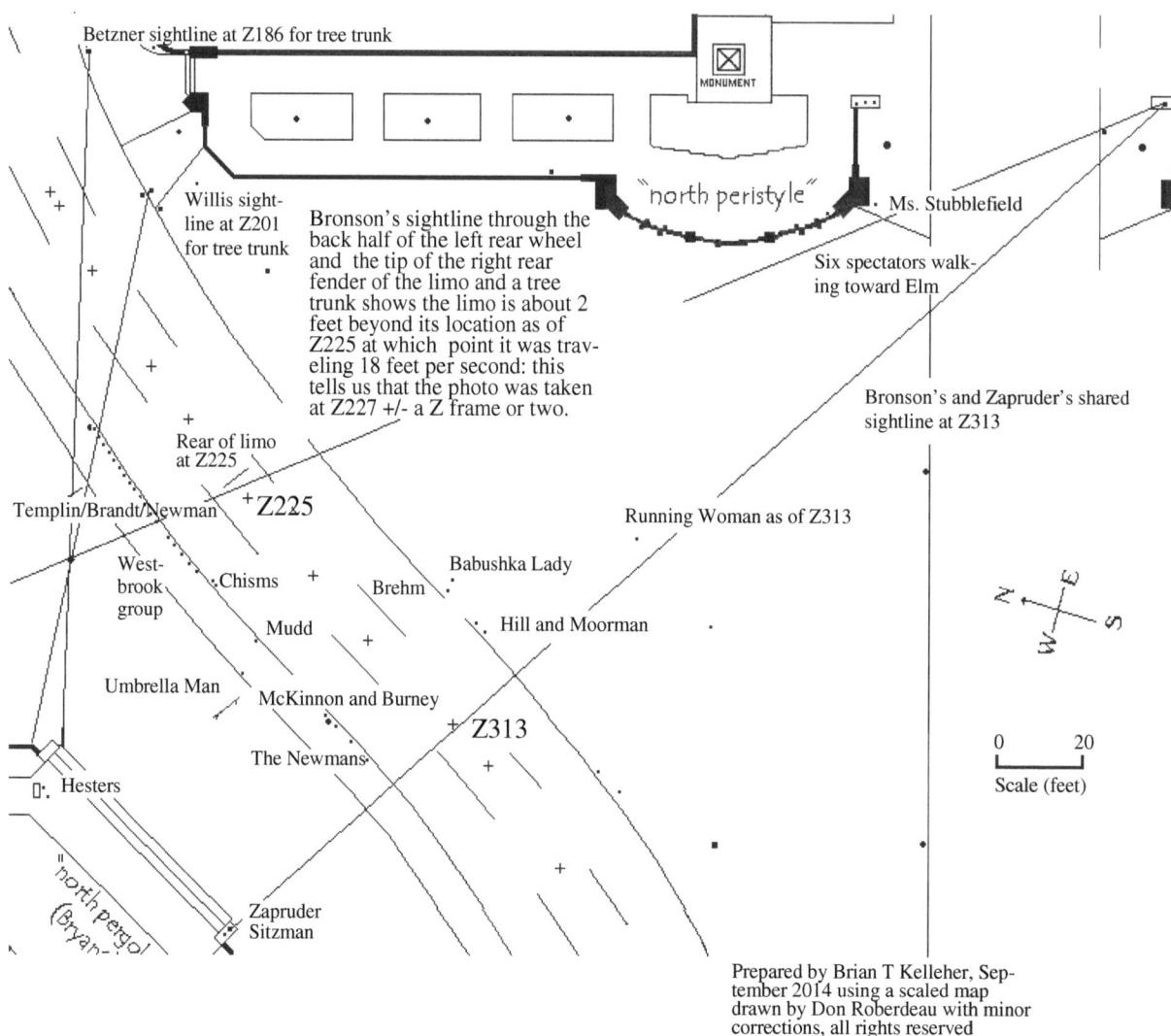

Figure 34
Charles Bronson's field of vision and key sightlines for his Z227 photo and assassination sequence - Given that the rear of the presidential limo is 6 feet or so behind the position of the president's head, the sightline through the trunk of the tree near the Thornton Freeway sign shows he took his photo of the limo under fire at Z227 plus or minus a Z frame or two. This tree trunk was not accurately located in the Roberdeau scaled drawing at hand, so I moved it.

7: The Bronson Assassination Sequence

Figure 35

The Bronson Z227 photo of the limo under fire - Spectators in view from camera left to right on the north side of Elm include Zapruder and Sitzman (west end of pergola), the Newman family, Burney and McKinnon, the Hesters (east end of pergola), the Umbrella Man, Mudd, two unidentified teens, the Chism family, the entire Calvary/Westbrook/Dishong group, Jean Newman, Brandt and Templin. Spectators in view on the south side of Elm from camera left to right include Moorman and Hill, Running Woman, Charles Brehm and son, and the Babushka Lady. On the heels of Running Woman, there is a group of six unidentified spectators including four men and two women who have just arrived from the intersection of Main and Houston and are rushing north across the infield toward the presidential entourage. According to Phil Willis's wife Marilyn, the woman that is still approaching the infield is her mother (Ms. Stubblefield). This is a cropped image that I photo edited to increase brightness and contrast (Charles Bronson, Bronson Family).

Figure 36

Bronson frame B21/Z325 and Clint Hill's sprint and revealing testimony - This is 0.7 second after the Z310/B10 head shot and 0.2 second before the Z328/B22 final shot. Ms. Kennedy's right arm is flipping up behind the president's head. From left to right on the south side of Elm, the Running Woman, Mary Moorman, Jean Hill and Charles Brehm are recoiling. From left to right on the north side of Elm, the following spectators are in blurry view: Zapruder, Sitzman, Bill and Gayle Newman and sons, Peggy Burney and Cheryl McKinnon. Those in blurry view in the Queen Mary include the following secret service agents: Kinney (driving); Roberts (right front seat), Ready (above Roberts on front of passenger side running board); McIntyre above Kinney on rear of driver's side running board); and Hickey (elevated left rear seat). Agents Landis (rear of right running board) and Bennett (right rear seat) are obstructed from view (by McIntyre and Hickey) as are the two presidential aides in the jump seats (by Jean Hill). Key motorcade witness Clint Hill is passing on foot in front of Bill Newman in an all-out sprint. He is just behind and between Motorcycle Officers Martin and Jackson and is fast approaching the rear of the presidential limo. The Bronson film images reveal that Agent Hill jumped off the front of the Queen Mary's driver's side running board at B03/Z300 and was still astride the Queen Mary as of B12/Z313. His desperate final sprint commenced at B14/Z316 in a reflexive reaction to the sound of the Z310/B10 shot. Hill reported he did not recall hearing the second shot and reasoned that this was due to the fact that he was running next to a motorcycle at the time. The Bronson film images confirm that Hill was running right next to Martin's motorcycle exhaust pipe as of B12/Z313. Between B03 and B14 (Z300-15), Hill covered about 12 feet in one second while running astride and between the Queen Mary's left front fender and the rear of Martin's cycle. Between B14 and B26 (Z316-35), however, Hill covered about 20 feet in one second in passing by Martin and Jackson. Hill reportedly heard the final shot ring out just before he reached the rear of the limo consistent with a shot fired at Z328 reaching the limo at Z330. Simultaneously with the sound, he reportedly saw the president's head driven forward to the left amidst a cranial eruption from the upper right side that spewed brain matter over the occupants of the car and the trunk. This is consistent with what we see in the Zapruder, Nix and Muchmore film images from Z331 to Z337. These same Zapruder, Nix, Muchmore images confirm that Agent Hill was looking directly at the president from a distance of about 5 to 8 feet as of Z328 to Z337. No assassination witness had a better view of the president during this interval than Agent Hill. For example, note that Brehm's view of the president during this interval was completely obstructed by Agent Hill. Brehm reportedly heard a final shot after seeing the president head explode at Z313 but presumed it missed because he could not see its effects. Agents Kinney and Roberts in the front seat of the Queen Mary reportedly could not tell which of the last two shots caused the head to explode because they were so close together. Agent Hickey in the Queen Mary's elevated rear seat reportedly saw both of the last two shots hit the president in the head. This is a cropped image that I photo edited to increase brightness and contrast (Charles Bronson, Bronson Family).

Chapter 8

Jiggle Analysis

It is a certainty that there are discernible blurs on the Zapruder film and the others resulting from involuntary startle reactions (flinches and camera jerks) caused by the loud reports of the shots fired during the assassination. For example, in reenactment testing conducted in 1967 by *CBS News*, amateur movie makers using Bell and Howell movie cameras identical to Zapruder's were asked to film a slowly moving car as a rifleman in a tower behind them and off to the side fired shots at the car in random sequence at the distance and angle of the Z313 head shot. In every case "a few frames after a shot was fired, the highlight [bright white points usually on the trim of the car from which sunlight reflects off shiny metal] turned to crescents of light [white streaks]" (White, 1968, p. 75 and CBS News Inquiry," June 25, 1967, Part 6: 6:35-7:55 out of 8.14 minutes, www.youtube.com/watch?v=P8p9UoQIe8.

As you are about to find out, this blurring was not startle induced. Given that it was taking Zapruder 8 frames to jiggle his camera after a shot was fired, it is occurring too soon. The CBS video images suggest that the rocking camera movement was occurring with the arrival of the ballistic shock waves.

To date, four experts using various techniques including two HSCA consultants have conducted jiggle investigations on the Zapruder film images and published or otherwise presented findings. As explained later in this chapter, there was no consensus opinion among the experts and much disparity.

In this chapter I have conducted an independent jiggle analysis using a different approach that involved accurately synchronizing to a single Z-frame equivalent all seven of the sequences that were taken as the shots rang out (two for Dorman). Using this much more rigorous approach, the jiggle analysis not only provided definitive scientific proof on shot timing and sequence, but established the location of the assassin. My findings in brief are as follows.

Tables 28 through 30 and Figures 37 and 38 follow and relate to the ensuing discussions.

Zapruder assassination sequence - I found conspicuous startle-induced blurring amid corresponding human-reflex reactions to combined muzzle-blast and shock-wave noise at Z227, Z318 and Z336. I found shock-wave-induced blurring at Z313/314 and Z331/332 that I attribute to the shock waves passing under the heavy camera as it was being nudged by shock waves hitting the camera.

Muchmore assassination sequence - I found conspicuous startle-induced blurring to muzzle-blast noise amid corresponding human-reflex reactions at M46 (Z317) and M63 (Z334). I interpret her ending her film at the equivalent of Z337 (M66) as an alarm reaction to this same muzzle-blast noise.

Nix assassination sequence - I found conspicuous startle-induced blurring to muzzle-blast noise amid corresponding human-reflex reactions at N029 (Z319) and downward camera movement at N47 (Z337).

Bronson assassination sequence - I found three frames of up and down camera movement amongst spectator reflex reactions from B16 to B18 (Z319 to Z322) that I attribute to the auditory reflex reaction to bullet shock wave noise. I attribute the blurry ending to the film commencing at B25/Z333 to a combination of bullet shock waves passing under and hitting the camera and the reflex reaction. I attribute the blurring in his Z227 photo of the limo under fire to bullet shock waves passing under and hitting his still camera at that frame.

Wiegman assassination sequence - I found conspicuous startle-induced signature blurring to muzzle-blast noise amid corresponding human-reflex reactions commencing at W080 (Z315) and W103 (Z332).

Dorman assassination sequences - I found conspicuous startle-induced signature blurring in response to combined muzzle blast and shock-wave noise amid corresponding human-reflex reactions commencing at D373, D396, and D411 (Z224/313/330). I also found downward shock-wave-induced blurring at D371/Z221 that I attribute to the bullet shock waves passing under the heavy camera as it was being nudged by the shock waves hitting the camera. I did not find such blurring in connection with the second and third shots suggesting that between the first and second Ms. Dorman moved back or to the left removing the camera from the shock-wave path.

The collective experts who have previously conducted jiggle analyses for the Z film completely overlooked the signature blurring in the other assassination sequences, and the gravity-enhanced shock-wave impacts on the heavy hand-held cameras. They also overlooked the telltale single-frame blurring at Z336. The blurring on the left side of frame Z336 is just as pronounced as the signature-blurring at Z227 and similar in nature. There is significant blurring on the right side of frame Z336 as well, but less so than for Z227.

Shock-wave-induced camera movement

The nature of ballistic shock waves - According to my somewhat intuitive understanding of the physics involved, a bullet traveling faster than the speed of sound (Mach 1), pushes the air and sound waves it is forming aside and creates bullet-length zones of high and low pressure air behind the bullet that radiate outward at the speed of sound. The effect is to propagate an expanding cone of densely compacted pressure waves off the rear of the bullet. Though the shock-wave front travels at the speed of sound and is audible, it is distinguished from ordinary sound waves by the fact that it is comprised of turbulent layers of highly compressed and decompressed air and is moving straight ahead. It is akin to the wave of water generated by a speeding motor boat and has a low pressure trough and a high pressure crest. The shock-wave front continuously loses energy as it expands. It can be envisioned as a stampede of sound-waves, the sonic boom. The best source of information I found on-line is Maher, Robert and Shaw, Steven, "Deciphering Gunshot Recordings," rob.maher@montana.edu, Montana State University.

The Mach Angle - The theoretical maximum angle of propagation of a ballistics shock wave for any given supersonic bullet is a function of the speed the bullet is traveling. Since the speed of the wave front is limited to the speed of sound, the angle of forward propagation is related to the ratio of the speed of the bullet to the speed of sound and is called the Mach angle or M angle. The M angle has two components that total 90 degrees: forward in the direction of the bullet and rearward. With respect to the forward component of the angle, a bullet traveling at Mach 1 or lower is not propagating shock waves and the M angle is zero.

In our case, the bullet was traveling at about 2,000 feet per second (Mach 1.78) as it generated shock waves that reached Zapruder and Bronson. With just this information, we know from an on-line calculator

8: Jiggle Analysis

that the supersonic bullet was propagating shock waves at a 55.8 degree angle relative to the plane of the bullet. The wave-front cone behind the bullet fanned out at Mach Angle of 34.2 degrees.

Which filmmakers were in the path of bullet shock waves? - For bullets fired at the president from the TSBD sniper's nest that propagated outward/forward in all directions at a 55.8 degree angle, my protractor revealed that Muchmore, Bronson and Nix were potentially within the path for all three shots and Zapruder for just the last two being about 13 feet south of the last of Z221shot shock waves. It further revealed that the shock-wave fronts that would have hit them were propagated at about Z160, Z177, Z185, and Z240, respectively. Muchmore and Nix, however, were protected by the columns of the north peristyle. Wiegman was too far east. Dorman would have had to have been holding her camera almost out of the window to be in the path of the waves. As discussed in Chapter 4, this appears to have been the case for just the Z221 shot. Figure 37 shows the first and second shot Mach Angles for Z223 and Z250 bullet positions.

Can ballistic shock waves produce camera jiggles? - According to Nobel-prize-winning physicist Luis Alvarez, the shock-wave front that reached Zapruder after traveling a distance of 80 feet at Mach 1 caused the blurred images that came amidst the Z313 cranial eruption. He argued that the force of the shock wave striking the camera was sufficient to create the necessary amount of movement. The appearance of identical blurring amidst the second cranial eruption at Z331 seems to confirm his conclusion.

In attempting to verify Alvarez's conclusion, I reviewed the following paper published in the *Journal of the Acoustical Society of America*: Dumond, et al, California Institute of Technology, "A Determination of the Wave Forms and Laws of Propagation and Dissipation of Ballistic Shock Waves," September 27, 1945. In concluding the report, the authors compared their numeric modeling results with actual field test data generated at the U.S. Army's Camp Irwin, California, training grounds. The model predicted that a shock wave propagated from a 1.5-inch-long bullet fired with sufficient speed to produce a 60 degree M angle would impart a force of 0.0044 atmosphere on a 38-inch-diameter microphone diaphragm after the shock wave had traveled 270 feet.

In calibrating their pressure-recording instrument for the field testing, a 50-gram weight (0.11 pound) placed on the diaphragm produced a pressure reading of 41-mm of mercury. The peak reading measured for the actual rifle shot was 3.5-mm of mercury. This translates to 0.009 pounds [(0.11x3.5)/41=0.009]. Thus, assuming the left side of Zapruder's camera was 6 by 4 inches (24 square inches), the instantaneous peak pressure on the right side of the camera was 0.006 pounds [(24/38)x0.009=0.0057]. This is about 3 grams, the weight of a penny. The data is for a bullet just fired, so the pressure peaks are significantly higher than for a bullet that already traveled 205 feet. On the other side of the coin, the Z310 and Z328 bullet shock waves only had to travel 80 feet to reach Zapruder.

Since the pressure was applied in a millisecond (0.001 second), it can be likened to a quick tap on the left side of the heavy camera. While this would not ordinarily be enough force to produce blurring in several Z frames, there is another much stronger force in play that Alvarez failed to recognize: the force of gravity.

What has to have been the primary force behind the camera movements we see at Z313/314 and Z331/332 is the effect of the shock waves that passed under the heavy hand-held cameras as they were receiving a nudge. In the same manner that the wake of a speed boat rocks a fishing boat that it passes by due to the force of gravity, these shock waves "rocked" the cameras. The expected camera movement and resulting blurring is primarily up and down.

The next blurring we see after Z313/314 when we know a shock wave entered Zapruder's ear canal is not until Z318. It defies reason that it would take Zapruder five frames to react. He reacted in the usual three frames to the muzzle blast from the Z221 shot.

Zapruder's shock-wave-induced blurring confirms the shot was fired at Z310 - Assuming the shock waves for the Z310 and Z328 shots fired from the TSBD sniper's nest struck his hand-held camera at a 55.8 degree left to right angle relative to the bullet's path at the speed of sound, my protractor revealed that the shock waves emanated from the bullet at about Z240. This point is about 200 feet from the sniper's nest and about 86 feet from Zapruder. At Mach 1 speed, the shock wave struck and passed under Zapruder's camera 0.18 second later which is 3.3 Z frames: [200/2,000=0.1], [86/1,125=0.08], [0.1+0.08=0.18] and [0.18x18.3=3.3]. Assuming the blurring started in mid frame Z313, this tells us the shot was fired during the first half of Z310: [312.5-3.3=309.2].

Bronson shock-wave-induced blurring - Assuming the N shock waves for the Z221/Z310/Z328 shots fired from the TSBD sniper's nest struck his hand-held camera at a 55.8 degree right to left angle relative to the bullet's path at the speed of sound, my protractor revealed that the N shock waves emanated from the bullet at about Z177. This point is about 140 feet from the sniper's nest and about 247 feet from Bronson. At Mach 1 speed, the shock wave struck and passed under Bronson's cameras 0.29 second later which is 5.3 Z frames:[140/2,000=0.07], [247/1,125=0.22], [0.07+0.22=0.29] and [0.29x18.3=5.3].

Shot-noise-induced human-reflex-reaction analyses (jiggle analysis) for the Zapruder, Wiegman, Dorman, Muchmore, Nix and Bronson films reveals the shot timing and assassin's location

In the prior five chapters, I precisely synchronized the 18.3 frames per second Z-film images with the images of the motion-picture sequences taken by Wiegman, Dorman, Muchmore, Nix and Bronson. In so doing, I provided a means of confirming exactly when the three shots were fired and where they were coming from. This involved using a scaled-drawing of Dealey Plaza on which I precisely plotted their positions relative to the president and sniper's nest at Z223, Z313 and Z330. See Figure 37.

Estimating the bullet speed - According to wound-ballistics' expert Larry Sturdivan, testing conducted with Oswald's rifle in April/May of 1964 at the US Army's Biophysics Lab at Edgewood, Maryland provided a reasonable estimate of 660 meters per second plus or minus 10 meters per second (2,165 feet per second plus or minus 30) initial velocity. Following the lead of assassination researcher Joe Elliot, I used an on-line ballistics calculator while assuming negligible wind effects to come up with the following expected speeds for the Z221, Z310 and Z328 shots. For the first shot, the expected speed as the bullet reaches Z223 at 180 feet from the sniper's nest is 1,980 feet per second and the average speed is 2,073 feet per second. For the second shot the expected speed as the bullet reaches Z313 at 260 feet from the sniper's nest is 1,900 feet per second and the average speed is 1,940 feet per second. For the final shot the expected speed as the bullet reaches Z330 at 270 feet from the sniper's nest is 1,885 feet per second and the average speed is 1,890 feet per second. Like Elliot, I used the trajectory calculator at JBM Ballistics.com. These results are not guaranteed accurate by the author or the ballistics web site.

Thus, for the Z221 shot and all points short of it, I will assume the average bullet speed is 2,100 feet per second. For the Z310 and Z328 shots, I will assume the average bullet speed is 1,900 feet per second. These estimates are considered accurate to 30 feet per second with any variations for individual shots introducing

8: Jiggle Analysis

a constant source of minor error that has no significant effect on the ability to synchronize the assassination films.

Calculating when the shots were fired and the time for the bullets to reach the president - As discussed in Chapter 2, the Zapruder film images inform us that shots struck the president at Z223, early in Z313 and late in Z330. Thus, assuming the shots were fired from the TSBD sniper's nest, all I need to know to calculate the travel time from the president to the rifle are the measured distances in feet from the TSBD sniper's nest at Z223, Z313 and Z330. Using our scaled Dealey-Plaza drawing and accounting for both the vertical and lateral components of distance, I determined that the president was located about 180, 260 and 270 feet southwest of the sniper's nest as the shots were fired. Thus, within plus or minus a frame:

The bullet that entered the limo in say mid frame Z223 (Z222.5) was fired in late frame Z221 (Z220.8) after a travel time of 0.09 second, which is 1.7 Z frames: [180/2,100=0.086] and [0.086x18.3=1.7] and [222.5-1.7= 220.8];

The bullet that entered the limo in say early Z313 (312.1) was fired in mid frame Z310 (309.6) after a travel time of 0.137 second, which is 2.5 Z frames: [260/1,900=0.137] and [0.137x18.3=2.5] and [312.1-2.5=309.6];

The bullet that entered and exited the limo late in frame Z330 (330) was fired in mid frame Z228 (327.4) after a travel time of 0.14 second, which is 2.6 Z frames [270/1,900=0.14] and [0.14x18.3=2.6] and [330-2.6=327.4].

Calculating the time for the muzzle-blast noise to reach the filmmakers - This is a straightforward calculation. I measured the distances in feet of each of the filmmakers to the sniper's nest taking into account, via a right angle calculator, the vertical and lateral components of distance and then divided by the speed of sound at 1,125 feet per second at 68 degrees Fahrenheit, which was the documented temperature at 12:30 p.m. This yields the total sound-wave travel time in seconds. For Zapruder, at a distance of 260 feet away, the travel time was 0.23 second, which is about 4.2 Z frames. The distances and times for the rest are as shown in Tables 28, 29, and 30 at the end of the chapter.

Estimating the reaction time to produce shot-induced blurring - A literature review available on-line conducted by Robert Kosinski of Clemson University, reports that the normal human auditory response time for major muscle groups is 0.14 to 0.16 second, which is 2.6 to 2.9 (three) Z frames (Kosinsky, 2008). Consistent with a 0.15 second human-reflex reaction time, the Zapruder-film images reveal that human-reflex reactions in the presidential limo where the shot noise was very loud were commencing by the end of Z316 which is three Z frames (0.1 to 0.17 second) after the bullet entered it say mid 313 (Z312.5).

A quick check of the Zapruder film images reveals that the signature blurring for the Z221 and Z310 shots occurs at Z227 and Z318, respectively. Knowing it took three Z frames (0.14 second) for shock waves to reach his ears for the Z310 shot and five frames (0.23 second) for the muzzle blast noise, his reaction time for the Z310 shot shock waves would be five Z frames assuming that was the impact he was responding to. This tells us that his camera jiggles for all shots are in response to muzzle blast sound waves arriving in five Z frames rather than shock waves arriving in three. This tends to confirm that the blurred images we see at Z313-314 and Z331-332 were indeed from the shock waves and that Zapruder's auditory reflex reaction time is the expected three frames (0.11 to 0.6 second).

In view of the above, I used the relative sound levels to which the filmmakers were exposed, and took into consideration normal auditory reflex-reaction times to predict the following reaction times for startle-induced blurring. For Zapruder at 260 feet away; Nix at 340 feet away and Bronson at 350 feet away, I allowed a reaction time of 0.14 to 0.19 second which is 2.5 to 3.5 Z frames from the time the muzzle-blast noise reached their ears. For Muchmore at about 220 feet away and Wiegman at about 120 feet away I allowed a reaction to of of 0.14 to 0.16 second which is 2.5 to 3 Z-frame equivalents. For Dorman at about 36 feet away, I allowed 0.11 to 0.14 second which is 2.0 to 2.5 Z-frame equivalents. Dorman was exposed to extremely high noise levels.

Projecting and confirming the onset of shot-induced blurring assuming the shots were fired from the TSBD sniper's nest - To predict the frame where the onset of startle-induced blurring would occur for each shot and each filmmaker, I added the projected reaction time (0.11 to 0.19 second (2.0 to 3.5 Z frame equivalents) to the calculated sound-wave travel time in seconds. After getting the films in frame-by-frame sync, I then checked the film images looking for signature blurring in the midst of human-reflex reactions to the shot noise. The projections and observations are shown in the tables at the end of the chapter.

Conclusions

The camera-jiggle evidence coupled with the contents of film images themselves as presented in Tables 28 through 30 at the end of the chapter and elsewhere in this book supports the following conclusions:

1. The Zapruder, Muchmore, Nix and Bronson film images of the assassination sequence can be easily synchronized to plus or minus one Z frame; they collectively record and confirm the Z313 cranial explosion and many associated human-reflex and alarm reactions including among others Jackie Kennedy's right-hand flip at Z324-28, and Motorcycle Officer Chaney's dramatic head turn back over his right shoulder commencing at Z333. In each case, the camera eye in these four films is focused on the president just before and after the Z310 and Z328 shots. All you need is two reliable points of correlation with the Z film spaced as far apart as possible to synchronize these films and there are plenty to pick from. On this basis alone, I find no merit in the arguments that have been raised over the years that the Zapruder film images have been tampered with to the point the film images cannot be relied on as evidence.

2. The Wiegman film images can be synchronized to plus or minus one Z frame using a simple sightline analyses and a verifiable camera recording speed of 32.0 frames per second - With just one reliable direct point of correlation via sight lines W330/264=Z447, we can establish that W001 = Z258.5 (mid frame Z259) and that W099/080=Z314.5 (mid frame Z315). See Chapter 3.

3. The Dorman film images for the fourth sequence can be synchronized to plus or minus one Z frame using sightline analysis coupled with derivation of camera speed. For the fifth sequence, they can be synchronized to plus or minus a few Z frames using sightlines and derivation of vehicle speed and camera speed and then calibrated to plus or minus one frame using signature blurring and human reflex reactions. See Chapter 4.

Dorman fifth sequence tentative sync - To establish the tentative start time of the all-important fifth sequence, I made use of the fact that both Wiegman and Dorman had the open-topped mayor's car in view as it passed in front of the north end of the reflecting pool. I used the respective sightlines and the car's known length to establish the location of the left rear of the car as of D377 and W034 when the right end of the rear bumper disappeared from Wiegman's view. Using Wiegman and Dorman sightlines, I found that as of W034 the left rear of the car was 8 feet shy of its position at D377 and that the car was traveling at an average speed of 15.66 feet per second. Thus, 0.51 second had elapsed between W034 and D377. Knowing Wiegman's film was re-recorded at a Z-film-calibrated 25.6 frames per second, this means that 13 W frames elapsed during this interval. Thus, as a close approximation D377=W046=Z291.

Dorman fourth and fifth sequences final sync - With respect to the fourth sequence, I made use of Dorman's first sequence and Marie Muchmore's fifth to establish that Dorman's camera was running at something very close to 16.0 frames per second. Then, using just the one direct point of correlation with the Z film via sightlines, D352=Z199, this gives us a definitive fourth-sequence start time of D336=Z182. With respect to the fifth sequence, from the onset of overt signature blurring and human-reflex reactions to the Z310 shot noise, I was able to establish that the exact start time is mid frames D377=W046=Z291.

4. The mathematical predictability of the shot-induced signature blurring and human-reflex reactions to shot noise as demonstrated in Tables 28, 29 and 30 at the end of the chapter and in Chapters 3 and 4 of this book proves that the Dorman and Wiegman film images are indeed synchronized to plus or minus one Z frame at Z191=W046=D377. The film images themselves, coupled with the ability to count frames and establish the exact locations of the filmmakers on a scaled drawing, are resolving the potential sources of error that would ordinarily prevent us from attaining this degree of precision in conducting a scientific analysis where there are multiple potential sources of error. The potential sources of error include variances in camera-recording speed and bullet-travel speed between shots and during the course of individual shots. As already stated, there are uncertainties inherent in using sightlines and vehicle-travel speed to establish close approximations of the sequence start times.

Second-shot verification at Z310/W073/D394 via human-reflex reactions - The overt signature blurring starting at W080 (Z315) of the W film is confirmed as shot induced by concurrent head turning commencing at W076 (Z313) for multiple spectators lining the north side of Elm directly in front of and below the TSBD sniper's nest. These human-reflex reactions to shot noise in the W film correlate exactly with the signature blurring commencing at D396 (Z313) of the D film given the confirmed camera speeds. They also correlate exactly with the the concurrent head turning commencing at D398 (Z315) for the spectators lining the opposite side of Elm. Note that Dorman is reacting in unison with the spectators on the north side of Elm because she is about the same distance away from the sniper as they are. The same goes for Wiegman with respect to the spectators on the south side of Elm. Moreover, the spectators on the south side of Elm at 115 feet from the sniper are reacting in near unison with the occupants of the presidential limo at 270 feet from the sniper because the bullet shock-wave noise arrived in the limo with the bullet traveling at 1,900 feet per second, while the muzzle-blast noise reached the spectators on the south side of Elm traveling at 1,125 feet per second.

Third-shot verification at Z328/W098/D409 via human-reflex reactions - If the ducking and diving within the presidential limo we see commencing Z333 was induced by a final shot that entered the limo late in Z330, and if the Z film is truly in sync with the W film and the assumed camera speeds and bullet-travel times are all correct, we must find in the Wiegman film concurrent spectator reactions commencing at W101 which is 26 W frames (one second) after W076. Not only that, this head turning must occur a few frames before a telltale camera jerk. This is exactly what we find. The spectator reactions commence at W101 (Z330) including dramatic hard looks back toward the TSBD by two of those in view. The signature blurring commences at W103 (Z332). Similarly, if the Z and W films are truly in sync with the D film, we must find signature blurring commencing at D411 which is 16 frames after D396 and concurrent spectator reactions commencing at D413 which is 16 frames after D398 (Z315). This is exactly what we find. The signature blurring does indeed commence at D411 (Z330) and the spectator reactions do indeed commence at D413 (Z333) comprised of concurrent looks to the right for six with two continuing up toward the sniper's nest.

5. The mathematical predictability of the shot-induced signature blurring and human-reflex reactions to shot noise proves that the Z221, Z310 and Z328 shots were fired from the TSBD. For each shot, the observed signature blurring occurred either exactly as mathematically predicted for a TSBD sniper's nest location or within one Z-frame equivalent of what was predicted. In addition, as covered in the prior chapters, in each and every case the signature blurring is occurring amidst mathematically predictable human-reflex-and-alarm reactions to the sound of the shots among at least most of those in view if not all.

6. For Bronson at about 350 feet away from the sniper's nest it was taking 9 Z-frame equivalents from the time a shot was fired to see startle-induced blurring. The mathematically predicted time was 9 Z frames. The travel time for the bullet muzzle blast noise to arrive at Bronson's ears accounted for 6 Z-frame equivalents and the startle-reaction time was 2.5 to 3.5 Z frame equivalents. With respect to Z-frame equivalents: 1 B frame = 1.53 Z frames [18.3/12=1.52].

7. For Nix at about 340 feet away from the sniper's nest it was taking 9 Z-frame equivalents from the time a shot was fired to see startle-induced blurring. The mathematically predicted time was 9 Z frames. The travel time for the bullet muzzle blast noise to arrive at Nix's ears accounted for 6 Z-frame equivalents and the startle-reaction time was 3 Z-frame equivalents. With respect to Z-frame equivalents: 1 N frame = 1 Z frame.

8. For Zapruder at about 260 feet away from the sniper's nest it was taking 7 to 8 Z frames from the time a shot was fired to see startle-induced blurring. The mathematically predicted time was 7.5 Z frames. The travel time for the muzzle blast noise to arrive at Zapruder's ears accounted for 4.2 Z frames and the startle-reaction time was 3 Z frames.

9. For Muchmore at about 220 feet away from the sniper's nest it was taking 7 Z-frame equivalents from the time a shot was fired to see startle-induced blurring. The mathematically predicted time was 7 Z-frame equivalents. The travel time for the muzzle blast noise to arrive at Muchmore's ears accounted for 3.5 Z-frame equivalents and the startle-reaction time was 3 Z-frame equivalents. With respect to Z-frame equivalents: 1 M frame = 1 Z frame.

10. For Wiegman at about 115 to 125 feet away from the sniper's nest it was taking four to five Z-frame equivalents from the time a shot was fired to see startle-induced blurring. The mathematically predicted time was 4.5 Z-frame equivalents. The travel time for the muzzle blast noise to arrive at Wiegman's ears accounted for 2 Z-frame equivalents and the startle-reaction time was 3 Z-frame equivalents. With respect to Z-frame equivalents: 1 re-recorded W frame = 0.71 Z frame [18.3/25.6=0.71].

11. For Dorman, who was by far the closest to the TSBD sniper's nest at about 36 feet away, it was taking two to three Z-frame equivalents from the time a shot was fired to see startle-induced blurring. The mathematically predicted time was 2.5 Z-frame equivalents. The travel time for the bullet shock waves to arrive at Dorman's ears accounted for 0.5 Z-frame equivalent and the startle-reaction time was 2.5 Z-frame equivalents. With respect to Z-frame equivalents: 1 D frame = 1.14 Z frames [18.3/16=1.14].

12. None of the three shots were fired from behind the grassy knolls perimeter fence. Zapruder was filming the assassination from the same area of the grassy knoll where certain conspiracy advocates contend that a second sniper fired over the perimeter fence. If any of the three shots had been fired by a grassy knoll

8: Jiggle Analysis

shooter at the alleged locations, Zapruder would have heard the shock-wave noise from a distance of 30 to 45 feet after the bullet had traveled just 40 to 60 feet. Using the average distances, the very loud bullet-shock-wave noise would have arrived at Zapruder ears, within 0.06 seconds (37.5/2,000] + 50/1,125] = 0.063) which is just 1.2 Z frames. Given the much-louder level of shot noise and the short distance, we would expect to see Zapruder's signature blurring for a shot from the knoll 3 to 4 Z frames after the shot rather than 7.5 to 8 frames. There would be similar effects on the onset of signature blurring in the other assassination sequences.

13. A bullet hit the president and governor within frame Z223 that was fired from the TSBD sniper's nest at Z220.5 plus or minus a Z frame. Amidst overt human-reflex and alarm reactions to a shot, there is pronounced horizontally oriented blurring at Z227 or equivalent in the two films for which jiggle analysis was conducted (Zapruder and Dorman). With the limo about 180 feet away from the rifle, the last of the bullet shock waves would have entered the pergola about 15 feet to the east of Zapruder. At 260 feet away, Zapruder would have heard the boom of the muzzle blast within frame Z224, Wiegman at 125 feet within Z222 and Dorman at 36 feet within Z221.

14. A bullet hit the president within frame Z313 that was fired from the TSBD sniper's nest at Z309.5 plus or minus a Z frame. Amidst overt human-reflex-and-alarm reactions to a shot, there is pronounced horizontally oriented blurring commencing at Z318 or equivalent in all six films for which jiggle analysis was conducted (Zapruder, Bronson, Nix, Muchmore, Wiegman, and Dorman). Assuming a 60-degree M wave and a speed of 1,125 feet, the shock wave would have reached Zapruder within frame Z313. At 260 feet away, Zapruder would have heard the boom of the muzzle blast within frame Z314 and Muchmore at 220 feet within Z313.

15. A bullet hit the president within frame Z330 that was fired from the TSBD sniper's nest at Z327.5 plus or minus a Z frame. Amidst overt human-reflex-and-alarm reactions to a shot, there is pronounced horizontally oriented blurring at Z336 or equivalent in five of the six films for which jiggle analysis was conducted (Zapruder, Nix, Muchmore, Wiegman, and Dorman). Bronson released the shutter eight frame after the final shot. Assuming a 60-degree M wave and a speed of 1,125 feet, the shock wave would have reached Zapruder at frame Z331. At 260 feet away, Zapruder would have heard the boom of the muzzle blast within frame Z332 and Nix and Bronson at 345 feet within Z333.

16. There was no first-shot miss. While there is plenty of potentially qualifying blurred Z-frame images prior to Z221, there is not one single signature-reflex-or-alarm movement among the presidential-security forces of the presidential entourage. This includes the two secret-service agents in the presidential limo, the four motorcycle-escort police, and the eight secret-service agents and two presidential aides in the Queen Mary. The Zapruder-film images reveal unambiguous concurrent signature-reflex and requisite-alarm reactions among this group for three shots and only three shots. The first concurrent signature reflex reactions are not seen until Z225/226 and the first concurrent signature alarm reactions among the presidential security forces are not seen until Z230. There was a second set of reflex reactions commencing at Z316 and a third set at Z333. There was a second set of alarm reaction commencing at Z321 and a third set at Z339. The Croft Z160 photo provides visual evidence that there was no first shot miss at Z152. See Figure 38.

17. There was no second-shot miss. There is no question that bullets entered the presidential limo at or very close to Z223 and Z313. During the interval between, there are no signature reflex or alarm reactions by the limo occupants other than those reasonably attributed to the sound and effects of the Z221 shot.

The Alvarez and *CBS-News* studies

Professor Luis Alvarez from the University of California, Berkeley, a recipient of a Nobel Prize in physics, who pioneered the development of what came to be known as "jiggle analysis," was the first to apply the technique as a forensic tool in the Kennedy assassination. In his original jiggle investigations prior to his work on the assassination he noted an intermittent three-cycle-per-second blur pattern that appeared to be characteristic of all movies made with handheld cameras, presumably due to neuromuscular reactions. He helped camera manufacturer Bell & Howell develop a damping system to counteract this intrinsic oscillation.

Alvarez's interest in the Kennedy assassination was piqued after viewing the sequential Zapruder frames *Life Magazine* had published in a 1966 cover story, "A Question of Reasonable Doubt." Using the set of Zapruder frames published by the WC when it released its report in 1964 (frames 171 to 334), Alvarez measured the differences in length of the horizontal spread of smear streaks in sequential frames to calculate the velocity of the change. In this fashion, he identified/measured potential startle reactions commencing at the following points: Z182, Z190, Z221, Z227, Z292, Z313, and Z318.

Reasoning that startle reaction to gunfire would tend to start the clock in the normal three-jiggle-per-second sequence, he identified reactions to possible shots corresponding to the blurs commencing at Z182, Z221, and Z313. The startle signature consists of a series of two to three sharply blurred frames separated by three to four clear frames.

It so happens, that Z180 corresponds to a point where the assassin had a brief opening through the oak tree otherwise blocking his view of the president. Alvarez speculated that the Z182 blur was associated with a missed shot that deflected off a branch. Such speculation ignores the fact that no one in the presidential limo or its police escort or follow-up car that was in Zapruder's view showed the slightest hint of reacting to this hypothetical Z182 missed shot.

Alvarez successfully approached *CBS* with the idea of verifying his conclusions as part of a *CBS* documentary series then in preparation titled, "The Warren Report." *CBS* retained Dr. Charles Wycoff, a photo-analyst expert from the firm Egerton, Germeshausen, and Greir, Inc., to check Alvarez's methods and findings using the slides the WC had transferred to the National Archives. Wycoff/*CBS* concluded the blurs commencing at Z190, Z227 and Z318 were the most likely associated with shots.

As part of the June 1967 documentary, *CBS* presented and expanded Alvarez's work. *CBS* cameramen were taken to a firing range where marksmen fired a MC rifle similar to Oswald's as part of an assassination recreation. The cameramen were put into position off to the side of the target at a distance and angle corresponding to where Zapruder was standing at the point the head shot struck (about Z313) relative to the TSBD sniper's nest and the presidential limo. Quoting from Walter Chronkite's narration:

The film taken by these cameramen showed the effects of the shots despite instructions to hold steady. Even in steadier hands, motion was always noticeable. This frame shows highlight dots around the cars windshield. In reaction to a shot, the dots changed to crescents [i.e. they were blurred]. And in the following frame they become streaks [more blurred], comparable to streaks found in some frames of the Zapruder film. White, 1968, p. 229.

8: Jiggle Analysis

In January 1976, Alvarez published an article in which he revisited and revised his original conclusions. Based on further considerations, he concluded that the jiggle commencing at Z313 was due to the bullet shock wave pressure front striking the camera and that the jiggles commencing at Z182 and Z221 were due to neuromuscular reactions to shots ringing out five to six frames earlier at Z178 and Z215.

The HSCA jiggle investigations

The HSCA conducted its own scientific analysis of the blur patterns in the Zapruder film. Two members of the photographic panel, William Hartmann and Frank Scott, conducted independent evaluations. Like *CBS*, Hartmann simply measured the elongation of small round features on the limo on a frame-by-frame basis, this time using the entire set of 353 frames (Z133 to Z486). Scott measured the vertical and horizontal displacement of non-mobile background features to identify blurs caused by changes in the direction the camera was pointing. On this basis, he concluded the blurring commencing at Z313 was likely not due to an auditory startle reaction. Please note that this finding lends supports to the shock waves causing the similar blurring at Z313 and Z331.

The HSCA photographic panel concluded that a series of extended and pronounced blurs at ten-frame intervals commencing at about Z331 are associated with Zapruder's witnessing the devastation of the head shot and repeatedly shouting "They killed him!" Like Alvarez, the panel concluded that the blur at Z318 was associated with a shot fired from the TSBD sniper's nest at Z310 that struck the president at Z312. They disagreed with Alvarez that the two-frame blur commencing at Z221 was associated with a shot. They further concluded that another shot was fired at about Z185 in connection with the series of blurs commencing at Z190 and other evidence. The panel also pointed to possible shots causing the blurs commencing at about Z158 and Z227, finally deciding that the one at Z158 was associated with a missed first shot at Z152 based on other evidence.

Collectively, the HSCA and Alvarez studies observed the onset of significant jiggles at the following frames: Z158, Z182, Z190, Z210, Z221, Z227, Z292, Z313, Z318, Z331, Z342, about Z350, and about Z360. They missed the telltale blurring at Z336 which came amidst concurrent human reflex reactions to bullet shock-wave and muzzle-blast noise.

The HSCA acoustics investigations

As mentioned in the introductory chapter, the HSCA dubiously concluded in 1979 that four shots were fired at the president in Dealey Plaza, three from the TSBD sniper's nest and a missed third from behind the grassy knoll perimeter fence. The committee based this faulty conclusion on expert analysis of four closely spaced cracks recorded on a police dictabelt during a 5-1/2 minute interval during which an unidentified Dallas Police motorcycle officer's radio microphone was inadvertently stuck open. It was believed at the time and later disproved that the stuck-open microphone was on Officer Hollis McLain's bike during the interval he was traveling north on Houston Street fast approaching the TSBD.

In field testing the theory, three sets of live firing tests were conducted by Dallas police officers in Dealey Plaza over a 5-hour period in August 1978 under the direction of Doctor James Barger, Chief Scientist with Bolt, Beranek & Newman acoustics consultants. They used the same make and model of Oswald's M.C. rifle to shoot four live rounds at sand bags located certain distances along the center of Elm corresponding to shots fired at about Z140, Z230, and Z313 using the Z313 sand bags for the last two shots. For each test, an array of twelve microphones were set up at different intervals along Houston and Elm to measure the amplitude of the shot noise in decibels. As set forth in the September 11, 1978, testimony of Doctor Barger (HSCA V2, pp. 22-23, 45, 49) the findings that are of most significance to the jiggle analysis are as follows. By measurements, the amplitude of the bullet shock wave noise at 10 feet from the trajectory (M angle) of the approaching bullet, decreases by just 1 decibel per 100-feet-per-second decrease in the bullet's supersonic speed. The amplitude of bullet shock-wave noise was measured at 130 decibels at 30 feet from the muzzle and 10 feet from the trajectory (M angle) of the approaching bullet. This represents the minimum noise level the limo occupants were exposed to and the approximate noise level the police escort and occupants of the presidential follow-up car were exposed to. Depending on the distances from the TSBD sniper's nest which were in the range of 70 to 300 feet, the peak muzzle-blast noise measured at street level ranged from 135 to 115 decibels. This reveals that the spectators lining Elm in front of the TSBD that were in Dorman's and Wiegman's view were exposed to shot noise of about 130 decibels and that those spectators in view of Zapruder, Nix and Muchmore were exposed to about 120 decibels. These are very loud levels that are known to ordinarily trigger the acoustic startle reflex.

Table 28

First shot jiggle analysis for the Zapruder and Dorman assassination sequences and the Bronson Z227 photo of the limo under fire confirms it was fired from the TSBD sniper's nest at Z221/D371 (muzzle blast noise in all cases except Bronson)

Filmmaker and the frame the shot was fired	Distance of filmmaker to rifle (feet)	Speed of sound (feet per second)	Sound travel time (seconds and frames)	Assumed reflex reaction time tolerance for range 0.11 to 0.19 sec (frames)	Predicted time from shot to blurred frame (frames)	Predicted blurred frame for shot fired at Z220.1 to Z221	Observed blurred frame # as recorded on film	Difference between estimated and actual reflex reaction time (frames)
Zapruder at Z220.5	260	1,125	260/1,125=0.23 = 4.2	2.5 to 3.5 (0.14-0.19 sec)	4.2+2.5 =6.7	220.1+6.7 = 226.8= Z227	**Z227**	0
Dorman at W371/Z220.5	36	1,125	36/1,125=0.03 = 0.5	2.0 to 2.9 (0.11-0.16 sec)	0.5+2.5 = 3	220.5+3 = 222.5 = Z223/D372	**Z223**/D372	0
Bronson Z227 photo for Z220.5 shot	Bullet speed = 2,000 feet/second; distance to president = 140 feet; distance from president to Bronson = 247 feet: [140/2,000=0.07], [247/1,125=0.22], [0.07+0.22=0.29] and [0.29x18.3=5.3]			Not applicable	5.3 = 6	220.5+6 = 226.5 = 227	Z227	0

Conclusions: Dorman's signature blurring for the Z221 shot comes four Z frames (~0.2 second) before Zapruder's because she is the equivalent of four Z-frames (~0.2 second) closer to the sniper's nest taking into account the distances involved, the speed of the bullet, the speed of sound and the level of noise. The result of the analysis for the Bronson Z227 photo confirms that blurring was the result of shock waves passing under and striking the camera.

8: Jiggle Analysis

Table 29

Second shot jiggle analysis for the Zapruder, Dorman, Wiegman, Muchmore, Nix and Bronson assassination sequences confirm it was fired from the TSBD sniper's nest at Z310/W073/D394/M39/N20/B10 (muzzle blast noise in all cases except Bronson)

Filmmaker and the frame the shot was fired	Distance of filmmaker to rifle (feet)	Speed of sound (feet per second)	Sound travel time (seconds and frames)	Assumed reflex reaction time tolerance for range 0.11 to 0.19 sec (frames)	Predicted time from shot to blurred frame (frames)	Predicted blurred frame for shot fired mid frame Z310 = Z309.5	Observed blurred frame as recorded on film	Difference between estimated and actual reflex reaction time (frames)
Zapruder at Z309.5	260	1,125	260/1,125=0.23 = 4.2	2.5 to 3.5 (0.14-0.19 sec)	4.2+3.5 = 7.7	309.5+7.7 = 317.2 = Z318	Z318	0
Wiegman at W073/Z309.5	125	1,125	125/1,125=0.11 = 2.0	2.5 to 3.0 (0.14-0.16 sec)	2.0+2.8 =4.8	309.5+4.8 = 314.3 = Z315/W080	Z315/W080	0
Dorman at D394/Z309.5	36	1,125	36/1,125=0.03 = 0.5	2.0 to 2.7 (0.11-0.15 sec)	0.5+2.5 = 3.0	309.5+3.0 = 312.5 = Z313/D396	Z313/D396	0
Muchmore at M39/Z309.5	220	1,125	220/1,125=0.20 = 3.7	2.5 to 3.0 (0.14-0.16 sec)	3.7+3.0 = 6.7	309.5+6.7 = 316.2 = Z317/M47	Z317/M46	0
Nix at N20/Z309.5	340	1,125	340/1,125=0.3 = 5.5	2.5 to 3.5 (0.14-0.19 sec)	5.5+3.2= 8.7	309.5+8.7 = 318.2 = Z319/N029	Z319/N029	0
Bronson at B10/Z309.5	Bullet speed = 2,000 feet/second; distance to president = 140 feet; distance from president to Bronson = 247 feet: [140/2,000=0.07], [247/1,125=0.22], [0.07+0.22=0.29] and [0.29x18.3=5.3]			2.5 to 3.5 (0.14-0.19 sec)	5.3+3.5=8.8	309.5+8.8 = 318.3= Z319/B16	Z319/B16	0

Conclusions: Dorman's signature blurring for the Z310 shot comes five Z frames (~0.3 second) before Zapruder's and two (~0.1 second) before Wiegman's because she is the equivalent of five Z-frames (~0.3 second) closer to the TSBD sniper's nest than Zapruder and the equivalent of two Z frames (~0.1 second) closer than Wiegman taking into account the distances involved, the speed of the bullet, the speed of sound, and the level of noise. Similarly, Wiegman is the equivalent of three Z frames (0.16 second) closer to the sniper's nest than Zapruder. Assuming the reaction time was 2.0 to 3.5 Z-frame equivalents (0.11-0.19 second) as assumed above, the results confirm the bullet was fired at Z309.5 plus or minus a Z frame equivalent.

Table 30

Third shot jiggle analysis for the Zapruder, Dorman, Wiegman, Muchmore, Nix and Bronson assassination sequences confirms it was fired from the TSBD sniper's nest at Z328/W098/D409/M57/N038/B22 (muzzle blast noise in all cases)

Filmmaker and the frame the shot was fired	Distance of filmmaker to rifle (feet)	Speed of sound (feet per second)	Sound travel time (seconds and frames)	Assumed reflex reaction time tolerance for range 0.11 to 0.19 sec (frames)	Predicted time from shot to blurred frame (frames)	Predicted blurred frame for shot fired at mid frame Z328= Z327.5	Observed blurred frame as recorded on film	Difference between estimated and actual reflex reaction time (frames)
Zapruder at Z327.5	260	1,125	260/1,125=0.23 = 4.2	2.5 to 3.5 (0.14-0.19 sec)	4.2+3.5 = 7.7	327.5+7.7 = 335.2 = Z336	**Z336**	0
Wiegman at W098/Z327.5	115	1,125	115/1,125=0.11 = 1.8	2.5 to 3.0 (0.14-0.16 sec)	1.8+2.6 = 4.4	327.5+4.4 = 331.9 = Z332/W103-04	**Z332**/W103-04	0
Dorman at D409/Z327.5	36	1,125	36/1,125=0.03 = 0.5	2.0 to 2.7 (0.11-0.15 sec)	0.5+2.0 = 2.5	327.5+2.5= 330 = Z330/D412	**Z330**/D411	0
Muchmore at M57/Z327.5	220	1,125	220/1,125=0.19 = 3.5	2.5 to 3.0 (0.14-0.16 sec)	3.5+2.7 = 6.2	327.5+6.2 = 333.7 = Z334/M63	**Z334**/M63	0
Nix at N038/Z327.5	340	1,125	340/1,125=0.3 = 5.5	2.5 to 3.5 (0.14-0.19 sec)	5.5+3.2=8.7	327.5+8.7 = 336.2 Z337/N047	**Z337**/N047 (faint)	0
Bronson at B22/Z327.5	Bullet speed = 2,000 feet/second; distance to president = 140 feet; distance from president to Bronson = 247 feet: [140/2,000=0.07], [247/1,125=0.22], [0.07+0.22=0.29] and [0.29x18.3=5.3]			2.5 to 3.5 (0.14-0.19 sec)	5.3+2.5= 7.8	327.5+7.8 = 335.7 = Z335.3	Bronson stopped filming at the equivalent of Z335	+1

Conclusions: Dorman's signature blurring for the Z328 shot comes six Z frames (~0.3 second) before Zapruder's and two (~0.1 second) before Wiegman's because she is the equivalent of six Z-frames (~0.3 second) closer to the TSBD sniper's nest than Zapruder and the equivalent of two Z frames (~0.1 second) closer than Wiegman taking into account the distances involved, the speed of the bullet, the speed of sound, and the level of noise. Similarly, Wiegman is the equivalent of four Z frames closer to the sniper's nest than Zapruder. Assuming the reaction time was 2 to 3.5 Z-frame equivalents (0.11-0.19 second) as assumed above, the results confirm the bullet was fired at Z327.5 plus or minus a Z frame equivalent.

8: Jiggle Analysis

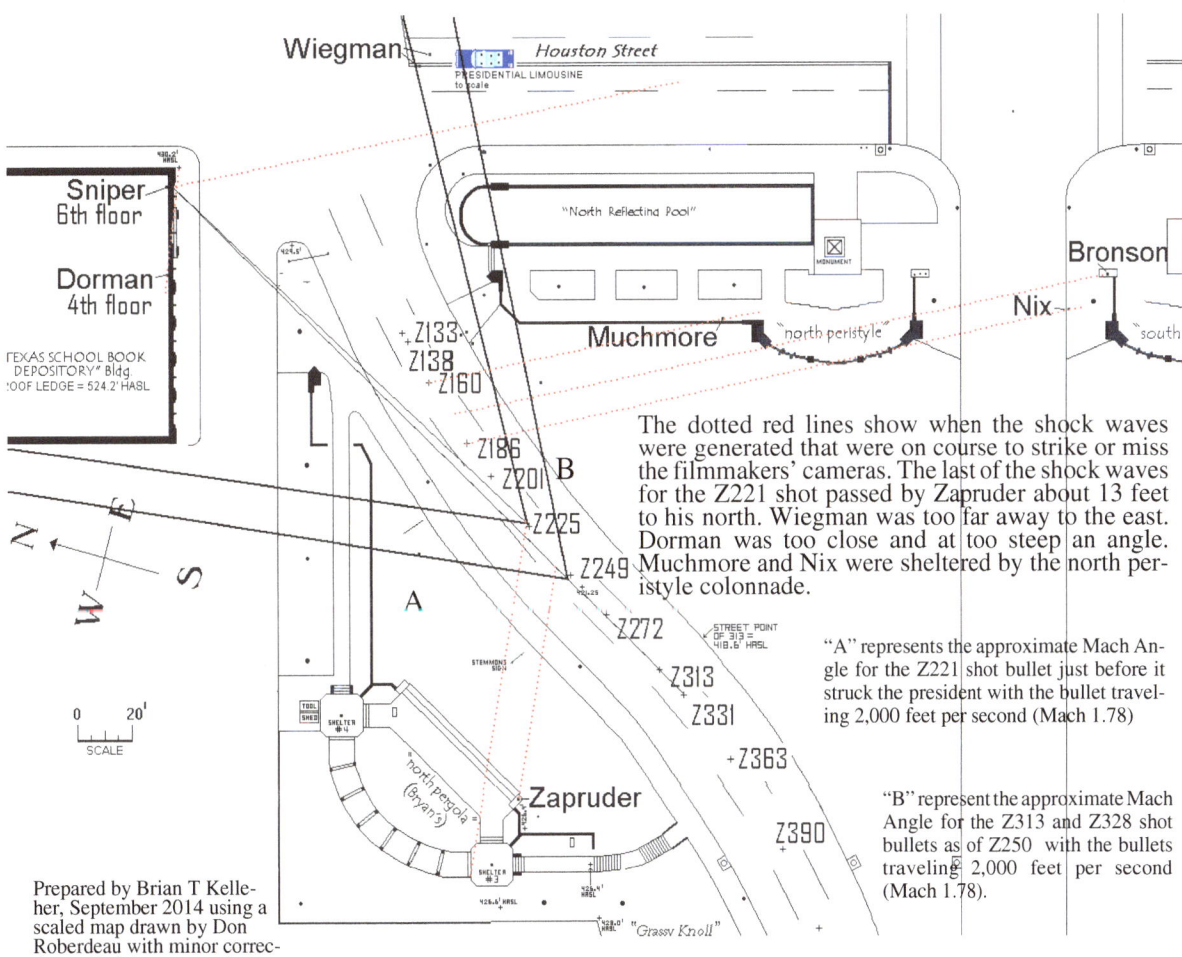

Figure 37

Scaled drawing of Dealey Plaza used for jiggle analysis - This is the scaled drawing of Dealey Plaza that I used when enlarged to make the measurement used in Tables 28, 29, and 30 and elsewhere in this book. The scaled base map that I used for this illustration was prepared by assassination researcher Don Roberdeau whose web site is found at droberdeau.blogspot.com. . . . See Figure 1 caption. Note that the trajectory lines for the Z310 and Z328 shots are superimposed/identical explaining why the rushed Z328 shot was on target without the need to re-aim. Zapruder was located within the path of bullet shock waves generated for the last two shots at the point the president passed about Z240. Bronson was located within the path of bullet shock waves generated for all three shots at the point the president passed at about Z177. The other filmmakers were either outside the path (Wiegman) or sheltered by the north peristyle colonnade (Muchmore and Nix). Dorman would need to have been holding her camera part way out the window which she apparently was doing during the first shot (see Chapter 4). For a bullet traveling at 2,000 feet per second (Mach 1.78) the Mach Angle via on-line calculator is 34.2 degrees and the shock waves are propagated outward/forward at a 55.8 degrees.

Figure 38
The Croft Z160 photo of the presidential limo heading west on Elm refutes the mythical Z152-first-shot miss
- This is the last of a sequence of three pictures the 20-year-old Mormon missionary took of the motorcade and was taken 3.3 seconds before the Z221 shot was fired. Croft turned over his undeveloped film to the Denver FBI the day after the assassination, having arrived there by train the prior evening. While handing it over, he told the FBI that he had snapped a fourth picture about the time he heard the first shot ring out. In developing the film, however, the FBI discovered that for one reason or another, the attempt had produced a blank image (Airtel to Director, FBI from SAC Denver, file #62-109060-1388, 11/23/63, cited in Trask, p. 225). According to the dubious opinions of HSCA forensic-panel experts and the current defenders of its conclusions, the Kennedys and Connallys are here exhibiting alarm reactions to a bullet fired from the TSBD sniper's nest at Z151 that missed the president and vanished. In truth, however, Croft was the last of the continuous line of the spectators along the street in the vicinity of the southwest corner of Houston and Elm. The president having recognized this a few seconds earlier, had already abruptly turned his head to the right to acknowledge the spectators clamoring for his attention on the other side of the street who we know included the Mary Woodward group from the *Dallas Morning News*. This group is just out of view to camera left and the president is giving them his signature radiant smile. Jackie is also poised to make an abrupt head turn to the right, but is giving Croft the courtesy of completing his picture before she too makes an abrupt turn to the right. Governor Connally is in the process of turning his head to the left, but is coming to the realization that there are no spectators to interact with, explaining his abrupt about-face. Agents and Greer and Kellerman in the front seat have not moved their heads since Z133 and do not for another 65 frames (per Zapruder film images) and not one of the spectators in view along the north side of Elm are exhibiting the least sign of alarm. The Croft Z160 photo confirms that the blurred images at Z frames 158/159 are not gunshot induced (Robert Croft, via David Von Pein's web site "The Kennedy Gallery").

Chapter 9

Evidence on Minimum Firing Time and Marksmanship

The evidence presented so far is telling us that bullets arrived at the presidential limo at Z223, Z313 and Z330, that the first two hit both the president and governor, and that the third hit the top of the president's head.

For a third shot fired at Z328 that hit the president, if Oswald did the shooting, he would have just 1 second (18 Z frames) to get the third shot off after firing the second at Z310. Assuming that the rifle was steadily aimed at the president's head from Z310 to Z328 as the evidence indicates, could Oswald have operated the bolt and fired this quickly using the rifle that was recovered at the scene? What were his chances for scoring hits on his first two shots spaced 5 seconds apart using this World War II vintage Italian-made rifle?

MC rifle test firing/minimum firing times/accuracy

The FBI, WC, the HSCA and others have conducted tests with Oswald's Mannicher-Carcano (MC) rifle or those of similar vintage to establish minimum-firing times and accuracy ratings for two consecutive shots. Here follows a quick summary of what has been done.

FBI field testing - On November 27, 1963, three FBI firearms experts (Killion, Cunningham, and Frazier) fired three shots at a stationary target fifteen yards (45 feet) distant using Oswald's MC rifle. The firing times were 9, 8 and 6 seconds, respectively and all the shots were high and to the right of the aiming point. Later that day, Robert Frazier fired two more series of shots "to determine how fast the weapon could be fired primarily, with secondary purpose accuracy" and had firing times of 4.6 and 4.8 seconds. Based on these last two firing tests, Frazier gave expert testimony to the WC that he believed that 4.6 seconds "is firing [three shots] as fast as the bolt can be operated" (WC interview, 3/31/64, [WRv.3Hpp404, 407]). As you will see below, Frazier's expert opinion on minimum-firing time is clearly flawed in that it does not take into account the possibility that Oswald fired using the iron sights rather than the telescopic sights, or fired while simply maintaining his aim. Frazier's carelessness in rendering such an important opinion doomed to failure the WC's investigations into the firing sequence and is an excellent example of what I was referring to in Chapter 2 in terms of not placing blind trust in the opinion of the FBI's experts. Frazier's 2.3-second minimum-firing time is woefully inaccurate.

On March 16, 1964, the FBI's Frazier fired three series of three shots at a stationary target a hundred yards away using Oswald's rifle. His firing times were 5.9, 6.2, and 6.5 seconds. Once again, all his shots were about 5 inches high and 5 inches to the right of the aiming point. In his WC interview, he explained that the inaccuracy was due to a problem with the telescopic sights.

US Army field testing - On March 27, 1964, the WC arranged for the US Army Ballistics Research Laboratory to conduct firing tests more closely matching the conditions in Dealey Plaza. Three marksmen (Hendrix, Staley and Miller) holding "Master" rifle ratings from the National Rifle Association fired at three silhouette targets located at distances matching those the FBI had established for shots fired during the assassination. They again used Oswald's rifle but first adjusted the telescopic sights by adding some shims. Each marksman fired two sets of three shots. The firing times were 8.25, 7.0, 6.75, 6.45, 4.6, and 5.5 seconds. The minimum firing time (by Miller) was 4.6 seconds and the average was 6.4 seconds. All the marksmen hit the first target and scored two out of three hits with all rounds, but none were able to hit all three targets with consecutive firing. Five of the six misses involved the second target, suggesting they were tending to rush the second shot and taking more time with the third. Miller fired a third round in 4.45 seconds using the standard sights instead of the telescopic sights, hitting the first two targets and missing the third badly.

***CBS News* field testing** - In 1967 as part of a news inquiry titled *The Warren Report*, televised in four parts commencing June 25, 1967, *CBS* had a group of eleven volunteer marksmen, some experts, some not, take turns firing three shots at a moving target during a recreation of the assassination sequence. They were unable to obtain Oswald's rifle and instead procured several MC rifles of the same make and model. Each of the marksmen were given time to practice with the weapon at a nearby rifle range. For the recreation, they had a tower and target track constructed at the H.P. White Ballistic Laboratory near Bel Air, Maryland. The tower provided the elevation of the TSBD sixth floor sniper's nest and the track was fabricated and angled to match precisely the angle and distances on Elm to the sniper's nest. The target was a standard FBI silhouette moved by electric motor at 11 miles per hour to approximate the speed of the limo. In each run, the first shot was fired with the target distance at 175 feet to correspond to the president's position at about Z210. In a series of thirty-seven attempts, there were seventeen runs in which the marksmen were not successful in getting off three shots due to difficulties operating the bolt. The minimum-firing time for all the completed series was 4.1 seconds and the average was 5.6 seconds. Of most significance:

> *The series of three shots was rarely evenly spaced, and a marksman often snapped off his second shot less than two seconds after his first, or his third shot less than two seconds after his second. The results, in short, were simply not consistent with those reported by the Commission. . . . CBS News cannot concede that 2.3 seconds is the minimum time for two shots, since time after time a sequence of two shots occurred in far less time than that interval. White, 1968, pp. 82-83 and 224-25.*

HSCA field testing - On March 22, 1979, the HSCA firearms panel conducted firing tests specifically intended to answer the question as to whether it would have been possible for Oswald to have fired two shots in less than 1.7 seconds. The tests were conducted at the Lorton Correctional Facility firing range in Virginia. The intent was to use Oswald's MC rifle, but during bench tests it was found to be in too-poor condition to be used. They used the same MC rifle used during acoustics tests conducted in Dealey Plaza in August 1978. The rifle was shot by four expert marksmen from the Washington, D.C. police department and two members of the HSCA firearms panel (Cornwall and Blakey). The latter had no formal training in the use of firearms. All shots were fired using the standard sights rather than the telescopic sights. The shots were fired from a two-story tower approximately 20-feet high at three targets stationed from left to right at distances of 143 feet, 165 feet and 266 feet from the tower.

Without getting into details, the following three conclusions were reached among others: (1) the weapon can be fired more rapidly using the regular sights rather than the telescopic sights; (2) it is difficult, but not impossible to fire three shots, at least two of which scored direct hits, with an elapsed time of 1.7 seconds or less between any two shots, though no shooter achieved this; (3) "it is not difficult to fire two consecutive shots from a MC rifle within 1.7 seconds, and to point aim if not carefully sight it on the target of each shot." Cornwall fired the rifle twice in 1.2 seconds and Blakey fired it twice within 1.5 seconds, with his second shot missing the silhouette by approximately 2 inches (Blakey memo dated March 22, 1979, HSCA Vol. VIII Addendum C).

Oswald's marksmanship and bolt-operating proficiency and practical considerations

Marksmanship - Oswald was an ex-marine and had received intensive training in the use and maintenance of bolt-action military rifles. His military test scores from 1956 and 1959 revealed that he was an average to below-average shot by Marine-Corps standards. According to FBI-rifle-specialist Robert Frazier, "when you shoot at 175 feet and 260 feet, which is less than 100 yards, with a telescopic sight, you should have no difficulty hitting your target. . . . I mean it requires no training at all to shoot a weapon with a telescopic sight; once you know that you must put the crosshairs on the target, that is all that is necessary" (WR, p. 190).

Toward the beginning of his initial interrogation by Dallas Police Captain, Will Fritz, Oswald could not refrain from bragging about his expertise in handling firearms: "I received an award for marksmanship as a member of the marine corps."

Master-Sergeant James Zahm, then in charge of the Marksmanship Training Unit in the Marine Corps School at Quantico, VA informed the WC that the shot which struck President Kennedy in the upper back at 177 to 191 feet was "very easy" and the shot which struck the president in the head at a distance of 265 feet was "an easy shot" (WR pp. 190-91).

Based on this expert testimony, in a 6-second duration shooting scenario where the first-two shots were separated by 5 seconds, any ex-Marine of average capability even out-of-practice would be expected to hit the first-two shots. There would be more than enough time to operate the bolt and carefully aim the second shot.

Bolt-operating proficiency - Oswald's wife Marina testified that she observed Oswald practicing the operation of the bolt of his rifle in May 1963 within approximately six months of the assassination (WR p. 192). There is also evidence that Oswald fired a single shot on April 10, 1963 when trying to assassinate anti-communist right-winger General Edwin Walker, who had apparently incurred Oswald's wrath by campaigning in the press for the military overthrow of Castro's Marxist Regime in Cuba (WR p. 404).

Additional practical considerations - Beyond establishing that Oswald practiced operating the bolt, the FBI and WC were not able to establish that Oswald had ever practiced shooting the rifle after purchasing it in March 1963, though he may very well have. One indication that he had practiced shooting is that, in searching his premises, law-enforcement personnel could not locate any extra bullets. The Western Cartridge Company bullets for Oswald's MC rifle came in boxes of twenty, and only three spent cartridges and one unfired bullet were recovered at the TSBD crime scene. Assuming Oswald purchased at least a single box of ammo for his rifle, there are at least fifteen cartridges that are unaccounted for.

On the question of whether Oswald would have deemed it necessary to fire an extraneous third shot given the visual devastation created by the Z310 head shot, the following considerations are relevant: (1) Oswald did not have Zapruder's vantage point: he could only see the relatively undamaged rear of the president's head at the moment of impact; (2) even if he did see the jettison from the cranial explosion, he would not have necessarily assumed the shot was fatal. In connection with considerations 1 and 2 above, it is relevant to point out that the effects of the head shot are not at all conspicuous in the Bronson, Muchmore, and Nix films or the Moorman Z316 photo; and (3) the evidence is telling us that with the final shot, Oswald's intent was to fire a final shot as quickly as possible while maintaining his aim. See Figure 37.

Oswald's ability to get a shot off in 1 second and score a lucky hit - Given the above and assuming he just needed to keep the rifle pointed in the same direction it was pointed at Z310, it is reasonable to believe that Oswald could have easily operated the bolt and fired the gun in the president's direction in exactly one second while simply maintaining his aim.

The lateral trajectory analyses for the Z328 head shot that I presented in Chapter 14, revealed that Oswald's rifle was still pointed at where the president's head was located at Z313. The vertical trajectory analysis revealed that he had inadvertently lifted the barrel just enough to score the lucky second hit. See Figures 97 and 98.

Should the reader have lingering doubts as to whether or not Oswald could have gotten a rapid-fire final shot off in less than 1.5 seconds, go to mcadams.posc.mu.edu/dealey.htm where assassination researcher John McAdams has published a film clip of conspiracy advocate Josiah Thompson's efforts to prove that Oswald could not fire two consecutive shots within the 2.3-second time limit the WC allotted based on flawed expert opinion. You can watch Thompson operate the bolt, aim and re-fire the MC rifle in exactly 1.5 seconds starting from the point he fired his initial dry-run shot.

To confirm that Oswald could have used the sling to rapid fire a final shot 0.8 second while maintaining his Z313-shot aim, view the following video posted on YouTube in 2010 by Mag30th titled "Rapid Firing the Mannlicher-Carcano Rifle: 6 Shots in 5.1 Seconds."

In providing some final words on the subject, I will cite the opinion of the person I have dubbed the preeminent eyewitness to the assassination. He was not only the best positioned of the witnesses to the first two shots, but from my perspective had the most relevant experience having participated in and been repeatedly shot at and wounded in the June 1944 D-Day invasion of Normandy:

World War II veteran Charles Brehm, approximately Z270, curb south side of Elm - *Since I have a history of using firearms, people have asked me what my opinion was regarding the ability to fire those shots. I have no doubt in my mind that almost anybody who had basic training like I had in the Ranger battalions would have no difficulty at all. And especially, the fellow was in the marines, who are ordinarily crackerjack people with firearms, would have no problem at all. And I understand that he had a full sling which actually melds the rifle to your body. You become one so that your re-aiming is not necessary. You have the rifle in your arms at the same position. So there's no doubt in my mind that he could have gotten off those shots (Sneed, 1998, p. 64).*

Chapter 10

Key Evidence as to the Location of the Assassin

One would logically expect that if a sniper fired three rifle shots at the President of the United States in broad daylight in front of hundreds of spectators and scores of law-enforcement and media personnel, some of those present would have taken note of the assassin's position. In this chapter you will see that such is indeed the case. This chapter provides a summary of the most compelling primary and corroborating secondary ear/eyewitness testimony that all three shots were indeed fired from the TSBD sniper's nest. It also includes a summary of the most compelling photographic evidence that the shots came from this location.

Figures 39 through 51 follow and relate to the ensuing discussions.

Key witness Howard Brennan heard and saw an assassin fire a rifle from the TSBD's southeast corner sixth-floor window

Constituting the most important eyewitness in the case with respect to the source of the three shots, spectator Howard Brennan, who was ideally positioned on the southwest corner of Houston and Elm, clearly observed a gunman firing a rifle in the direction of the president at the exact time he was assassinated. Brennan quickly relayed his observations to the Dallas police present on the scene. The information and description that Brennan provided, were it not for the delayed response of the policeman he first told in getting the building sealed off, might have resulted in the arrest of Oswald at the scene. I am disregarding the testimony of Amos Euins because I could not verify the information he provided to the WC as to where he was standing when he allegedly saw the shooter. The Dorman film shows him standing along the curb on the west side of Houston about halfway between Main and Elm.

Brennan is visible in frames 133 to 207 of Zapruder's footage exactly where he said he was in his testimony. He was sitting on the wall of the reflecting pool near its northeast corner.

Commencing at 12:33:52 p.m. on police-radio channel 2, Dallas Motorcycle Officer Bobby Hargis, based on information provided by Brennan, transmitted the following information to police headquarters and the officers assigned to the motorcade: "A passerby [Brennan] says . . . the Texas School Book Depository . . . stated the shots came from that building." Similarly, at 12:45 p.m. Dallas Police Sergeant Sawyer, who had just taken charge of the crime scene, reported to dispatch and then posted an all-points bulletin: "The wanted person in this is a slender white male, about 30, 5-feet-10, 165, carrying what looks to be a 30-30 or some type of Winchester."

Three key witnesses Jarman, Norman, and Williams on the fifth floor of the TSBD

The Dillard and Powell photographs taken within 10 to 30 seconds of the final shot from camera car 3 and the southeast corner of Houston and Elm, respectively, show three young male TSBD employees looking out of open windows on the fifth floor of the TSBD directly below the TSBD sniper's nest. If three shots were indeed fired from the TSBD sniper's nest, we would certainly expect these three witnesses to have noticed and such is indeed the case. As they departed the building within about 5 minutes after the shooting, they were immediately identified to Dallas Police Officer Barnett by Howard Brennan as the spectators he saw looking out the windows under the sniper's nest. After confirming that they had been on the fifth floor and heard shots fired from above them, two of the three were immediately placed in protective custody and taken to the sheriff's office where Williams and Jarman gave sworn statements. In March 1964, all three were interviewed on location by the WC.

Three key witnesses Cabell, Couch and Jackson that saw a rifle projecting from the TSBD southeast corner window during the shooting

There is highly credible ear/eyewitness testimony for three participants of the motorcade of looking up at the sniper's nest either during or in the seconds after the shooting in time to see the barrel of the assassin's rifle projecting in the president's direction. They were riding in open-topped convertibles (the mayor's car and camera car 3) and were just entering the intersection with an ideal vantage point just after a shot rang out.

The same photographic evidence that confirms that these witnesses were exactly where they said they were supports the "bang . . . . . bang/bang" shooting sequence with a 5-second pause following the first shot. It confirms that the mayor's car arrived at the south side of the intersection of Houston and Elm at approximately Z220. It confirms that camera car 3 arrived at this same point 5 seconds later at about Z310. See Figure 39.

The observations and actions of Motorcycle-Officer Marion Baker

There was a strong Dallas Police Department and Sheriff's Department presence in Dealey Plaza when the shots rang out. Of all these law-enforcement personnel, just one immediately came to the conclusion that the shots came from the TSBD. He was riding off the right-rear fender of camera car 3. His entry into the TSBD within 20 seconds of the final shot is documented by movie footage taken from camera car 3 by *WFAA-TV News* cameraman Malcolm Couch. See Figure 51.

Photographic evidence that supports all three shots came from the TSBD sixth floor southeast corner window

The Altgens Z253 photo - This photo captures a collective look to the right rear toward the TSBD for three of the ten secret service agents in the presidential follow-up car, namely Agents John Ready and Paul Landis on the right-side running board and Agent George Hickey on the left side of the rear seat. The photo also helps us establish the location of the mayor's car as the first shot rang out. See Figure 40.

The Zapruder-film images - Frames Z133 to Z240 suggests that the collective head turns toward the TSBD that are evident in the Altgens Z253 photo commenced at approximately Z230 which is 0.44 second

10: Key Evidence as to the Assassin's Location

after the first shot struck the president at Z223. These film images also help us establish the location of the mayor's car and the camera cars as the three shots rang out. See Figure 5.

The Tom Dillard post-assassination photos - Dillard took two photos from the rear seat of camera car 3 within 10 to 20 seconds of the assassination that verify that three key ear/eyewitnesses to the location of the shooter were positioned exactly where they said they were at the time of the shooting: on the fifth floor of the TSBD directly below the sixth floor SE corner window sniper's nest. The photos also verify the claims of several occupants of the car that they observed a rifle barrel extending from the window immediately after the final shot rang out. See Figure 44.

The James Powell post-assassination photo - This photo taken from the curb near the southeast corner of Houston and Elm approximately 30 seconds after the assassination documents and verifies Powell's claim that some spectators in the area were pointing toward the building as the source of the shots. See Figure 45.

Dorman-film images - Frames D413 to D421 (Z332-41) document that there were two spectators in business suits, including picture-taker James Towner, standing along the curb on the south side of Elm directly across the street from the southeast corner of the TSBD who looked up in the direction of the sniper's nest within a split second of the final shot. The film images also help us establish the location of the mayor's car, camera car 3 and Motorcycle Officer Baker as the shots rang out. See Figure 43.

Wiegman-film images - Frames W101 to W111 (Z330-37) document that there was a young man standing in front of the TSBD who turned his head hard right rear toward the TSBD sniper's nest within a split second of the final shot. The film images also help us establish the location of the mayor's car as the first shot rang out and where camera car 3 and Motorcycle Officer Baker were located as the final shots rang out. See Figure 42.

Couch-film images - The first four seconds of the Couch film taken about 15 to 18 seconds after the head shot confirm that Dallas Police Motorcycle Officer Marion Baker entered the TSBD on the run just after the shots rang out. They also serve to document that there was at least one spectator wearing a Stetson hat positioned in front of the TSBD who looked up in the direction of the sniper's nest immediately after the shots rang out. The film images confirm that camera car 3 came to a stop within the intersection and also help us establish the location of camera car 3 and Motorcycle-Officer Baker as the final shots rang out. See Figure 51.

Muchmore and Nix-film images - Frames M62-M66 (Z333 to Z337) of the Muchmore Film and N058 to N064 (Z348 to Z352) of the Nix film document that north-of-Elm-spectator "Flying Tackle Man" reacted as if the shots were fired from the direction of the TSBD and not the grassy knoll. He ran for and took cover directly in front of the so-called picket-fence shooter area endorsed by HSCA experts and in the exact location where the so-called "Black Dog" assassin was lurking according to certain conspiracy advocates. These same Muchmore frames M62-M66 (Z333 and Z337) and Nix frames N043 to N060 (Z333 to Z350) capture a collective hard look to the right rear toward the TSBD for all four motorcycle officers flanking the rear of the presidential limo (Martin, Hargis, Chaney and Jackson) commencing at Z333 to Z339 within 0.16 to 0.44 second of the final shot. See Figures 33 and 41.

Dallas police crime-lab photographs - The crime lab investigators took a number of photos within an hour of the shooting that document the discovery of the assassin's lair, his rifle and three spent cartridges lying on the floor directly behind the sixth floor southeast corner window. See Figures 46 through 50.

Ballistics evidence relating to the shooter's location

In the aftermath of the assassination, the FBI conducted investigations using standard protocols that provided sufficient ballistics evidence to link the three spent shells and the so-called stretcher bullet to the World-War-II-vintage Italian-made rifle discovered on the sixth floor of the TSBD.

The FBI also conducted investigations using neutron-activation analysis that provided sufficient evidence to conclude that the bullet fragments recovered from the limo and from Governor Connally's right forearm and wrist came from the same production lot as the stretcher bullet and the unfired bullet in the rifle.

Key ear/eyewitness testimony to the source of the shots (Figure 39)

One witness at the southwest corner of Houston and Elm that saw the assassin fire the last shot

Howard Brennan, 45-year-old steam fitter with Wallace & Beard Construction, southwest corner of Houston and Elm - *I was sitting on a ledge or wall near the intersection of Houston Street and Elm Street near the red-light pole. I was facing in a northerly direction looking across the street from where I was sitting. I take this building across the street to be about seven stories. Anyway in east end of the building and the second row of windows from the top I saw a man in this window. I had seen him before the president's car arrived. He was just sitting there looking down apparently waiting for the same thing I was, to see the president. I did not notice anything unusual about this man. He was a white man in his early 30s, slender, nice looking, slender and would weigh about 165 to 175 pounds. He had on light-colored clothing but definitely not a suit. I proceeded to watch the president's car as it turned left at the corner where I was and about 50 yards from the intersection of Elm and Houston and a point I would say the president's back was in line with the last windows I have previously described I heard what I thought was a backfire. It run in my mind that it might be someone throwing firecrackers out the window of the red brick building and I looked up at the building. I then saw this man I have described in the window and he was taking aim with a high-powered rifle. I could see all the barrel of the gun. I do not know if it had a scope or not. I was looking at this man in this window at the time of the last explosion. Then this man let the gun down to his side and stepped out of sight. He did not seem to be in a hurry. I could see this man from about the belt up. There was nothing unusual about him at all in appearance. I believe I could identify this man if I ever saw him again.* Sheriff's Department affidavit, 11/22/63 (WRv.24Hp.203).

Note - According to the testimony of Secret Service Agent Forest Sorrels, Brennan told him on location at about 1:15 p.m., that he looked up and saw the sniper in response to hearing a second shot. WC Deposition, May 7, 1964.

Three witnesses on the fifth floor of the TSBD that heard the shots and looked up toward the sniper's nest

Harold Norman, 25-year-old order filler, fifth floor looking out the first window from the east end - *(1) He stated that about the time the car in which the president was riding turned onto Elm Street, he heard a shot. He said he thought the shot had been fired from the floor directly above him. He further stated at that time he stuck his head out from the window and looked upward toward the roof but could see nothing because small particles of dirt were falling from above him. He stated two additional shots were fired after he pulled his head back in from the window.* FBI interview, 11/26/63. *(2) Just after the president passed by, I heard a shot and several seconds later I heard two more shots. I know the shots had come from directly above me, and I could hear the expended cartridges fall to the floor. I could also hear the bolt action of the rifle. I also saw some dirt*

10: Key Evidence as to the Assassin's Location

fall from the ceiling of the fifth floor and I felt sure that whoever had fired the shots was directly above me. I saw all of the people down on the street run toward the west side of the building, so I went to that side with Williams and Jarman, and looked out the west-side window. We discussed the shots and where they had come from and decided we better go downstairs. Affidavit prepared for the secret service, 12/4/63 (WRv.17Hp.208).

Bonnie Ray Williams, 20-year-old order filler, fifth floor looking out the second window from the east end - *(1) I went to work today at 8 a.m. this morning. I worked on the sixth floor today with Mr. Bill [Shelley], Danny [Arce], Charles [Givens] and a Billy Lovelady. . . . We worked up until about 10 minutes to 12. Then we went downstairs. We rode the elevator to the first floor and got our lunches. I went back on the fifth floor with a fellow called Hank and Junior. I don't know his last name. Just after we got on the fifth floor we saw the president coming around the corner on Houston from Main Street. I heard two shots [he did not realize the first noise was a shot] it sounded like they came from just above us. We run to the west end of the building. We didn't see anybody. We looked down and saw people running and hollering. We stayed there and in a little while some officers came up. They left and then we took the elevator to the fourth floor. We stayed there a little while and then went out.* Sheriff's Department Affidavit, 11/22/63 (WRv.24Hp.229). *(2) Well the first shot I really did not pay any attention to it, because I did not know what was happening. The second shot, it sounded like it was right in the building, the second and third shot. And it sounded . . . it even shook the building, the side we were on cement fell on my head. . . . Harold was sitting next to me and he said it came right from over our head . . . . [He said] "I can even hear the shells being ejected from the gun hitting the floor."* WC testimony, 3/24/64 (WRv.3Hp.175).

James Jarman, 34-year-old order checker, fifth floor looking out the fourth window from the east end - *After the motorcade turned, going west on Elm, then there was a loud shot, or backfire, as I thought it was then. . . . And then the second shot was fired, and that is when the people started falling to the ground and the motorcade jumped forward, and then the third shot was fired right behind the second one. Well after the third shot was fired, I think I got up and I run over to Harold Norman and Bonnie Ray Williams and told them . . . that it wasn't a backfire or anything; that someone was shooting at the president. Hank said . . . that he thought the shots had come from above us, and I noticed that Bonnie Ray had a few debris in his head. It was sort of white stuff, or something, and I told him not to brush it out, but he did.* WC Testimony, 3/24/64 (WRv.3Hp.204).

Three witnesses in the motorcade that saw the rifle extending from the sniper's nest in the president's direction just after a shot rang out

Elizabeth Cabell (Mayor Cabell's wife), left side of rear seat in sixth car of the motorcade (mayor's convertible) - *The position of our car was such that when that first shot rang out, my position was such that I did not have to turn to look at the building. I was directly facing it. . . . I heard the shot, and without having to turn my head, I jerked my head up. . . . Because I heard the direction from which the shot came, and I just jerked my head up. I saw a projection out of one of those windows . . . on the sixth floor. . . . It was a rather long-looking projection. . . . and I turned around to say to Earle, "It's a shot," . . . . And [as he started to say] "Oh, no; it must have been a . . . ," the second two shots rang out. I was acutely aware of the odor of gunpowder.* WC interview, 7/13/64 (WRv.7Hp.486).

Notes - Camera car 1 was two cars back of the mayor's car. The Wiegman assassination sequence begins at Z259 with the rear-two-thirds of the mayor's car in view just short of completing the hard left turn off Houston onto Elm at a point directly opposite the sniper's nest. By reasonably assuming the mayor's car was traveling at approximately the same speed as Wiegman's car, we can project that as the Z221 shot rang out, the mayor's car was located where Wiegman's was located as the Z310 second shot rang out 5 seconds later. Camera car 1 was just starting the left-hand turn with the front of the car just about to face the sniper's nest at a distance of about 125 feet which is an ideal vantage point. By the time the second and third shots rang out 5 to 6 seconds later, they were approaching the grassy knoll. See Figure 12.

Robert Jackson, 29-year-old Dallas Time Herald photographer in ninth car of motorcade (camera car 3), sitting on the right side of the top of the back of the rear seat with Malcolm Couch - *And as we heard the first shot, I believe it was Tom Dillard from Dallas News who made some remark as to that sounding like a firecracker . . . and before he actually finished the sentence, we heard two other shots. Then we realized it was gunfire, and then we could see at this point it was the president's car. We were still moving slowly . . . . Then after the last shot, I guess all of us were just looking all around and I just looked straight up ahead of me, which would have been looking at the School Book Depository, and I noticed two Negro men in a window straining to see directly above them, and my eyes followed right on up to the window above them and I saw the rifle or what looked like a rifle approximately half the weapon, I guess I saw, and just as I looked at it, it was drawn fairly slowly back into the building, and I saw no one in that window with it. . . . I said, "There is a gun," or "It came from that window." I tried to point it out. But by the time the other people looked up, of course, it was gone, and about that time we were beginning to turn the corner.* WC testimony, 3/10/64 (WRv.2Hp.158-59).

Notes for Jackson and Couch - We know from Wiegman's sightlines that as of Z313, camera car 1 was just starting the left turn from Houston onto Elm and that the front of camera car 3 was about 50 feet shy of the front of camera car 1. Assuming that Jackson saw the rifle 4 seconds after the Z310 shot and that his car was traveling at an average speed of 12 feet per second, he was just starting the turn when he saw the rifle. As it turns out, the mayor's car and Jackson's car were at about the same location during the rifle-barrel sightings.

Malcolm Couch, 25-year-old WFAA-TV cameraman, ninth car of motorcade (camera car 3), sitting on top of the back of the rear seat with Robert Jackson - *We had just made the turn [onto Houston from Main] and I heard the first shot. . . . as I say, the first shot I had no particular impression; but the second shot, I remember turning - several of us turning and looking ahead of us. It was unusual for a motorcycle to backfire that close together, it seemed like. And after the third shot, Bob Jackson who I recall was on my right yelled something like, "Look up in the window! There's the rifle!" And I remember glancing up to a window on the far right, which impressed me as the sixth or seventh floor, and seeing about a foot of a rifle being the barrel brought into the window. I saw no one in the window, just a quick one-second glance at the barrel. . . . I recall seeing uh some people standing in some of the other windows about roughly, third or fourth floor in the middle of the south side. I recall one; it looked like a Negro boy with a white T shirt leaning out one of those windows looking up-up to the windows above him.* WC testimony, 4/1/64 (WRv.6Hp.156-57).

Marion Baker's observations and actions

Marion Baker, 33-year-old Dallas Police Officer riding motorcycle escort on the east side of the dignitary cars of the motorcade - *(1) Friday November 22, 1963, I was riding motorcycle escort for the President of the United States. At approximately 12:30 p.m. I was on Houston Street and the president's car had made a left turn from Houston unto Elm Street. Just as I approached Elm Street and Houston I heard three shots [and saw pigeons depart en mass from the roofs of two buildings at the corner of Houston and Elm]. I realized those shots were rifle shots and I began to try to figure out where they came from. I decided the shots had come from this building on the northwest corner of Elm and Houston. This building is used by the Board of Education for book storage. I jumped off my motor and ran inside the building.* Affidavit, 11/22/63. *(2) We approximated it [his position at the first shot] was 60 to 80 feet north of the north curb line of Main on Houston. It hit me all at once that it was a rifle shot because I had just come back from deer hunting and I had heard them pop over there for about a week.* WC Testimony, March 25, 1964 (WRv.3Hp.246).

Notes - As shown in Figure 39, Baker was escorting the camera cars and was fast approaching the intersection of Houston and Elm when the last two shots rang out. He might have overheard Jackson's shouts about a rifle in the window. The Dorman film picks up his partner McLain starting the turn at about Z392 on the west side of the intersection which is 4.5 seconds after the Z310 shot.

10: Key Evidence as to the Assassin's Location

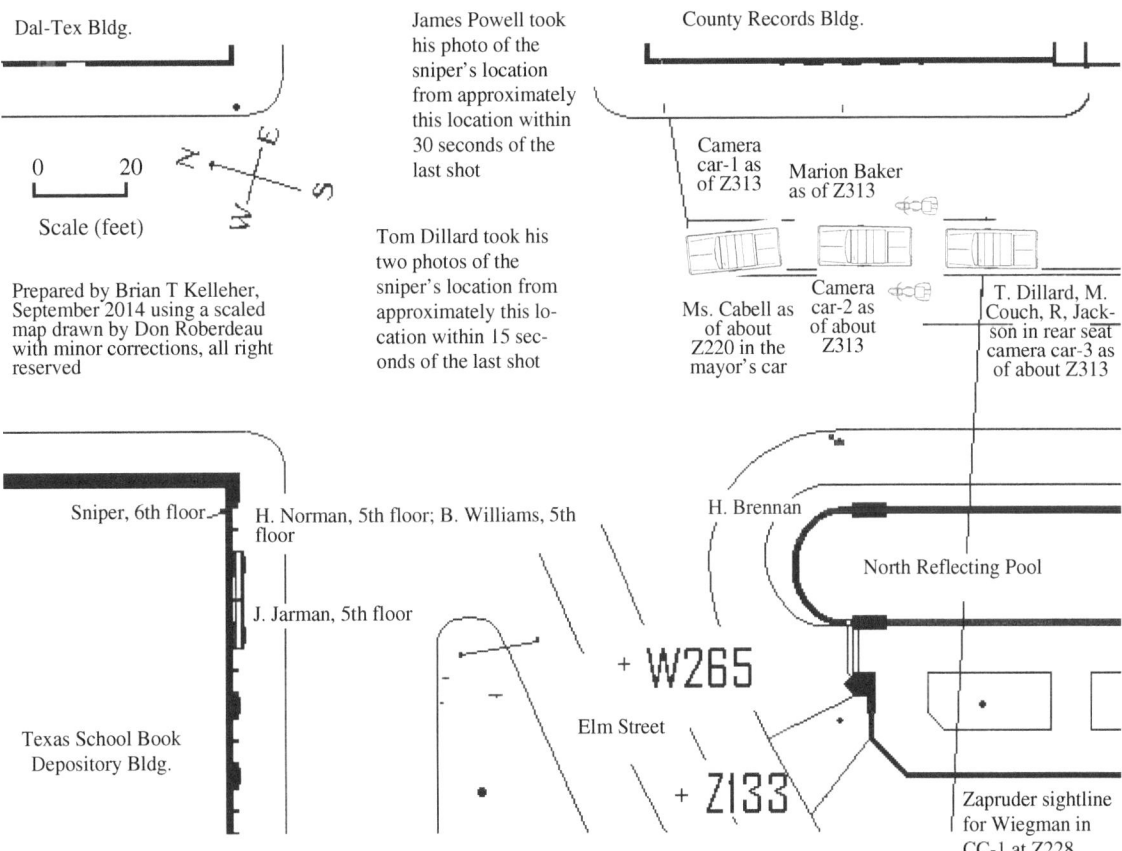

Figure 39

Location of key witnesses to the source of the three shots - Here we have the exact location of Wiegman in camera car 1 as of Z313 and the approximate locations of camera cars 2 and 3. According to Zapruder's sightline for Wiegman's camera position at Z228, as the first shot rang out at Z221, the mayor's car, which was two cars ahead of camera car 1, was located very close to where camera car 1 was located as of Z313. The sketch of the camera cars and their motorcycle police escort is from Trask, 1994, p.306.

Figure 40
Altgens Z253 photo head turning toward the TSBD sniper's nest (cropped) - Bettman/CORBIS

Figure 41
Muchmore frame M66/Z337 Flying Tackle Man heads for shelter in the alleged picket-fence shooter area as Officers Martin and Chaney look right rear (cropped) - (Marie Muchmore/AP Television News)

Figure 42
Wiegman frame W111/Z337 head turning toward the TSBD sniper's nest (cropped)

Figure 43
Dorman frame D421/Z342 head turning and looking up toward the TSBD sniper's nest (cropped) - (Dorman Family Collection/Sixth Floor Museum at Dealey Plaza)

Figure 44
Tom Dillard photo of the TSBD sniper's nest taken 10 to 15 seconds after the last shot - (Tom Dillard)

Figure 45
James Powell photo of the TSBD sniper's nest taken about 30 seconds after the last shot (cropped)

10: Key Evidence as to the Assassin's Location

Figure 46
Dallas police crime lab photo of the sniper's nest 11/25/63 with the boxes repositioned after they were moved - See photo credit for Figure 50.

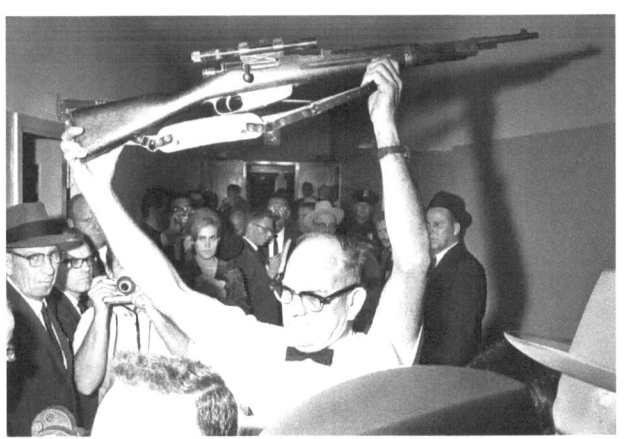

Figure 47
Press photo showing Dallas police crime lab's Lieutenant Carl Day holding Oswald's Carcano rifle above his head, 11/22/63

Figure 49
Dallas police crime lab photo of the sniper's rifle just after it was discovered, 11/23/63 - See photo credit for Figure 50.

Figure 48
Dallas police crime lab photo of the sniper's nest showing three spent shell casings, 11/23/63 - See photo credit for Figure 50.

Figure 50
Dallas police crime lab photo of the sniper's nest from the rear, 11/23/63 - Dallas Police Department photograph, R.W. "Rusty" Livingston Collection/Sixth Floor Museum at Dealey Plaza www.jfk.org

Figure 51
Couch film frame 83 showing officer Marion Baker and Roy Truly heading for the TSBD entrance as Stetson Hat Man looks up at the TSBD sniper's nest - The young man that took a hard look back over his left shoulder between Wiegman frames W101 and 111 (Z332-337) is at camera left looking west down Elm. Roy Truly is two spectators to camera left of the upward-gazing Stetson Hat Man and is heading toward Baker. Officer Baker is to camera left of Stetson Hat Man's head. This is 3.5 seconds after Couch began filming his Dealey Plaza-post-assassination sequences and an estimated 21.7 seconds after the Z310 shot rang out. This is a cropped image that I photo edited to increase brightness and contrast (Malcolm Couch, Lyndon B. Johnson Museum, via *WFAA TV*).

Chapter 11

Key Witness Testimony for the First Shot

The Zapruder-film images collectively provide compelling evidence that the first shot was fired at Z221. The evidence lies in the governor's signature jolting and concurrent visible reactions of the members of the presidential entourage commencing Z225 and Z230. To verify the photographic evidence, we need to examine the relevant testimony of these key ear/eyewitnesses where it exists to see if it correlates with the story that the film images tell. These seventeen key witnesses comprising the presidential entourage include: (1) five surviving occupants of the presidential limo; (2) four motorcycle-escort policemen; and (3) eight of the ten occupants of the Queen Mary (the other two did not provide relevant testimony). There are seventeen in this motorcade group. See Figure 52.

To conduct a proper, systematic evaluation of the available stationary ear/eyewitness testimony regarding the timing and effects of the first shot, I first separated the wheat from the chaff by identifying the witness groups/populations who were optimally located to make reliable and meaningful observations that are pertinent to the questions at hand. Only by tallying such evidence, can one draw meaningful conclusions and properly judge the merits of any individual witness statements within the context of the whole.

With this purpose in mind, I identified an additional twenty-four ideally positioned spectators meriting primary status on the basis they provided unambiguous testimony relating to the question of exactly where the president was located on Elm when the first shot rang out: (1) nine spectators who were lining the north side of Elm as the president passed by them within 20 feet between Z190 to Z215; (2) six spectators who were lining the north side of Elm as the president passed by them within 20 feet between Z215 and Z230; (3) five spectators who were positioned opposite or within the grassy knoll and saw the president react to the first shot from a distance of within 50 to 100 feet as he approached them; and (4) four spectators who were lining Main or Elm within 70 to 230 feet of the president as of Z223 who snapped still photos just before or just after the shooting started and testified to that effect. There are twenty four in this stationary witness group. See Figure 52.

Despite the mountain of evidence described in the prior chapters that the first shot was fired at Z221, the consensus of opinion among the HSCA experts and today's lone-gunman advocates is that there was a first shot fired at about Z152 that missed the limo. I further rebut this premise in this chapter.

Figures 52 through 55 follow and relate to the ensuing discussions.

Conclusions

The testimony provided by the above forty one key ear/eyewitnesses with respect to the timing and effects of the first shot correlates closely with the photographic evidence and provides overwhelming support for the first shot being fired at Z221 and wounding the president when his limo had just passed the Thornton Freeway sign. As such, it unequivocally refutes a first shot fired prior to Z200. See summary in Chapter 1.

Among the forty one that provided relevant testimony, there is not a single credible statement that supports a first shot fired prior to Z200. Agent Greer who was driving the presidential limo, testified he heard the first shot just prior to passing the TSBD. This falls anywhere from pre Z133 to about Z210 depending on whether or not he was including its western annex. He further testified that he paid no heed to the first-shot noise and at the time was looking with concern at the many spectators atop the triple underpass. Moreover, before the second shot rang out, Greer was clearly aware from all the commotion in the car that the president was wounded by the Z221 first shot and was told so. He is among those who looked into the back seat after the first shot, albeit because his attention was aroused by Kellerman's advising him they were hit.

Resolving the perplexing testimony of Governor Connally that he was hit in the back by the second shot - To the day he died, the governor insisted that he heard a first shot before he was wounded and was hit in the back immediately after by a second shot that he did not hear. Based on his own frame-by-frame review of the Zapruder film, he testified to the WC that he was struck in the back at about Z233 as he was turning in his seat to look back out of concern for the president. Based on the FBI's then recently established minimum-firing time of 2.3 seconds (42 Z frames), Connally estimated that the president was hit by the first shot at about Z190.

First and foremost, as will be discussed in detail in Chapter 12, his trusted-wife Nellie from the onset was adamant that the president was hit by the first shot and that the governor was nearly shot dead by the second. As discussed in Chapter 2, the Z-film images reveal that Ms. Connally had every good reason for mistakenly believing this was the case.

Also of critical significance, the governor testified under oath to the WC that he lost consciousness just after he heard the shot that hit the president in the head. The Z-film images confirm this. They show him slamming his head into a metal bar atop the front seatback at Z324 in completing his frantic lunge forward after the Z310 shot, and then collapsing left-shoulder-first onto his wife's right shoulder and lap from Z325 to Z339 as if he had just been shot dead. This dramatic reaction is why Ms. Connally, who was looking away from the president at the time of the Z313 cranial eruption, believed from the onset that her husband was hit by the second shot she heard rather than the first. Ms. Connally associated the final shot with brain matter raining down on her, which the Z/N/M-film images reveal occurred between Z331 and Z337 as a result of the Z330 shot. If Governor Connally had heard all three shots there would have been no doubt in his mind that he and the president were both struck by the first shot.

Another reason the governor was adamant in his opinion has to do with the fact that neither he nor the FBI ever endorsed the single-bullet theory and were completely at odds with the WC on this particular issue. In attempting to align his wounds, Connally and his doctors believed that for a single bullet to have caused all five of his wounds (back, chest, forearm, wrist, and thigh) he needed to be in the position he was sitting at about Z234 at which point he was facing straight ahead with the bullet's exit point below and inside his right nipple pointing toward its final resting place on the inside of his left thigh at the same time the back of his raised right forearm was in the vicinity of the exit wound in the chest. As will be discussed in detail in Chapter 12, the collective evidence is overwhelming that the governor's right-forearm wound was created by the damaged bullet that exited the president's head at Z313.

Rebuttal of arguments that a first shot missed the limo at Z152/153 - Those who argue the case for a Z152 first-shot-miss cite the following evidence: (1) pronounced Zapruder film jiggles at frames 158/59; (2) Governor Connally's dubious testimony as to the timing of the first shot; (3) Agent Glen Bennett's dubious testimony as to the visible effects of the second shot; (4) 10-year old Rosemary Willis' dubious and distant recollections as to why she might have stopped running along the sidewalk at about Z190 while looking back over her shoulder toward the TSBD; (5) the concurrent head turns of the Kennedys and Connallys commencing Z155 to Z165; and (6) the abrupt movements of south-of-Elm spectator 10-year old Rosemary Willis.

Prior to the shooting, the Zapruder film shows Governor Connally continuously looking to the right except from Z160 to Z164 when he took a quick glance to the left and then abruptly turned back to the right from Z165 to Z170. This is just after the president spun his head from looking forward-left to forward-right from Z155 to Z160. Jackie Kennedy who had been interacting with spectators on the south side of Elm also turned her head quickly to her right between about Z170 and Z174. Also commencing Z165, Ms. Connally looked back over her right shoulder and was looking toward the president from Z180 until disappearing from view at about Z200. While such concurrent movements are suggestive of reflex or alarm reactions to a shot fired at about Z150, the careful observer will conclude that the Kennedys and Connallys made their turns at about the same time because the line of spectators at the curb on the south side of Elm had come to an abrupt end at the point the president passed at about Z160.

The careful researcher will also note that Nellie Connally told the WC that just seconds before the first shot rang out she turned and looked back toward the president and said "Mr. President, you can't say that Dallas does not love you." This head turn and 2-second-long communication occurs from Z165 to Z200.

The careful observer will also arrive at the conclusion that the scampering 10-year-old Rosemary Willis stopped running and turned to look back over her right shoulder commencing about Z190, because her 14-year-old sister Linda was hollering and/or whistling at her to stop. From Z135 to Z155, Linda, in her blue dress, was standing off the northwest corner of the reflecting pool looking in Rosemary's direction with her hands cupped to her mouth in megaphone fashion. From Z175 to Z185, Agent Hickey from his position in the elevated left-rear seat of the Queen Mary also appears to be admonishing Rosemary to stop running, picking up where Linda left off. See Figure 53.

Most telling, not a single one of the secret service agents or policemen in the presidential entourage turned their heads in alarm until Z230 at which point most, if not all, did so in unison with Ms. Connally.

Key stationary ear/eyewitness testimony to the first shot

Figure 52 shows the location of the ear/eyewitnesses covered here. The only witnesses whose first-shot testimony is cited in this chapter are those individuals that provided unambiguous information as to either the president's reaction to the shot, or the location of the president relative to themselves at the time of the first shot. The testimony of the grassy knoll witnesses and the presidential entourage regarding the second and third shots is covered in the next chapter.

The specific locations for some of the fifteen spectators lining the north side of Elm from Z190 to Z237 involved a minor amount of guesswork. Where I could not confirm the witness' exact location within a group, I relied to some extent on the witness locations shown on the most-up-to-date map of Dealey Plaza produced and published by assassination researcher, Don Roberdeau. I used an asterisk to identify my reliance on Mr. Roberdeau's research. I disagree with some of the locations he was depicting as of September 2014 including Burney, Hawkins, Mudd, and Jean Newman.

Nine along the north side of Elm from Z190 to Z215

Billie Clay, about Z190, curb north side of Elm, 57-year-old TSBD employee with co-workers Dickerson, Hendrix and Williams - *Just a few seconds after the car in which President John F. Kennedy was riding passed the position where I was standing, I heard a shot. . . .* FBI interview, 3/23/64 (WRv.22Hp.641).

    Notes for Clay, Hendrix and Millican: assuming Z223, they heard the shot 1.7 seconds after the president passed by.

Ruth Hendrix, about Z190, curb north side of Elm near lamp pole, 51-year-old TSBD employee with co-workers Clay, Dickerson and Williams - *I recall that just seconds after the car in which President John F. Kennedy was riding passed the position where I was standing, I heard a shot.* FBI interview, 3/24/64 (WRv.22Hp.649).

A. J. Millican, about Z190, curb north side of Elm, plumbing company employee that was working in the railroad yards - *Just after the president's car passed, I heard three shots come up from toward Houston and Elm right by the TSBD Building . . .* Undated statement on sheriff's department letterhead, presumably 11/22/63 (WRv.19Hp.486).

Mary Woodward, about Z192, *Dallas Morning News* reporter, curb north side of Elm, with Alonzo, Brown and Donaldson - *Just as the President and Mrs. Kennedy went by, they turned and waved at them. Just a second or two later, she heard a loud noise.* FBI interview, 12/6/63 (WRv.24Hp.520).

    Note: Assuming Z223, she heard the shot 1.6 seconds after the president passed her.

Ann Donaldson, about Z190, 26-year-old *Dallas Morning News* reporter, curb north side of Elm, with co-workers Alonzo, Brown and Woodward - *When I heard the first shot, I'd say the president was about 1:00 or 1:30. He definitely was not directly opposite.* Atterberry e-mail communication to author, 9/6/04.

    Notes for Donaldson and Berry: at Z223 the president was about 20 feet past them at 1:45.

Jane Berry, about Z200*, curb north side of Elm, 23-year-old TSBD employee with co-worker Betty Thornton - *She was standing just west of the building . . . Just as the car was passing her, she heard a rifle shot.* FBI interview, 3/19/64 (WRv.22Hp.637).

John Templin, about Z207, curb north side of Elm, 25-year-old military reservist with Earnest Brandt (shipping clerk for Graybar Electric Company) - *And just about, I would say 30 feet past us, we heard what I personally thought was a motorcycle backfire, and . . . the president kind of threw his shoulders up a little bit and laid his head back on the back of the seat . . .* Transcript of interview by Bob Porter, 7/8/95, Sixth Floor Museum at Dealey Plaza Collection Oral History Program.

    Notes for Templin and Brandt: at Z223 the president was about 12 feet past them.

Earnest Brandt, about Z208, curb north side of Elm, 37-year old veteran with John Templin (salesman for Consolidated Copperstate Motor Lines) - *. . . was two years in the Navy, came back in 46 . . . And I think the limousine was about 60 or 70 feet past us, 3 or 4 seconds from the time . . . then bam! The first shot was fired. . . . The first shot he did like this (raising arms to neck) and slumped forward a little bit . . .* Transcript of interview by Bob Porter, 5/12/94, Sixth Floor Museum Oral History Collection.

    Notes - Given that Brandt testified to seeing the president react to the first shot by raising his arms to his neck, his wide error in recalling the distance the limo had traveled after passing him is ignored.

Jean Newman, about Z210, curb, north side of Elm, 21-year-old Rheem Manufacturing Company employee near Brandt and Templin - *. . . after he had just passed, there was a loud report, it just scared me, and I noticed that the president jumped . . . I saw him put his elbows like this, with his hands on his chest.* Dallas County Sheriff's Department statement, 11/22/63 (WRv.19Hp.489).

11: Key First Shot Witness Testimony

Note: at Z223 the president was about 15 feet past her.

Six along the north side of Elm from Z215 to Z250

Karen Westbrook, about Z223*, curb north side of Elm, 18-year-old TSBD employee with co-workers Calvary, Hicks and Reed - *(1) I saw the president's hair fly up . . . I knew he was hit.* (Kent Biffle interview, 11/22/63, "Assassin Crouched and Took Deadly Aim," Dallas Morning News 11/23/63 section 4 p 1). *(2) The car he was in was almost directly in front of where I was standing when I heard the first explosion. I did not immediately recognize this sound as a gun shot.* FBI interview, 3/19/64 (WRv.22Hp.679).

Notes for the Westbrook group: at Z223 the president was approximately right in front of them at a distance of about 20 feet.

June Dishong, about Z224, curb north side of Elm, 55-year Dal Tex building employee within the Westbrook/Calvary group - *He drops his arm as they go by possibly 20 feet. Suddenly, a sound. . . . The president bent forward into his wife's lap as his arm slipped off the side of the car.* Excerpts from her 11/22/63 diary entry, Mark Wrolstad "Eyewitness to Murder," Dallas Morning News, 11/22/98.

Gloria Calvary, about Z226*, curb north side of Elm, 21-year-old TSBD employee with co-workers Hicks, Reed and Westbrook - *The car he was in was almost directly in front where I was standing when I heard the first shot.* FBI interview, 3/29/64 (WRv.22Hp.638).

Karen Hicks, about Z228*, curb north side of Elm, 19-year-old TSBD employee with co-workers Calvary, Reed and Westbrook - *The car he was in was almost directly in front of where I was standing when I heard the first explosion.* FBI interview, 3/20/64 (WRv.22Hp.650).

Carol Reed*, about Z230, curb north side of Elm, 20-year-old TSBD employee with co-workers Calvary, Hicks and Westbrook - *At the time President Kennedy was shot I was standing on the curb of Elm Street about mid-way between the TSBD Building and the Elm Street railroad overpass.* FBI interview, 3/19/64 (WRv22Hp.668).

Note: Reed's testimony is not considered relevant because it is not specific enough.

Faye Chism, about Z235, curb north side of Elm, 19-year old homemaker with her husband and 3-year-old son - *As the president was coming through, I heard this first rifle shot, and the president fell to his left.* Dallas County Sheriff's Department statement, 11/22/63 (WRv.19Hp.472).

Notes for the Chisms: at Z223 the president was about 12 to 15 feet short of them.

Arthur Chism, about Z237, curb north side of Elm, 23-year-old cook at Marriot Hotel, with his wife and 3-year-old son - *When I saw the motorcade round the corner, the president was standing and waving to the crowd. And just as he got just about in front of me, he turned and waved at the crowd on this side of the street, the right side. At this point, I heard what sounded like a shot, and I saw him, the president, sit back in his seat and lean his head to the left side.* Dallas County Sheriff's Department statement, 11/22/63 (WRv.19Hp.471).

Five along the north or south side of Elm from Z250 to Z310 (grassy knoll)

Charles Brehm, about Z280, just off the curb, south side of Elm - *(1) The first shot rang out and I was positive when I saw the look on his face and saw him grab his chest and saw the reaction of his wife that he had been shot . . .* Radio interview at curb about 12:35-45 p.m., November 22, 1963. *(2) When the president's automobile was very close to him and he could see the president's face very well, the president was seated, but was leaning forward when he stiffened perceptibly at the same instant what appeared to be a rifle-shot sounded . . .* FBI interview 11/25/63 (WRv.22Hp.837).

Note: at Z223 the president was about 50 feet short of him.

Gayle Newman curb, about Z295, north side of Elm - *. . . the car was just up a piece from us and this shot fired out and I thought it was a firecracker. And the president kind of raised up in his seat . . . .* Video tape of live TV interview by Jay Watson, WFAA TV, at about 1:20 p.m., 11/22/63, "The Story Behind the Story," Belo Interactive, 2003, DVD, track 8.

Notes for the Newmans: at Z223 the president was about 60 to 70 feet short of them.

Bill Newman curb, about Z300, north side of Elm - *The president's car was some 50 feet still in front of us coming toward us when we heard the first shot and the president jumped up in his seat. I thought it scared him . . .* Recording of live TV interview by Jay Watson, WFAA TV, about 1:10 p.m., 11/22/63, "The Story Behind the Story," Belo Interactive, 2003, DVD, track 7.

Marilyn Sitzman, about Z313, pergola, north side of Elm - *I heard the first shot . . . he slumped over in his seat.* Darwin Payne, Dallas Times Herald reporter telephoned notes tear sheets, November 22, 1963, Sixth Floor Museum and interview by the Sixth Floor Museum, 1996.

Notes for Sitzman and Zapruder: at Z223 the president was about 100 feet from them.

Abraham Zapruder, about Z313, pergola, north side of Elm - *It was about halfway down there, I heard a shot, and he slumped to the side like this (indicating).* Recording of live TV interview by Jay Watson WFAA TV, at about 2:30 p.m., 11/22/63, "The Story Behind the Story," Belo Interactive, 2003, DVD, track 14.

Four key stationary witnesses that took pictures of the limo between Z133 and Z350

James Altgens, about Z350, curb, south side of Elm - *I made one picture [the Z253 photo] at the time I heard a noise that sounded like a firecracker. . . the shot was just a fraction ahead of my picture. . . . Well it sounded like it was coming from behind the car . . . .* WC interview, 7/22/64 (WRv.7Hp.517).

Note: he took the Z253 photo 2 seconds after Z223 at which point the president was about 100 feet short of him. See Figure 9.

Hugh Betzner, about Z133, sidewalk, south side of Elm - *I was standing on the southwest corner of Houston Street as the motorcade came along. I began taking pictures, one on Houston Street and one as the president's car rounded the corner. I took another picture of the limousine [the Z186 photo] as it drove off down the hill. And I had just lowered the camera and was rewinding the film when I heard the first shot.* On scene interview by UPI, "Motorcade Took Off In Hurry," Hamilton [Ontario] Spectator, 11/23/63.

Notes: The Zapruder and Dorman films collectively show that Betzner finished rewinding his camera after taking his Z186 shot at about Z205 at which point he sprinted further west down Elm. This is just under a second before the first shot rang out. The president was 90 to 100 feet past him at Z223. See Figures 53 and 54.

Charles Bronson, about Z290, pedestal, south side of Main - *I was waiting till the limousine got into full view at about right angles [to his camera's eye], but the shot rang out just before. I wasn't quite ready, but I had my finger on, and I had enough pressure on it so when the shot rang out . . . I instinctively jumped [flinched] and snapped it [the Z227 photo] at the same time, and that's the reason you will notice that the picture is a little blurred up and down.* Richard Trask interview, 11/23/85, cited in Trask, 1994 p. 283.

Notes: At Z177 the president was about 247 feet away from Bronson and about 140 feet from the sniper. With the bullet traveling 2,000 feet per second and shock waves and sound traveling at 1125 feet per second, it would take the shock waves about 0.29 second to reach him and create camera movement. This is six Z frames putting the expected impact for a shot fired at Z221 exactly at Z227. See Figures 34 and 35.

11: Key First Shot Witness Testimony

Phil Willis, about Z150, curb, south side of Elm - *(1) Willis advised that just about the same time that the limousine carrying President Kennedy was opposite the Stemmons Freeway road sign, he heard a loud report and knew immediately it was a rifle shot and knew also the shot had hit.* FBI interview, 6/18/64 (CD 1245). *(2) That picture [the Z201 photo/Willis photo # 7] was made at the very instant that the first shot was fired . . . In fact, the shot caused me to squeeze the camera shutter, and I got a picture of the president as he was hit with the first shot . . . As a matter of fact, the fellow standing on the ledge [Zapruder] under the right-hand corner of the Stemmons Highway sign . . . his pictures . . . showed that at this instant [Z201] he had already grabbed his throat . . . You see the highway sign that he has the rear of [at Z226] . . . I have the front of [at Z201] . . . It proves without question that at this instant [Z201] the president had been hit.* WC interview, 7/22/64 (WRv.7Hpp.493-94).

Notes: I concluded the Willis photo was taken at Z201 based on my own sightline analysis using Z film images and a scaled drawing of the limo. At Z223 the president was about 70 feet past Willis. Allowing three Z frames for reaction time based on Wiegman's who about the same distance, Willis' claim that the sound of the first shot caused him to squeeze the camera shutter would equate to it being fired at about Z197. His statement is considered rationalization and is therefore disregarded. He squeezed the shutter very close to the time of the sound of the shot and reasonably assumed the sound had an effect. Supporting this conclusion is that Willis' claim seems to have arisen from his over-simplified and incorrect sightline comparison of the position of the Stemmons Freeway sign from his perspective at Z201 versus Zapruder's at Z226. See Figure 55.

Key-motorcade-eyewitness testimony to the first shot

Figure 52 shows the location of the ear/eyewitnesses covered in this section.

At Z152, the president's car, closely followed by the motorcycle escort and Queen Mary, had just completed the left turn off Houston onto Elm and was heading down hill toward the triple underpass. The rear seat of the limo was slightly past the middle of the TSBD where the row of spectators lining the curb on the south side of Elm abruptly ended and the sparsely occupied grass infield began. This point is about 65 feet west of a point in the middle of the intersection extending from the edge of the curb on the west side of Houston. The president was almost directly in front of picture takers Willis and Croft, who were standing where the sidewalk ends on the south side of Elm. The Queen Mary was directly in front of the middle of the TSBD proper.

At Z221 the rear seat of the limo was about 150 feet west on Elm as determined above. The presidential limo had just passed the Thornton Freeway sign where the grassy knoll begins and was opposite the sparsely occupied grass infield on the south side of Elm. The president had just passed north-of-Elm spectator Jean Newman and was directly in front of the Calvary/Westbrook/Dishong group. The Queen Mary was in front of the Thornton Freeway sign.

Five in the presidential limo

Agent William Greer, driver - *(1) The president's automobile was almost past this building and I was looking at the overpass that we were about to pass under in case someone was on top of it, when I heard what I thought was a backfire of what I thought was a motorcycle behind the president's automobile. . . .* Undated signed report (WRv.18Hp.723). *(2) Well, when we were going down Elm Street I heard a noise that I thought was a backfire of one of the motorcycle policemen . . .* WC interview, 3/9/64 (WRv.2Hp.117).

Notes - The Zapruder film images confirm that Greer paid no heed to the first shot until looking back toward the governor from Z280 to Z289 at the time Kellerman was turning back to the front and advising him they were hit and to get out of there. Kellerman specifically told Greer that the first shot wounded the president.

Agent Roy Kellerman, right-front seat - *As we turned off Houston onto Elm ... there was a sign on the side of the road [Thornton Freeway sign] ... we no more than passed that and you are out in the open, and there is a report which rang like a firecracker pop ... and as I turned my head to the right to view whatever it was or see whatever it was, I heard a voice from the back seat...* WC testimony, 3/9/64 (WRv.2Hp.73).

Note: Kellerman turned and looked back at the president from Z240 to Z270.

First Lady Jacqueline Kennedy, left-rear seat - *So I was looking to the left. I guess there was a noise, but it didn't seem any different noise really because there is so much noise, motorcycles and things. But then suddenly Governor Connally was yelling, "oh, no, no, no."* .. WC testimony, 6/5/64 (WRv.5Hp.180).

Note: Ms. Kennedy was looking ahead to the right but to the left of the president from about Z220 to Z246.

Nellie Connally, left jump seat - *When we got past this area [of heavy crowds on Elm], I did turn to the president, and said "Mr. President, you can't say that Dallas doesn't love you ..." it seems to me very soon that I heard ... a frightening noise, and it came from the right. I turned over my right shoulder and looked back and saw the president as he had both hands at his neck....* WC testimony, 4/21/64 (WRv.4Hp.147).

Note: Ms. Connally turned and looked back at the president a few seconds before the first shot from about Z170 to Z200. She turned to look back at the president after the first shot commencing Z230.

John Connally, right jump seat - *(1) And then we had just turned the corner, we heard a shot; I turned to my left. I was sitting in the jump seat. I turned to my left to look in the back seat. The president had slumped.* Martin Agronski interview at Parkland Hospital, 11/27/63, transcript obtained from National Archives, record number 180-10098-10246. *(2) After rounding the corner at Elm and Houston, we ... had gone, I guess, 150 feet, maybe 200 feet, I don't recall how far it was, heading down to get on the freeway ... when I heard what I thought was a shot, I instinctively turned to my right because the sound appeared to come from over my right shoulder ... and I saw nothing unusual except just people in the crowd, but I did not catch the president in the corner of my eye .... so ... failing to see him .... I was turning to look back over my left shoulder into the back seat, but I never got that far in my turn.... I felt like someone had hit me in the back....* WC testimony, 4/21/64 (WRv.4Hpp.132-33).

Notes - The Zapruder film images show the president and governor grimacing and exhibiting concurrent involuntary right-arm and shoulder movements commencing at about Z223 while confirming that the governor first appears to feel the painful effects of the shot at about Z234 almost two-thirds-of-a-second after the bullet entered the limo at Z223.

Also consistent with his WC testimony, the governor by all appearances made an initial failed attempt to turn and look back at the president over his left shoulder from Z230 through Z239. Commencing Z240 he then made a concerted and successful effort to look back at the president over his right shoulder by leaning back and swiveling in his seat.

The trajectory analyses performed here and by the WC, HSCA, and other assassination researchers reveals that the bullet passing back to front through the president at Z223 was on course to cause the wounds to the governor's right side and chest. See Figures 69, 70, 74, and 95.

Four motorcycle-escort police

Officer Bobby Hargis, off left-front fender of Queen Mary at Z150-220 - *... so I was next to Mrs. Kennedy when I heard the first shot, and at that time the president bent over, and Governor Connally turned around .... a real shocked and surprised expression on his face ...* WC deposition, 4/8/64 (WRv.6Hp.294).

Notes - The Zapruder film images confirm that Hargis turned his head from looking forward to looking to the right commencing Z230 and that he was looking toward the president and governor from Z235 to Z275.

11: Key First Shot Witness Testimony

The governor commenced swiveling around in his seat to look back over his right shoulder toward the president at Z240.

Officer B.J. Martin, off left-front fender of Queen Mary at Z150-220 - *Yes sir; I heard a shot.... I looked back to my right... at the building on the right there [TSBD].... I looked at the president after I heard the first shot and he was leaning forward. I could see the left side of his face. At the time he had no expression on his face.* WC deposition, 4/3/64 (WRv.6Hpp.290-91).

Notes - The Zapruder film images confirm that Martin turned his head from looking forward to looking to the right commencing Z230 and that he was looking toward the president and governor from Z235 to Z275.

Officer James Chaney, off right-front fender of Queen Mary from Z150-220 - *We heard the first shot. I thought it was a motorcycle backfiring, and, uh, I looked back over to my left and also President Kennedy looked back over his left shoulder...* Recording of Bill Lord interview broadcast on WFAA-TV, 11/22/63, cited in Trask, 1998, pp. 155 and 119.

Notes - The Zapruder film images and the Altgens Z253 photo confirm that Chaney turned his head from looking forward to looking to the left presumably commencing Z230 and that he was looking into the limo as of Z253. The president started slumping to his left at Z245.

Officer D.L. Jackson, off right-front fender of Queen Mary from Z150-220 - *... we turned west on Elm Street: drove only a short way traveling very slowly. About that time I heard what I thought was a car backfire and I looked around and then into the president's car.* Quoted from a hand-written diary Jackson reportedly wrote the night of 11/22/63, cited in Savage, 1993, pp. 362-63.

Notes: The Willis Z201 photo shows all four motorcycle-escort police including Jackson looking pretty much straight ahead. He presumably started looking around in alarm at Z230 concurrent with the other alarmed members of the presidential entourage. See Figure 55.

Eight in the Queen Mary

Agent Sam Kinney, driver - *As we completed the left turn and on a short distance, there was a shot.... I saw the president lean toward the left and appeared to have grabbed his chest with his right hand.* Written report, 11/22/63 (WRv.18Hp.732).

Note for all the occupants of the Queen Mary that mention this movement: the president started leaning to his left with his elbows splayed commencing Z245.

Agent Emory Roberts, right-front seat - *12:30 p.m.: first of three shots fired at which time I saw the president lean toward Mrs. Kennedy...* Written statement, 11/29/63 (WRv.18Hp.734).

Agent Clint Hill, front-left running board - *On the left-hand side was a grass area with a few people scattered along observing the motorcade passing, and I was visually scanning these people when I heard a noise similar to a firecracker. The sound came from my right rear and I immediately moved my head in that direction. In so doing, my eyes had to cross the presidential automobile and I saw the president hunch forward and slump to his left...* Written statement, 11/30/63 (WRv.18Hp.742).

Note: Hill started turning his head to the left commencing Z230.

Agent William McIntyre, rear-left running board - *... the first shot was fired, followed in quick succession by two more. I would estimate that all three shots were fired within 5 seconds...* Written statement, 11/29/63 (WRv.18Hp.747).

Note: McIntyre's testimony is not considered relevant because it is not specific enough.

John Ready, 36-year-old secret service agent on the right running board of the presidential follow-up car (3rd car in motorcade) in front of fellow-agent Landis - . . . *After the initial shot I attempted to locate the area from where they had come from but I was not able to.* Written statement 11/22/63 (WRv.18Hp.750).

Note: In an undated report, Ready stated "I immediately turned to my right rear" (WRv.18Hp.749).

Agent Paul Landis, rear-right running board - . . . *the president's car and the follow-up car had just completed their turns and both were straightening out. At this moment I heard what sounded like the report of a high-powered rifle from behind me, over my right shoulder. My first glance was at the president as I was practically looking in his direction anyway. I saw him moving in a manner which I thought was to look in the direction of the sound . . . I immediately turned my gaze over my right shoulder, toward the modernistic building [TSBD] I had observed before.* Written statement, 11/27/63 (WRv.18Hp.758).

Note: The Zapruder film images and the Altgens Z253 photo confirm that Landis and Agent Ready who was standing next to him turned their heads from looking forward to the right rear presumably commencing Z230.

Kenneth O'Donnell, 39-year-old WW-II veteran, left jump seat of the presidential follow-up car (3rd car in motorcade), (special assistant to president) - *We turned, I remember the overpass. And then the shots occurred-which at that time I did not know were shots. My first impression was it was a firecracker. And then someone said "he has been hit," or I noticed the slump. He had been waving out the right side of the car, and I noticed him slump toward Mrs. Kennedy, and I realized then that they had been shots. But as fast as that realization occurred, I saw the last shot hit. . . .* WC deposition, 5/18/64 (WRv.7Hp.447).

Note: O'Donnell's testimony is not considered relevant because it is not specific enough.

Presidential Aide David Powers, right jump seat - *We then turned off Main Street onto Houston and made the sharp swing to the left up Elm. . . . Shortly thereafter the first shot went off and it sounded as if it were a firecracker. I noticed then that the president moved quite far to his left . . . .* Written statement, 5/18/64 (WRv.7Hp.473).

Agent George Hickey, left-rear seat - *Just prior to the shooting, the presidential car turned left at the intersection and started down an incline toward an underpass followed by 679X. After a very short distance I heard a loud report which sounded like a firecracker. . . . I stood up and looked to my right and rear in an attempt to identify it . . . .* Written statement, 11/30/63 (WRv.18Hp.762).

Note - The Zapruder film images and the Altgens Z253 photo confirm that Hickey turned his head from looking forward to the right rear presumably commencing Z230.

Agent Glen Bennett, right-rear seat - *The president's auto moved down a slight grade and the crowd [on the right side of Elm] was very sparse. I heard a noise that immediately reminded me of a firecracker. I immediately upon hearing the supposed firecracker looked at the boss's car. At this exact time I saw a shot that hit the boss about 4-inches down from his right shoulder; a second shot followed immediately and hit the right-rear high of the president's head.* Hand-written report, 11/22/63 (WRv.24Hp.542).

Notes - Bennett testified that he thought the first shot missed given that he "saw" a bullet hit the president in the upper back. This testimony is in conflict with the photographic evidence showing him bent over looking toward the right out over the grassy knoll from Z201 to Z253. It is also in conflict with his recollection that the first shot sounded when the crowds had thinned on the north side of Elm, which commences at about Z230. In reporting he "saw" the second shot hit the president in the back, he presumably saw a bloody area on the president's upper back when he came into view at about Z320 at the tail end of his rearward head snap. He would have gotten the impression that the Z313 bullet's impact drove him forward.

11: Key First Shot Witness Testimony

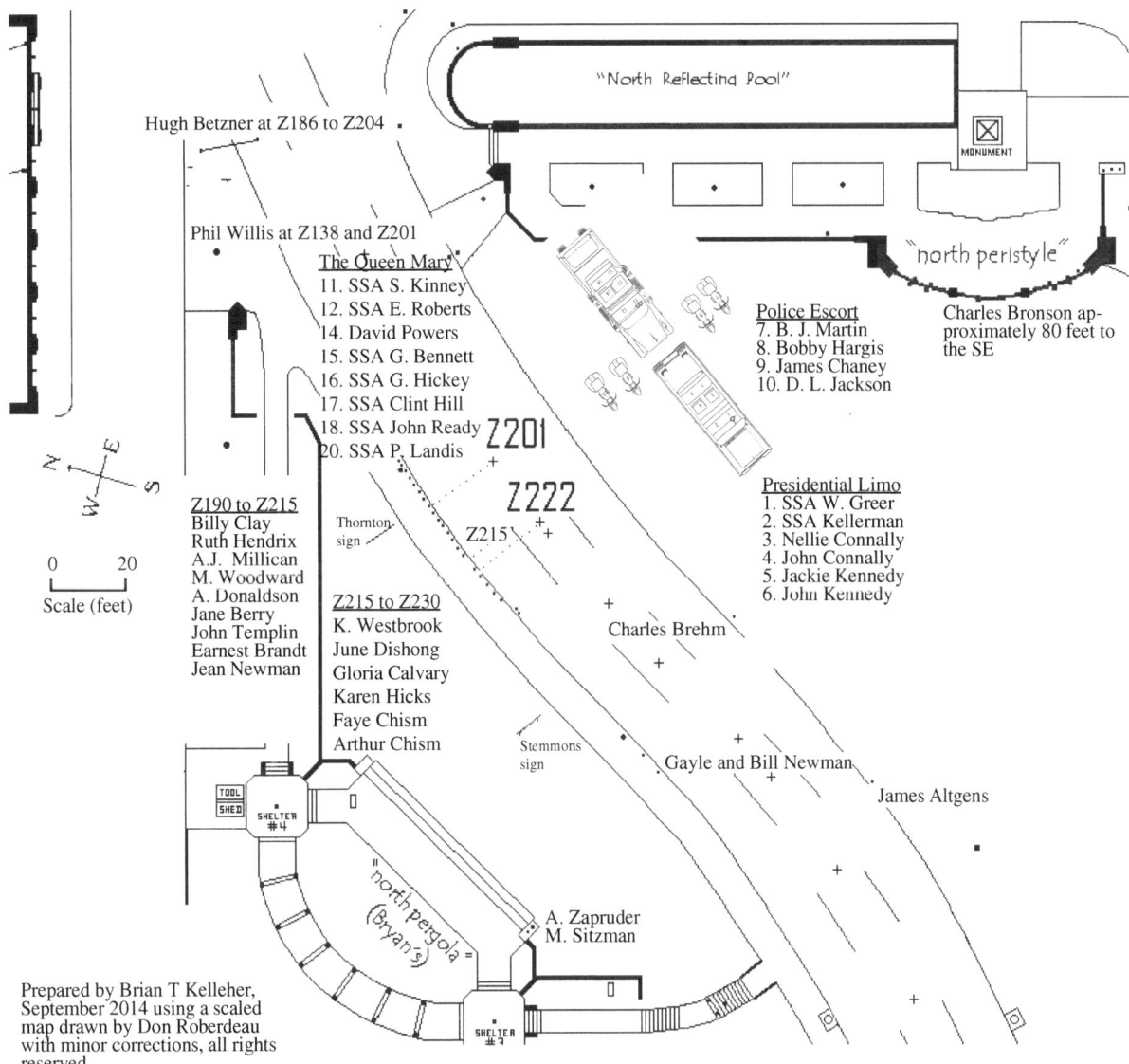

Figure 52

Key first-shot witness locations - This group includes twenty four stationary ear/eyewitness located within 100 feet of the president as of Z223 and seventeen of the twenty members of the presidential entourage. The individual and collective key-witness testimony coupled with the photographic evidence provides compelling proof that the first shot struck the president at Z223 just after the presidential limo passed the Thornton Freeway sign. I used Zapruder, Bronson and Nix sightlines to pinpoint most stationary witnesses' locations. I used the Willis Z201 photo for the Chisms. The drawing of the limo, Queen Mary and the police motorcycles is from Trask, 1994, page 63 and is enlarged relative to scale.

Frame 87 Dorman 3rd sequence showing Rosemary and Linda Willis running past key witness Howard Brennan.

Frame 105 Dorman 3rd sequence showing Linda coming to a stop as Rosemary continues on.

Z150 showing Rosemary still running and Linda with her hands cupped to her mouth presumably yelling at her sister to stop running.

Z178 showing Rosemary looking back toward Agent Hickey and/or her dad. Linda has lowered her hands.

Figure 53

Photographic evidence refuting a first-shot miss at Z151 - Dorman-third-sequence frame 87 shows 14-year-old Linda Willis and 10-year-old Rosemary Willis running past key witness Howard Brennan as they chased after their picture-taking father Phil Willis (not in view). Dorman third sequence frame 105 shows where Linda slowed to a stop when she came opposite her father's curb position while looking in his direction. She seems to have an Argus camera case strapped around her neck. Zapruder frames Z150 and Z178 collectively show that the left to right head turns between Z150 and Z175 by the president, the governor, and their first ladies were due to the line of spectators ending on the south side of Elm. Picture-taker Richard Croft is the last in line and is located at the point the president passed at Z160. Frame Z150 further shows Linda with her hands to her mouth in megaphone fashion, presumably shouting at Rosemary to stop running. Frame Z178 further shows Secret Service Agent George Hickey leaning his head in Rosemary's direction from his position in the left-rear seat of the Queen Mary. By all appearances, he is admonishing her to stop running. Note that as of Z150 Hickey appears to be shooing Phil Willis off the curb and that Rosemary is looking toward them both at Z178. These are cropped images that I photo edited to increase brightness and contrast (Elsie Dorman Collection and Zapruder Family Collection/The Sixth Floor Museum at Dealey Plaza http://www.jfk.org).

11: Key First Shot Witness Testimony

Figure 54
The Betzner Z186 photo of the presidential limo and Queen Mary heading west down Elm - This photo was taken two seconds before the first shot rang out. Despite appearances, the presidential limo is still approaching the Thornton Freeway sign and the president is about to come opposite the first lamppost and the Mary Woodward group, who are obstructed from view by Agents Ready and Landis. Zapruder and Sitzman are in view in the background just to the right of the Stemmons Freeway sign and the so-called "Black Dog Man" is peering over the end of the masonry wall extending to camera left of the sign. Of the six occupants of the presidential limo, only the president is in view and he is looking forward-right toward the Calvary/Westbrook/Dishong group who, from Betzner's vantage point, are standing in front of the right side of the Stemmons sign. Seven of the ten occupants of the Queen Mary are in clear view and appear very much on alert. Just one of the four motorcycle policemen are in view (Jackson). Hugh Betzner, via Mary Ferrill Foundation.

Figure 55

The Phil Willis Z201 photo of the presidential limo and Queen Mary heading west down Elm - This photo was taken just one second before the first shot rang out. Despite appearances, the presidential limo is still approaching the Stemmons Freeway sign and the president has just come opposite the Thornton Freeway sign and a group of a half dozen or so TSBD female employees that included key first-shot witness Jane Berry. From right to left on the north side of Elm, the following other key first and second shot witnesses are in view among others: A.J. Millican; the Mary Woodward group; Earnest Brandt, John Templin, the last of the Calvary/Westbrook/Dishong group, the Chisms, Umbrella Man, F. Lee Mudd, Cheryl McKinnon, Peggy Burney, the Newmans, Flying Tackle Man and Red Shirt Man. The fact that Emmett Hudson is not in view standing next to Flying Tackle Man suggests that he is the shadowy figure that resembles a black dog who is behind the end of the masonry wall, and that he was heading down the stairs to get a closer view. More likely, Hudson is obstructed from view by the second lamppost and the small sign bolted to it. Zapruder and Sitzman are in view in the background just to the right of the Stemmons Freeway sign and the Hesters are in view on the opposite side of the pergola. Four of the six occupants of the presidential limo are in view including the president and his wife who are both looking forward-right toward the Chisms who, from Willis' vantage point, are standing in front of the Stemmons sign. Eight of the ten occupants of the Queen Mary are in clear view and appear very much on alert. Three of the four motorcycle policemen are in view (Martin, Hargis and Jackson). In comparing the unchanged positions of the presidential entourage in the Z186 Betzner and Z201 Willis photos which were taken about a second apart, we see no indications of any reactions to gunshot noise. Phil Willis Collection/The Sixth Floor Museum at Dealey Plaza http://www.jfk.org.

Chapter 12
Key Witness Testimony for the Final Two Shots

In Chapters 2 through 7 we covered the photographic evidence of shot-noise-induced human-reflex reactions for members of the presidential entourage that revealed shots fired at Z310 and Z328. Accordingly, we used the following motorcade witness groups/populations as corroborating ear/eyewitnesses in order of relative importance expecting and finding close correlation: (1) the five surviving occupants of the presidential limo; (2) the four motorcycle officers flanking the rear of the presidential limo; and (3) the ten occupants of the presidential follow-up car, collectively the presidential entourage. There are nineteen in this motorcade group.

There is just one stationary ear/eyewitness group that merits prime-status ranking relating to the question of exactly where the president was located on Elm when the last two shots rang out and the effects of those shots (jolts and cranial eruptions). This group is comprised of the spectators on or opposite the grassy knoll who had a largely unobstructed view of the president from within 70 feet during the interval Z250 to Z370. It is further limited to those that provided timely testimony as to where the president was located when the last two shots rang out and their effects. There are twelve in this sub group: five on the south side of Elm and seven on the north. Beyond the above, there are six others, further distant, that testified to seeing the head shot who were well enough positioned to see the effects of the last two shots and provide timely credible testimony. There are a total of eighteen in this stationary witness group.

Figures 56 through 59 follow and relate to the ensuing discussions.

Conclusions

The overall testimony provided by thirty seven key witnesses to the second and third shots provides overwhelming support for the second shot causing the Z313 cranial explosion and a rapid-fire third-shot striking the president's head late in frame Z330 causing a jolt forward and a second jettison of brain matter from the open cranium. See summary in Chapter 1.

Uncertainty as to which of the shots hit the president's head - It goes without saying that, if the TSBD sniper fired a rapid-fire final shot at Z328 that caused a second cranial eruption at Z331 just one second after the first at Z313, there would be conflicting opinions or uncertainty among our key eyewitnesses as to which shot struck the president in the head. Given what we see in the Zapruder film images, we would expect those who witnessed just the Z313 explosion to describe the rearward head movement, the upward jettison of blood, and the unnatural movement of the president's scalp. We would expect those who witnessed just the Z330 eruption to describe the president's head and upper torso being driven forward and out of view amid the forward and rearward jettisons of brain matter.

Just seven of the key eyewitnesses described the Z313 cranial eruption - The Z313 cranial eruption was seen primarily by north-of-Elm (grassy knoll) witnesses including from east to west: John Templin, Bill and Gayle Newman, Zapruder, Sitzman, and Emmett Hudson. Charles Brehm and Marilyn Willis witnessed it from the south side of Elm and Officer James Foster from atop the triple underpass. Explaining why so few saw it: (1) the jettison could only be seen for 0.1 second; (2) the motion pictures of the limo under fire show that most members of the presidential entourage were not looking directly at the president at Z313; and (3) those witnesses who observed the rearward head snap from behind the president were under the impression that he had simply straightened back up in his seat (see testimony of Jean Hill, Hargis and Hickey).

Nine key eyewitnesses to the Z330/331 cranial eruption - The following key witnesses were looking directly at the president's head from relatively close proximity at Z330/Z331 and individually and collectively testified in so many words that as the final shot rang out, they witnessed a cranial eruption when he was positioned as he appears at Zapruder frames Z330 to Z342 rather than Z313 through Z325: south-of-Elm *AP* photographer James Altgens, Motorcycle-Escort Officers Hargis and Chaney, Secret Service Agents George Hickey, Clint Hill, Paul Landis, William McIntyre and Emory Roberts; and Aide Kenneth O'Donnell. I would have included Toni Foster (The Running Woman) here, if she had provided her testimony of witnessing the rearward jettison of brain matter with the final shot in a timelier basis. She did not come forward until 1996 (interview with Deborah Conway, 1996, *Kennedy Assassination Chronicles Magazine*, Summer 2000, Vol. 6, Issue 2).

Testimony of Secret Service Agent Glen Bennett concerning the second shot that was disregarded for just cause - Agent Bennett was in the passenger side of the elevated rear seat of the Queen Mary with a clear view of the president, but only when he was sitting straight up and facing forward. He dubiously testified that he "saw" the second shot hit the president in the back. This testimony is disregarded because it is not only impossible for Bennett to have seen a bullet traveling at 1,900 feet per second hit the president in the back, but also because his claim is refuted by the photographic evidence. The Betzner Z186, Willis Z201 and Altgens Z253 photos collectively reveal that Bennett was not looking in the president's direction at Z223 when we know he received the bullet in his upper back (see Chapter 11). Correlating the collective photographic evidence with his testimony, Bennett who was bent over looking hard to the right of his car as of Z186 and Z201 apparently spent about 5 seconds looking around trying to determine the source of the shot. With the president's upper back finally in view at about Z320 after he straightened up in the seat, Bennett apparently saw a bloody spot on the president's back at the tail end of his rearward head snap. He would have gotten the impression the Z310 shot hit the president in the back and knocked him forward. He then raised his eyes and saw the president's bloodied head driven forward amidst jettisons of forward and rearward brain matter just as the Z328 final shot rang out.

Resolving the perplexing testimony of the Connallys - With respect to the governor, first and foremost as mentioned in Chapter 11, the governor testified that he was heavily influenced by the unwavering opinion and sworn testimony of his wife Nellie. She was adamant that she looked back in response to the first shot noise and saw president Kennedy with his hands to his neck just before her husband was shot nearly dead by a second shot. Also, of critical significance is that the governor testified under oath to the WC that he lost consciousness just after he heard the Z310 shot hit the president in the head. The Z-film images confirm this. They show him slamming his head into a metal bar atop the front seatback at Z324 in completing his frantic lunge forward and then collapsing, left-shoulder-first, onto his wife as if unconscious by from Z325 to Z332. If Governor Connally had heard all three shots, there would have been no doubt in his mind that he and the president were both struck by the first shot.

12: Key Second and Third Shot Witness Testimony

Correlating Ms. Connally's testimony to the Zapruder-film images, and recognizing she was looking away from the president during and after the points his head exploded at Z313 and Z330, it is obvious that at the time of the shooting Ms. Connally, for every good reason, thought the president was hit in the head by the shot that she heard at Z330 and was under the mistaken impression that her husband had been shot near-dead by the shot she heard at Z313. The frantic movements and shouting she described as occurring in the immediate aftermath of the second shot occurs from Z295 to Z324 during which time the governor spun to his right and lunged forward while shouting, "Oh my God, they are going to kill us all."

From Ms. Connally's contemporary diary prepared within a few weeks of the event and published in her book *From Love Field* (2003) p. 164 - *John had turned to the right at the first shot to look back to see the president. and had then wheeled to the left to get another look, realized the president had been shot, said, "no, no, no," was hit himself by a second shot [the Z310 shot], and said, "My God, they are going to kill us all," wheeled back to the right, crumpling his shoulders to his knees in the most helpless and pitiful position a tall big man could be in [from Z316 to Z327].*

From Ms. Connally's 1978 interview by the HSCA - *. . . [Describing the governor's reaction to the Z310 second shot and how she herself reacted] he lunged forward [from Z316 to Z324] and then just kind of collapsed [from Z325 to Z339]. . . . I thought he was dead. When you see a big man totally defenseless like that, then you do whatever you think you can do to help the most and the only thing I could think of to do was to pull him down out of the line of fire [from Z316 to Z332].*

From Ms. Connally's televised live interview with Larry King aired November 22, 2003 - *"What did the third one do?" Nellie: "Well, I couldn't see because I had the weight [from Z327 to Z332]. I had pulled John over on my lap [from Z316 to Z332] to get him out of the line of fire. And I couldn't move.*

It is further evident that Ms. Connally was unaware that the Z313 shot hit the president in the head because of the timing in which she was showered with the fallout of brain matter. According to the collective testimony of Ms. Connally and Agent Kellerman, the raining down of brain matter occurred in the jump seat and front seat commencing at about Z331. Remarkably, though no one seems to have noticed, the Zapruder, Nix and Muchmore film images actually show Ms. Connally being showered with a spray of brain matter during the interval Z331 through Z337. See Figures 7, 8, 27, 28, 31 and 32. The film images corroborate her testimony that she felt the impact.

From Ms. Connally's contemporary diary prepared within a few weeks of the event and published in her book *From Love Field* (2003) p. 164 - *I reached over and pulled him to me and tried to get us both down in the car [from Z316 to Z332]. Then came a third shot with John in my arms and still trying to stay down [from Z330 to Z332]. I did not see the third shot hit, but I felt something falling all over me [from Z331 to Z337]. My sensation was of spent buckshot. My eyes saw bloody matter in tiny bits all over the car [commencing Z331]. John was bleeding badly all over the front of his shirt. He was not moving in my arms. I thought my husband was dead [he was unconscious when the final shot arrived].*

From Ms. Connally's 1978 interview by the HSCA - *. . . Then, I heard a third shot [the Z328 shot] and felt matter cover us [from Z331 to Z337] . . . I heard three shots and had three reactions, three separate reactions. The first shot [the Z221 shot], then I looked and saw the president; the second shot [the Z310 shot], John; and third [the Z328 shot], all this matter all over us."*

From Ms. Connally's televised live interview with Larry King aired November 22, 2003 - *. . . I couldn't move. But I heard the third shot [the Z328 shot] and then bloody matter, like buck shot, little pieces were all over the interior of the car, all over our clothes.*

Contributing to the illusion that the president was struck in the head just by the Z328 shot was the fact that he did not begin his final collapse forward until Z333 just after the Z328 shot rang out. In fact, the president was starting his final collapse about the same time Ms. Connally was lunging her upper body toward the center of the car in response to the sound and effects of the final shot.

Collectively, this fully explains the perplexing testimony of the Connallys. Ms. Connally's testimony, in particular, provides very compelling proof that a third shot entered the limo at Z330 and hit the president in the head for a second time. Ms. Connally's diary entries confirm her husband was unconscious as the final shot arrived consistent with what the governor told the WC.

Key stationary ear/eyewitness testimony to the second and third shots
(Figure 56)

Seven along the north side of Elm from Z250 to Z370

F. Lee Mudd, about Z250, curb north side of Elm near the umbrella man and Stemmons Freeway sign, owner Southside Ranch Clothing Store, Shreveport, LA - *When the president's car was some 50 or more feet away from him [past him], he heard what sounded like two gunshots, and he saw the president slump [commencing at Z333]. Immediately thereafter, he observed the president's car pull out of the line of the parade and continue west on Elm toward the underpass. When the president's car came abreast of Mudd [at about Z250], he could see the president slumped down toward his wife, who was leaning over him. He recalled seeing another man in the car whom he did not recognize at the time but whom he later learned was Governor Connally and this man appeared to be holding one arm to his side. However, he did not notice this man much because his attention was focused on the president. Mr. Mudd stated he definitely recalls hearing two shots probably less than a second apart. He said there may have been a third shot fired, but he could not be sure of this. He stated that immediately after the shots were fired, some of the spectators along the side of the street dropped to the ground, and he did so himself insomuch as the shots alarmed him and he did not know what had happened or where the shots had come from.* FBI interview, 11/24/64 (WRv.24Hp.538).

Notes - Mudd only recalled hearing the rapid-fire Z310 and Z328 shots. He was unsure if he heard the Z221 shot. Mudd's location on Elm is evident from his testimony. His head and/or raised right arm are visible in Zapruder frames Z226 through Z243. He is visible in the Bronson Z227 photo standing near Umbrella Man. Mudd was about 50 feet from the president at Z313. Except for his having difficulty specifically recalling the sound of the Z221 shot, his testimony when properly interpreted correlates closely with the Z221/310/328 sequence. Several post-assassination films and photos confirm his testimony that he hit the ground after the shots and was sitting for a period at the edge of the sidewalk next to the Umbrella Man. See Figure 59.

Peggy Burney, about Z285, curb north side of Elm, Dal Tex Building/Zapruder employee - *I was standing at the curb on Elm about a third the way from Houston Street near the overpass.... The car had passed about 15 feet beyond me when I heard the first shot. I did not realize it was a shot: I thought it was a backfire. The president ducked.... Then I heard a second shot. I noticed that Jackie didn't duck. The car momentarily stopped [slowed] then veered slightly to the right and speeded off.... Everyone realized the shots were coming from up high.... My employer, Mr. Zapruder was making a movie at the time it happened.* Castleberry, "I Saw Him Die Woman Cries," Dallas Times Herald, 11/23/63. Castleberry identifies herself as the author in an interview by Hugh Aynesworth, moderator, 11/20/93, cited in Hlavach and Payne, Reporting the Kennedy Assassination, 1996, p. 55.

Notes - Like Mudd, Burney only recalled hearing the rapid-fire Z310 and Z328 shots. Her location on Elm is evident from her testimony and is consistent with the location of the rest of Zapruder's employees. She is visible in the Bronson Z227 photo standing to camera left of a streetlight pole near the Newmans. She also can be seen in the Wiegman first sequence running down the sidewalk in his direction. Like Mudd, she did not recall hearing the first shot ring out. About 3 or 4 o'clock that afternoon, she gave an eyewitness account via telephone to her cousin Vivian Castleberry, a reporter for the *Dallas Times Herald*.

12: Key Second and Third Shot Witness Testimony

Gayle Newman, about Z295, curb north side of Elm - *. . . the car was just up a piece from us and this shot fired out and I thought it was a firecracker. And the president kind of raised up in his seat . . . . And all of a sudden, this next one pops and Governor Connally grabbed his stomach and kind of laid over to the side [from Z316 to Z324] and then another one, it was all so fast, and President Kennedy reached up and it looked like he grabbed his ear and blood started gushing out . . . It was just right by us when it all happened, just right in front of us . . .* Video tape of live TV interview by Jay Watson, WFAA TV, at about 1:20 p.m., 11/22/63, "The Story Behind the Story," Belo Interactive, 2003, DVD, track 8.

Notes - The last two shots rang out immediately after the president passed them. The sightlines show that the Newmans had an unobstructed view of the president and governor at Z221 and Z310 and continuing on until about Z325 when Motorcycle-Officers Chaney and Jackson began partially obstructing their views of the presidential limo as they passed within 5 to 10 feet of them. Based on her testimony, her eyes were drawn back and forth between the president and governor during this interval. In the Nix film, Gayle is looking into the limo at the equivalent of Z290 to Z317 when she disappears from view to camera right. Except for the fact that she, like Ms. Connally and Aide David Powers, fell under the impression that the governor was struck by the Z310 shot, her testimony correlates strongly with the Z221/310/328 sequence. See Figure 59.

Bill Newman, about Z300, curb, north side of Elm - *The president's car was some 50 feet still in front of us coming toward us when we heard the first shot and the president jumped up in his seat. I thought it scared him . . . And as the car got directly in front of us, well a gunshot apparently from behind us hit the president in the side of the temple . . . I don't recall a third shot . . .* Recording of live TV interview by Jay Watson, WFAA TV, at about 1:10 p.m., 11/22/63, "The Story Behind the Story," Belo Interactive, 2003, DVD, track 7.

Notes - In the version of the Nix film contained in *Discovery Channel's* Death in Dealey Plaza, Mr. Newman is visible through Z339. Between Z321 and Z333 he turns slightly to his left and crouches. From Z334 to Z339 he spins to his left and as he disappears from view appears to be reaching down to gather up his child. He was looking at the president at Z313 but not at Z330. Except for the fact that he could not specifically recall the sounds of both of the last two rapid-fire shots, his testimony correlates strongly with the Z221/310/328 sequence.

Marilyn Sitzman about Z313, pergola, north side of Elm - *I heard the first shot . . . he slumped over in his seat . . . second shot hit pres right in the temple.* Darwin Payne, *Dallas Times Herald reporter telephoned notes tear sheets, November 22, 1963, Sixth Floor Museum and interview by the Sixth Floor Museum's Oral History Program, 1996.*

Note - Except for her not recalling hearing a third shot, Ms. Sitzman's testimony correlates strongly with the Z221/310/328 sequence.

Abraham Zapruder, about Z313, concrete pedestal, north side of Elm - *(1) . . . M. heard three shots. After first one president slumped over and grabbed stomac . . . two more shots looked like head opened up . . . Jackie first reached over to the president and after second shot . . . she crawled over to back of car . . .* Interview by Darwin Payne, *Dallas Times Herald, 11/22/63*, photocopy of notes found within the Dallas Times Herald photographic collection by Trask in 1992, cited in Trask, 1998, p. 149. *(2) I thought I heard two, it could be three, because to my estimate I thought he was hit [in the head] on the second I really don't know. . . . I never even heard a third shot. . . . I thought it came from behind me. . . . I have no way of determining which direction the bullet was going [from the sound]. . . . There was an echo that gave me sound all over.* WC interview, 7/22/64 (WRv.7Hp.571-72).

Notes - Zapruder was about 70-feet north of the president at Z310 with a completely unobstructed view of the two head shots. Zapruder's earliest testimony correlates exactly with the Z221/310/328 sequence and is considered most relevant. The severe blurring at Z331-332 explains why he did recall seeing a second cranial eruption. Allowing for his subsequent uncertainty as to whether he heard a third shot just before Ms. Kennedy started climbing onto the trunk, his testimony is still considered strongly supportive. Zapruder's lingering doubt as to whether he heard the Z328 shot presumably stems from the fact that his employees Sitzman, Burney, Beatrice Hester and her husband Charles could only recall two.

Emmett Hudson, about Z370, concrete steps, north side of Elm - *The first shot rung out and, of course, I didn't realize it was a shot, what was taking place right at that present time, and when the second one rung out, the motorcade done got further on down Elm, and you see, I was trying to get a good look at President Kennedy. I happened to be looking right at him when that bullet hit him, the second shot. Yes, it looked like it hit him somewhere along about a little bit behind the ear and a little above the ear. . . . when that third shot rung out . . . I was close to the ground . . .* WC deposition 7/22/64 (WRv.7Hp.559-60).

Notes - The sightlines show that Hudson, from his elevated position, had an unobstructed view of the president for all three shots. Hudson who was standing on the steps next to Flying Tackle Man is just starting to run up the stairs at the time he and Red Shirt Man come into Nix's view from N063 to N092 (Z353-82). Red Shirt Man has also just started running but has tripped over Hudson's foot and is beginning to fall as he disappears from view. Hudson is still on his feet as of Z382 refuting his testimony that he heard the final shot when he was close to the ground. Except for his faulty recollection of when he fell to the ground, his testimony correlates exactly with the Z221/310/328 sequence.

Five along the south side of Elm from Z280 to Z355

Charles Brehm, about Z280, just off the curb, south side of Elm - *(1) [after witnessing the president's dramatic reaction to the first shot]. . a few seconds later the second shot rang out and he just absolutely went down in the seat of the car . . . there was a third shot that went and by that time I had grabbed my little 5-year-old boy and ran away from the scene of the thing. . . .* Radio interview at curb about 12:35-45 p.m., November 22, 1963. *(2) When the president's automobile was very close to him and he could see the president's face very well, the president was seated, but was leaning forward when he stiffened perceptibly at the same instant what appeared to be a rifle shot sounded. According to Brehm the president seemed to stiffen and come to a pause when another shot sounded and the president appeared to be badly hit in the head. Brehm said when the president was hit by the second shot, he could notice the president's hair fly up, and then roll over to his side [commencing Z331] . . . Brehm said a third shot followed . . .* FBI interview 11/25/63 (WRv.22Hp.837). *(3) The third shot really frightened me! It had a completely different sound to it because it had really passed me, as anybody knows who has been down under targets in the Army or been shot at like I had been many times. You know when a bullet passes over you, due to the cracking sound it makes, and that bullet had an absolute crack to it. I do believe that shot was wild.* Larry Sneed interview, 1987, cited in Sneed, 1998, p. 61.

Notes - The 38-year-old World-War-II veteran and carpet salesman for Montgomery Ward was about 30-feet east of the president at Z310. The sightlines show he had an unobstructed view of the president's head at Z313, but could not see it at Z330 because Officers Martin and Hargis were in the way as well as Agent Hill. Brehm had substantial first-hand experience with the operation and sounds of WW-II vintage rifles and had been shot at and wounded himself as a member of the Ranger Battalions that participated in the D-Day invasion. For this reason, in voicing an opinion on the timing and effects of the three shots, Brehm along with Zapruder is aptly considered a preeminent ear/eyewitness.

Mary Moorman, about Z297, curb, south side of Elm - *As President Kennedy was opposite me I took a picture of him [the Z316 photo]. As I snapped the picture of President Kennedy, I heard a shot ring out. President Kennedy sort of slumped over. Then I heard another shot ring out and Mrs. Kennedy jumped up in the car and said "My God he has been shot" . . . I heard three or four shots in all.* Sheriff's Department interview, 11/22/63 (WRv.19Hp.487).

Notes - The Zapruder film shows Moorman was looking toward the president at Z313 through her viewfinder. The Nix and Muchmore films show she might have been looking at him at Z330. Moorman only clearly recalled hearing the rapid-fire Z310 and Z328 shots. From her excellent unobstructed vantage point, Moorman took her famous photo of the limo under fire at the equivalent of Z316 just after the president had

12: Key Second and Third Shot Witness Testimony

been struck in the head. Except for her not specifically recalling the sound of the Z221 shot and her mentioning the possibility of a fourth shot, her testimony correlates closely with the Z221/310/328 sequence. See Figure 57.

Jean Hill, about Z295, curb, south side of Elm - *The president's car came around the corner and it was over on our side of the street. Just as Mary Moorman started to take a picture [the Z316 photo], we were looking at the president and Jackie in the back seat.... Just as the president looked up toward us two shots rang out and I saw the president grab his chest and fall forward across Jackie's lap and she fell across his back and said, "My God, he has been shot." There was an instant pause between the first two shots and the motorcade seemingly halted for an instant and three or four more shots [presumably echoes] rang out.* Sheriff's Department interview, 11/22/63 (WRv.24Hp.212).

Notes - The Zapruder film shows that Hill was looking toward the president at Z313. The Nix and Muchmore films show she might have been looking at him at Z330. Like Moorman, Hill only clearly recalled hearing the rapid-fire Z310 and Z328 shots. Hill's recollections of the number of shots and where they came from evolved with time, so only her very earliest testimony is considered relevant. Frames Z288 through Z312 of the Zapruder film show Ms. Hill looking toward the president until he passed her at which point she began looking toward motorcycle officer Hargis. Hargis subsequently caught up to the president due to the slowing of the limo, allowing Hill to witness the president's head snapping back commencing at Z316. Except for her not specifically recalling the sound of the Z221 shot and identifying echoes as additional shots, her earliest testimony correlates closely with the Z221/310/328 sequence.

James Altgens, about Z350, curb, south side of Elm - *I made one picture [the Z253 photo] at the time I heard a noise that sounded like a firecracker... the shot was just a fraction ahead of my picture.... I wasn't keeping track of the number of pops that took place, but I could vouch for No. 1, and I can vouch for the last shot, but I cannot tell you how many shots were in between. There was not another shot fired after the president was struck in the head. That was the last shot, that much I will say with a great deal of certainty.... I was looking at the president, just as he was struck, it caused him to move a bit forward [commencing at Z331]. He seemed as if at the time, well, he was in a position, sort of immobile. He wasn't upright. He was at an angle but when it hit him, it seemed to have lodged, it seemed as if he were hung up on a seat button or something like that. It knocked him just enough forward that he came right on down [commencing at Z333]. There was flesh particles that flew out the side of his head in my direction so much so that it indicated to me that the shot came out of the left side of his head. Also . . . blood on his forehead or face ....* WC interview, 7/22/64 (WRv.7Hp.517-18).

Notes - The 44-year-old *AP* photographer was about 36 feet south of the slumped president at Z313 with his view obstructed by the Connallys and Ms. Kennedy. Altgens was about 25 feet south of the president at Z328 and had the stricken president in camera view from about Z325 to Z345 as the president was struck in the back of the head by the Z328 final shot. His testimony vividly and accurately describes what we see in the Zapruder film during this interval including a second cranial eruption spraying brain matter in his direction that landed on the Connallys. From this excellent vantage point on Elm directly opposite the grassy knoll, Altgens took his famous photo of the limo under fire at the equivalent of Z253. As he enters Zapruder's view at Z343, he is in the midst of a weak-kneed recoil supporting his lament that he was too shocked by the sound and effects of the final shot to operate the shutter of his camera. Although he did not specifically recall the sound of the Z310 shot and fell victim to the illusion that the final shot was the only shot that struck the president's head, his testimony correlates closely with the Z221/310/328 sequence. See Figure 58.

Malcolm Summers, about Z355, just off the curb, south side of Elm - *(1) The president's car had just come up in front of me when I heard a shot and saw the president slump down in the car and heard Mrs. Kennedy say "Oh no," then a second shot and then I hit the ground as I realized these were shots.* FBI interview, 11/23/63 (WRv.19Hp.500). *(2) The first reaction that I saw when the first shot was fired was the secret-service men kind of looking around and down at the people... I heard three shots all together and was standing practically right beside the car after he had already been hit just a few feet up above me there.... I'm not* *sure about which one hit him. . . . the second and third. . . . As to the spacing of the shots, there was much more time between the first one and the second two; the second and third, they were real close. . . . When the president got the head wound, he still hadn't come up to me yet. I was still looking directly at him. Then the third one, he was right beside me or something to that effect. I'd say when he got the head wound, I'm guessing that he would have been 10 to 12 feet away. And then the other one came, which led me to believe it was several people shooting rather than just one. . . . A lot of people question that they could do it that quickly, especially those last two shots. Certainly I had some doubt at that time that they were from the same gun because they were real close.* Larry Sneed interview, 1987, cited in Sneed, 1998 pp. 86 and 106-7.

Notes - The 39-year old Korean-War veteran was standing about 5-feet off the curb just to the west of picture-taker James Altgens. Summers was about 38-feet south of the slumping president as of Z310, but his view was largely if not completely obstructed by the Connallys and Ms. Kennedy. The president was about 20 feet from Summers when he passed by him at about Z350 and was lying face down on the rear seat completely out of his view. Summers comes into Zapruder's view at Z345 and between this point and when he disappears at Z361 he is dropping to the ground in unison with Ms. Kennedy crawling part way onto the presidential limo's trunk. His testimony correlates closely with the Z221/310/328 sequence.

Six others who testified to seeing the head shot

Hugh Betzner, about Z160, curb, south side of Elm near where the sidewalk ends at the edge of the grass infield - *I took another picture [the Z186 photo] as the president's car was going down the hill on Elm Street. I started to wind my film again and I heard a loud noise. . . . Then I ran around so I could look over the back of a monument and I either saw the following then or when I was standing back down on the corner of Elm Street. I cannot remember exactly where I was when I saw the following: I heard at least two shots fired and I saw what looked like a firecracker going off in the president's car. . . .* Dallas County Sheriff's Department statement, 11/22/63 (WRv.24Hp.200).

Notes - The 22-year-old railway-express employee and accounting student can be seen winding his camera in the Zapruder film through Z207 and Dorman film through Z206. The Dorman film reveals he began running down Elm about Z206. It is evident that he ran far enough west to obtain a good view of the rear of the presidential limo as the last two rapid-fire shots rang out. Mr. Betzner's testimony correlates closely with the Z221/310/328 sequence.

Linda Willis, about Z160, curb, south side of Elm near where the sidewalk ends at the edge of the grass infield - *Yes, I heard one. Then there was a little bit of time, and then there were two real fast bullets together. . . I heard the first shot come, and then he slumped forward, and then I couldn't tell where the second shot went, and then the third one, and that was the last one that hit him in the head.* WC deposition, 7/22/64 (WRv.7Hp.498).

Notes - The 14-year-old high-school student can be seen in the Dorman film's fourth sequence between Z210 and Z221 as she walks or runs west down Elm approaching the edge of the grass infield presumably to join or fetch her younger sister Rosemary. This put her in a good position to observe the president at Z313 to Z330. Ms. Willis' testimony correlates closely with the Z221/310/328 sequence.

John Templin, about Z210, 25-year-old military reservist, curb north side of Elm - *. . . the president kind of threw his shoulders up a little bit and laid his head back on the back of the seat, and I thought, well, he's just playing and playing the crowd and acting silly, you know. . . . But the second shot was probably another 40 to 50 foot further down, and it blew the right side of his head off, as near as I could tell. I was close enough that I could see that. I could see his hair depart from his head actually. That was the second shot, sir, and some say it was the third shot that killed him, but as I recall, and I'll believe it to my dying day, it was the second shot . . . I was still in the military reserves at the time.* Transcript of interview by Bob Porter, 7/8/95, Sixth Floor Museum at Dealey Plaza Collection Oral History Program.

12: Key Second and Third Shot Witness Testimony

Note - Templin's testimony correlates closely with the Z221/310/328 sequence.

Marilyn Willis, about Z270, near NW corner Houston and Main, looking toward Elm through last window of colonnade with her parents the Stubblefields (wife of Phil Willis) - *Mrs. Willis advised when the motorcade passed on Elm Street in front of where she was standing she heard a noise that sounded like a firecracker or backfire. A few seconds following this, she stated she heard another report and saw the top of President Kennedy's head blow off and ringed by a red halo. She stated she believe she heard another shot following this.* FBI interview, 6/19/64 (CD 1245).

Note - Ms. Willis' testimony correlates closely with the Z221/310/328 sequence.

J.E. (Bill) Decker, 66-year-old Chief of the Dallas County Sheriff's Department in the right-rear seat of the lead car (1st car in motorcade) alongside Secret Service Agent Sorrels, with Chief of Police Curry and Agent Lawson in front seat - *As the motorcade was proceeding down Elm Street, I distinctly remember hearing two shots. As I heard the first retort, I looked back over my shoulder and saw what appeared to be a spray of water come out of the rear seat of the president's car.* Written report, undated (WRv.19Hp.458).

Note - Except that he recalled hearing only one of the two rapid-fire final shots, Sheriff Decker's testimony correlates closely with the Z221/310/328 sequence.

James Foster, patrolman, atop Elm Street RR overpass with about a dozen Union Terminal Company employees and fellow officer J.C. White who was on the west side of the overpass - *Just as the vehicle in which President Kennedy was riding reached a point on Elm Street just east of the overpass, Patrolman Foster heard a noise that sounded like a large firecracker. He stated his attention was directed to President Kennedy and he realized something was wrong because of the movement of the president. Another report was heard, . . . and about the same time the report was heard, he observed the president's head appear to explode and immediately thereafter, he heard a third report which he knew was a shot. . . He stated the shots sounded as if they came from the direction of the TSBD Building. . .* FBI interview, 3/25/64 (CD 897).

Note - Foster's testimony correlates closely with the Z221/310/328 sequence.

Key-motorcade-eyewitness testimony to the second and third shots (Figure 56)

At Z313 during the president's first cranial eruption, the rear seat of the limo was about 230 feet west on Elm at a point off an imaginary line extending across the intersection along the western edge of Houston. The president was directly opposite Zapruder's position on the north side of Elm and off the middle of the sparsely occupied grass infield on the south side of Elm. The limo, closely trailed by the police escort and Queen Mary, had just passed north-of-Elm spectators Gayle and Bill Newman and south-of-Elm picture-taker Mary Moorman and her friend Jean Hill.

The five survivors in the presidential limo

Agent William Greer, driver - *. . . Well, when we were going down Elm Street I heard a noise that I thought was a backfire of one of the motorcycle policemen. . . . And then I heard it again. And I glanced over my shoulder. And I saw Governor Connally like he was starting to fall. Then I realized something was wrong. I tramped on the accelerator, and at the same time Mr. Kellerman said "Get out of here fast." And I cannot remember even the other shots or noises there was. I cannot quite remember any more. I did not see anything happen behind me any more, because I was occupied with getting away. I know there was three that I heard . . . [There were] 3 or 4 seconds [between the first two shots] . . . . the last two seemed to be just simultaneously, one behind the other. . . .The second one didn't sound any different much than the first one but I kind of got, by turning around, . . . a little concussion of it, maybe when it hit something. . . . [He heard the final shot] Just* *as soon as I turned my head back from the second shot, right away I accelerated right then. It was a matter of reflexes to the accelerator...* WC testimony, 3/9/64 (WRv.2Hp.117-18).

Notes - The Zapruder film shows Greer looking back into the rear seat twice during the 5-second interval between the first and second shots and then reacting dramatically to the blasts of the Z310 and Z328 shots. Greer's first look back occurs from Z280 to Z289 as Kellerman is shouting "Let's get out of here, were hit." He turns back forward from Z290 to Z294. His second look back occurs from Z300 to Z305 and appears to be in response to the governor's shouting commencing Z295 "Oh my God." He is looking directly into the governor's face as the president's head explodes at Z313. He frantically turns forward from Z316 to Z320 and, with his shoulders hunched, is leaning/ducking forward toward the steering wheel from Z321 to Z332. The Zapruder, Muchmore and Nix films show him leaning/turning his head slightly to the right and cringing from Z333 to Z339. His revised testimony including feeling the concussion of the second shot on his face and hearing the third shot just as he turned back and stomped on the accelerator pedal correlates exactly with the Z221/310/328 sequence.

Agent Roy Kellerman, right-front seat - *... [Having turned around in response to the first shot] There was enough time for me to verify the man was hit. So, in the same motion, I come right back ... and said to the driver "Let's get out of here; we are hit," and grabbed the mic and I said, "Lawson, this is Kellerman ... we are hit; get us to the hospital immediately." Now in the seconds that I talked just now, a flurry of shells come into the car [later in his testimony he clarified he heard just two come in].... [Describing the time between the last two shots that came when he was talking into the mic] ... a plane breaking the sound barrier: bang, bang. [Describing when brain matter rained down on him] When I have given the orders to Mr. Lawson, this is when it all came between the driver and myself ... let's say you take a little handful of matter, I am going to use sawdust for want of a better item, and just throw it.* WC testimony, 3/9/64 (WRv.2Hp.73/76/78).

Notes - The Zapruder film shows Kellerman looking back into the rear seat just once during the 5-second interval between the first and second shots and then reacting dramatically to the blasts of the Z310 and Z328 shots. Kellerman swivels left in his seat from Z245 to Z269 and looks at the president from Z270 to Z279. As he turns back to the front from Z280 to Z289 he looks toward Greer while he was reportedly shouting, "Let's get out of here, we are hit." From Z290 to Z299 he reaches forward and grabs the radio mic. From Z300 to Z315 he is talking into the radio mic. Commencing Z316 he frantically hunches his shoulders and ducks forward against the dash while presumably still talking into the mic. From Z333 to Z336 of the Muchmore film he turns/ducks rapidly to his left and commencing Z337 dives down and to his left toward the center of the seat. His testimony is consistent with his movements and correlates exactly with the Z221/310/328 sequence.

First Lady Jacqueline Kennedy, left-rear seat - *... [Having diverted her attention from the governor] I turned to the right. And all I remember seeing of my husband, he had this sort of quizzical look on his face, and his hand was up, it must have been his left hand. And just as I turned and looked at him, I could see a piece of his skull, and I remember it was flesh colored.... No blood or anything ... And then he sort of did this (indicating), put his [right] hand to his forehead and fell in my lap. And then I just remember falling on him and saying ... "Oh, my God, they have shot my husband." ... I don't recall climbing out on the back of the car.... Well there must have been two because the one that made me turn around was Governor Connally yelling. And it used to confuse me because first I remembered there were three.... But I used to think that if only I had been looking right, I would have seen the first shot hit him, and then I could have pulled him down, and the second shot would not have hit him. But I heard the governor yelling and that made me turn around. ... And those were the only two I remember.* WC testimony, 6/5/64 (WRv.5Hp.180).

Notes - The Zapruder film shows Ms. Kennedy paid little heed to the sound of the first shot until her slumping husband's left elbow contacted her right arm commencing at Z247 as she was waving at the Chisms or Mudd. The film shows her reacting dramatically to the blasts of the second and third shots. As she began to turn toward the president at about Z248, her eyes were drawn to the governor who had turned around and was shouting, "Oh, no, no, no." From Z290 to Z293, she diverts her attention back to the wounded president

12: Key Second and Third Shot Witness Testimony

and by Z312 has lowered and turned her head to look at his neck. In the aftermath of the Z313 cranial explosion, from Z316 to Z324 she spontaneously pushes the president away with her right forearm which flips up behind his back from Z325 to Z328 after losing contact with the top of his left shoulder. From Z322 to Z332 Ms. Kennedy straightens back up in her seat while inspecting the damage to her husband's head as he slumps forward onto her chest. In response to the sound and effects of the Z328 shot, from Z333 to Z338 Ms. Kennedy visibly cringes and recoils with her eyes wide open and her mouth agape leaning back and slightly to her right while jerking her right forearm to the rear. She begins to frantically rise from her seat at Z339 and has both hands on the trunk by Z370. Her inability to recall the sound of the Z328 shot correlates with her inability to recall fleeing the car. Therefore, in all respects, her testimony correlates closely with the Z221/310/328 sequence.

Nellie Connally, left jump seat - . . . *As the first shot was hit and I turned to look at the same time, I recall John saying, "Oh, no, no, no." Then there was a second shot, and it hit John [on the right forearm], and as he recoiled to the right, just crumpled like a wounded animal to the right he said, "My God, they are going to kill us all." . . . I never again [after Z290] looked in the back seat of the car after my husband was shot. . . . I just pulled him over into my arms [from Z316 to Z332] . . . The third shot that I heard I felt. It felt like spent buckshot falling all over us, and then of course, I too could see that it was brain matter.* WC testimony, 4/21/64 (WRv.4Hp.147).

Notes - The Zapruder film images coupled with her testimony on when she took her final look back and heard her husband's final remarks make it clear that during the shooting, Ms. Connally thought her husband was nearly killed by the Z310 shot. Her first look back over her right shoulder occurred from Z230 to Z240 and she is looking at the president through Z269. From Z270 to Z279 she takes a quick look toward Kellerman. From Z280 to Z289 she takes a final glance back toward the president. From Z290 to Z300 she is looking at the rear of her husband's head as he leans back toward her and rests his head on her right shoulder. From Z301 to Z315 she is lowering her head toward the left side of his face as he is mouthing the words, "Oh my God." From Z316 to Z325, in response to the blast of the Z310 shot, Ms. Connally recoils and leans to her left toward the front of the limo to get her head down. From Z326 to Z332 she is hunkering up against the door with her arms in front of her as her seemingly unconscious and half-dead husband collapses left-shoulder first onto her right side, pinning her up against the inside of the door. We can see brain matter raining down on her from Z331 to Z337. In response to the blast of the Z328 shot, from Z333 to Z336 she turns/ducks her head to her right and leans back allowing her unconscious husband commencing Z333 to collapse left-shoulder-first onto her lap. From Z337 to Z345, while Ms. Kennedy is rising up and the president is into his final collapse forward, Ms. Connally dives her upper body toward the center of the car. She ends up on her right shoulder with her head behind her husband's lower back and her left arm extending protectively over his right side. North-of-Elm spectator Gayle Newman and Presidential Aide Robert Powers also thought the governor was wounded by the Z310 shot based on his dramatic reactions. Allowing for her understandable belief that the Z310 shot nearly killed her husband and that only the last of the two final shots struck the president in the head, Ms. Connally's testimony correlates exactly with the Z221/310/328 sequence and provides compelling proof in support. As far as I am concerned, Nellie Connally has been vindicated by the evidence presented in this book.

John Connally, right jump seat - . . . *[After realizing he had been shot through the back and chest] So I merely doubled up and then turned to my right again . . . and Mrs. Connally pulled me over into her lap . . . . then, of course, the third shot sounded, and I heard the shot very clearly. I heard it hit him. . . . I immediately when I was hit, I said, "Oh, no, no, no." And then I said, "My God they are going to kill us all." . . . . After the third shot . . . I heard Roy Kellerman tell the driver, "Bill, get out of line." And then I saw him move, and I assume he was moving a button or something on the panel of the automobile, and he said, "Get us to the hospital quick." At about that time, we began to pull out of the cavalcade, out of the line, and I lost consciousness [by all appearances at Z325] . . .* WC testimony, 4/21/64 (WRv.4Hp.133).

Notes - The Zapruder film shows the governor reacting as if he were struck by the Z310 shot and losing consciousness commencing Z325. In the aftermath of his collective reactions to the first shot and presumably in response to hearing Kellerman shouting out they were hit, we see the governor mouthing the words "Oh my

God" from Z295 to Z307 while he is leaning back against his wife and looking straight ahead out the right side of the car. From Z308 to Z312 as he continues to shout, he turns his head forward in the direction of Kellerman who has just grabbed and started speaking into the radio mic. From Z316 to Z324 the governor reacts to the Z310 shot very much as if he had been shot by spinning to his right and lunging forward. Having slammed his head against a metal bar on the back of the front seat at Z324, from Z325 to Z332 he slumps left shoulder first toward the left side of the car and onto Ms. Connally's right side pinning her up against the inside of the car door. From Z333 to Z339, the unconscious governor collapses left-shoulder first onto his wife's lap into the area she has just cleared by leaning back. He remains motionless in this position through Z369. Allowing for his understandable belief that the Z221 shot did not cause his wounds given to his wife's confidence in her recollections and the fact that he was unconscious when the final shot passed over his head at Z330, his testimony correlates strongly with the Z221/310/328 sequence.

The four motorcycle-escort police

Officer Bobby Hargis, off left-rear fender of presidential limo at Z313 - *(1) I thought Governor Connally had been hit when I saw him turn toward the president with a real surprised look. The president then looked like he was bent over or that he was leaning toward the governor talking to him. As the president straightened back up, Mrs. Kennedy turned toward him, and that is when he got hit in the side of the head, spinning it around... I was splattered with blood..* Sunday News, New York, November 24, 1963, p. 21. *(2) ... then as the president raised back up like that (indicating) the shot that killed him hit him. I don't know whether it was the second or third shot. Everything happened so fast... [two] is all that I can recall remembering ... I was splattered with blood and brain, and kind of a bloody water...* WC deposition, 4/8/64 (WRv.6Hp.294).

Notes - Hargis is among those key witnesses who interpreted the rearward head snap from Z316 to Z325 as the president straightening up in his seat. The Zapruder film wide-screen version including the images between the sprocket holes ("Image of an Assassination") have him in view looking out to the right in alarm from about Z235 to Z275 and again from Z307 through Z313 when the president's head explodes. He did not notice the Z313 cranial explosion but did see the rearward head snap. After darting his head slightly to his right and upward between Z315 to Z317 in response to the Z310 shot, commencing Z321 he resumes looking out to the right at the Hudson Group. Commencing Z326, he darts his head to the left and is looking directly at the president when his head explodes at Z330. Between Z333 to Z336, in response to the Z328 shot, Hargis darts his head to his left then right and is again looking directly at the stricken president before disappearing from view behind Agent Hill at Z337-38. The Nix film confirms these rapid head movements. In the Muchmore film images we can discern whitish fluids engulfing him from about Z335 to Z337. The Zapruder film and Nix film images collectively show Hargis further respond to the Z328 shot by quickly coming to a stop between Z339 and Z344 at which time he also turns his head hard-right. As he disappears from Nix's camera view at Z363, he appears to be looking at Flying Tackle Man and getting set to dismount. Allowing for his inability to recall the sound of both of the final shots, his testimony correlates closely with the Z221/310/328 sequence. See Figure 57.

Officer B.J. Martin, off left-rear fender of presidential limo at Z313 - *... [After turning his head toward the president in alarm from Z230 to Z275] ... and he was leaning forward. I could see the left side of his face. At the time he had no expression on his face. [after looking back toward the TSBD and then off to the right] Yes sir, two more shots. ... I noticed there were blood stains on the windshield of my motor and then I pulled off my helmet and noticed there were blood stains on the left side of my helmet ...* WC deposition, 4/3/64 (WRv.6Hp.291-92).

Notes - According to his testimony, Martin observed the president's reaction just to the first shot which occurs from Z245 to Z290 and not the final two. He is in Nix's camera view from the equivalent of Z316 to Z372 but the Muchmore film provides a better view from Z300 to Z337 capturing his two tell tale darts of the head between Z316 to Z319 and Z333 to Z336. Except during the head darting, he is looking off to the right

12: Key Second and Third Shot Witness Testimony

of the limo until Z325 when, like Hargis/Chaney/Jackson, he darts his head to the left and is looking toward the president as of Z330 with his view obstructed by Hargis. Commencing Z339 he looks hard to the right and continues to do so through Z352. It is significant that the blood stains he mentioned were only on the left side of his helmet because it reveals he ran into the fallout of the cranial explosion at some point after he turned his head hard to the right commencing Z339 just after Hargis and Agent Hill were hit with bloody brain matter. Allowing for his understandable confusion as to which of the last two shots caused the head wound, his testimony correlates closely with the Z221/310/328 sequence.

Officer James Chaney, off right-rear fender of presidential limo at Z313 - . . . *[After looking over his left shoulder after the first shot and returning his eyes forward] Then, uh, the second shot came [causing Chaney to take a quick glance to the right from Z316-18], well then I looked back [from Z326 to Z333] just in time to see the president struck in the face by the second bullet [the third shot]. He slumped forward into Mrs. Kennedy's lap, and uh, it was apparent to me that we were being fired upon. . . . [as to the source of the sounds] it was back over my right shoulder.* Recording of Bill Lord interview broadcast on WFAA-TV, 11/22/63, cited in Trask, 1998, pp. 155 and 119.

Notes - Like Hargis, Chaney is among the many key witnesses that got the impression that the president was killed by the shot that rang out at Z330 and drove him forward onto his wife's lap rather than by the shot that hit him in the head at Z313. He is in Nix's camera view from the equivalent of Z307 to Z351 and is in Muchmore's view from Z320 to Z337. The Nix film images show Chaney looking forward as of Z313 indicating he did not witness the first cranial explosion. The Muchmore and Nix films collectively show that in response to the Z310 shot, Chaney completes a glance to his right between Z316 and Z319 and then looks out to the right toward the Hudson Group commencing about Z321. Like Hargis, Chaney, and Jackson from Z326 to Z333 he darts his head hard left toward the president in time to witness the Z330 cranial eruption. Between Z333 and Z336 he darts his head hard right and commencing Z337 quickly brings his motorcycle to a stop by Z343 while taking a very telling hard look back over his right shoulder. He is still looking right when he disappears from view at Z353. Allowing for his understandable confusion as to which of the last two shots killed the president, his testimony correlates exactly with the Z221/310/328 sequence. See figure 57.

Officer D.L. Jackson, off right-rear fender of presidential limo at Z313 - . . . *[After hearing the first shot and looking back and then returning his eyes forward] . . . and then into the president's car in time for the next explosion and saw Mr. Connally jerk back to his right and it seemed he looked at me [from Z255 to Z307] and I could see a shocked expression on his face and I thought someone is shooting at them. I began stopping my motor [starting Z337] and looked straight ahead, first at the triple overpass and saw only one policeman standing on the track . . . I looked back toward the president and saw him hit in the head; he appeared to have been hit above the right ear . . . the top of his head flew off away from me . . . I knew that the shooting was coming from my right rear and I looked back that way [commencing Z337] but I never looked up.* Quoted from a hand-written diary Jackson reportedly wrote the night of 11/22/63, cited in Savage, 1993, pp. 362-63.

Notes - Jackson was in Nix's camera view from the equivalent of Z309 to Z356. The Nix film images show Jackson mimicking Chaney's movements as the final two shots rang out. Jackson is looking straight forward toward the underpass as of Z313 indicating he did not witness the Z313 cranial explosion. The images show that in response to the Z310 shot noise, Jackson completes left/right/left darting of the head between Z316 and Z319 and then turns his head forward/right and looks out over the knoll toward the Hudson Group. Commencing Z326 through Z333 he turns his head left toward the president and is looking directly at him at Z330. Between Z333 and Z337 he darts his head hard to the right. He disappears from Nix's view behind Chaney from Z338 to Z344 as they both slow to a crawl with Chaney briefly stopping. When he comes back into view, he is looking toward the presidential limo again through Z350. With the exception of his faulty recollection that he was looking into the limo as the second shot sounded rather than toward the underpass, and that he began slowing his cycle just after the third shot sounded rather than just before, Jackson's testimony correlates with the Z221/310/328 sequence.

Ten in the Queen Mary

Agent Sam Kinney, driver - . . . *[After watching the president slump to the left after the first shot]* There was a second of pause and then two more shots were heard . . . . I saw one shot strike the president in the right side of the head. . . . I did hear three shots but do not recall which [of the last two] shots were those that hit the president [in the head] . . . Written report, 11/22/63 (WRv.18Hp.732).

    Notes - Kinney is in view for six frames at the very end of the Muchmore film corresponding to Z332 to Z337 during which time he darts his head hard right commencing Z333 in response to hearing the noise of the Z328 final shot. The Nix and Muchmore film images show him already looking to the right when he comes into view at Z331 revealing that he did not see the Z328 shot effects. Allowing for his understandable confusion as to which of the last two shots caused the head wounds, his testimony correlates closely with the Z221/310/328 sequence.

Agent Emory Roberts, right-front seat - *(1)* . . . *[After watching the president slump to the left after the first shot]* I knew he was hit. Just as the first or second shot was fired, Hill ran from the follow-up car to the president's car. After SA Hill got on rear step of president's car *[commencing at Z337]*, it appeared SA John Ready was about to follow and go for the right-rear step. However, I told him not to jump, as we had picked up speed, and I was afraid he might not make it. Written report, 11/22/63. *(2) I do not know if it was the next shot or third shot that hit President Kennedy in the head, but I saw a small explosion on the right side of the president's head, saw blood, at which time the president fell further to his left. Mrs. Kennedy was leaning toward the president, however, she immediately raised up in the seat . . . .* Written statement, 11/29/63 (WRv.18Hp.734).

    Note - Roberts was in and out of Bronson's blurry view. He is concisely describing the effects of the Z328 shot. Allowing for his understandable confusion as to which of the last two shots caused the head wounds, his testimony correlates closely with the Z221/310/328 sequence.

Agent Clint Hill, front-left running board - *(1)* . . . *[After watching the president slump to the left following the first shot and presumably hearing Agent Kellerman shouting at Greer that they were hit and/or the governor's shouting]* I jumped from the follow-up car [at Z300] and ran toward the presidential automobile. I heard a second firecracker-type noise, but it had a different sound-like the sound of shooting a revolver into something hard. I saw the president slump more to his left [commencing Z331]. . . Written statement, 11/30/63 (WRv.18Hp.842). *(2) Between the time I originally grabbed the hand hold [at Z337] and until I was up on the car [initially at Z340] . . . the second noise that I heard had removed a portion of the president's head, and he had slumped noticeably to his left [from Z331 to Z340]. Mrs. Kennedy had jumped up from the seat [from Z339 to Z370] . . . The second one had almost a double sound-as though you were standing against something metal and firing into it, and you hear both the sound of a gun going off and the sound of the cartridge hitting the metal place, which could have been caused probably by the hard surface of the head. But I am not sure that is what caused it.* WC testimony, 3/9/64 (WRv.2Hp.138/144).

    Notes - Other than Ms. Kennedy and the Connallys, Agent Hill was the closest to the president as of Z330 and was looking right at him. He was close enough to hear the bullet strike the skull. Hill is in and out of Bronson's camera view from the equivalent of Z298 to Z331 and the last third of the Muchmore assassination sequence from the equivalent of Z315 to Z337. During these intervals we see him leap from the Queen Mary's running board and hit the ground running at Z300 and then assume full speed at Z316 in a reflex reaction to hearing the sound of the Z310 second shot. With the sound of the Z328 final shot, he leaps forward at Z333-36 and was just about to grab the rear hand hold with his left hand as the Muchmore film ends at M66/Z337. Hill's sworn testimony that he heard a final shot about the time he reached the rear of the limo and witnessed it striking the president in the head and driving him forward and to the left amidst a cranial eruption, is very powerful evidence of a Z328 final-shot that struck the top right of the president's head.

12: Key Second and Third Shot Witness Testimony

Agent John Ready, front-right running board - *(1) . . . [After hearing the first shot and looking back over his shoulder to look for the source] At this time the secret-service follow-up car seemed to slow and I heard someone from inside the car say "he's shot." I left the follow-up car in the direction of the president's car but was recalled by ATSAIC Emory Roberts (Secret Service) as the cars increased their speeds.* Written report, 11/22/63 (WRv.18Hp.749). *(2) He thought the first shot was a firecracker thrown from behind them. He said the second and third shots were closer in time than the first and second shots.* HSCA deposition, 3/10/78.

Notes - The Nix film images show Ready responding to the Z328 shot by turning his head slightly left and ducking from Z333 to Z336 and then squatting into a ready-to-jump position commencing Z337. He remains in this position until disappearing to camera right about Z350. Ready is in and out of Bronson's camera view from the equivalent of Z296 to Z331 and appears to be looking forward. Ready's testimony, however, indicates he was not looking in the direction of the president when any of the shots rang out. His testimony correlates closely with the Z221/310/328 sequence.

Agent William McIntyre, rear-left running board - *The presidential vehicle was approximately 200 feet from the underpass when the first shot was fired, followed in quick succession by two more. I would estimate that all three shots were fired within 5 seconds. After the second shot, I looked at the president and witnessed him being struck in the head by the third and last shot . . .* Written statement, 11/29/63 (WRv.18Hp.747).

Notes - McIntyre is a classic example of a witness whose eyes were drawn toward the president by the sound of the Z310 second shot, and got the impression that the president was killed by the Z328 final shot. McIntyre is visible in the last three frames of the Muchmore film during the interval equivalent to Z335 to Z337 during which time he is ducking down and turning his head to the right, presumably commencing Z333 in response to the sound of the Z328 shot. He is in an out of view in the Bronson assassination sequence but we see his reflex reaction at Z316 to Z317. As of Z313, he was presumably distracted by Agent Hill who had jumped off the running board at about Z300 and was running alongside the car. His testimony correlates closely with the Z221/310/328 sequence.

Agent Paul Landis, rear-right running board . . . *[After hearing the first shot and noticing the president starting to react as he looked back to locate the source] . . . I began to think the sound had been that of a firecracker, but I hadn't seen any smoke. In fact, I recall Special Agent Jack Ready saying "What was it, a firecracker?" I remarked, "I don't know; I don't see any smoke." So far the lapsed period of time could not have been over 2 or 3 seconds. All during this time, I continued to scan the crowd, returning my gaze towards the president's car. It must have been another second or two before the next shot was fired because . . . I then thought that maybe one of the cars in the motorcade had a blowout that had echoed off the building. I looked at the right-front tire of the president's car and saw it was all right. I then glanced to see the right-rear tire, but could not because the follow-up car was too close. . . . I glanced toward the president and he still appeared to be fairly upright in his seat, leaning slightly toward Mrs. Kennedy with his head tilted slightly back. . . . It was at that moment I heard a second report and saw the president's head split open and pieces of flesh and blood flying through the air. I also remember Special Agent Clinton Hill attempting to climb onto the back of the car at the time the second shot was fired. I would guess the time between the first and second report must have been about 4 or 5 seconds. My reaction at this time was that the shot came somewhere towards the front, but I did not see anyone on the overpass . . . I do not recall hearing a third shot.* Written statement, 11/27/63 (WRv.18Hp.758-59).

Notes - The Altgens Z253 photo shows Landis looking hard-right-rear toward the TSBD. He is not in anyone else's camera view. From his testimony it is evident that Landis is among those whose eyes were drawn to the president by the sound of the Z310 second shot and came under the impression that the Z328 third shot killed him. As the last shot rang out he witnessed the second cranial eruption and the president being driven forward commencing Z331 and recalled it rang out just as Hill reached the limo. Except for his inability to recall hearing both of the final shots, his testimony correlates closely with the Z221/310/328 sequence and provides strong evidence that the Z328 final shot hit the president in top of the back of the head.

Aide Kenneth O'Donnell, left jump seat - . . . *he had been waving out the right side of the car, and I noticed him slump toward Mrs. Kennedy, and I realized then that they had been shots. But as fast as that realization occurred, I saw the last shot hit. I saw the third shot. It was such a perfect shot, I remember I blessed myself. . . . the first two came almost simultaneously. . . . She turned toward him, and then the third shot hit. Obviously she then knew what happened. She turned, looking at the backup car. Meanwhile, Agent Hill had gotten off the car and started running up. She was clambering toward the back . . . .* WC deposition, 5/18/64 (WRv.7Hp.448).

Notes - O'Donnell, who was not in anyone's camera view except Phil Willis' (looking forward), is yet another example of a witness whose eyes were drawn toward the president by the sound of the Z310 second shot and witnessed him being hit in the head by the Z328 final shot which he presumed killed him. Because O'Donnell is among just a few ear witnesses that recalled hearing the first two shots bunched, his testimony as to the timing of the second shot is considered too conflicted to be of any use.

Aide David Powers, right jump seat - . . . *[After hearing the first shot and noticing the president slump to the left]. . . . There was a second shot and Governor Connally disappeared from sight [from Z316 to Z333] and then there was a third shot which took off the top of the president's head . . . . The total time between the first and third shots was about 5 or 6 seconds.* Written statement, 5/18/64 (WRv.7Hp.473).

Notes: It is evident from his testimony that with the sound of the Z310 shot, Powers, who was not in anyone's camera view except for Altgens/Betzner/Willis (looking forward in all three), noticed the governor diving forward as the president leaned back. He then witnessed the president being hit in the head by the Z328 final shot and saw the second cranial eruption. Allowing for his understandable confusion as to which of the last two shots killed the president, Powers testimony correlates closely with the Z221/310/328 sequence.

Agent George Hickey, left-rear seat - . . . *Perhaps 2 or 3 seconds elapsed from the time I looked to the rear and then looked at the president. He was slumped forward and to his left, and was straightening up to an almost erect sitting position as I turned and looked. At the moment he was sitting erect [at Z325] I heard two reports which . . . were in such rapid succession that there seemed to be practically no time element between them. It looked to me as if the president was struck in the right-upper rear of his head. The first shot of the second two seemed as if it missed because the hair on the right side of his head flew forward and there didn't seem to any impact against his head. The last shot seemed to hit his head and caused a noise at the point of impact which made him fall forward [commencing at Z331] and to his left again. Possibly 4 or 5 seconds elapsed from the time of the first report and the last.* Written statement, 11/30/63 (WRv.18Hp.762).

Notes - In the Altgens Z253 photo Hickey is looking hard right over his right shoulder directly at the TSBD entrance in response to the noise of the first shot. He is not visible in the Nix or Muchmore films. Hickey is in and out of Bronson's camera view during the equivalent of Z296 to Z331 and appears to be looking forward with an unobstructed view of the president. He did not witness the Z313 cranial explosion but did observe the president's head snapping back from Z316 to Z325 immediately afterward. He thought he was simply straightening up in his seat. He witnessed the second cranial explosion at Z330/331 and saw the president's head driven forward and left. Allowing for his understandable confusion as to which of the last two shots caused the head wounds, his testimony correlates exactly with the Z221/310/328 sequence.

Agent Glen Bennett, right-rear seat - . . . *[After hearing the first shot] . . . I immediately upon hearing the supposed firecracker looked at the boss' car. At this exact time I saw a shot that hit the boss about 4-inches down from his right shoulder; a second shot followed immediately and hit the right rear high of the president's head.* Hand-written report, 11/22/63 (WRv.24Hp.542).

Notes - Based on his testimony, Bennett is also among those whose eyes were drawn to the president by the sound of the second shot and came under the impression that the third killed him rather than the second. See second page of this chapter.

12: Key Second and Third Shot Witness Testimony

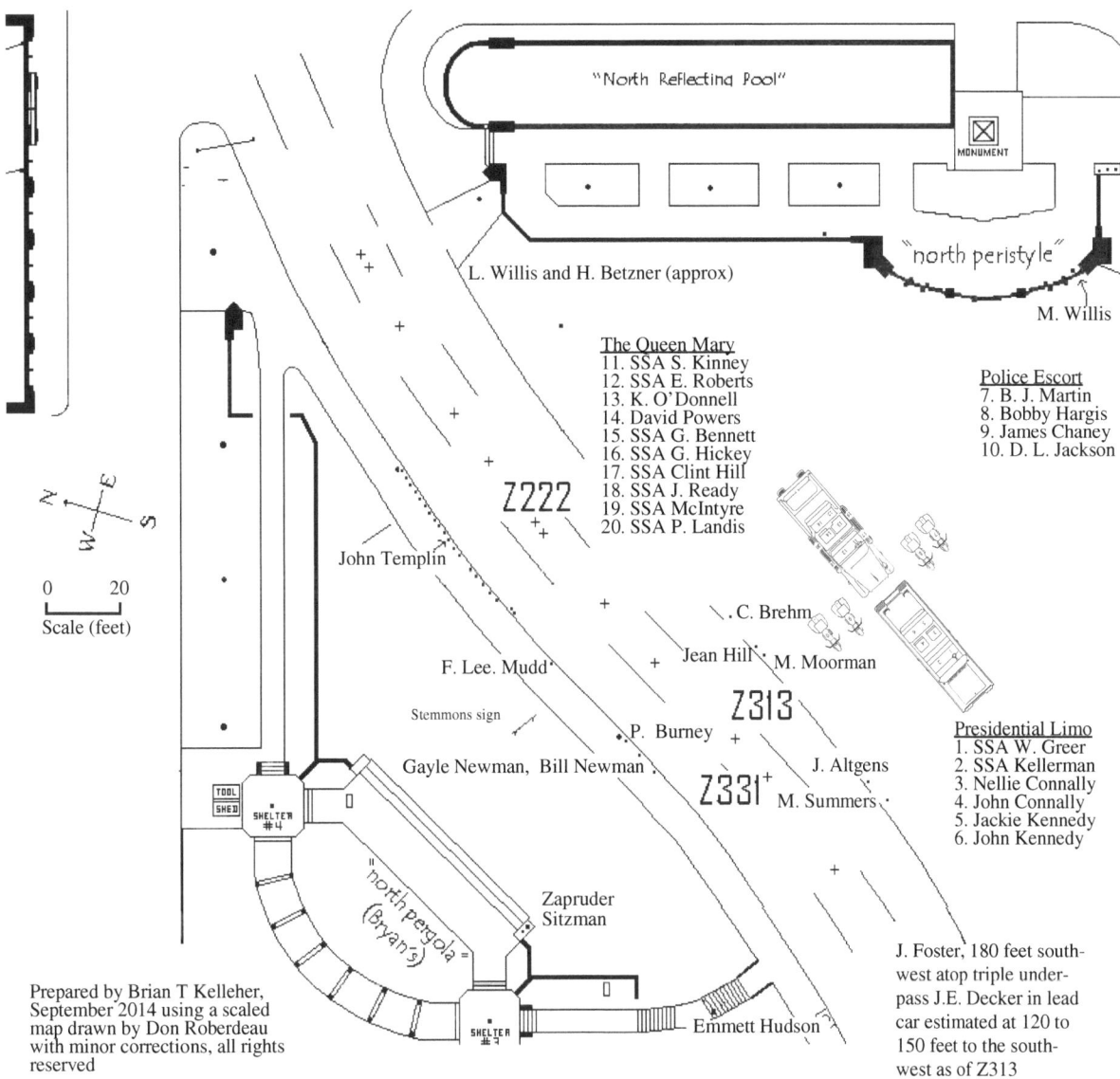

Figure 56

Locations of key second-and-third-shot witnesses - This group includes eighteen stationary ear/eye witnesses located within 25 to 180 feet of the president as of Z313 and all twenty of the presidential entourage. The individual and collective key-witness testimony coupled with the photographic evidence covered in prior chapters provides compelling proof that the second shot struck the president in the head at Z313, and that a rushed final shot struck the president's head at Z330. I used Zapruder, Bronson, Nix and Moorman sightlines to pinpoint most of the stationary witness locations. I used the Dorman-film images and their respective testimony to approximately position Linda Willis and Hugh Betzner as of Z313 since they moved from where they were as of Z200. I used Shaw-trial testimony to position Linda's mother Marilyn Willis. The drawing of the limo, Queen Mary and the police motorcycles is from Trask, 1994 page 63 and is slightly enlarged relative to scale.

Figure 57
The Mary Moorman Z316 photograph of the limo under fire and the revealing testimony of Motorcycle Officers Hargis and Chaney - The Z316 identification is my own based on scrutiny of Zapruder frames Z313-16 and particularly the positions of the president's right shoulder and the degree of leftward rotation of Agent Kellerman's head. The president's right shoulder is raised because he has just started jerking his right arm up toward his face. This is the frame where auditory reflex reactions commence among all the limo occupants as well as Motorcycle-Officers Hargis and Chaney who are riding off the limo's left and right-rear fenders, respectively. The Zapruder film images have Hargis in view looking out to the right in alarm from about Z235 to Z275 and again from Z307 through Z313 when the president's head explodes. He did not notice the Z313 cranial explosion but did see the rearward head snap. After darting his head slightly to his right and upward between Z315 to Z317 in response to the Z310 shot, commencing Z321 he resumes looking out to the right at the Hudson Group. Commencing Z326, however, he darts his head to the left and is looking directly at the president when his head explodes at Z330. The Muchmore and Nix films establish that Chaney, who was looking forward as of Z313 through Z316, completed a quick glance to his right between Z317 to Z318 in response to the second shot noise meaning that he also did not witness the Z313 cranial eruption. Between Z320 and Z325 he began looking out to the right, but consistent with what he reported to news media within an hour of the shooting, from Z326 to Z329 Chaney darted his head to the left and between Z330 and Z333 was looking directly at the president as the final shot hit him in the head, knocking him forward onto his wife's lap. All four motorcycle police darted their heads toward the limo from Z326 to Z330, presumably in response to the roar of the engine when Greer stomped on the accelerator pedal and/or the governor's shouting. This is a cropped image that I photo edited to increase brightness and contrast (Mary Moorman, Bettmann/CORBIS).

12: Key Second and Third Shot Witness Testimony

Figure 58
The James Altgens Z253 photo of the limo under fire showing the Queen Mary and the police motorcycle escort and alarm reactions to the Z221 first shot and the misperceptions of Agent Glen Bennett - The Z253 identification is my own and is based on the relative positions of the governor's head, the president's left hand and the first lady's two gloved hands. The Zapruder film images reveal that Ms. Kennedy's right hand was resting on the back of the president's left as of Z255 and thereafter. This precludes the long-standing Z255 identification. Those in the midst of exhibiting alarm reactions to the sound of the Z220 first shot that are either known or assumed to have commenced at Z230 include the following from left to right and forward to rear: Motorcycle Escort Officers Martin, Hargis and Chaney; Agents Hill and McIntyre on the Queen Mary's driver's-side running board; Agents Ready and Landis on the passenger-side running board; and Agents Hickey and Bennett in the rear seat. From the collective photographic evidence it is clear that Bennett who is bent over looking to the right as of Z253 did not have the president in view as of Z222. As such, the photographic evidence refutes Bennett's testimony that he "saw" the second shot hit the president in the upper back. The collective evidence suggests that Bennett saw the bloody effects of the Z221 shot as the Z310 shot rang out and—as was the case with Altgens and others—saw the president hit in the head by the Z328 final shot and did not realize he had already been hit at Z313. This is a slightly cropped image of that available in the public domain (*AP Worldwide* via David Von Pein's blog site "The Kennedy Assassination Gallery").

Figure 59
Life Magazine **Photographer, Art Rickerby's post-assassination photo of a mix of key grassy knoll eyewitnesses and press photographers taken from camera car 2 within a minute of the shooting** - Going from left to right the following are in view: Motorcycle Officer Clyde Haygood; *NBC* Cameraman, Dave Wiegman filming Cheryl McKinnon; *UPI* photographer, James Altgens running up the sidewalk; Bill and Gayle Newman lying on the ground; *CBS* Cameraman, Tom Craven and White House Cameraman, Tom Atkins, both from camera car 1, filming the Newmans; Cheryl McKinnon lying on ground; Zapruder, Sitzman and the Hesters in the pergola shelter; Mudd and the Umbrella Man, sitting; *UPI* Cameraman, Tom Cancellari from camera car 2 walking toward the Newmans; and Faye Chism running (Art Rickerby, *Life/Time Warner, Inc.*, via David Von Pein's blog "The Kennedy Gallery").

Chapter 13

Tracking Down the "Lost Bullet"

The proof of a third shot entering and exiting the presidential limo at Z330 is not limited to photographic evidence of a signature jolt, a second cranial eruption, signature reflex and alarm (Figure 61) reactions and ear/eyewitness testimony. There is also concrete ballistics evidence. Figures 60 through 67 follow and relate to the ensuing discussions.

With the knowledge that a final shot passed through the top of the president's head at Z330, I was hot on the trail of the "lost bullet." To track it, I first positioned the limo at Z330 relative to the curving trend and slope of the street on my scaled drawing of Dealey Plaza (Figure 63). In plotting the lateral trajectory of a bullet fired from the TSBD sniper's nest, I discovered that this bullet passed through the presidential limo at precisely the same point the president's head was struck at Z313. This finding is consistent with Oswald simply operating the bolt and squeezing a shot off as fast as he possibly could while maintaining his aim. I found that in the absence of lateral deflection, after exiting the president's head the bullet would have exited the driver's side window or vent window. Extending the trajectory line about 90 feet south, I found documentation of a conspicuous gouge located on the top south corner of a storm-sewer catch basin that forms part of the curb on the south side of Elm at the point that the stricken president had passed at approximately Z400. In examining a close-up photo of the gouge, I could see that the bullet bounced off the curb in end-over-end fashion and deflected to the right. Following this trail by extending the line another 146 feet in the direction in which the tail end of the scar is pointing, I intersected the curb along the south side of Main at the exact location where the FBI cut out a section of curb which had a small scar smeared with lead. This scar is aligned with the tail end of the catch-basin gouge. Knowing a spectator (James Tague) standing on the south curb of Main about 15 east of the scar had been wounded by a concrete chip, I looked for and found a picture of the wound (Figure 64) and noted the chip struck him at a 65 degree descending angle from a point to the rear of his left shoulder. Following this trail by extending the line upward from the cheek, I encountered the rectangular concrete column separating Commerce and Main (Figure 65). Looking for and finding a post-assassination photo showing this area of the column (Figure 66), I found a telltale bright spot at a point about 17 feet up along its rounded northeast edge. Traveling to Dealey Plaza on Google Maps/Earth, taking advantage of the zoom feature, I found evidence of another deflection to the right (Figure 67) and the likely spot where at least part of the bullet is still lodged in the span of concrete running 15 feet above the west-bound lane of Main.

My vertical trajectory analysis revealed that, en route to the catch-basin gouge, the bullet had deflected upward in passing through the top of the president's head and just barely cleared the head of the hunched down Nellie Connally. As was the case with the lateral trajectory analysis, I found that Oswald in taking his rapid-fire final shot had by all appearances simply maintained his Z310 second shot aim with just a slight rise.

The catch-basin gouge was discovered by a sharp-eyed Dallas police officer within 20 minutes or so of the shooting. The small scar on the south curb of Main Street was discovered by a sharp-eyed deputy sheriff within the same time frame. Though government investigators and experts and most assassination researchers are aware of the gouge in the catch basin, and notch on the curb, nobody ever realized their true significance.

The initial discovery and investigation of the catch-basin gouge

One of the key stationary ear/eyewitnesses to the shots mentioned in Chapter 12, Dallas Police Officer James Foster, had watched the assassination from atop the triple underpass. He was under orders to keep the area clear of pedestrians but allowed a dozen or so Union Terminal rail-yard employees to remain with him since it was railroad property. Foster was convinced that the shots came from the vicinity of the TSBD and within a few minutes of the shooting raced across the railroad yards in the area to the north of the picket fence that forms the northeast boundary of Dealey Plaza. By the time he arrived in the area northwest of the TSBD building, Chief Inspector H.J. Sawyer had taken charge of securing the building. After informing Sawyer of his observations, Foster walked down Elm to search the area of the shooting for signs of the bullets. This search might have been prompted by some of those standing near Foster atop the triple underpass who claimed that they saw a bullet strike the street resulting in a spray of concrete.

> **Royce Skelton, Union Terminal Employee, atop the triple overpass nearby Dallas Patrolman James Foster** - *I heard two more shots. I heard a woman say "Oh no" or something and grab a man inside the car. I heard another shot and saw the bullet hit the pavement. The concrete was knocked to the south away from the car. It hit the pavement in the left or middle lane.* Sheriff's Department statement, 11/22/63 (WRv.19Hp.496).

What Royce Skelton and several of his companions were describing is most likely the spray of brain matter resulting from the Z313 or Z331 cranial explosions rather than a spray of concrete from a bullet strike on the street or curb. Whatever the reason for Foster conducting his prompt search, he quickly found a fresh scar near the top south corner of a storm-sewer catch basin on the south side of Elm at about Z400 that was largely obstructed from view. He was tipped off to the scar by the fact that, in bouncing off the concrete structure, the bullet had dislodged a patch of sod where the lawn encroached on the concrete. From his testimony there was no doubt in Foster's mind that one of the last two shots he heard created the scar.

> **Dallas Police Officer James Foster atop the triple underpass near Royce Skelton** - *(1) Found where one shot had hit the turf there at that location [pointing at a photo of the top of the concrete basin] . . . they caught the manhole cover right at the corner . . . this looks like the corner here where it penetrated the turf right here (indicating) . . . [the bullet struck] on the concrete, right in the corner [and] ricocheted on out.* WC interview 4/9/64 (WRv.6Hp.252). *(2) The plaza had been freshly mowed the day before, thus I noticed this clump of sod that was laying there and was trying to find out what caused the clump of grass to be there. That's when I found where the bullet had struck the concrete skirt by the manhole cover and knocked that clump of grass up. Buddy Walthers, one of the sheriff's deputies, came up and talked to me about it, and we discussed the direction from which the bullet had come. It struck the skirt near the manhole cover and then hit this person [James Tague] who had stood by the column over there on Commerce Street. He came by and had a cut on his face where the bullet had struck the column. You could see about where the bullet had come from by checking the angle where it scraped across the concrete and the column where it struck the pedestrian. It appeared to have come from the northeast, approximately from the bookstore area, but we were never able to find the slug. When I first found the scrapped concrete and torn up sod, I contacted my sergeant, C.F. Williams. He told me to remain there until they got down there and had some pictures taken, which they did. I don't know what went on from there in regard to that, other than the FBI was supposed to have gone down there*

and taken out a section of the curbing. I probably got away from there about four o'clock. Sneed, 1998, pp. 212-13.

Figure 60 shows Foster and Deputy Sheriff Buddy Walthers investigating the catch-basin area within nine minutes of the assassination. Foster is presumably telling Walthers that in his opinion the shots came from the TSBD. The investigations in progress at 12:39 apparently led to Foster's discovery of the catch-basin gouge. It presumably also preceded Walthers discovery of the scar on the south curb of Main following his conversation with James Tague. During a March 31, 1964, interview with the FBI, 58-year-old U.S. Postal Worker John Martin advised that he noticed the scar and told a police officer he should inform his supervisors. He is presumably referring to Foster who was guarding the area (cited in Trask, p. 573).

The initial discovery and investigation of the scar on the curb near Tague

Deputy Sheriff Buddy Walthers played a substantial role in the Dallas Sheriff's Department investigation of the Kennedy assassination and Tippet murder starting within a minute of the final shot. Quoting from his supplementary report:

Deputy Sheriff, Buddy Walthers, just east of northeast corner of Houston and Main - *I was standing at the front entrance of the Dallas Sheriff's Office when the motorcade with President Kennedy passed. I was watching the remainder of the president's party when . . . I heard a report and immediately recognized it to be a rifle shot. I immediately started running west across Houston Street and ran across Elm Street and up into the railroad yards. . . . Upon reaching the railroad yards and seeing other officers coming, I immediately went to the triple underpass on Elm Street in an effort to locate marks left by stray bullets. While I was looking for possible marks [with Officer Foster], some unknown person [Tague] stated to me that something had hit his face while he was parked on Main Street . . . . Upon examining the curb and pavement in this vicinity, I found where a bullet had splattered on the top edge of the curb on Main Street . . . .* Supplemental Report, 11/22/63 (WRv.19Hp.518).

After discovering the scar, he reportedly went immediately to the vicinity of the TSBD and alerted those law officers present that the shot that struck the curb appeared to have come from that building. Within a few days thereafter, he reportedly resumed his bullet-strike investigation this time (by appearances) within the Commerce Street underpass. The results were negative:

Deputy Sheriff, Buddy Walthers - *. . . me and Allan Sweatt two or three days after the assassination did go back down there and make a pretty diligent search in there all up where that bullet might have hit, thinking that maybe the bullet hit the cement and laid down on some of them beams, but we looked all up there and everywhere and I never did find one. I never did in all of my life tell anybody I found a bullet other than where it hit.* W.C. testimony, 7/23/64 (WRv.7Hp.550).

The Secret Service and FBI fail to find the catch-basin gouge but further investigate the scar on the curb

The Secret Service investigated the scar in early 1964 but failed to find it. A February 1964 memorandum by Agent Forrest Sorrels who was in charge of Dallas operations references one of the photos taken by the Dallas Police crime lab with a considerable degree of misplaced contempt for what Foster had reported:

Secret Service Agent Forrest Sorrels - *Someone [Officer Foster] reported that a bullet had ricocheted off the concrete slab in the corner next to the word "sewer" stamped on the manhole cover and for this reason the photograph was taken. However, it was never verified that a bullet hit it [because the FBI took over the investigation and either failed to find the gouge or decided it was not important]. The spot was personally examined by me and I did not see any mark that in my opinion could have been caused by a bullet and I did* *not see how it could have been possible for any fragment of any of the three bullets that were fired to have hit this concrete slab.* SAIC Sorrels, Memorandum, 2/13/63, CE 2111.

I cannot find any record of the FBI investigating the gouge on the catch basin after they took over the investigation from the city and county. In June and July 1964, the FBI rather reluctantly investigated the scar at the curb on the south side of Main at the insistence of the WC. After denying the scar existed in July 1964, in August 1964 they ended up taking some photographs of it before cutting the scarred area out and shipping it to the FBI crime laboratory in Washington D.C. Also at the WC's request, in September 1964, the FBI investigated an alleged area of kicked-up turf near the catch basin by sweeping with a metal detector a half-mooned-shaped area extending away from the curb that was centered at the catch basin (WC document # 1518, FBI Robert Gemberling Report which includes a half-page report dated 9/18/64 summarizing the results of a sweep of a 300-square-foot area by Special Agents Pinkston and Barrett using a Detectros Model 27, metal detector).

J. Edgar Hoover to Warren Commission General Counsel J. Lee Rankin - *Reference is made to your letter dated July 7, 1964. This mark was located and was found to be 23 feet, 4 inches from the abutment of the triple underpass. This mark corresponds with photographs taken by James Underwood and Tom Dillard. Small foreign metal smears were found adhering to the curbing section within the area of the mark. These metal smears were spectrographically determined to be essentially lead with a trace of antimony. No copper was found.* FBI letter dated August 12, 1964.

It was on the basis of these minimal FBI and Secret Service investigations that the WC reached the following erroneous conclusion in misstating Foster's testimony which is the official last word:

Warren Report page 116 - *Dallas Patrolman J.W. Foster, who was also on the triple underpass, testified that a shot hit the turf near a manhole cover in the vicinity of the underpass. Examination of this area, however, disclosed no indication that a bullet struck at the locations indicated by Skelton or Foster.*

A more-careful look at the evidence of the two curb strikes

In examining close-up photographs of the scar at the corner of the concrete catch basin, it is clear to me that the bullet that created it looked exactly like CE-399, the so-called magic bullet, and measured 0.53 to 0.65 cm wide by 3 cm long. It is also clear to me that it arrived from the direction of the TSBD sniper's nest at a downward trajectory relative to the horizon of about 4 degrees and a minus 19 degree angle relative to the back (southeast) wall of the basin. I can see where the nose first made contact and penetrated a short distance. I can see that the oblique impact with the hard concrete surface caused the intact bullet to immediately topple forward and to the right and then flip over again as it bounced off at a 2 degree angle relative to the back of the basin leaving a double impression. See Figures 60, 61, and 63.

The exit end of the gouge on the catch basin is perfectly aligned with the scar along the curb on the south side of Main near Tague. According to my protractor, the angle of the strike on the curb is approximately minus 32 degrees relative to the plane of the curb. See Figure 62 and 63.

The true significance of the wounding of James Tague's LEFT cheek and evidence relating to the fate of the Z328 bullet

Based on the location and orientation of this smaller scar on the south curb of Main, the bullet could have entered the Commerce Street underpass or deflected high in the air and out of Dealey Plaza. According to Walthers' investigations in November 1963, however, it did not enter the underpass.

13: Tracking Down the "Lost Bullet"

The wounding of James Tague provides evidence that the bullet did neither. In this respect, I find it amusing, and very much in tune with some of my other "surprise" findings, that Mr. Tague always emphasized that his scratch was on his right cheek in the face of compelling conflicting photographic evidence that it was on the left. Given he was looking northeast toward the motorcade, Tague presumably could not fathom that the bullet that struck the curb to his right could have generated a chip in the concrete that hit him on the left side of his face. Although Tague's claim that the wound was on his right cheek is supported by the recollection of Motorcycle Officer Clyde Haygood who reported seeing a "slight cut on his right cheek" (WC testimony April 9, 1964), the photographic evidence for the left cheek is much more compelling. Moreover, during his filmed March 30, 1999, interview for The Sixth Floor Museum at Dealey Plaza's Oral History program, Tague pointed to his left cheek when explaining where his wound was located. What I see in the photo is a small piece of red-hot concrete or lead barely grazing the cheek and creating a linear burn.

What this misrepresented/neglected wound-ballistics evidence is actually telling us, however, is that the concrete chip that hit Tague did not come from the curb; it came from the rectangular concrete column he was standing in front of. How fortunate that this important evidence is preserved in *Dallas Times Herald* Photographer William Allen's black and white photograph of key south-of Elm grassy knoll witness Charles Brehm taken within 15 minutes of the assassination. Allen's photograph inadvertently captured the slightly wounded left side of James Tague's face and is telling us approximately where we can hopefully still find the long-lost Z328 slug. I am not aware of who first noticed the scratch on Tague's left cheek in the Allen photo. The earliest reference to it I found is Groden, 1993 p. 41. See Figures 64 and 65.

Given what we see in the Allen photograph, after the tumbling bullet struck the curb to the east of Tague, it deflected about 20 to 30 degrees to the right and struck the concrete abutment right behind him at a point somewhere above his left shoulder. This abutment separates the Main and Commerce Street underpasses. The 27-year-old Dodge salesman was giving his initial statement to the Dallas Police when Oswald was brought in. The fate of the document is a mystery to me. Tague was interviewed by the FBI on December 16, 1963, and reported hearing three shots with the last two "in quick succession." He was interviewed by the WC on July 23, 1964, giving testimony that in combination with the findings of the FBI investigations conducted in July-August 1964 led the commission to conclude that one of the three shots went wild and hit the curb near where Tague was standing. At the time of his WC interview, Tague could not say for certain whether he was wounded by the second or third shots. He reported that he was not looking in the president's direction when the last two shots rang out disqualifying him for inclusion as a key eyewitness in the prior chapter.

In his self-published book, *Truth Withheld, A Survivor's Story: Why We Will Never Know the Truth About the JFK Assassination* (2003), Tague concludes it was the final shot that missed, drawing from the testimony of some of the same witnesses I cite in the prior chapter who related that the last two shots came very close together at the time the president's head exploded. From his own experiences, he concluded that the FBI attempted to subvert evidence that a third shot missed wild. Tague was among those that denounced the single-bullet theory, believing that at least one of the shots came from the grassy knoll picket-fence area and that there was a conspiracy and cover-up that involved the U.S. government.

Identification of the exact location of the missing Z328 bullet

If the bullet did indeed strike the concrete abutment, it was presumably tumbling as it made initial impact. Whether the bullet entered the concrete and became embedded or bounced off, this impact would have left a clearly visible scar in the weathered gray of the concrete column. The scar would have been identifiable as a rapidly fading bright spot for a week or two. That is how Deputy Walthers discovered the scar on the curb on the south side of Main and how Officer Foster could tell the gouge on the catch basin cover was fresh. If there were a similar conspicuous scar in the concrete column separating Main and Commerce, it stands to reason that it would have been similarly quickly discovered. The fact that it was not discovered tells me that the scar was up too high to be noticed and that the bullet did not bounce off intact.

Sure enough, a photo *Dallas Morning News* Chief Photographer Tom Dillard took from the rear of the second dignitary car as he was exiting Dealey Plaza shows a conspicuous white spot on this very column that is far enough up (about 17 feet) to escape notice. What's more, the spot is the size I would expect to see (about an inch). If this white spot on the column is the impact point of the Z328 bullet after it deflected off the curb on Main, it would require about a 30 degree left to right deflection and 36 degree upward deflection. These angles are more than reasonable given the curb-scar's orientation. See Figure 66.

Most significantly, my protractor reveals that if a concrete chip that jettisoned from the white spot in the Dillard photo caused the scratch to Tague's left cheek, it would have arrived at a 65 degree descending angle. The Allen photo confirms that the chip that hit Tague produced a scratch that starts off at a 65 degree descending angle. See Figures 65 and 68.

Although the trajectory of the column strike as depicted in Figure 63 is just about straight on (90 degrees), the point the bullet struck is along the rounded right edge of the east face. As such, it likely deflected to the right. Examining the abutment span area immediately to the right of the column using Google Maps/Earth, it appears that at least a portion of the slug is lodged in the span about 6 feet to the right of the scar. There is what appears to be a classic perforation at this location of about the right diameter with subsequent erosional beveling primarily on the side facing the column. Since the bullet may have arrived at or departed the column in pieces, there are additional scars and notches on the face of the column and the span that should be checked for fragments or residues. See Figure 67.

Just before publishing the first edition of this book, I provided the location of the hole in the concrete to the Dallas FBI and Police Department and copied the *Dallas Morning News*, *CBS* and The Sixth Floor Museum at Dealey Plaza on the communication. As of December 2016, I have not heard back.

Fate of the missing portions of the Z310 bullet

There is good reason to believe that most of the mass comprising the bullet that exited the president's head deflected off the governor's right radial bone and that the bullet was still intact. There is also good reason to believe that it broke apart when it struck the trim above the rearview mirror. Thus, knowing the bullet arrived from the right rear, the evidence is further indicating that whatever escaped the limo most likely deflected to its left rear. This raises the possibility that what bounced off the chrome trim created the "area of bullet shot on curb" identified by a licensed surveyor on a survey map of Dealey Plaza prepared for the WC. The bullet-strike area is in front of where Charles Brehm and the Babushka Lady were standing. The large fragment that was found on the front seat of the limo with the governor's flesh attached would also have ricocheted out of the limo to the rear if it had not struck the back of the rearview mirror. If the remnants of the Z310 bullet did indeed strike the curb at this point, they might still be found in the adjacent area of infield.

13: Tracking Down the "Lost Bullet"

Figure 60
Three pictures of the bullet-strike investigations of the storm-sewer catch-basin area taken November 22, 1963 - The first photo was taken by free-lance press photographer Jim Murray at 12:39 p.m. and shows Dallas Police Officer Foster pointing Deputy Sheriff Walthers to the TSBD. The second two are Dallas Police Crime Lab photos taken later that day after Foster reported his findings to his superiors. He remained guarding the area until they arrived. Foster marked the close-up on the right with an arrow to show his skeptical Warren Commission interviewer the location of the strike. The arrow is visible (see my red arrow), but the gouge itself is hidden from view by the dark shadows the encroaching lawn is casting along the edge of the concrete. Foster testified that the bullet had knocked a piece of sod out of place as it ricocheted off the concrete. Foster's arrow is pointing to the same conspicuous gouge shown in Figure 61 (first, Jim Murray Film, second and third Dallas Police Crime Lab via Robin Unger's JFK Assassination forum).

Figure 61
The bullet-strike gouge at the Z400-storm-sewer catch basin's south corner as it appears today - As I am indicating in the close-up and in Figure 63, the bullet that created this gouge had to be the one fired from the TSBD sniper's nest at Z328; the portion of the Z310 bullet that left the limo was not intact. From its length, configuration and orientation, the careful observer will discern that the intact bullet left its full impression twice as it flipped over upon impact and then bounced off toppling in end-over-end fashion. This is also why it knocked the piece of encroaching sod shown in Figure 60A loose. The bullet deflected slightly to the right because the left side of the nose made first contact. The scar's twisted alignment shows the bullet exited the gouge directly on course to its next point of contact on the south curb of Main about 15 feet east from where the slightly wounded south-of-Main spectator James Tague was standing (photographer of relatively recent date unknown, via Robin Unger's JFK Assassination forum).

203

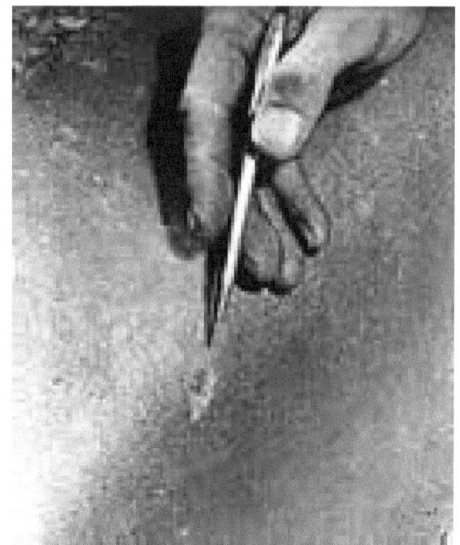 

Tom Dillard Collection/Dallas Morning News/The Sixth Floor Museum at Dealey Plaza

Figure 62
The bullet strike on the south of Main curb 23 feet east of the triple underpass abutment - The first two images were shot on Saturday, November 23, 1963, by James Underwood (motion picture) and Tom Dillard (photo), former occupants of camera car 3. The third shows Tague's position and was taken within a few minutes of the shots by Tom Cancellari former occupant of camera car 2 with his lens focused for a close-up. Note that both pens are following the trajectory of a scar pointing toward the catch-basin scar. The angle of approach relative to the plane of the curb is about minus 32 degrees (see Figure 63) (bottom Tom Cancellari, Bettmann/CORBIS).

13: Tracking Down the "Lost Bullet"

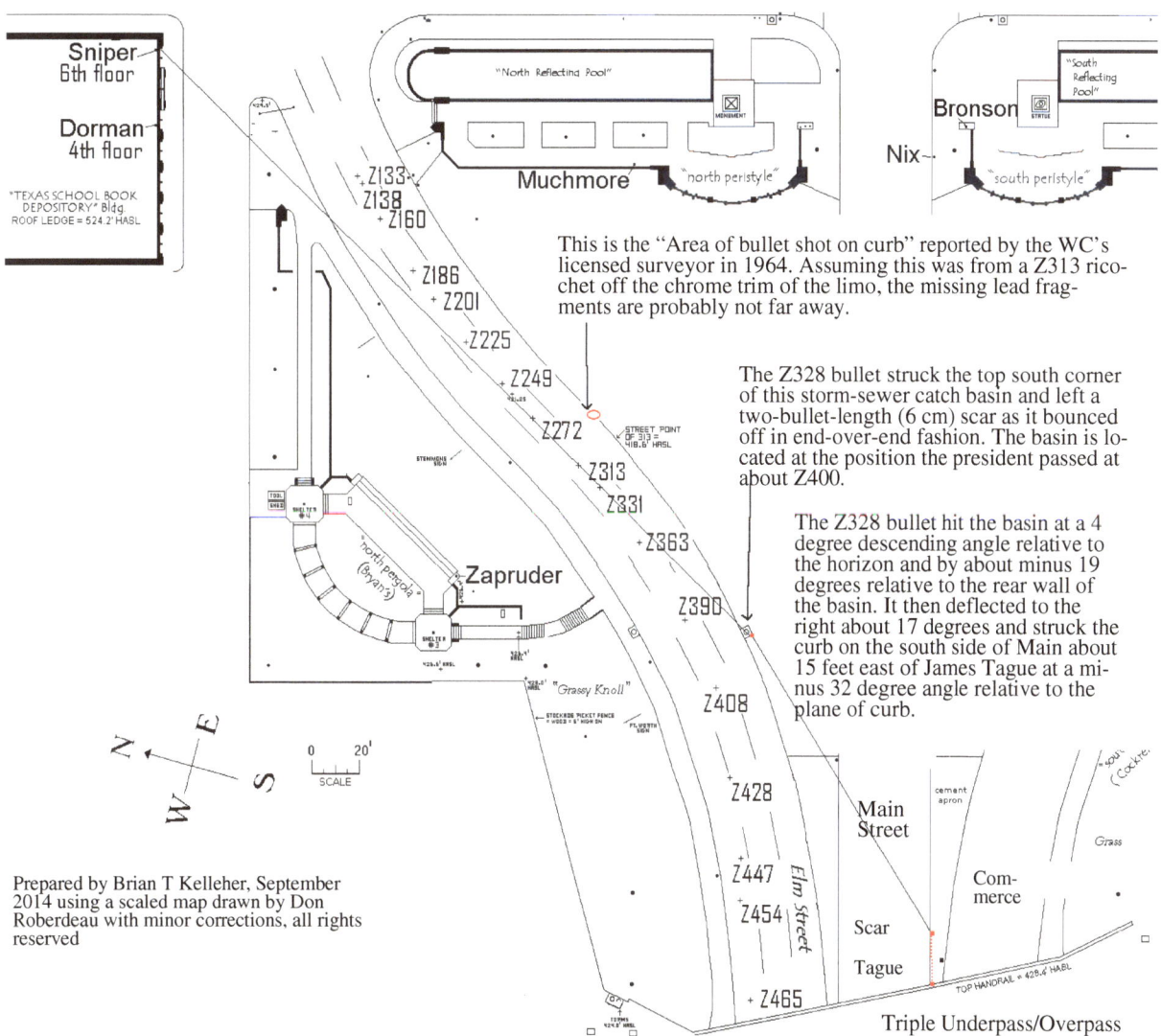

Figure 63
Lateral trajectories of the Z328 strikes on the curbs - The bullet arrived at the catch basin traveling at about a minus 19 degree angle to its rear wall. This is about a 6 degree right to left angle relative to the plane of the limo as of Z313. The tail end of the twisted scar on the catch basin is exactly aligned with the scar on the curb on the south side of Main Street. This scar is about 23 feet from the triple-underpass concrete column separating Commerce and Main at an angle of approach of about minus 32 degrees to the plane of the curb. See also Figures 60, 61, 62, 97 and 98.

The scratch descends at a 65 degree angle

Figure 64

Which of James Tague's cheeks were wounded? - The image on the left is cropped from a photo taken by *Dallas Times Herald* Photographer William Allen at the foot of the grassy knoll within 5 to 10 minutes of the shooting. It captures Charles Brehm giving what was likely his first detailed eye-witness account to a throng of spectators, media and law enforcement personnel. You can see what appears to be a scratch at the exact location Tague is pointing to in the photo on the right, but on the opposite cheek. Deputy Sheriff Buddy Walthers is in the foreground with a cigarette dangling from his mouth. He would soon be interviewing Tague, leading to the discovery of the scar on the south curb of Main Street near where Tague had watched the motorcade. They have just learned from Brehm that the president was shot twice with the second shot causing his head to explode. Given the photographic evidence, I conclude that Tague was rationalizing rather than remembering in pointing to his right cheek. Most significantly, based on where he was standing as he watched the motorcade, the orientation of the scratch reveals that Tague was struck by a concrete chip that arrived at his left cheek from his left rear at a roughly 65 degree descending angle. It just so happens, that there is visual evidence of a bullet strike in the concrete column he is standing in front of at exactly this angle of deflection. The photo (cropped) on the left was taken by William Allan (*Dallas Times Herald Collection*/The Sixth Floor Museum at Dealey Plaza. I found the figure on the right at Jefferson Morley's JFKfacts.org. See also Figure 66.

Figure 65

The true location of the wound to James Tague's cheek and its significance - The evidence is telling us that the concrete chip that created the scratch on Tague's left cheek came from the Z328 bullet striking the right edge of the rectangular column directly behind him following two deflections. I am predicting that at least a portion of the so-called "lost bullet" is to be found embedded in the concrete about six feet to the right of where it nicked the right edge of the column. This image of Tague is a frame from a clip that *Fox4 News* aired on the 50th anniversary of the JFK Assassination during which they interviewed Tague.

13: Tracking Down the "Lost Bullet"

Figure 66
Concrete photographic evidence of the "Lost Bullet" - *Dallas Morning News* Chief Photographer Tom Dillard took this photo within a minute of the assassination. In it, he captures the three camera cars departing Dealey Plaza with White House Cameraman Tom Atkins chasing after camera car 1 (now second in line). Dillard took the photo from the rear of the second dignitary car, a white Mercury Comet convertible, just after leaping aboard uninvited via the trunk. The car contained three Texas congressmen and presidential aide, Lawrence O'Brien. Dallas Police Officer James Foster is visible in this photo atop the underpass leaning over the hand rail. Dave Wiegman (center frame with Fedora hat) and Robert Jackson (to camera left looking right) are also in view. Dillard was originally located in the rear seat of camera car 3 (foreground) which he departed immediately after taking his two famous photos of the TSBD sniper's nest within 15 to 30 seconds of the assassination. Fortunately, this high resolution photo captures the central eastern face of the triple underpass in the background. I am identifying a conspicuous bright spot located about 17 feet up the rectangular concrete column separating Main and Commerce Streets as the location of a scar on the rounded right edge of the face of the column where the Z328 bullet struck and deflected to the right (see red arrow). To reach this location, the bullet would have to have deflected about 30 degrees left to right and 36 degrees upward after striking the rounded top section of the curb. This is consistent with the bullet's foot-level trajectory and oblique angle of approach to the curb (see Figure 63). As you can see, south-of-Main spectator James Tague's left cheek is in harm's way of any related concrete splatter that reached him at a descending angle of 65 degrees. The fresh scratch on his cheek descends forward down his cheek at a 65 degree angle. Using Google Maps/Earth, I can see what appears to be a bullet hole with erosional beveling along primarily the side facing the column about 6 feet away. It is in the concrete span extending above Main Street. There are other gouges and scars in the general area, suggesting the bullet might have arrived in pieces (Tom Dillard, *via Robin Unger's web site "JFK Assassination Forum"*).

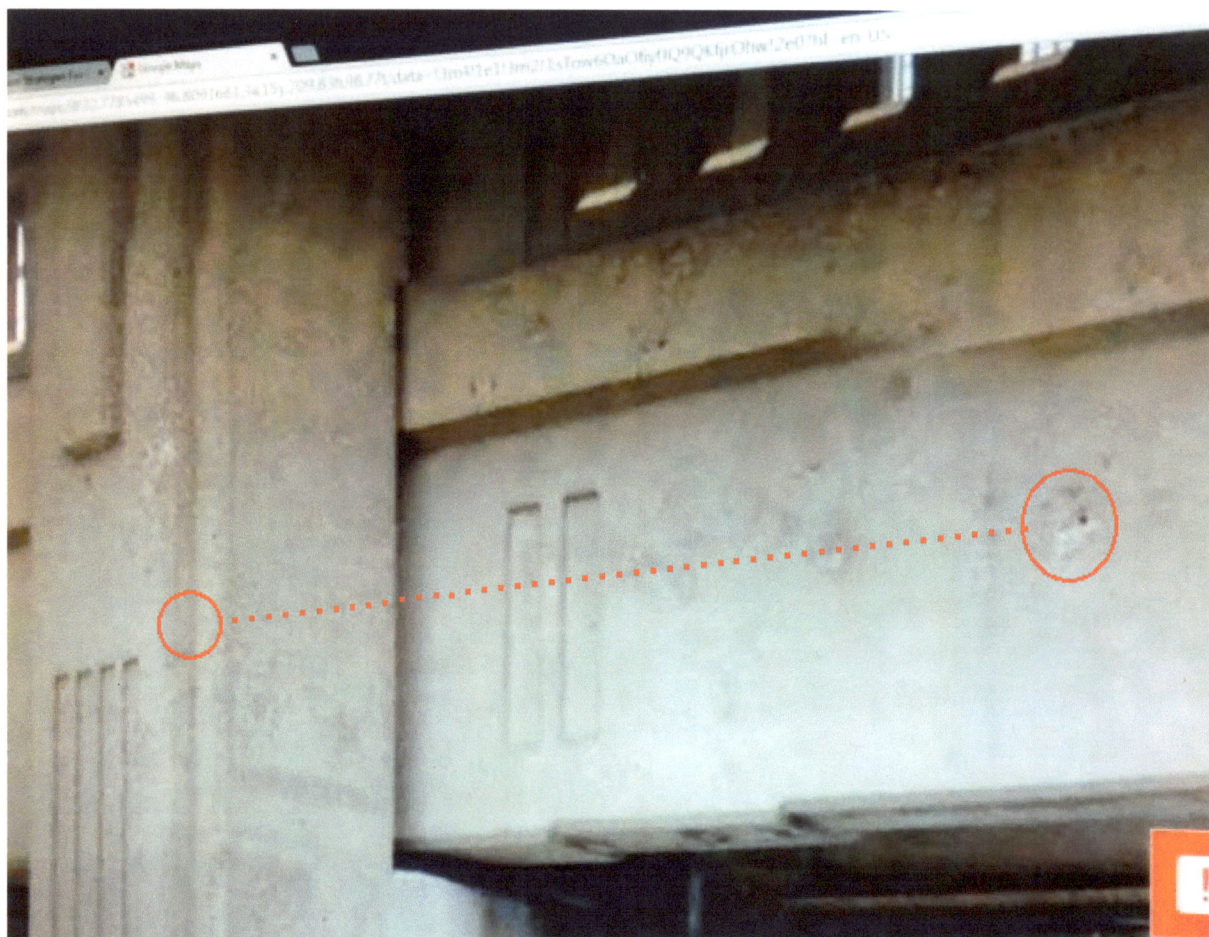

Figure 67
Possible bullet and or fragment strikes on the triple underpass concrete abutment - This is the area of interest identified in Figure 66. What appears to be a bullet hole shows beveling primarily on the side facing the column. This beveling presumably occurred well after the event, the result of fractures radiating from the hole. All the scars and holes in this general area should be investigated for lead smears and fragments. It is a cropped photograph I took of my computer screen during my first virtual visit to Dealey Plaza via Google Maps/Earth using the zoom feature (Phuong Vu, September 2013, all rights reserved).

Chapter 14

Resolving the Evidence on Wound Locations

The conclusions I reached in this chapter relied almost entirely on the photographic evidence including the assassination films and photos and autopsy photos and sketches. I also made use of the autopsy report and the drawings prepared by the WC and HSCA medical experts. Given all the new visual shot-identifier evidence I had on hand, I was able to provide what I am confident are the most accurate descriptions of the wounds made to date.

As part of this effort, I conducted my own very revealing vertical and lateral trajectory analyses to confirm the wound locations and to confirm all three shots came from the TSBD sniper's nest. I start this chapter off with the vertical analysis for the Z221 and Z310 shots and end it with the lateral for all three shots and vertical for Z328.

For starts, I will prove that the so called "magic bullet" did not change course and strike the back of the governor's right forearm, whereas the Z310 head-shot bullet did change course and strike the forearm.

Figures 68 through 98 follow and relate to the ensuing discussions.

Vertical trajectory analysis shows that the Z310 shot caused the wounds to the president's head and governor's right forearm and wrist and that the Z221 shot caused the rest of the wounds - Figures 68/69/70/71

The Z310 shot - My vertical trajectory analysis for Z312 produced a big surprise. I found that upon striking the back of the president's head at a descending angle of 15.6 degrees at a point 1.4 inches above the external occipital protuberance and 1.1 inches to the right of the midline, the bullet fired from the TSBD sniper's nest at Z310 deflected downward 7 degrees and exited the right side of the head at a 22.6 degree descending angle. The outshoot was about 4 inches above the president's right temple just inside the coronal suture and 1.4 inches below the crown. My analysis further shows that after glancing off the top of the governor's right radial bone, the bullet deflected upward and forward at an angle of about 16 degrees and hit the chrome trim above the rearview mirror where it broke apart. The nose portion hit the back side of the rearview mirror and ended up in the middle of the front seat with the governor's torn-away flesh embedded in it (CE-567). Most of the bullet's lead was deflected out of the limo to the left rear. See Figures 68 and 71.

The Z221 shot - My vertical trajectory analysis using Z222 and Z225 revealed that a bullet fired from the TSBD sniper's nest at Z221 was traveling on course at a descending angle of 20.5 degrees to cause, without any significant deflection, the wounds to the base of the president's neck and just the governor's right side, chest and thigh. This explains why it ended up intact and only slightly deformed. For the top side of the right forearm to be involved, the governor would have been either holding it at an impossibly odd angle in front of and just below his chest wound or down between his legs at a point tangential to the thigh wound. Such is not the case. A portion of the bright-white right shirt cuff is visible at frame Z222 at the level of the governor's mid lapel and to the right of and above the chest wound eliminating these possibilities.

Additional evidence that the single bullet theory needs to be revised with respect to the governor's forearm and wrist wounds - Figures 72/75/76/77

One of the two Parkland Hospital doctors, Charles Francis Gregory, who treated Connally's wounds reported that the bullet that struck the back of his right forearm created a jagged quarter-inch wide by inch-long gash with substantial missing flesh on the gaping upper end. He reported the top of the transverse wound was about 2 inches up from the main crease of the wrist. He further reported that the bullet completely severed the tendon serving the governor's right thumb and partially severed its nerve. He described the wound on the bottom of the wrist as a hard to see half-inch long slit that was about a half-inch above the main crease and ran parallel to it (WC Testimony of Dr. Charles Francis Gregory, pp. 7-8).

Consistent with the findings of my trajectory analyses, I found a great deal of additional evidence that a damaged bullet exiting about 4 inches above the president's right temple caused the glancing wound to the back of the governor's right forearm before ending up in the front seat with mangled pieces of his flesh attached to it (CE-567).

Further proof in the Zapruder film images that the Z310 shot struck the forearm - The careful Z-frame observer will confirm the following: (1) the governor's bright-white right shirt cuff jumps at least an inch forward and away from him between Z313 and Z314; (2) blood begins to appear on the cuff at Z317; (3) the governor is losing his grip on his hat as of Z320 and has lost consciousness by Z325; and (4) by Z332 the right cuff is a bloody mess. I consider the evidence of the signature jolt sufficiently definitive in and of itself to confirm the results of the trajectory analyses. See Figure 77.

Human-tissue analyses for Commission Exhibit CE-567 conducted to date is inconclusive and further testing would potentially confirm the tissues came from the top of governor's forearm - Figure 71 shows the two mangled portions of the Z310 bullet recovered from the front seat and front floor. CE-567 as it is known, originally weighed 41.5 grains thereby comprising about a quarter of the spent bullet's presumed original total mass of about 161 grains. It also includes a portion of the copper jacket and lead from the nose area.

CE-567 also includes four pieces of human flesh that were originally attached to the jagged fragment. This tissue was the subject of forensic investigations conducted in 1998 at the recommendation of the ARRB. The actual analytical report of the DNA testing said very little and was summarized in a NARA press release on January 21, 2000, as follows:

Although mtDNA was successfully extracted and amplified from the specimens, inconclusive sequence information was obtained for these four core samples. Additional amplification and sequencing attempts using the four paraffin-embedded samples remaining from the histological examination also proved inconclusive. As a result no comparison of the questioned human tissue with known sources is currently possible. NARA press release, January 21, 2000, "Lab Tests on Kennedy Assassination Now Complete."

Since the mtDNA analyses was inconclusive, why not conduct nuclear DNA analysis on tissue specimen # 3? I raise this question because the report says specimen # 3 showed "flattened superficial epithelium [skin] with well preserved nuclei" that were considered "extraordinarily well preserved"(Zimmerman, M. R., and

14: Resolving the Evidence on Wound Locations

Spencer, J.D., Maimonides Medical Center "Final Report of John F Kennedy Assassination Evidence," September 16, 1998. This is one of several appendices to a NARA report dated December 14, 1999 entitled, "Further Scientific Examination of the JFK Assassination Evidence."

I further note that the report of the microscopic examination which identified the four samples as human skin, makes no reference to a dense network of hair follicles. This is negative evidence that it came from the wound 4 inches above the president's temple which is just inside the hairline.

Commission Exhibit CE-567 fiber analyses conducted to date is inconclusive and further testing would potentially confirm the fibers came from the governor's damaged tendons and nerves - The 1999 NARA report covering the DNA testing also summarized the results of various analyses that were conducted to identify certain off-white fibers that were imbedded in the mangled lead of CE-567. These fibers were suspected by some of being from the governor's clothing. Because they were embedded in the metal, I suspect the fibers were fibrous connective tissues from the governor's right forearm. I suspect the embedded fibers were originally holding what ended up as four loose pieces of human flesh to the mangled lead fragment. Paper fibers cannot embed themselves in metal.

The doctors that NARA asked to conduct the analyses concluded that most of the fibers were similar to tissue paper: "a thin sheet of randomly oriented wood-pulp paper fibers." Mixed in, was what was described as a distinctly different fibrous material comprised of "a few long, slightly crimped, transparent, yellowish bundles with fibrils." This latter material was tested and determined to be protein (NARA report dated December 14, 1999 entitled, "Further Scientific Examination of the JFK Assassination Evidence, pp. 3-4).

Given all the evidence that the flesh came from the gash in the governor's forearm, I am going out on a limb and identifying both the tissue-paper-like material and the yellowish bundles with fibrils as being either from the governor's torn tendon and nerve or the sheath of fibrous connective tissue underlying them.

The forearm wound's jagged margins and presence of extensive coat fibers suggest a somewhat damaged bullet - Dr. Gregory was very skeptical that the magic bullet caused the forearm wound for multiple reasons. "I am not persuaded that this is very probable." He said the wound was very ragged and littered with fibers from the governor's coat consistent with CE-567 or CE-569. "One of these, it seems to me, could conceivably have produced the injury which the governor incurred in his wrist" (WC Testimony of Dr. Charles Francis Gregory, pp. 11-12)." These two fragments were presumably attached at the time of the wrist injury and broke apart upon striking the chrome trim above the rearview mirror. See Figures 68-71.

The NAA test results are consistent with the Z310 bullet striking the forearm - Contrary to what is stated in several articles by assassination researchers Kenneth Rahn and Larry Sturdivan as summarized in Mr. Sturdivan's book on assassination myths, the collective antimony data from Neutron Activation Analysis (NAA) does not provide scientific proof that the magic bullet struck the back of Connally's right forearm. To the contrary, the antimony levels in samples collected from a fragment from Connally's forearm (CE-842) are statistically similar to the antimony levels in samples from the magic bullet (CE-399). Additionally, the antimony levels are statistically similar for the following five fragments: one found in the front seat of the presidential limo (CE-567) that is definitely from the Z310 shot; one found inside the president's skull (CE-843) that is definitely from the Z310 shot; and three found on the passenger-seat floor (CE 840-1, 2, 3) that are definitely from the Z310 shot via Connally's forearm and wrist. This NAA data is telling us that the two bullets that struck the president and governor came from the same melt/ingot/box and have similar bimodal antimony levels. As such, the very limited test data shows a near certainty that at least some of the missing portion of the bullet lead that hit the president in the head at Z313 (CE-567) had antimony levels similar to that found in the magic bullet (CE-399). Consistent with this conclusion, according to the massive data-base that the FBI has assembled to conduct statistical analysis of bullet lead, the antimony levels within individual bullets are not typically uniform. Rather, the antimony levels are either "bimodal, or are mixtures of unimodal distribution" (National Academy of Sciences, *Forensic Analysis: Weighing Bullet Lead Evidence*, Chapter 3 Statistical Analysis of Bullet Lead Data, p. 46). See Figure 75.

The evidence is telling us that three bullet fragments recovered from under the left jump seat were associated with the governor's forearm and wrist wounds - The FBI report documenting the recovery of the three CE-840 fragments from the limo reveals they were found under the left jump seat. Given what we see in the Z film between Z313 to Z350, it is easy to envision how these three fragments would have ended up there if they were associated with the governor's forearm and wrist wounds. Indeed, there was a small exit wound on the bottom side of the governor's wrist where a fragment which exited at Z313 would have been on a direct course for the floor in front of the left jump seat. A bounce off the floor and rebound off the front seatback would have landed it under the left jump seat. The Zapruder film images show that the governor's bleeding right forearm was suspended above the left jump seat floor from Z313 to Z340 and was very likely resting on the floor under the left jump seat commencing at about Z341. The forearm and wrist wounds ostensibly shed the other two fragments during this interval. On the other hand, given the relative positions of the top of the president's head and the governor's head and upper body, my trajectory analysis reveals that, absent a torturous path, the three fragments could not possibly have ended up under the left jump seat without striking and damaging the front seatback and/or wounding the governor. See Figures 68 and 75.

The Z310 bullet entry hole is in the right occipital bone

I found two views among the autopsy photos published in Robert Groden's 1993 *The Killing of a President* and elsewhere confirming the inshoot location and dimensions, one taken before and one after the scalp was reflected. The one taken before the scalp was reflected is referred to by the ARRB as view 6; it was labeled by the autopsy surgeons in November 1966 for archival purposes as "wound of entrance in the right-posterior occipital region." The one taken after the scalp was reflected is referred to as view 7; it was labeled "missile wound of entrance in posterior skull, following reflection of scalp." See Figures 78, 79 and 80.

I used the butt end of the 2.75 cm wide (1.08 inch) ruler that the surgeons placed near the inshoot wound in views 6 and 7 to make sufficiently accurate measurements on the photos. My key findings based on these measurements are as follows:

Unraveling misunderstood autopsy photo view 6 - Figure 78

There is not the least question that view 6 is the rear of the president's head before the scalp was reflected showing both bullet wounds of entrance. According to the ruler in view on the Dox drawing of one of the color versions, the Z313 scalp defect measures 6.5 by 15 mm just as reported by the autopsy surgeons. There is a substantial triangular notch comprising the tip of the defect that helps orient view 6 and identify and orient view 7 with the scalp reflected (see below). There is a second smaller notch a little lower and to the right that serves likewise. The Z330 wound is visible along the rear margin of the greater scalp defect 2.6 inches above the Z313 inshoot's perforation.

Making use of the ruler - The Z313 wound in view 6 appears to the casual eye to be in the center of the head and high up because the head is rotated left and tilted. According to my measurements, however, the center of the wound is only about 4 inches from the rear hairline at all points. The crown of the president's

14: Resolving the Evidence on Wound Locations

head was about 8 inches above the mid-rear hairline ignoring the cowlick-area curvature. The cowlick area is centered about 7 inches above the hairline and lies within the curvature. According to view 6, the Z313 inshoot wound is halfway up the back side of the head.

Consistent with what the view-6 ruler is telling us, the autopsy face-sheet and Rydberg drawing both show the Z313 inshoot wound location about halfway up the back side of the head - In the autopsy face-sheet and WC's Rydberg drawing, the Z313 entrance wound is shown with the back of the president's head in what is referred to in medical terminology as the anatomically correct position. This means he is standing facing straight ahead with the top of his eyebrows even with the top of the ears (no tilting). As depicted, the wound is slightly to the right of center just at or slightly above the level of the top of the ears. See Figures 86 and 89.

Recreating autopsy photo view 6 - With my associate's assistance, I recreated autopsy view 6 using a trial-and-error approach including different camera angles. I started off by taping a half-inch square piece of paper to a point located 1 inch to the right of center and 4 inches above the rear hairline with my head tilted left and slightly back in the position it appears in view 6. While lying on my left shoulder, my associate took photos at various angles as I rotated my head to the left and tipped it. We easily attained a position where the location of the wound in the photo closely matched view 6. The distance to the hairline was about 4 inches at all points and the paper appeared to lie high up in the center of my head. The paper was about 2 inches above my external occipital protuberance (EOP), the pronounced bump about 2.5 inches above the mid-rear hairline. My associate and I were surprised to find that when I sat up straight with the half-inch patch still in place and adjusted my head into the anatomically correct position, the paper defect moved as if it knew exactly where it was supposed to go. It ended up roughly 1 inch to the right of center, 1.5 inches above the center of the EOP, 3.7 inches above the mid-rear hairline, and 2.5 inches from the hairline at a point behind the right ear. In short, the paper defect had moved into the same location that the autopsy face-sheet shows it relative to the hairline, EOP and top of the ears.

Why the Z313 defect appears to move downward - The 0.3 inch downward movement of the defect in un-tilting the head to achieve the anatomical position is due to the folding of the scalp and skin into the available space above and below the EOP.

Why the Z313 defect appears to move to the right - The 2 inch lateral movement of the view 6 defect toward the right ear in rotating the head into the anatomical position is attributable to the steeply convex shape of the sides of the skull.

The view 6 optical illusion - After spending several minutes making comically failed attempts to photo-recreate view 6 with the half-inch square paper taped at the position of the HSCA's cowlick entry point, my associate quit on me. There was no way; not even close. Those who see a wound in the cowlick area when they look at view 6 are experiencing an optical illusion. The hair above the wound is brushed forward/upward to expose it.

Unraveling the perplexing autopsy photo view 7 - Figures 79 and 80

According to an ARRB interviewer who had just asked puzzled Autopsy Surgeon Thornton Boswell to orient autopsy view 7: "Everyone that looks at these photographs [two versions of view 7] has a hard time orienting it (ARRB deposition of Dr. J. Thornton Boswell, February 26, 1996, pp. 77-82)." In January 1967, the Clark Panel re-labeled autopsy view 7 as "the other half of the margin of the exit wound and also showing the beveling of the bone characteristic of a wound of exit." The first half of the margin was considered to be located in two of three fragments that arrived from Dallas late during the autopsy. As already mentioned, the medical experts retained by the Rockefeller Commission in 1975 and HSCA endorsed this revised interpretation. They should not have!

I am 100 percent certain that autopsy view 7, as correctly identified by the autopsy surgeons in November 1966 when they still recalled taking the photo, is a landscape view of the rear of the president's head with the scalp reflected, showing the Z313 bullet hole in the right side of the upper occipital bone and the under surface of the section of scalp bearing the right half the Z330 inshoot defect. The key identifying anatomical features include the following among others: (1) the top of the president's left ear; (2) the very bottom of the president's right ear; (3) the upper-right portion of the back of president's neck in the area immediately below the right ear; (4) the severed mastoid muscle where an incision was made extending down along the rear hairline behind the right ear; (5) the far-right side of the highest nuchal line (suprema linea); (6) remnants of the fibrous occipitalis muscle in the area behind the right ear; and easiest to see (7) the Z313 inshoot wound with the same two triangular notches at or near its tip that are seen in view 6: the smaller one at about 2:00 o'clock to the tip.

The view 7 optical illusion - The leading edge of the reflected scalp flap in view is propped up to the point that the attached bone fragments that were lifted off the crown of the head lie almost on the same plane as the Z313 defect. This orientation creates a convincing illusion of looking down into an empty cranial cavity.

Orienting the president's rightward-tilted head - From the relative position of the ears and the orientation of the two triangular notches at and near the tip, we can tell the president's head is tilted to the right to the maximum extent with the neck held straight (about 30 degrees) and rotated about 15 degrees to the right. He is presumably lying on his left side with a surgeon propping his head up at the desired angle. If you draw a line from the upper-left corner to the lower-right corner of view 7 in landscape orientation, you are following the approximate midline of the back of the president's head from top to bottom.

The diameter of the Z313 perforation in the bone and absence of shelving is a tip off - According to the ruler in view 7, the perforation measures 6.5 mm by 7 mm. There is a complete absence of the type of shelving described in the autopsy report for the defect on the inner surface of the occipital bone.

The incisions surrounding the Z313 perforation including those used to collect tissue samples are a tip off - The careful observer will discern that to show the bullet's path through the scalp, the autopsy surgeons made an oval incision about a quarter-inch from the right perimeter of the scalp wound to preserve some of the underlying tissues surrounding it. There are gaps in the rim at both sides where the surgeons collected tissue samples subsequent to view 6 and prior to view 7. The supplemental autopsy report confirms the collection of tissue samples from the wound in the occiput in summarizing the results of a microscopic examination that showed several small fragments of bone at its margin.

The Z313 inshoot tunneling and its orientation is a tip off - The 8 mm long tunnel/gash through the rim of scalp that the surgeons left behind extends off the bottom and top of the perforation. With the president's head nodding left and rotated left as it appears at Z313, the open mouth of this tunnel into the cranium is aligned with the TSBD sniper's nest and the tip is aligned with the exit wound. It is slanted about 11 degrees to the right with the head in the anatomical position. According to Dr. Boswell, "I remember one picture [view 7] that shows the tunneling very well" (ARRB deposition of Dr. J. Thornton Boswell, February 26, 1996, P. 80).

The dimensions of the Z313 defect in the scalp and the distance below the rear margin of the greater defect are a tip off - The sum of the diameter of the 6.5 to 7 mm wide perforation and the 8 mm long tunnel is 15 mm. Views 6 and 7 are both showing an oval-shaped wound of entrance that measures 6.5 by 15 mm. According to the ruler, the oval defect is about 2.8-inches below the rear margin of the greater exit defect.

The bone fragments attached to the leading edge of the reflected scalp are a tip off - The skull fragments in the foreground of view 7 that are alleged to be intact frontal bone with an exit defect and v-shaped notch are in fact the several loose fragments of posterior parietal bone that can be seen in the lateral X-ray. They appear at the crown of the head along the rear margins of the greater skull defect and are a result of the impact of the Z328 shot. Humes testified in so many words that after extending the existing scalp lacerations down toward the president's ears, he took the existing loose flaps of scalp visible in the superior and lateral views 1, 2, and 3 and pealed them further back with the mobile bone fragments still attached. View 7 clearly shows the same flaps seen in the top and right side autopsy views after they were peeled further back just far enough to expose the Z313 inshoot in the skull. The front portion of the fragment with the semi-circular defect on its front margin is still facing up because this is how it was positioned when the flap was lifted up and peeled back. The bone fragment was detached from the scalp for just a few inches back from its front margin and the scalp was creased and weakened at this point due to being folded back by the force of the cranial explosion. To repeat, this semi-circular beveled exit defect is on a bone fragment removed from the crown of the head rather than frontal bone and is obviously from the Z328 shot, not the Z310 shot.

Lateral and anterior/posterior autopsy X-rays show two inshoot wounds and one outshoot wound - Figures 81/83

Though I have no training or qualifications as a radiologist, by checking for a defect 1 inch to the right and 1.4 inches above the EOP, I readily identified the Z313 wound of entrance on the enhanced lateral and anterior/posterior (AP) X-rays published by Groden and elsewhere. Once you know where to look, it is surprisingly conspicuous in both views. The AP view confirms the defect is 1.1 inch to the right of the midline. Both confirm that it is about 1.4 inches above the EOP.

In examining the X-rays, I can see exactly why one team after another of some of the most highly qualified medical and forensic experts in the country reached the clearly erroneous conclusion that the cowlick-entry wound is the location of the Z310 inshoot. They all had the AP and lateral X-ray misaligned by 2 degrees due to an understandable misinterpretation of a so-called 6.5 mm bullet fragment (see below). Moreover, they were completely unaware that there was a third shot fired at Z328 that struck the president in the upper head at Z330.

I conclude that what the forensic pathologists determined was a cowlick entry wound for the Z310 shot was in fact the inshoot wound for the Z328 shot which defected upwards and made its exit through the apex of the skull just a few inches forward of where it entered. I conclude that what the forensic pathologists identified in autopsy view 7 as a portion of the wound of exit from the Z310 shot is actually a portion of the wound of exit from the Z328 shot in the top of the head. The so-called bullet fragment in the cowlick area in the lateral X-ray lies outside the skull and is presumably a bone fragment associated with a fracture emanating from the Z330 perforation. See Figure 83.

Resolving the 6.5 mm fragment - Figures 83/84/85

I conclude with 100 percent certainty that the conspicuous "6.5-mm fragment" that appears behind and a little above the right eye in the AP view was incorrectly measured and was actually about 5.3 cm in diameter allowing for magnification. Objects on the front of the skull including the orbits were magnified by about 20 percent due to the angle at which the X-ray beams passed through in reaching the film. There is overwhelming evidence that this fragment was recovered by Autopsy Surgeon James Humes when he dissected this exact area after noticing the object on the AP X-ray. It was apparently wafer-thin in some places and broke apart during its recovery and subsequent handling by the FBI with a portion of it disintegrating. According to Humes' WC testimony "We dissected carefully in this area and in fact located this small fragment which was in a defect in the brain tissue at precisely this location . . . I find going back to my report, sir, that we found in fact two small fragments in this approximate location. The largest of these measured 7 by 2 mm; the smaller 3 by 1 mm" (Humes WC testimony, p. 7).

I conclude that in the AP view, the thin lead fragment was lying up against the damaged right orbital roof at the point it made contact for the following reasons: (1) given it was located in disrupted brain tissue, the object could easily have shifted its vertical position between X-rays and apparently did so; (2) there are brightness signals at this point of the orbital roof and just below it in both the AP and lateral views; (3) the object lying just below the bright spot in the orbital roof in the lateral view, resembles the rounded object in the FBI's photograph of the fragment; (4) there are overt fractures in the right orbital roof, right orbital floor and right cheek bone radiating from this exact location; (5) in his WC testimony, Humes stated he recovered a 7 by 2 mm lead fragment from this very location; (6) the autopsy report describes a separate bullet track in the disrupted brain tissue ending at this very location; (7) the Rydberg drawing shows this track and the fragment itself at this very location; and most telling of all (8) the shadow the object is casting in the photo that the FBI took of it upon its arrival at the crime lab, shows it was rounded on the reverse side. Thus, with the right amount of tipping and rotation, the object easily matches what is seen in the AP view also partly explaining its much greater brightness in the AP view than the lateral view; it is identifiable as a piece of the very tip of the bullet's nose. See Figures 84 and 85.

The Z310 bullet's exit point in the parietal bone and the greater defect - Figures 86 through 90

According to the sketch attached to the autopsy face-sheet, the greater defect created by the two cranial explosions was about 7 inches long and covered the entire right side of the top of the head from the front hairline to the cowlick entry point. Within this area starting at the coronal suture, the bone was blown out of the head by the Z310/Z328 shots in a roughly 13-cm long (5-inch) zone. In his sketch, Boswell seems to be showing the extent of the defect after the scalp was reflected and is including as "missing" the area of displaced fragments extending from the rear margin of the greater defect (see Figures 88 and 90). The area actually blown out at Z313 is about half this size. This is evident from the Zapruder film images and the fact that seven large pieces of loose fragmented bone, along with multiple smaller fragments, were found still attached to the scalp in the area surrounding the large cranial opening. See Figure 90.

Confirming the findings of the HSCA and autopsy surgeons, I found evidence that the Z310 bullet's exit point was in parietal bone 4 inches above the right temple along the inside of the coronal suture. According to the HSCA's scaled drawing of the president's skull, it lay about 1.4 inches below the crown of the president's head at the coronal suture. The key evidence is in the largest of the three fragments that arrived from Dallas late in the autopsy and the X-ray of the fragment.

The notion that autopsy view 7 shows a semi-circular portion of the exit defect in a flat piece of frontal bone a few inches above the right eye, is at odds with the HSCA conclusion that the exit wound lay along the inside of the coronal suture. It also conflicts with what is stated in the autopsy report. This is further proof that autopsy view 7 shows the inshoot wound in the outer surface of the skull with the scalp reflected.

Lateral trajectory analyses for the Z221 and Z310 shots confirms that both shots came from the TSBD sniper's nest and caused all the wounds except the Z330 wounds - Figures 94/95/96

The Z310 shot - To confirm that the Z310 shot came from the TSBD sniper's nest, I first used my scaled drawing of Dealey Plaza to determine that as of Z313, a shot fired from the TSBD sniper's nest would have struck the back of the president's head from the right rear at about a 6 degree right to left angle. I then determined that, relative to the anatomically straight-ahead position, the bullet that created the inshoot and exit wounds passed through the president's head at a left to right angle of 11 degrees. To make this determination, I used autopsy information on wound locations, AP-view and lateral-view scaled drawings of the president's skull prepared by the HSCA medical panel, and an on-line right-angle calculator. From these measurements and all else being equal, I conclude that if the shot came from the TSBD sniper's nest and there was no deflection, the president's head would have to have been rotated 17 degrees to the left as of Z312 [11+6=17]. See Figure 94.

In examining Z312, the president's head is nodding forward and left and his entire upper body is tilting left complicating the determination of the degree of anatomic leftward rotation of the president's head. Based on Dale Myers' 3-D simulation, he concluded the president's head was rotated about 26 degrees to the left as of Z312, plus or minus 2 percent. The HSCA's Thomas Canning, a NASA scientist, estimated the leftward rotation at 25 degrees. I used a trial and error approach. I assumed the president was unconscious. I allowed my head to nod forward until my chin was on my chest, leaned left and noticed that by the force of gravity my head nodded left and rotated left to just a limited extent. Carefully maintaining the angle of rotation, I assumed the anatomical straight ahead position and measured the leftward rotation at 15 to 20 degrees. Looking straight down into the limo at Z312, the president's head appears to be rotated left 25 degrees relative to the plane of the limo based on the direction his nose his pointing, but that is not the result of head rotation alone.

From the above findings I confirmed that at Z313 the president's head was rotated left about 17 degrees relative to the anatomic position, with the top of the slanted gash in the scalp pointed at the exit wound above the right temple, and the bottom pointed at the TSBD sniper's nest.

As demonstrated in Figure 68 and mentioned previously, the Z312 images show that the back of the governor's right forearm was in harm's way of the bullet exiting the president's head at a 23 degree descending angle including the 7 degrees downward defection between the inshoot and outshoot. While I can only approximately place the governor's forearm in the lateral plane as being forward of the president's left shoulder, Myers' 3-D simulation indicates that the bullet that exited the top right side of the president's head en route to the dent in the chrome trim above the rearview mirror, passed directly over the wounded section of the governor's right forearm.

The Z221 shot and source of the myth that the magic bullet deflected substantially to the right in passing through the governor's chest - According to my protractor, a shot fired from the TSBD sniper's nest would have struck the president at the base of the back of his neck from the right rear at about an 8 degree right to left angle. To conduct my horizontal trajectory analysis, I took advantage of the work conducted by NASA Scientist Thomas Canning in his dubious attempt to show that a shot that entered the limo at about Z190 caused all of the governor's wounds and the wounds to the base of the president's neck.

For a single bullet to have exited near the middle of Kennedy's neck and to have caused the wounds to the governor's right torso and left thigh, the governor had to be seated just enough inboard of the president. Accordingly, I have included in Figure 95 showing the Z223 lateral trajectory, the HSCA forensic panel's Z186 sightline analysis which was conducted using the Betzner Z186 photo. I was able to determine that the president's position was correct. I was also able to determine that Canning had the governor's right shoulder positioned a few inches too far inboard on the drawing by adding Zapruder's sightlines for frames Z183, Z186 and Z193. I also provide a rare photo (Robinson) and film image (Powers) that I found on the John McAdams' web site and added the sightlines for pictures taken on Houston by Marie Muchmore and James Altgens. Thus, what I have provided in Figure 95, hopefully leaves no reasonable doubt that both the president and governor were correctly positioned at Z223 to receive all of the wounds to their respective lower neck, torso and inner left thigh without any magical deflections in the lateral plane. See Figures 95/96.

The president's sitting position and wound locations at Z223 - Relative to the anatomic position, the HSCA concluded the bullet entered 4.5 cm (1.8 inches) to the right of the midline of the president's upper back and exited 0.5 cm (0.2 inch) to the left, just below his Adam's apple. The autopsy records, including autopsy view 5 and Humes' notes of his conversation with Parkland Hospital on the morning of November 23, 1963, reveals the outshoot wound involved the right wall of the trachea and was about 0.5 cm (0.2 inch) to the right of center. My best estimate is that the bullet traveled forward about 15 cm (6 inches) along the y axis in traversing the president's torso. According to a right-angle calculator, using distances of 1.6 inches for the x axis and 6 for the y axis, the bullet passed through at a 16 degree right to left angle. Given the known angle of approach from the TSBD was 8 degrees, this means the president's shoulders were rotated about 8 degrees to the right when he was struck in the back at Z223 [16-8=8]. This is consistent with what we see with the naked eye at Z225. See Figure 70.

According to the HSCA experts, the wounds were approximately anatomically opposite each other in the vertical plane. Knowing that the bullet from the sniper's nest struck him at a 20.5 degree descending angle, the president had to have been slouching/leaning forward about 20.5 degrees. This is consistent with what we see with the naked eye at Z225 [20.5-0=20.5]. See Figures 38 and 70.

The governor's sitting position and wound locations at Z223 - In providing their April 21, 1964, WC testimony, Doctor Shaw and Governor Connally put the bullet entrance point in the right shoulder a half-inch inside and a half-inch above the apex of the crease of the right armpit. This puts it about 8 inches from the midline of the back and 3 inches inside the outside of the right shoulder assuming a shoulder width of 11 inches. They put the bullet exit point about 2 inches inside the right nipple near the inner edge of an approximately 2-inch diameter hole. This large hole was created by the bullet striking and passing through the fifth rib in transverse fashion spraying bone fragments out perpendicular to the path of the bullet through the bone.

In the absences of a scaled drawing of the governor's torso, my best estimate is that the bullet traveled forward about 9 inches (y axis) in traversing the governor's chest and exited at a point about 3.5 inches from the midline which is 4.5 inches inside the entrance wound (x axis). This puts the right to left angle through the chest at 45 degrees. These distances could have been 8 inches and 4 inches and the like to yield this 45 degree angle.

Given the known angle of approach from the TSBD sniper's nest was 8 degrees, the 45 degree right to left angle means that, absent any deflection, the governor's shoulders would be rotated about 37 degrees to the right when he was struck in the back at Z223 [45-8=37]. According to Dale Myers' 3-D model, the governor's shoulders were rotated about 37 degrees to the right confirming there was no deflection.

14: Resolving the Evidence on Wound Locations

The Parkland doctors measured the descending angle through the governor's chest at 25 degrees which is also consistent with Dale Myers' 3-D model which has it at 26 degrees. Knowing the bullet's angle of descent was 20.5 degrees, this tells us the governor was leaning slightly back in his seat at about a 5 degree angle. This is consistent with what we see with the naked eye at Z223 [25-20.5=4.5]. See Figure 69.

The governor's distance inboard - We know from a scaled drawing of the presidential limo that the distance between the president's and governor's inshoot wounds (y axis) was about 27 inches. Thus, using a right-angle calculator, assuming both a lack of deflection and that the governor was struck at the same 8 degree right to left angle as the president, the governor's inshoot wound to his right shoulder was located about 4 inches inboard of the president's inshoot wound to his upper back. This is just as depicted in Figure 95 and confirms that the governor was seated as shown. According to this same figure, the midline of the governor's back was about a foot inboard of the center line of the president's back and the outer edges of their respective right shoulders were also a foot apart. See Figure 95.

Exposing and debunking single bullet theory mythology as it relates to the governor's forearm and wrist wounds

Single bullet theory (SBT) myth # 1, there is uncertainty as it relates to the governor's right wrist at the moment of impact creating the possibility that it was in the path of the Z221 shot - In opening this chapter, I pointed out that the governor's right shirt cuff is in view as of Z222 and that it is above the nipple level and well to the right. On that basis alone, there is no possibility that the bullet exiting an inch below and medial to the right nipple struck the top of the radial bone. See Figure 69.

SBT Myth # 2, there is a flip of the right lapel at Z223 caused by the exiting bullet - In opening this chapter, I pointed out that the signature downward/forward jolt of the governor's right shoulder commencing Z223 caused the suit to buckle and crease at the usual folding point along the lapel. Moreover, my trajectory analysis shows the bullet did not pass through the front side of the coat. The hole in the coat could only have been from the jettison of bone fragments perpendicular to the path of the exiting bullet.

SBT Myth # 3, the bullet deflected to the right when it contacted the fifth rib - I have demonstrated in this chapter that a Z223 trajectory line drawn through accurately placed wound locations reveals there was little if any deflection whether or not the bullet was tumbling.

SBT Myth # 4, the bullet could have struck the president and governor earlier than Z223 and created the president's wounds and governor's torso wounds - Using the actual wound locations, the geometry only works at Z223 plus or minus a frame or two. For example, using a properly scaled drawing, a bullet hypothetically hitting the president in the upper back at Z190 as proposed by the HSCA forensic panel would have arrived at a 14 degree right to left angle putting the outshoot wound to the front of the president's neck well to the left of the midline. See Figure 95.

SBT Myth # 5, the bullet exited directly below the governor's right nipple - To arrive at this clearly erroneous conclusion, one needs to completely ignore the evidence that was provided to the WC in April 1964 by Governor Connally and Doctor Shaw. Here is exactly what the governor told the members of the commission: [the bullet] "exited about 2 inches toward the center of my body from the right nipple of my chest (WC testimony, 4/21/64, WRv.4Hp.137).When Doctor Shaw was specifically asked where along the 20-cm long scar the bullet exited, he pointed to the same location about two inches medial to the nipple while providing the following description.

> **Robert Shaw, MD** - *The wound of exit was beneath and medial to the nipple. Here is the V [at the base of the front of the rib cage] that I was indicating. It is almost opposite that. . . . The entire surgical incision runs . .*

. just lateral to the . . . condral arch, and then extends laterally under the nipple . . . curving up into . . . the posterior lateral wall of the chest . . . 20 centimeters (8 inches). . . . All of the rest of this incision [extending away from the bullet's exit point] was necessary to gain access . . . for removing all the destroyed tissue because of the passage of the bullet. WC testimony, 4/21/64 (WRv.4Hp.137).

SBT Myth # 6, the bullet itself did not pass through the lung - Doctor Shaw perpetuated this myth. During the operation, he somehow got the clearly false impression that the bullet had tunneled transversally through the middle of the fifth rib for 4 inches after it made its initial contact. He blamed the damage to the lung itself on jettisoned bone fragments. This is not possible. According to the rules of geometry, to create the wounds he described, the bullet had to have passed through the extreme right-front right side of the lung creating distinct entrance and exit perforations in the fifth rib that were located about 7 inches apart.

Vertical and lateral trajectory analysis for the Z328 shot proves that Oswald fired the shot - Figures 97/98

Figures 97 and 98 show the findings of my trajectory analysis for the Z328 third shot. The results reveal that Oswald scored a remarkably lucky hit with the final shot only because, other than a slight inadvertent rise, he kept the barrel of the rifle steady while operating the bolt and firing as quickly as he possibly could while maintaining his second shot aim. The fact the bullet escaped the limo and caused the gouge on the curb proves it was fired from the TSBD sniper's nest at the exact same 6 degree right to left angle as the Z310 head shot and almost the same descending angle, 15 degrees vs. 15.6 degrees representing a very slight rise. It could not have come from anywhere else based on the trail it left behind.

To cause the catch-basin gouge in passing through the president's head, the bullet had to deflect upward by about 11 degrees and leave the limo at a descending angle of about 4 degrees.

To cause the catch-basin gouge without entering the limo and deflecting, the bullet would have had to have missed the president's head by about 10 feet on the high side at a descending angle of about 13 degrees. As discussed, there is a great deal of solid evidence that the Z328 shot did indeed pass through the president's head en route to the catch basin. I consider the signature jolt and cranial eruption at Z330/Z331 as confirmed by the Muchmore and Nix film images sufficient proof of this.

Notes on Illustrations - Figures 68 through 98

The medical evidence that I reproduced for use in the following illustrations are all in the public domain and were primarily obtained from the Mary Ferrill Foundation.

The illustrations that I generated to show the trajectories of the three shots were prepared with as much accuracy as possible. The photo-editing software I used (Corel Paint) to show trajectory lines is limited to one degree and the scale of the drawings does not allow for any more than that degree of precision.

14: Resolving the Evidence on Wound Locations

A red trajectory line is descending 16 degrees relative to the horizon from the barrel of the rifle in the TSBD sniper's nest to a point about 4 inches above the mid-rear hairline and an inch to the right of center in occipital bone. The black lines are to show the head was tipped downward 33 degrees.

Brian T Kelleher, September 2014, all rights reserved

The president's head is tilted 33 degrees downward relative to the horizon with 4 degrees due to the grade of the road.

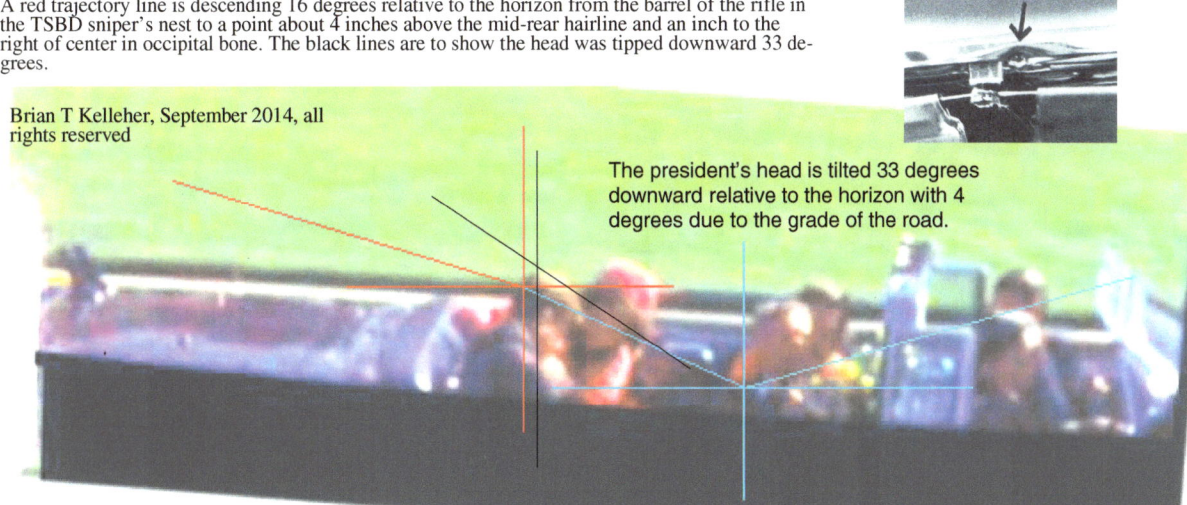

The aqua-blue line shows the bullet's path with the extra 7 degree downward deflection through an exit wound 4 inches above the temple. It also shows the 16 degree upward deflection off the surface of the governor's fractured radial bone that explains the dent in the chrome trim above the rearview mirror and the distribution of bullet fragments in the front compartment of the limo. A portion of the bullet bounced off the back of the mirror and landed on the front seat with some hairless flesh embedded in it.

Figure 68

Vertical trajectory analysis for the Z310 shot using Zapruder frame Z312 reveals it struck the back of the governor's forearm as well as the president's head - The dent shown in the inset is above the rearview mirror the back side of which was also dented and damaged. Using my photo-editing software, I cropped frame Z312 to focus attention on the president's position at impact. To account for the downward pitch of the road, I started off by using my photo-editing software to make the limo and curb level with the horizon. I then used the street elevations at Z250 (421.25') and Z313 (418.6') to establish that the downward grade in this 41-foot interval is 3.7 degrees and rotated the drawing clockwise by that amount. I used my properly scaled drawing to establish that the president's head was 250 feet from the base of the TSBD at a point directly below the sniper's nest as of Z313 and used this distance for my y axis. I then used the surveyed elevations for the street at Z313 (418.6') and the window sill elevation in the sniper's nest (490.9') to arrive at a gross elevation difference of 72.3 feet. I added 1.2 feet to compensate for the height of the rifle above the sill. I subtracted 3.5 feet to account for the president's slumped position in the rear seat to arrive at a net 70.0 feet difference in elevation and used this for my x axis. According to an on-line right-angle calculator, the bullet that hit the president at a point halfway up the back of the head arrived at a descending angle of 15.6 degrees relative to the horizon after traveling 260 feet. I then plotted the wound locations on the scaled drawing of the president's skull in HSCA Exhibit F-137 (see Figure 94) and determined that with the head in the anatomical position, the bullet traveled upwards at a 24 degree angle in passing through the head. Knowing the bullet struck the back of the head at a 15.6 degree descending angle relative to the horizon, this tells us that in the absence of defection, the president's head would have had to be tipped forward 40 degrees relative to the horizon if the shot was fired from the TSBD sniper's nest. Applying a protractor to Z312, the president head is tilted down about 33 degrees which includes 3.7 degrees forward tilt due to the slope of the road. This equates to a 7 degree downward deflection [40-33=7]. As you can see, with this 7 degree downward deflection, the bullet is traveling on course to cause the transverse glancing wound to the back side of the governor's right forearm and the small exit wound on the inner side of the wrist. Assuming an expected upward and forward deflection off the radial bone and with the evidence of the dent, the bullet is then on course at an ascending 16 degree angle to hit the chrome trim above the rearview mirror explaining the deformed fragments and sections of hairless skin found on the mid-front seat and/or front floor. In conducting my vertical trajectory analysis, I reviewed WC Exhibits CE-882, 883 and 884 covering the FBI's Z313 trajectory analysis (see Figure 92). I also reviewed the HSCA forensic panel's figures II-27 and II-28 covering theirs. See Figure 93 (Zapruder Family Collection/The Sixth Floor Museum at Dealey Plaza http://www.jfk.org).

The Complete Unraveling of the JFK Assassination

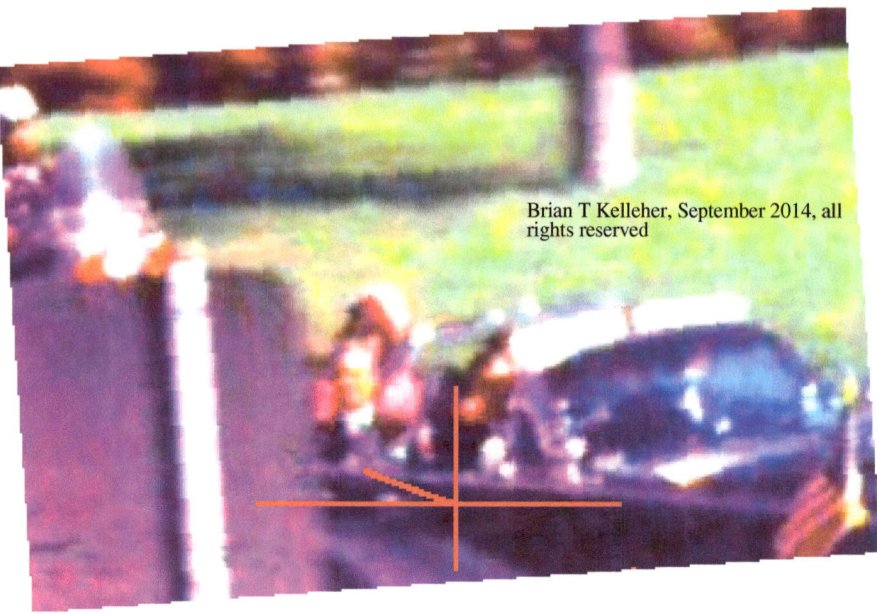

A red trajectory line that is descending at 21 degrees from the barrel of the rifle in the TSBD sniper's nest is shown exiting a point an inch below and an inch or two inside Connally's right nipple ending at a point on the inside of his left thigh about 5 to 6 inches above the knee. Zapruder was tilting the camera a little to the right and showed the grade of the road with an 8 degree downward slope when it is actually about 4 degrees. I therefore rotated the cropped image 4 degrees counter clockwise to offset his tilting.

Figure 69

Vertical trajectory analysis using Zapruder frame Z222 confirms the Z221 shot did not cause the wounds to the governor's right forearm or wrist - Using my photo-editing software, I cropped frame Z222 to focus attention on the governor's position at the exact moment he was struck by the bullet. Fortunately his right shirt cuff is barely in view showing the back of his right forearm is located slightly above and well to the right of the right nipple. Although my red trajectory line appears to originate just below the white cuff, I started the line to represent a location about an inch below and an inch inside his right nipple. I used the length of his face to estimate the distance below his chin. The back of the governor's wrist and forearm are clearly out of harm's way. Zapruder was filming the limo's approach from a distance of about 100 feet providing a view of the downward slope of Elm. However, according to my protractor he has the limo traveling on a descending angle of 8 and 7 degrees, respectively at Z222 and Z225 instead of 4 degrees. To compensate for the extra tilt, I rotated the cropped Z222 image 4 degrees counter clockwise. I then confirmed that the distance from the president's head at Z222 to the base of the TSBD at a point under the sniper's nest is 170 feet using a properly scaled drawing and used this for my y axis. I assumed a distance of 172 feet for Connally. I used the surveyed elevation for the TSBD window sill (490.9') and interpolated from the street elevations near Z210 (423.7') and Z250 (421.25') to establish a gross difference in elevation of 67.8 feet [490.9-423.1= 67.8]. I added 1.2 feet to compensate for the height of the rifle above the sill. I subtracted 3.5 feet to account for Connally's sitting position in the rear seat of the limo to arrive at a net 65.5 feet difference in elevation and used this for my x axis. According to the on-line right-angle calculator, the bullet that hit the governor in the right side between the shoulder blade and the crease of his right armpit arrived at a descending angle of 20.5 degrees relative to the horizon. As you can see, the exit wound under the governor's right nipple and its final resting place at the inside of his right thigh 5 to 6 inches above the knee are confirmed to lie approximately along the bullet's projected path, but not so for the wrist wounds. Though this illustration's primary purpose is to demonstrate that the so-called magic bullet could not have caused the wounds to the governor's forearm and wrist, in conjunction with Figures 70 and 95, this trajectory analysis provides solid photographic evidence that the Z221 shot caused all the wounds to the president's lower neck and just the wounds to the right side of the governor's torso and his inner left thigh (Zapruder Family Collection/The Sixth Floor Museum at Dealey Plaza http://www.jfk.org).

14: Resolving the Evidence on Wound Locations

Zapruder was tilting the camera a little to the right and showed the grade of the road with a seven degree downward slope when it is actually about 4 degrees. I therefore rotated the cropped image 3 degrees counter clockwise to offset his tilting.

Brian T Kelleher, September 2014, all rights reserved

Figure 70

Vertical trajectory analysis using Zapruder frame Z225 confirms the Z221 shot caused the wounds to the base of the president's neck and the governor's torso and left inner thigh - Since Z222 and Z225 were recorded just three Z frames apart (0.16 second) and the president and governor have not yet appreciably changed their relative sitting positions excepting the governor's dropped right shoulder, I applied the 21 degree-downward trajectory calculated for frame Z222 to frame Z225 to demonstrate that the bullet exiting Connally's chest was on course to the TSBD depository sniper's nest via the wound locations at the base of the front and back of the president's neck. The actual angle for a would-be shot striking the president and governor at Z225 is 20.2 degrees given a net difference in elevation of 65.8 feet and a distance of the governor to the base of the TSBD at a point under the sniper's nest of 176 feet. Since I can only plot to the nearest degree, this illustration would look much the same if I plotted that trajectory (The Zapruder Family Collection/The Sixth Floor Museum at Dealey Plaza http://www.jfk.org).

Figure 71

WC Exhibits CE-567 and CE-569 mangled bullet fragments and four pieces of skin and underlying flesh - At top is CE-569. At bottom left is the mutilated fragment recovered from the front seat that presumably originally had a single piece of flesh attached. The single piece ended up as the four pieces in the lower right. The evidence is telling us the flesh came from the top of the governor's forearm rather than the president's head.

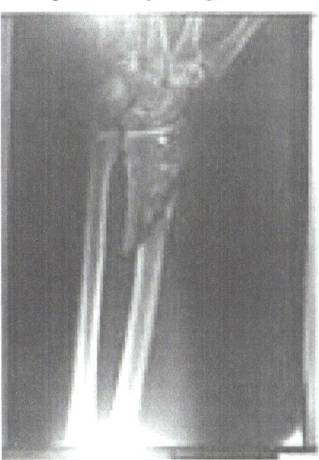

Figure 72

HSCA Exhibit F-83 X-ray of Governor Connally's right forearm - The 1 inch long by quarter-inch wide wound is on the back of the inner side of the right forearm beginning 2 inches above the crease of the wrist. The radial bone has a conspicuous compound fracture but there is just a tiny bullet hole through it. This fracturing represents a glancing wound. One would logically expect the bullet to have deflected off the top of the radial bone in an upward and forward direction. A tiny fragment passed through explaining the exit wound near the crease on the under side of the wrist.

The Complete Unraveling of the JFK Assassination

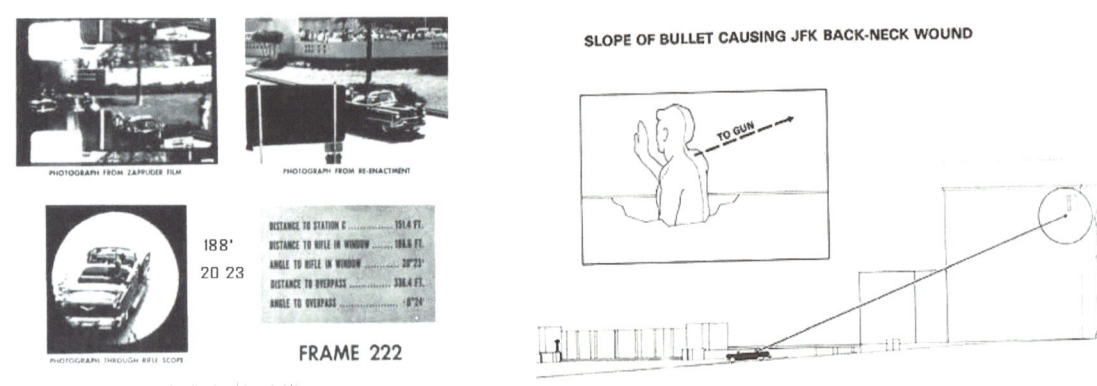

Figure 73

CE-894 and HSCA Exhibit F-142 showing the incorrect slope of bullet causing JFK back and neck wounds
- The WC exhibit is for Z222 and was prepared by the FBI. It has a 2 percent error presumably stemming from the incorrect assumption that the TSBD is 100 feet wide when it is actually 98 feet. It shows the distance from the rifle to the president at 188 feet when it is actually 184 feet and shows the bullet descending at 20.4 degrees when the angle is actually 20.5 degrees. The HSCA drawing is for Z190 and was prepared by Thomas Canning. It has a 5 percent error stemming from the use of an inaccurate topo map. It shows the distance from the rifle to the president at 171 feet when it is actually 163 feet and shows the bullet descending at 22 degrees when the angle is actually 23.4 degrees.

According to Dale Myers' web site, his model projects that at Z223 the president was located 200 feet from the sniper's nest and that the bullet struck the president at a 10 degree right to left angle. This tells me that Myers used the HSCA's flawed topo map to construct his model.

I rotated the image 4 degrees clockwise to adjust for the downward slope of the road. Representing a shot fired from the TSBD sniper's nest at Z221, I added a line that passes through the president's upper back wound at a 21 degrees descending angle relative to the horizon.

Figure 74

Dale Myers' 3-D computer-graphics simulation of the president's and governor's position in the limo at Z223 - The depiction looks reasonable except the governor's right arm is too low. Mr. Myers is showing the location approximately as it appears as of Z225. At Z222, we can see the entire top side of the white shirt cuff, putting it about 6-inches higher at the moment the so-called magic bullet struck Connally. The impact of the Z221 shot on the governor's right side caused enough of a downward and forward jolt to the right shoulder and arm to make the shirt cuff disappear between Z222 and Z223 (Dale Myers, all rights reserved).

14: Resolving the Evidence on Wound Locations

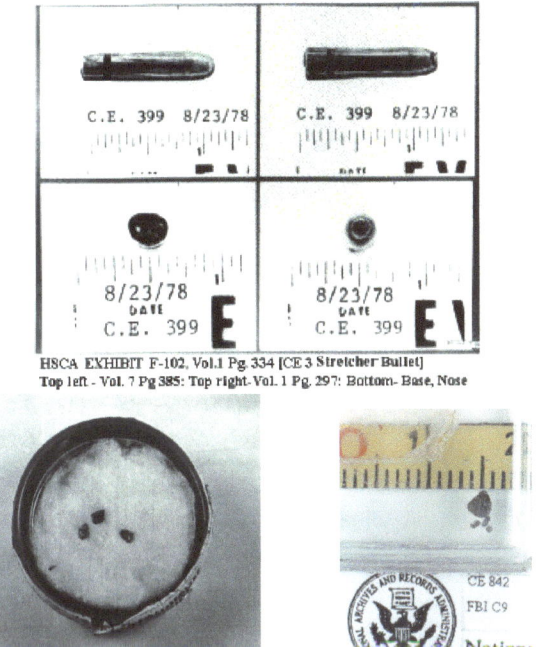

Figure 75

CE-399, 840, and 842 showing the magic bullet, three bullet fragments recovered from under the left jump seat, and the bullet fragments recovered from Connally's forearm - According to the forensic testing that was conducted via NAA, the antimony levels detected in samples collected from the magic bullet and the various fragments reveal that the two bullets that struck the president and governor at Z223 and Z313 came from the same production lot. The antimony concentrations in the two bullets matched in bimodal fashion.

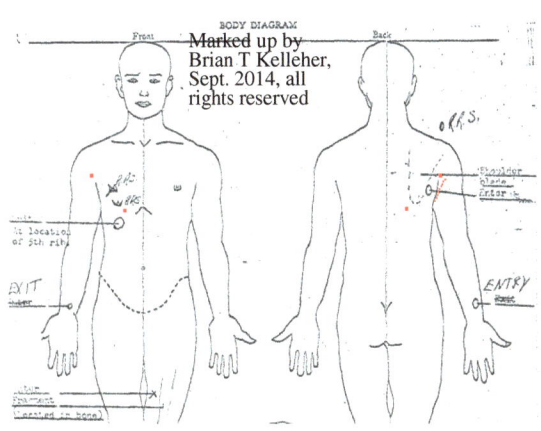

Figure 76

WC Exhibit Shaw # 1 showing the governor's wounds (cropped) - This un-scaled diagram of a teen male was handed to Shaw during his first WC interview. Shaw did not prepare it. I have put red dots on the approximate actual wound locations which are about 4.5 inches apart in the lateral plane. The entrance wound is shown about 2 inches too low and 2 inches too far to the inside. It is placed in the upper back rather than the base of the right shoulder where is can be discerned at Z340-346. The bullet exit point is near the inner margin of the 2-inch diameter hole located under and just inside the right nipple. With the inshoot correctly placed, it is evident that the bullet passed through the body at a 45 degree right to left angle and did not deflect to the right.

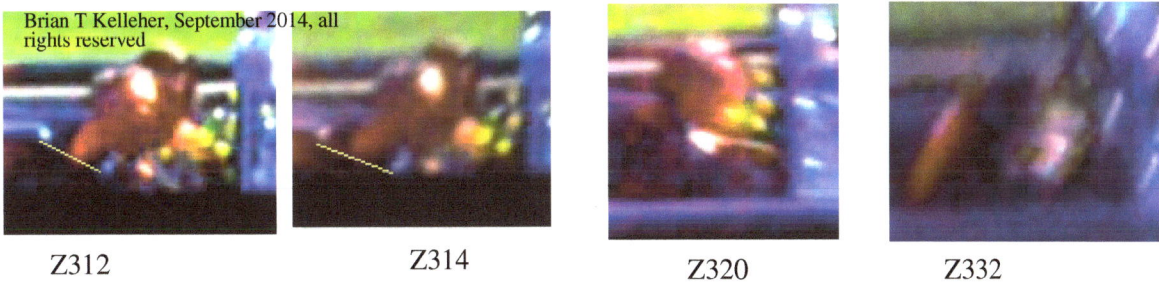

Figure 77

Photographic evidence in the Z Film images that Connally's wounds to his right forearm and wrist occurred at Z313 - Between Z313 and Z314, the bright-white right shirt cuff jumps forward and to the right at least an inch concurrent with similar movement to the president's head. As of Z320, the governor is losing his grip on his Stetson hat because his thumb is no longer working. He is just about to slam his head into the metal handrail atop the front seatback which occurs at Z324/Z325. By Z332, his right shirt cuff is a bloody mess and his right wrist with the rest of his body is limp. He is collapsing left-shoulder first onto his wife's right shoulder as if he had just been shot dead (The Zapruder Family Collection/The Sixth Floor Museum at Dealey Plaza http://www.jfk.org).

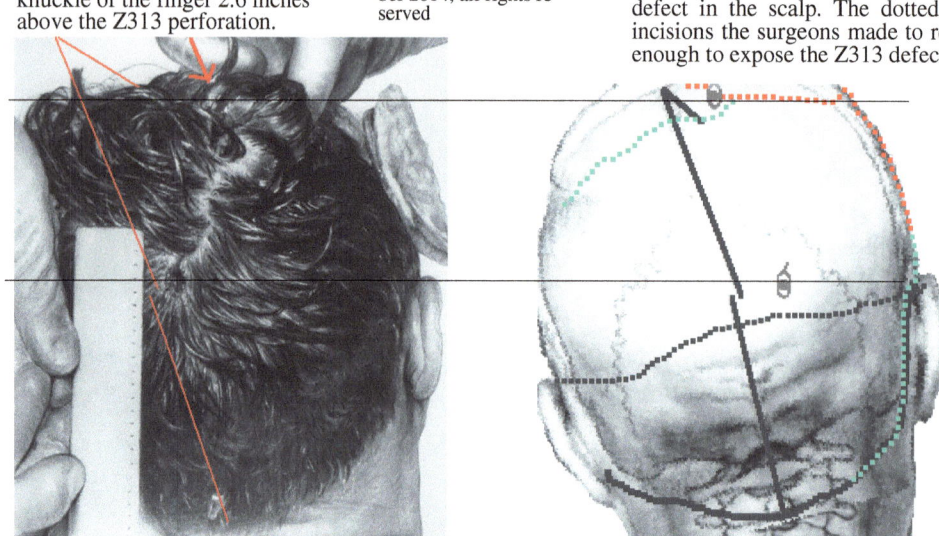

In view 6, the president's head is tilted to the left and rotated slightly right which collectively moves the Z313 wound slightly up and to the left. If you undid this tilting and rotation, it would move the wound to exactly where I am showing it on the Dox drawing of the back of the head. If you rotated and tilted the president's head to the left as it appears as of Z313 and then looked at the head from a point directly behind it, the top of the 6.5 by 15 mm defect in the scalp would be pointing toward where the bullet exited the skull 4 inches above the right temple and the bottom would be pointing back at the sniper's nest. If you then rotated and un-tilted the head into the anatomical straight ahead position, the wound would be angled left to right about 11 degrees.

Figure 78

Unraveling misunderstood autopsy view 6 of the two entrance wounds in the back of the head using HSCA Exhibit F-307 - Because of the camera angle and the fact that the hair above the wound is combed upwards to expose it, the oval Z313 inshoot wound appears higher up on and more toward the center of the head than it actually is. The autopsy surgeons took great pains to provide a flat-edge ruler with half-centimeter graduations to avoid any confusion on the Z313 wound's location and size. According to the ruler, the center of the wound is 9.8 cm (3.9 inches) above the lowest point of the rear hairline at the middle of the back of the neck. Also according to the ruler, the Z313 perforation lies about 2.6 inches below what appears to be the Z330 scalp defect in the cowlick area which lies along the rear margin of the greater scalp defect. This puts the Z313 wound in upper occipital bone about halfway up the back of the president's head at a point about a third of an inch above a line drawn across the tips of the ears and about 1.4 inches above the EOP. The president's head was about 8 inches long at the back measured from the rear hairline to the vertex. It is steeply sloped at the top in the cowlick area, the middle of which is about 7 inches above the hairline. Picture placing a book level to the top of the president's head and measuring the distance from the book's bottom straight down to the middle of the entrance wound. The distance is about 4 inches. The Z313 wound measures 6.5 mm across and 15 mm long confirming the 6 by 15 mm measurement recorded in the autopsy report and its face-sheet. Of critical significance, please note that the wound has a conspicuous triangular notch at the top. Because the president was hit with his head rotated and tilted left and downward, the bullet created a tunnel of sorts (gash) as it entered which lies along the line of its trajectory. As noted above, this tunnel is slanting left to right with the president's head in the anatomically straight ahead position. I see indications in autopsy views 6 and 7 of efforts by those taking the photos to mask the fact that the entrance wound was angled to the right rather than to the left explaining why they are so difficult to orient. This is further evidenced by the depiction of the wound on the autopsy face-sheet. It shows it slanting to the left rather than to the right. The surgeons apparently thought that to depict a wound caused by a shot from the right rear it was necessary to show it slanting right to left. See Figure 89.

14: Resolving the Evidence on Wound Locations

I added dashed red lines to both views to show the incisions made to reflect the scalp. I added a dashed yellow line to view 6 to show the rear margin of the greater scalp defect. The red arrows point to the Z330 inshoot defect in the scalp.

In view 7 as photographed, the head is tilted to the right to the maximum extent and rotated to the right to the maximum extent bringing the wound closer to the right ear. Here I have rotated the view 7 photo 20 degrees to the left to facilitate comparison with view 6.

Because a surgeon is pulling the president's hair forward out of camera view, we see the under side of the right half of the Z330 scalp inshoot defect along the rear margin of the greater exit defect.

The top of the left ear is pushed away from the head by a bone fragment.

The semi-circular notch to the left of the Z313 inshoot is half of the outshoot skull defect for the Z328 shot which exited near the crown of the head.

Brian T Kelleher, September 2014, all rights reserved

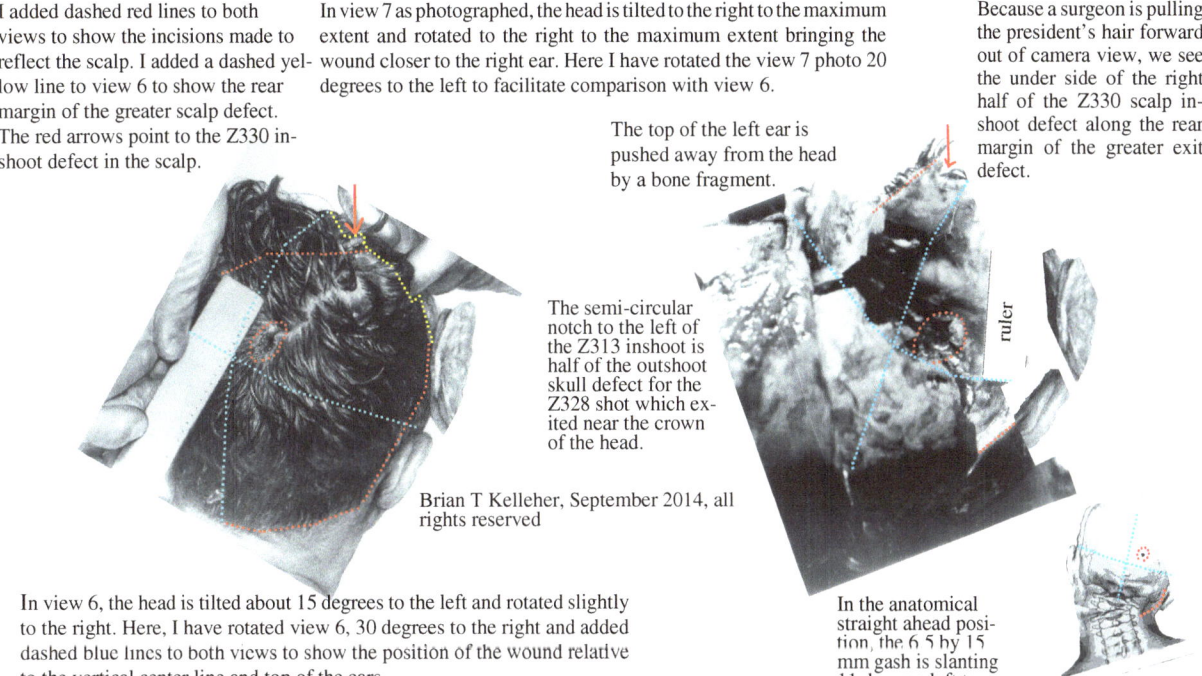

In view 6, the head is tilted about 15 degrees to the left and rotated slightly to the right. Here, I have rotated view 6, 30 degrees to the right and added dashed blue lines to both views to show the position of the wound relative to the vertical center line and top of the ears.

In the anatomical straight ahead position, the 6.5 by 15 mm gash is slanting 11 degrees left to

Figure 79

Syncing autopsy views 6 and 7, the entrance wounds without and with the scalp reflected - To facilitate comparison I rotated view 6 by 30 degrees to the right and view 7 by 20 degrees to the left and copied view 6's right ear and skull flap to view 7. The match is not perfect because there are different camera angles and different degrees and directions of tilting. The key identifying features for the perplexing view 7 close-up include: (1) the Z313 entrance wound itself which is the focus of the eye of the camera and the subject of the ruler in both views; (2) the two telltale triangular notches at/near the tip of the wound; (3) the top of the president's left ear which is pushed away from the head by reflected scalp and loose bone; (4) the very bottom of his right ear at the back edge of the jaw; (5) the severed right mastoid muscle; and (6) the right side of the president's neck in the area directly below his right ear. Once the incisions were made as depicted above left, the flaps of scalp in the side and top view of the president's head that had bone fragments attached along their rear margins were simply peeled back and to the right from the top of the head just enough to expose the Z313 inshoot in the skull. This explains the bone fragments that are in view in the foreground of view 7 one of which bears a portion of the exit defect from the Z330 shot. The two views are showing the same 6.5 by 15 mm wound of entrance at a point 3.9 inches above the rear hairline. With the aqua blue line that I added to show the anatomic horizontal midline, please note that the tip of the defect in the scalp is pointing about 11 degrees to the right consistent with a shot fired from the TSBD sniper's nest at Z310. The Z330 inshoot defect in the scalp can be discerned in both views. In view 6, it is along the rear margin of the greater exit defect in the scalp. In view 7 we see the under side of just the right side. The left side and top was along the rear edge of a scalp flap and was peeled back.

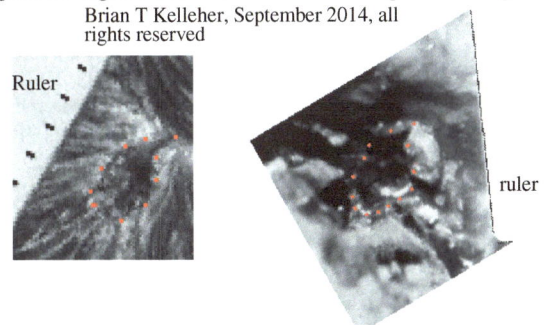

Brian T Kelleher, September 2014, all rights reserved

Figure 80

Close-ups of the view 6 and view 7 same Z313 scalp defect - I added red dots along the perimeter and adjusted the wound to the same scale to ease comparison. In both images the wound measures 6.5 by 15 mm. Tissue samples appear to have been collected from both sides of the rim left in place around the wound.

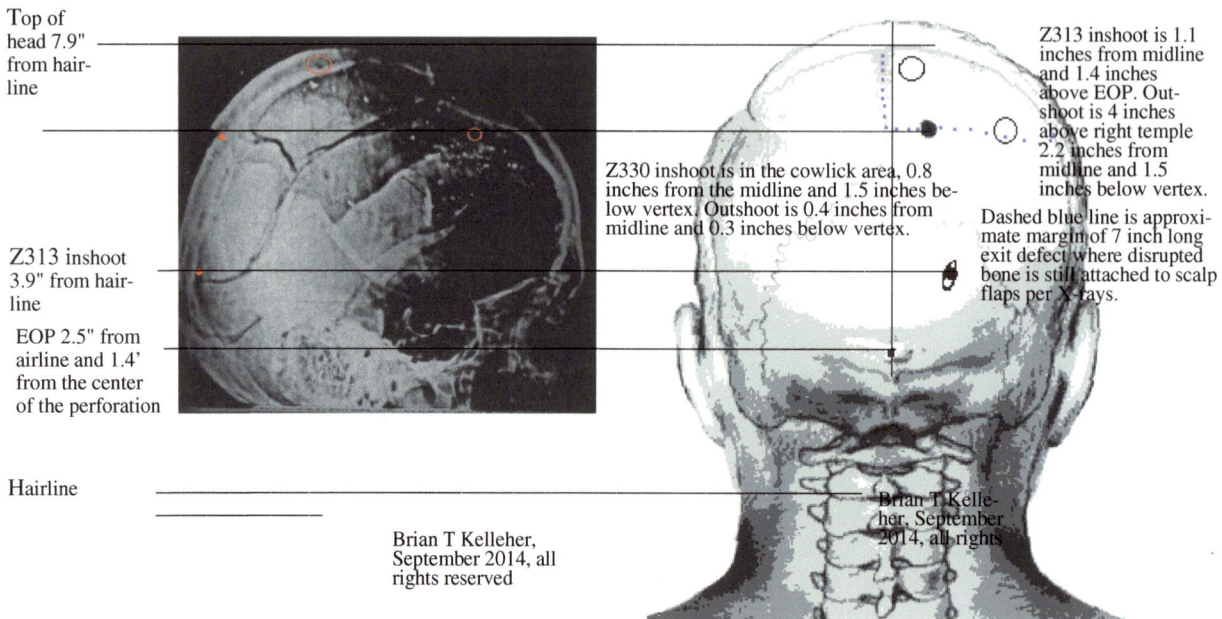

Figure 81

The exact location of the two inshoot and two outshoot wounds on the lateral X-ray and HSCA Exhibit F-307 - Drawing F-307 shows the HSCA wound locations. The Z313 inshoot's position is exactly as depicted on the autopsy face-sheet except for the slant direction. See Figure 89.

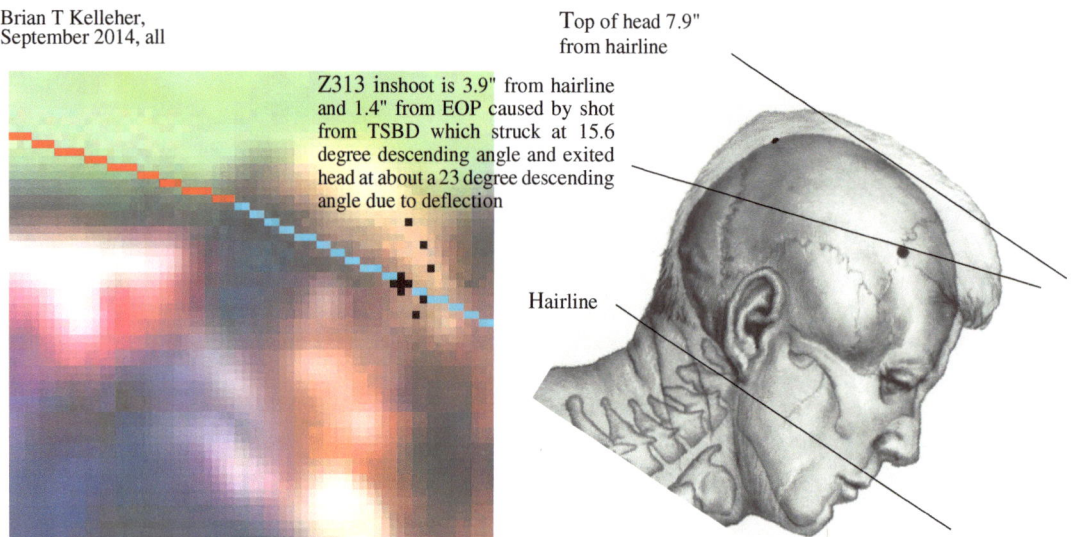

Along with the president's head being tilted down 33 degrees, it is rotated to the left about 17 degrees and tilted to the left preventing an exact match especially with respect to the location of the exit wound. Note how low in the face the president's nose and right eye appear and how close the crown is to the top of the ear and that extending the redline would put the exit defect at the crown of the head (Zapruder film images courtesy The Sixth Floor Museum at Dealey Plaza http://www.jfk.org).

Figure 82

The path of the bullet through the president's head at Z313 and HSCA Exhibit F-66 - I rotated HSCA Exhibit F-66, a side view drawing of the president's head 33 degrees clockwise to match Z313. See credit for Figure 68.

14: Resolving the Evidence on Wound Locations

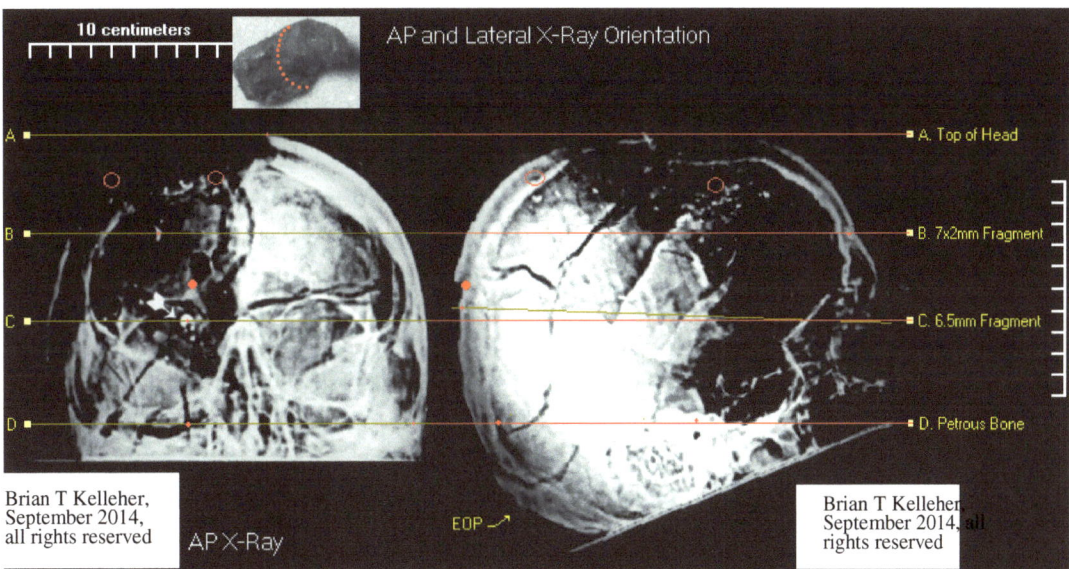

The inshoot perforation for Z313 is along the yellow/red line D labeled petrous bone and the 6.5 mm fragment is behind the roof of the orbit of the president's right eye. I used solid red circles to show the locations of the two inshoots and open red circles for the two outshoots. I have the cowlick entry a little higher up than the HSCA experts.

Figure 83

Syncing the anterior-posterior and lateral X-rays to identify the entrance and exit wound locations and to explain the 6.5 mm lead fragment - I adapted this drawing from an illustration published on the John McAdams' web site from a paper dated April 2000 by Joe Durnavich titled "Making Sense of the Head X-rays." With his orientation, Mr. Durnavich followed the lead of the HSCA medical experts and assumed that the 6.5 mm bullet fragment that is in clear view on the AP view lies in the rear scalp just below the alleged cowlick entry point. To sync the two views, he used the 6.5 mm fragment and another lead fragment he calls the 7x2 mm fragment that appears to be embedded in frontal bone a few inches above the right eye. My orientation follows the autopsy report and reasonably assumes that the 6.5 mm fragment is behind and just below a bright area of the damaged right orbital roof at or near its apparent point of contact. I used the same 7x2-mm fragment as well as the inshoot wound itself for my syncing orientation as well as the bright area of the orbital roof. This required a 2-degree clockwise rotation of the lateral view without changing its size. From the collective visual information, the Z313 inshoot wound lies along the inner end of an approximately 3 cm long (1.3 inch) outward radiating fracture that is conspicuous on the AP view and shows up in the lateral as a conspicuous dark area resembling in my eye a bullet hole. The lateral view shows a similar concentric fracture below it that is out of view low on the AP view. This dark bullet-hole-like area has a fracture extending out toward the right side of the head and then all the way up to the boundary of the large exit defect. Only part of this fracture is visible in the AP view. There is a second fracture in clear view on the AP view that extends straight up from the entrance perforation. This fracture is discernible on the lateral emanating from the inner side of the dark area. The inshoot is slightly above and inboard of where the bullet hole appears to lie in the lateral. According to the scale Mr. Durnavich provided, it is located at a point about 2.8 cm (1.1 inches) from the centerline, and 7.4 cm (2.9 inches) below the point the HSCA identified as the cowlick-entry point. This puts it about 1.4 inches above the EOP which is not visible in the AP view because the head is tilted back too far. I conclude that the HSCA cowlick entry is the inshoot for the Z328 shot. I conclude that the Z328 outshoot defect showing beveling on the outer surface is in view at center stage in autopsy view 7. I conclude it was located 2.4 inches forward of the Z328 inshoot near the vertex of the head. Based on the beveling the medical experts reported seeing in the lateral view, I interpret what appears to be a half-inch diameter upward and inward extension of the Z330 inshoot defect in the AP view as signature beveling and shelving on the inner surface of the bone. This beveling's orientation is consistent with an upward deflection of the bullet toward its point of exit. Mr. Durnavich credited Jim Felzer, author of *Assassination Science* (1998) for the copies of the X-rays he used.

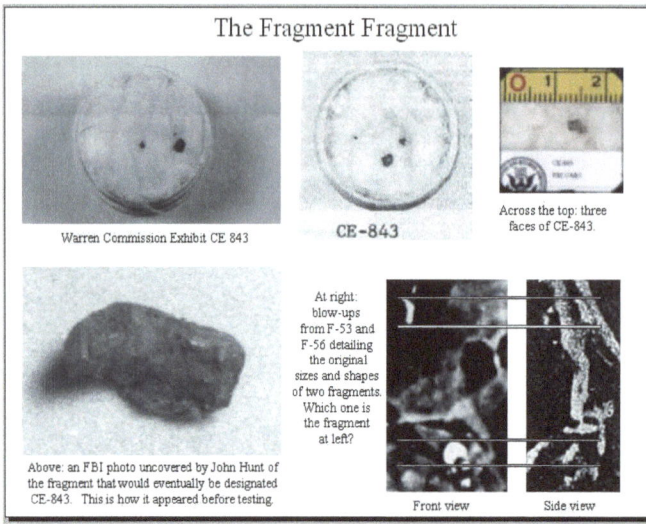
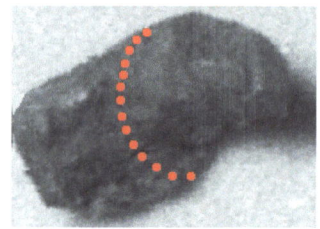

Figure 84

WC Exhibit CE-843 and its FBI photo, lead fragments recovered from the president's brain tissues - The FBI damaged the 7 by 2 mm fragment that Humes recovered behind the right eye before it was officially entered into evidence to the point it measured just 3 mm in diameter. This suggests it was wafer thin in places. Assassination researcher John Hunt located the above photo taken upon the fragment's arrival at the FBI crime lab. To the casual eye, this club-shaped object appears far different in appearance than the round object in the AP view. To the careful observer, it is obvious that they are one and the same. The shadow the object is casting off one side shows it is rounded. Thus, viewed from the flip side and allowing for some rotation and tipping, it will exactly match what is seen in the AP X-ray (see inset and Figures 83 and 85). Source: JFK Lancer.

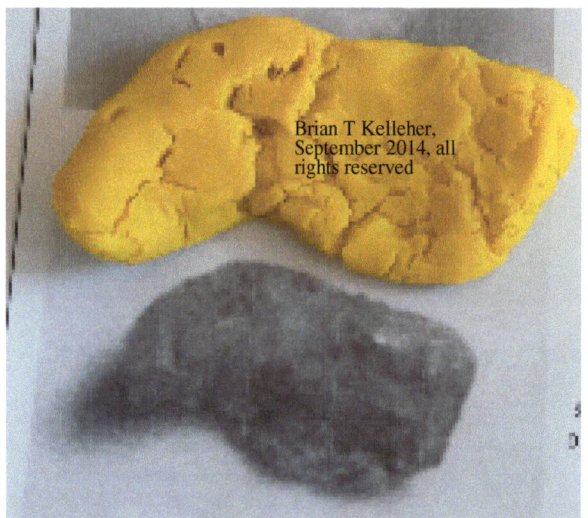

Figure 85

Sculpting the photo of CE-843 to confirm it is the "6.5 mm" fragment in the AP X-ray - Using some "Play-Doh," I was able to create a pretty close albeit crude match of what the FBI photo shows. I then flipped it over and adjusted the position to get the point of the wing at the right location and rotated it clockwise along its vertical axis until we got a close-enough match to prove the point. This also explains why the object was so bright in the AP view. The fragment is identifiable as a piece of the tip of the nose which is 5.3 mm in diameter (Phuong Vu, all rights reserved).

14: Resolving the Evidence on Wound Locations

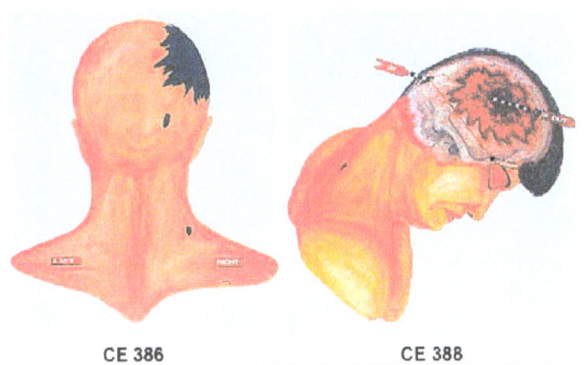

Figure 86

WC Exhibits 386 and 388: the Rydberg Drawings of the head wounds - The rear view drawing is reasonably accurate. The inshoot wound is about a third of an inch higher than shown. The side view drawing shows the greater exit defect with all the loose bone fragments removed. It also shows the tract of the "6.5 mm" diameter bullet fragment that was recovered. I highlighted the track in red and enlarged the fragment. These drawings were made without access to the autopsy photos and X-rays.

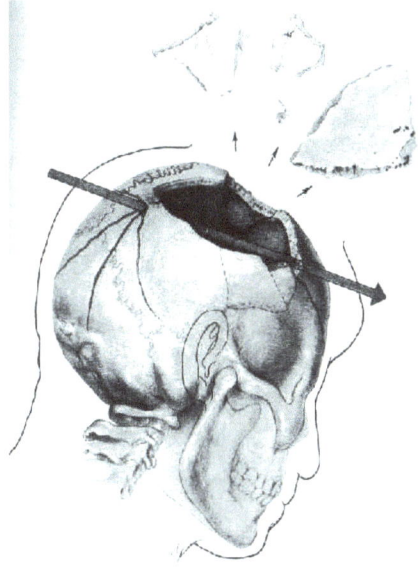

Figure 87

HSCA Exhibit F-66, the Dox drawing of the bullet's path through the president's head (cropped) - This drawing shows a bullet entering the Z328 inshoot and exiting the Z313 outshoot. The president's head is not tilted down enough to correlate with what we see at Z312/Z313. This drawing was prepared from autopsy photos and X-rays.

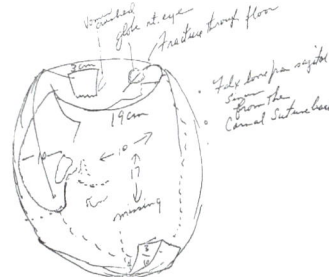

Figure 88

Boswell sketch of the top of the president's head - It is roughly portraying the area of missing and disrupted bone primarily on the top-right side of the head but also extending into the left. On the top-right side, the 10 by 17 cm (4 by 5 inches) missing area starts at the coronal suture and extends rearward through the disrupted cowlick area. Boswell shows four large bone fragments that were detached and dangling from the scalp: one at the right front in frontal bone; one on the left side of the head at the crown that was 10 cm in diameter, and two to the rear extending into the cowlick area, one of which was triangular in shape and measured 3 by 4 by 6 cm. The autopsy X-rays and photos show another bone flap on the right side of the head. There is a fracture extending from the Z313-bullet outshoot area through the roof and floor of the right orbit and into the right cheek. The volmer bone is crushed at the back of the nose.

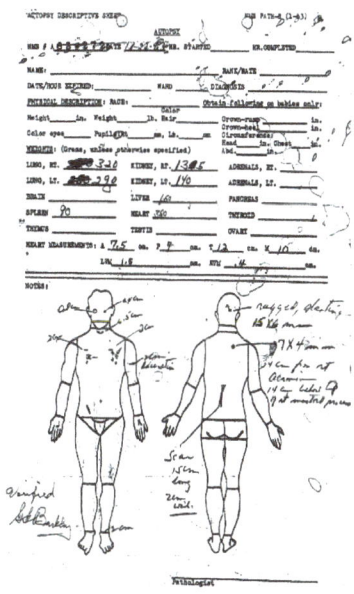

Figure 89

HSCA Exhibit F-44, JFK autopsy face-sheet - It shows the approximate wound locations which are supported by measurements, X-rays and photos.

231

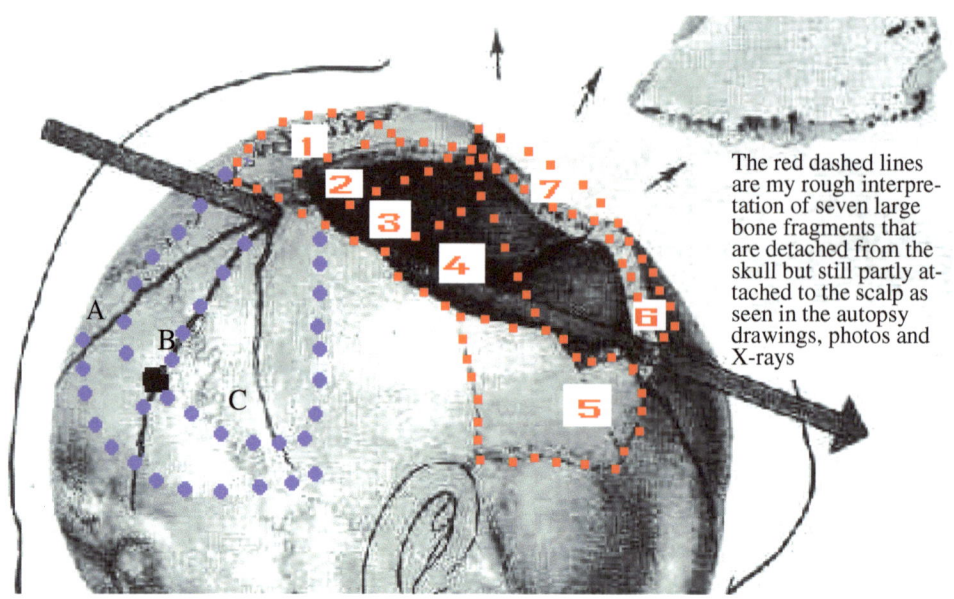

The fractures labeled A B C on the BOH are per the HSCA medical experts based on their interpretation of the AP X-ray. I think these fractures are actually on the front of the head involving the volmer bone, right orbit and right cheek respectively..

The blue dashed lines are my rough interpretation of the fractures radiating from the Z313 in-shoot per the X-rays.

The red dashed lines are my rough interpretation of seven large bone fragments that are detached from the skull but still partly attached to the scalp as seen in the autopsy drawings, photos and X-rays

Brian T Kelleher, September 2014, all rights reserved

Figure 90

Markup of HSCA Exhibit F88 (Dox drawing) showing the locations of the greater exit defect and main fractures - My red-dashed lines show seven bone fragments that were loose of the skull but still attached to the scalp per the autopsy drawings, photos and X-rays. Fragments 5/6/7 were out as of Z313 with just #5 in Zapruder's camera view. The Z328 shot caused the disruption in the cowlick area and crown of the head creating loose fragments 1/2/3/4 and other fracturing. When the side view and top view autopsy photos were taken, # 3 was dangling above the right ear. When the view 6 photos and lateral X-ray were taken, #3 was back in and # 5 was dangling. The AP X-ray shows Fragments 1, 2 and 3 dislodged and displaced and dangling inside the cranial cavity. Fragments 1, 2 and 3 can be seen in autopsy view 7 with # 2 at center stage bearing a portion of the beveled exit of the Z328 shot.

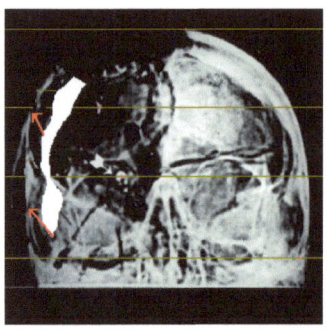
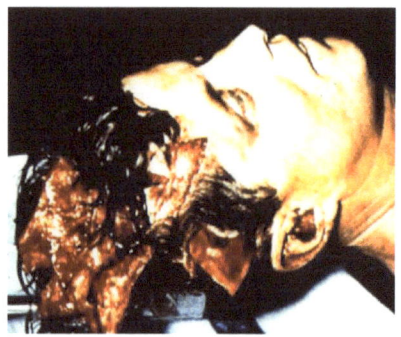

In autopsy view 2, the so-called v-shaped notch is formed by the edges of displaced bone fragments 4 and 6 as labeled in Figure 90 above. There is no v-shaped notch on the top edge of Fragment 5. Fragment # 3 is dangling above the president's right ear and is keeping # 5 in place. When # 3 is put back in behind #4, # 5 swings out.

Figure 91

Autopsy view 2, right side of the president's head and clarification of the so-called v-shaped notch via the AP X-ray - From the AP X-ray we see that the left side of the V is a portion of the top edge of displaced Fragment # 4 which is dangling within the cranial cavity and pressed up against its right side as revealed by the AP X-ray. The right side of the notch is part of the frontal bone fragment that is dangling from the scalp flap that comprises what is left of the president's front hairline. This bone fragment is perched on the top edge of fragment 4. I photo edited the AP X-ray and put Fragments 2, 3, 4 back where they belong further to the outside and higher in the head.

14: Resolving the Evidence on Wound Locations

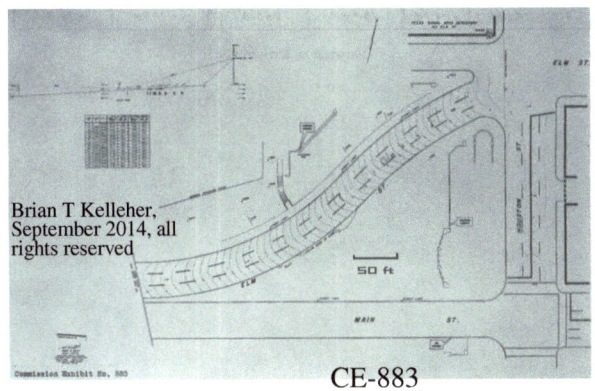

CE-883   CE-884

Figure 92

Source of 2 percent error in the WC/FBI trajectory analysis for Z313 - CE-883 is a surveyor's plat that was prepared for the WC and is accurately drawn to scale. It depicts the results of the FBI's May 1964 trajectory analyses for Z161 through Z313. The data table is repeated in CE-884. Unfortunately, the drawing is barely legible and contains no scale legend. I added the scale legend using the known widths of Elm Street (40 feet) and the reflecting pool (20 feet). For Z313, CE-884 shows the calculated line-of-sight distance from the president to the tip of the rifle barrel as 265.3 feet at an angle of 15 degrees 21 min. By the rules of geometry, this means that the distance to the foot of the TSBD at a point below the sniper's nest was determined to be 256 feet. It puts the assumed difference in elevation between the tip of the rifle and head wound at 70 feet which matches my estimate. According to the 50-foot scale that I added to CE-883, however, the distance from the president as of Z313 to the base of the TSBD at a point directly below the sniper's nest is about 250 feet which is the same number I obtained using Roberdeau's scaled drawing. I am guessing that the person who did the FBI analysis used an assumed width of 100 feet for the TSBD to calculate his distances. I initially made the same mistake only to find the distance is actually 98 feet across, a 2 percent error. At a distance of 260 feet, the 5-foot discrepancy is 2 percent off. This slight error does not make a significant difference in demonstrating the angle of approach or descent. See Figure 68.

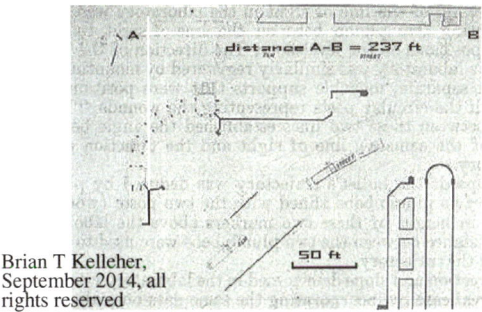
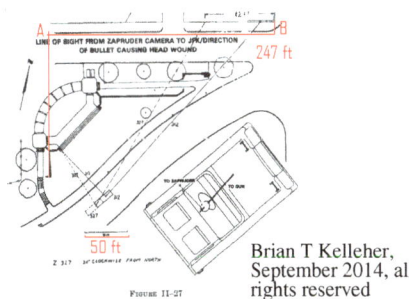

Figure 93

Source of 5 percent error in the HSCA trajectory analysis for Z313 - The barely legible drawing on the left is the surveyor's plat of Dealey Plaza that was prepared for the HSCA. It is accurately drawn to scale. I added the scale legend using the known widths of Elm Street (40 feet) and reflecting pool (20 feet). Figure II-27 from the HSCA report appendices, is the drawing that the forensic panel prepared on their own to show the results of their trajectory analysis. It is drawn inaccurately and therefore is impossible to accurately scale. Using the properly drawn surveyor's plat, the distance from the president to the foot of the TSBD at a point directly below the sniper's nest is about 250 feet which is the same number I obtained using the Roberdeau scaled drawing. Using the 50-foot scale on Figure II-27, the distance is about 265 feet. Using line A-B to scale the drawing, this distance is 256 feet and the TSBD is 100 feet wide. This suggests to me that the drawing was reconstructed to make it fit the FBI's calculated distance of 256 feet thereby compounding the FBI's original minor error.

The Complete Unraveling of the JFK Assassination

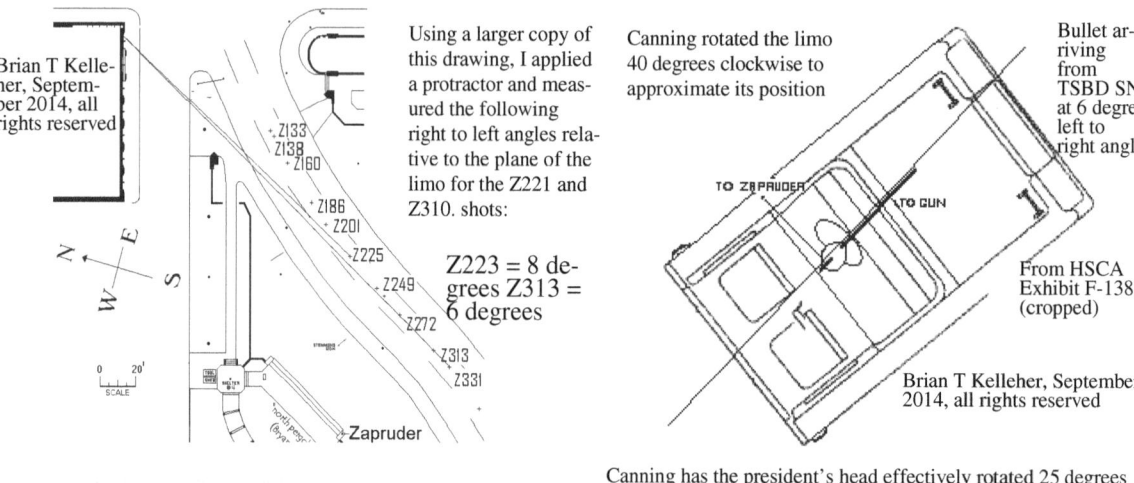

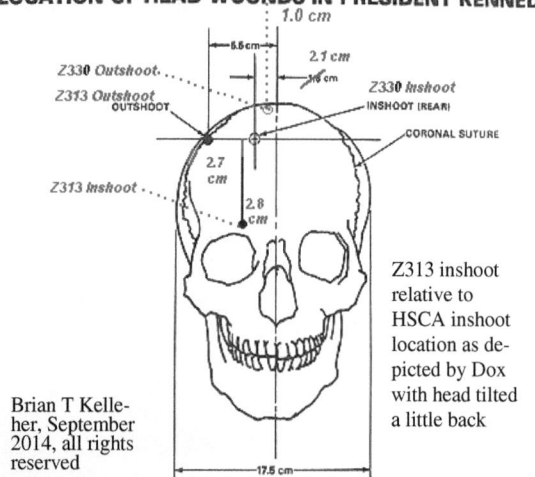

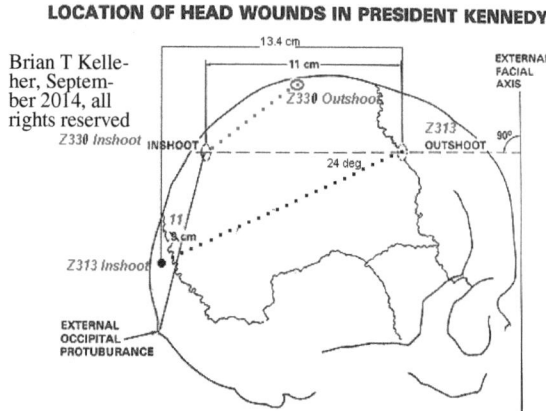

HSCA Exhibit F-147 (markup)   HSCA Exhibit F-137 (markup)

Figure 94

A simple lateral trajectory analysis for the Z310 shot using HSCA exhibits 137, 138 (in part) and 147 - I started off by applying a protractor to my scaled drawing of Dealey Plaza to establish that a shot from the TSBD sniper's nest would have arrived from the right rear at a 6 degree right to left angle. I then used the above HSCA exhibits and added the actual inshoot location to establish that the inshoot and exit wounds were 2.7 centimeters apart along the x axis and 13.4 centimeters apart along the y axis. Given these distances, according to an on-line right-angle calculator, the bullet passed through the president's head at an 11.4 degree left to right angle. This means that if the shot came from the sniper's nest at a 6 degree angle and there was no deflection, the president's head had to be rotated 17.4 degrees to the left as of Z312 [11.4+6=17.4]. Though this does not jive with the output of Dale Myers' 3-D simulation from which he concludes the president's head was rotated about 26 degrees to the left as of Z312, my own trial and error approach confirmed the president's head was rotated about 17 degrees left. The combination of leaning left and nodding left produces apparent leftward rotation looking down into the limo and accounts for the difference. As discussed previously, it was the downward tipping of the president's head at Z312 that caused the Z310 bullet to create a 6.5 by 15 mm gash in the tissues of the scalp at the point of impact. See also Figures 79 and 80.

14: Resolving the Evidence on Wound Locations

Frame from the Dave Powers film shot from the Queen Mary showing the limo leaving Love Field (mcadams...)

Duane Robinson photo of the limo on Cedar Creek (cropped) (mcadams...)

Brian T Kelleher, September 2014, all rights reserved

James Altgens photo of the limo starting down Houston Street (cropped)

Frame from Muchmore first sequence of limo entering the intersection of Main and Houston (cropped)

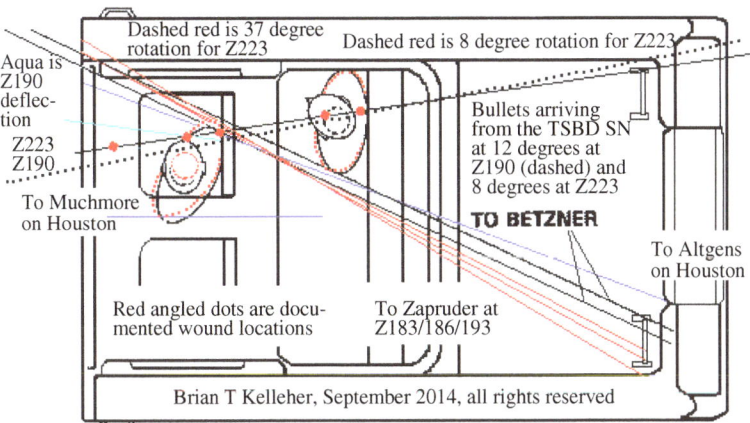

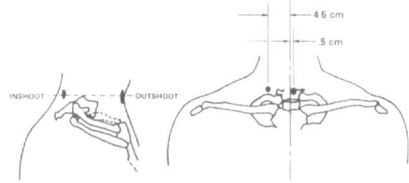

HSCA Exhibit F-376 - Drawing of the wounds to the base of the president's neck - The outshoot was 0.2 inches to the right of center (not the left as depicted) and involved the right wall of the trachea. The inshoot was 1.8 inches to the right of center. In the anatomic position the wounds were about 1.6 inches apart on the x-axis and 6 inches apart on the y. Thus, the bullet passed through at a 16 degree right to left angle.

I adjusted the seating positions drawn by Canning using sightlines for Altgens and Muchmore on Houston and for Zapruder for frames Z183, Z186 and Z193. I have also added the paths of bullet fired from the sniper's nest entering the limo at Z190 and Z223 which entered the base of the president's neck at a point a few inches to the right of the mid line at 12 and 8 degrees right to left angle relative to the plane of the limo.

Figure 95

A simple lateral trajectory analysis for the Z221 shot using HSCA Figure II-23 - Thomas Canning was basing his trajectory analysis on Z190 which is 1.7 seconds before Z223. The sightlines tell me that the governor's right shoulder was several inches outboard of where Canning has it. As of Z223, the president was turned about 8 degrees to the right versus 5 degrees at Z190 as Canning had it and the governor was turned about 37 degrees to the right versus 30 degrees as Canning had it at Z190. I used red-dashed lines to correct the location of the governor's shoulders and approximate the respective positions at Z223.

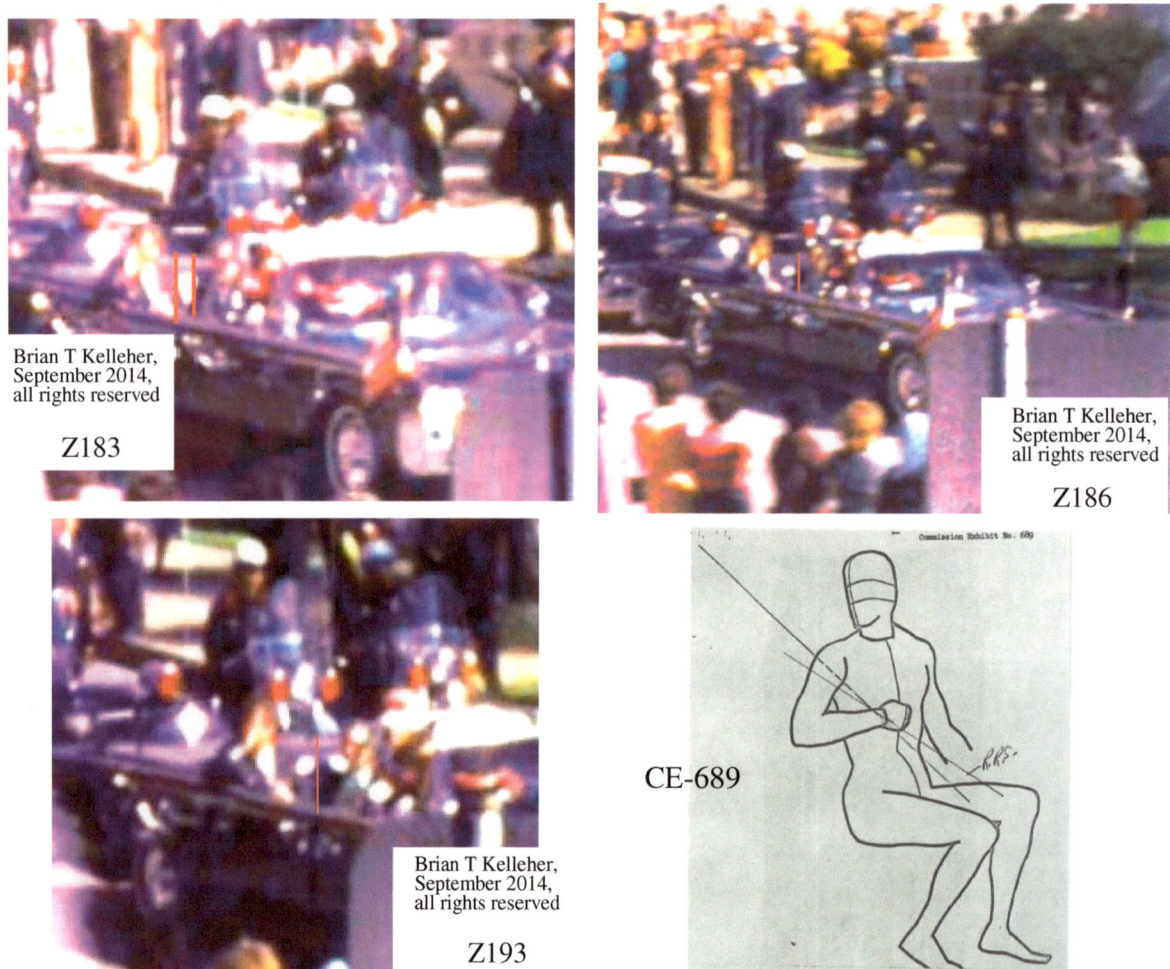

Figure 96
Zapruder sightlines for Z183, Z186 and Z193 for positioning the president and governor for the Z221 shot and WC Exhibit CE-689 showing the correct and incorrect wound locations and bullet path through the governor's torso - The sightlines show the governor's right shoulder is several inches outboard of Canning's seating alignment. The soon-to-be outshoot wound to the middle of the president's neck is 4 inches to the right of the soon-to-be inshoot wound to the extreme right side of the governor's back. As of Z223, the wounds lay along the path of a bullet fired from the TSBD's sniper's nest at a 20.5 degree descending angle and 8 degree right to left angle; so did the outshoot wound to the governor's chest and the inshoot wound to the inside of his left thigh. The trajectory analysis when properly conducted clearly shows that the Z221 bullet performed no magic. It did not deflect at impossible angles and did not strike the governor's right forearm. During his April 21, 1964, interview by the WC, also attended by Governor Connally, Doctor Shaw who was the Parkland doctor who had treated the wounds to the governor's torso, was asked to endorse a vertical and lateral trajectory that fully supported the single bullet theory. Shaw used a red pencil to accurately plot the true path of the bullet through the governor's torso. His line passes through an inshoot wound located at the base of the rear side of the right shoulder, enters the rib cage just inside the crease of the right armpit, and exits the front wall of the chest a few inches inside and about an inch below the right nipple. The bullet is exiting the chest too far inboard and too low to involve the back of the governor's right forearm. Please note that as of Z193, the governor's suit coat is buttoned very low and that there is no possible way that a bullet exiting 2-inch inside and an inch under the right nipple could pass through a hole in the right side of his coat that is 6 inches from the midline (Zapruder Family Collection/The Sixth Floor Museum at Dealey Plaza http://www.jfk.org).

14: Resolving the Evidence on Wound Locations

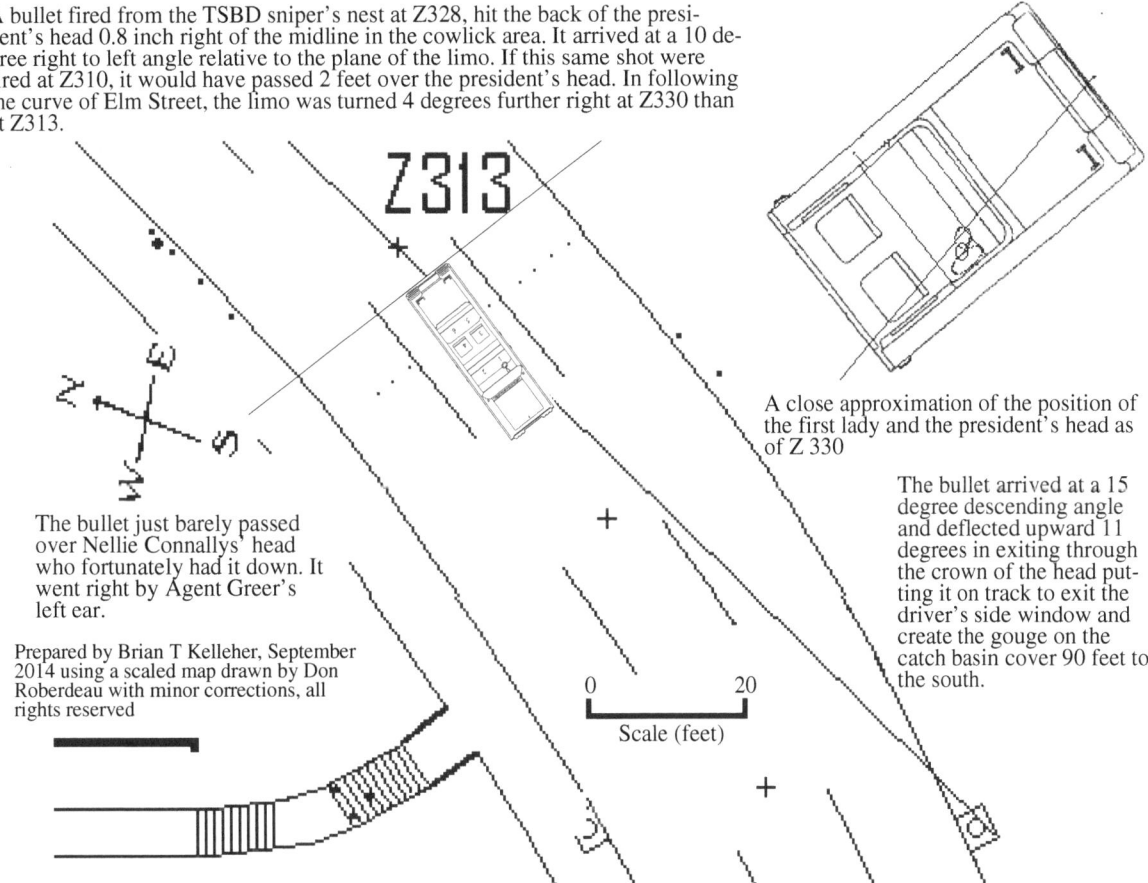

Figure 97
Lateral trajectory analysis for the Z328 shot - In order for a bullet to have passed through the top of the president's head at Z330, and then to have escaped the limo and created the gouge on the Z400 catch basin's top south corner, the limo would have had to be oriented as shown above and the bullet had to have been fired from the TSBD sniper's nest at the exact same 6 degree right to left angle and almost the same descending angle at which the Z310 shot was fired from the TSBD sniper's nest (15 degrees rather than 15.6 degrees). In passing through the head, the bullet needed to deflect upward about 11 degrees. Thus, the collective evidence for the Z328 head shot is proof that Oswald scored a remarkably lucky hit with his rushed final shot only because he did not change aim between shots. In exiting at the open driver's side window at about a 4 degree descending angle, the screaming bullet barely missed Nellie Connally and Agent Greer as a result of their respective hunkering down postures. It barely missed Agent Hill and Jackie Kennedy in entering the limo.

A bullet arriving from the TSBD sniper's nest at a 15 degree descending angle struck the president in the cowlick area 0.8 inch right of center. Upon striking the skull at an oblique angle, it deflected upward 11 degrees and exited the limo at a 4 degree descending angle putting it on course to create the gouge on the south corner of the storm sewer catch basin 90 feet to the south.

Figure 98

Vertical trajectory analysis for the Z328 shot - Using my photo-editing software, I cropped frame Z330 to focus attention on the president's position at impact. To account for the downward pitch of the road, I started off by using my photo-editing software to make the limo and curb level with the horizon. I then used the street elevations at Z250 (421.25') and Z313 (418.6') to establish that the downward grade in this 41-foot interval is 3.7 degrees and rotated the drawing clockwise by that amount. I used my properly scaled drawing to establish that the president's head was 262 feet from the base of the TSBD at a point directly below the sniper's nest as of Z330 and used this distance for my y axis. I then used the surveyed elevations for the street at Z313 (418.6') and the window sill elevation in the sniper's nest (490.9') to arrive at a gross elevation difference of 72.3 feet. I added 1.2 feet to compensate for the height of the rifle above the sill. I subtracted 3.5 feet to account for the president's slumped position in the rear seat to arrive at a net 70.0 feet difference in elevation and used this for my x axis. According to an on-line right-angle calculator, the bullet that hit the president in the cowlick area arrived at a descending angle of 15 degrees relative to the horizon after traveling 270 feet. I know from the bullet strike gouge on the Z400 catch-basin cover that the bullet had to have left the limo at about a 4 degree descending angle. This is telling us that it deflected up about 11 degrees in passing through the president's skull [15-4=11]. As shown, a bullet following this trajectory (blue line) would have barely missed Nellie Connallys' head. We can see that given the orientation of the president's head at Z330 and assuming this 11 degree upward deflection, the bullet wound have exited at the crown of the head just a few inches forward of the inshoot. This is consistent with what the X-rays are showing. This trajectory analysis confirms that Oswald defied the low odds of a final shot hit because he simply cocked and fired without changing his aim (Zapruder Family Collection/The Sixth Floor Museum at Dealey Plaza http://www.jfk.org).

Chapter 15

Oswald Acted Alone

My detailed evaluation of the evidence in the JFK case did not extend to the specifics of the case against Oswald or conspiracy because I believe there is sufficient evidence already on the record. I agree with the WC, Gerald Posner and Dale Myers as to who assassinated the president and murdered Police Officer Tippet that day in Dallas. I recommend the *Warren Report*, *Case Closed* and *With Malice* to those who want to see the entire body of evidence. The evidence that he was not a patsy is overwhelming. This chapter explains in brief why I have come to the conclusion that Oswald acted alone as a radical Marxist extremist.

Figures 99 through 100 follow and relate to the ensuing discussions.

Oswald was a self-described radical Marxist seeking out others of similar vein

Oswald was not a "lone nut." He read extensively and authored a manifesto. His writings show he was a passionate political extremist/activist who was honestly convinced the U.S. was headed for economic disaster and a political/social upheaval, which he wanted to be in the thick of. For those who want medical-professional insight into *The Mind of Oswald*, I recommend Dallas Psychologist Diane Holloway's well-written book by that name.

Shortly after receiving his mail-order weapons, Oswald wrote down the radical Marxist thought process he had adopted to justify assassinations of political figures such as General Walker and JFK in the course of becoming in his own mind a working-class hero:

Lee Harvey Oswald about April 1963 - *It is readily foreseeable that a coming economic, political or military crisis, internal or external, will bring about the final destruction of the capitalist system. Assuming this, we can see how preparation in a special [violently radical] party could safeguard an independent course of action [for the leaders of the working class] after the debacle, an American course . . . .* WC Exhibit CE-779 cited by Holloway, 2000, p. 138.

Writings such as the above and his street-agitation work and political correspondence prove that Oswald was actively seeking out others of similar vein to foster political/social upheaval in the U.S. From these writings, it is evident that Oswald, given the opportunity, would have eagerly taken part in an assassination conspiracy amongst any pro-Castro revolutionaries or any left-wing political organizations or individuals with radical or violent tendencies. These are exactly the types of like-minded individuals he was seeking to join in forming a "special party" of assassins and terrorists to hurry along and lead the revolution. The famous backyard photos provide grim evidence that he was ready, willing and able to kill political leaders or commit what we today call terrorist acts to promote his political ideals and ambitions. See Figure 99.

Oswald shot the president from his place of employment and had no need to participate in a conspiracy or any opportunity to

The fact that Oswald shot the president from his place of employment is evidence on its own that he was acting opportunistically for reasons touched on above. Moreover, the opportunity to assassinate Kennedy from his place of employment arrived completely by chance and the evidence is that he did not become aware of the chance until just two or three days before he committed the violent act. The motorcade route was not revealed by Dallas newspapers until Tuesday, November 19th and Oswald most likely read the news upon arriving at work the next morning. Consistent with the above, the evidence shows that Oswald was so frustrated by his inability to find recruits for his "special party" or a decent job that he had decided to move to Cuba to participate in Castro's revolution. If he had his way in late September 1963 with the Cuban or Russian ambassadors in Mexico, he would have been in Cuba in November 1963.

Oswald's admitted presence alone on the upper floors during the shooting and obvious guilt

In his final interview on Sunday November 24, 1963, just before he was shot dead by Jack Ruby, Oswald admitted, in so many words, that he was on the upper floors of the TSBD assassinating the president when the shooting occurred.

> **Harry Holmes, Postal Inspector, U.S. Post Office, Terminal Annex, Dallas, Texas** - *When asked about his whereabouts at the time of the shooting, he stated that when lunch time came, and he didn't say which floor he was on, he said one of the Negro employees [Charles Givens] invited him to eat lunch with him and he stated: "You go down and send the elevator back up and I will join you in a few minutes." Before he could finish whatever he was doing [assassinating the president], he stated, the commotion surrounding the president took place and when he went downstairs a policeman questioned him as to his identification and his boss stated "he is one of our employees"....* Memorandum of Oswald's November 24, 1963, interview, December 17, 1963. Holmes related the same information during his 4/2/64 WC testimony (WRv.7Hp.302).

WC critics make much of the fact that there is somewhat convincing evidence that Oswald made a brief appearance in the first floor domino room at around noon and had a quick bite to eat. He told his interrogators he did so and I tend to believe from the evidence that he did indeed make a brief appearance in the domino room. Assuming this to be true, however, there is no question from what he stated in his final interview, that upon finishing his lunch, as most everyone else prepared to watch and cheer the president, Oswald went right back up to the sixth floor using the stairs or elevator, completed his task, and then came back down to the second floor within a minute or so of when the president was shot dead with the mail-order rifle he brought to work that day.

The TSBD employee who Oswald was referring to in his final interview was 38-year-old order filler, Charles Givens. Commencing at 8:00 that morning, Mr. Givens and four other employees (Danny Arce, Billy Lovelady, William Shelley and Bonnie Ray Williams) were laying new floor in the southwest corner of the sixth floor. During the prior days they had moved many cases of books out of the area and stacked them on the opposite corner of the building unwittingly constructing Oswald's sniper's lair.

> **Bonnie Ray Williams, 20-year old TSBD order filler** - *We had to move these books to the east side of this building, over here ... I would say this would be the window Oswald shot from. We moved these books kind*

15: Oswald Acted Alone

of like in a row like that, kind of winding them around. Williams WC testimony, 4/8/64 (WRv.3p.167) which is confirmed by Givens WC testimony 4/7/64 (WRv.6Hp. 350).

Knowing the president's motorcade was due to pass by, the entire group broke for lunch about 15 minutes early and took both the passenger (east) and freight (west) elevators along the rear (north) side of the building down to the first floor. On the way down, Givens, who was in the east elevator which had openings that one could look out through, observed Oswald on the fifth floor in the vicinity of the elevator and exchanged a few words with him about sending the freight elevator back up (WC testimony, 4/8/64, WRv.6Hp.349).

Shelley testified to seeing Oswald at the time during his WC testimony on April 7, 1964 (WRv.6p.328). Arce (WRv6Hp.364-65), Lovelady (WRv.6Hp.337-38) and Williams (WRv.3Hp.186) testified to hearing this interchange during their April 7/8, 1964 WC interviews.

After reaching the first floor and washing up in the restroom, Givens realized he left his cigarettes upstairs in his jacket and went back up in the east elevator. After retrieving his jacket he was about to get back on the elevator when Oswald approached him from the direction of the sniper's nest holding his clipboard, giving the appearance that he was busy filling orders. This was just 5 minutes or so before noon. When Givens asked Oswald if he wanted to go down for lunch, he declined the offer and asked him to close the gates on the freight elevator when he got downstairs so he could call it up (WC testimony 4/7/64 WRv.6Hp.349-53).

In the meantime, key witness Harold Norman finished his lunch in the domino room and met up with co-worker James Jarman to go outside to watch the motorcade (WC testimony 3/24/63 WRv.3Hp.189). Oswald told his interrogators that he saw these two walking away from the domino room as he was eating his lunch alone which tends to confirm he was there at approximately noon.

After departing the building, Norman and Jarman stood on the sidewalk on the north side of Elm just west of where Roy Truly and O.V. Campbell were standing on the street in front of the entrance to the building. They were joined there by Danny Arce. At about 12:15 p.m., with the crowd thickening, Norman and Jarman decided they could get a better view from the upper floors of the building. They entered the rear door and took the west elevator up to the fifth floor (Norman WC testimony 3/24/64 WRv.3Hp.189-90).

Shortly after Givens had returned with his cigarettes to the first floor via the east elevator, key witness Bonnie Ray Williams took the east elevator back up to the sixth floor where he ate his somewhat famous lunch of a bone-in fried-chicken sandwich, Fritos and Doctor Pepper at the third window from the east. The residues of his lunch confirmed his testimony in this respect. From prior conversations, Williams was expecting that at least some of his co-workers would be joining him. Though he was not far from the sniper's nest, Williams could not see Oswald in the SE corner due to the stacked boxes. He neither saw nor heard anyone walking about before taking the east elevator down to the fifth floor presumably at about 12:20 p.m. There he found his two co-workers James Jarman and Harold Norman in the SE corner windows and joined them (Williams WC testimony 4/8/64, WRv.3Hpp.169-71).

The collective evidence including the above coupled with the admissions of Lee Harvey Oswald himself indicate that Oswald was alone on the sixth floor in the area of the SE corner window as of Williams' departure at about 12:20 p.m. through 12:30 p.m., at which point Oswald fled the scene of the crime. If Oswald did make a cameo appearance in the domino room it would have been at about noon shortly after Givens left him behind, leaving plenty of time for his return trip to the sixth floor.

The evidence that Oswald did all the shooting is overwhelming

Besides the above, there is a mountain of evidence telling us that Oswald laid his simplistic plans to assassinate the president all by himself on Thursday, November 21, 1963, spent a restless night with his wife, and then carried out his abominable plan on Friday improvising as the day went on. He used the sixth-floor-SE-corner window because the books happened by chance to be stacked high in the area and improvised his unlikely brief escape. He left a farewell note to his wife in the form of his wedding ring and almost all his cash, came to work carrying his disassembled rifle in a make-shift paper bag, was seen walking away from the sniper's lair at about noon, was seen firing the rifle in the president's direction as the last shot rang out at 12:30 p.m., left a palm print on the box he was sitting on in the sniper's lair, fled the scene of the crime, shot and killed a police officer that stopped him on the street for questioning, fled that crime scene, etc.

Critics will howl that it is impossible for Oswald to have fired two shots in one second and hit a moving target as small as the president's head almost 100 yards away. The collective evidence, however, clearly shows he did. The bullet left a trail and could not have come from anywhere else. All Oswald had to do was maintain his aim while operating the bolt and pressing the trigger. It was a miracle that the bullet did not hit Ms. Kennedy or Ms. Connally, or Agent Greer.

The fact that Jack Ruby shot Oswald dead while he was being transferred to County jail on the Sunday after the assassination raises suspicions of complicity. Given the circumstances of the shooting, however, there is no possibility that Ruby planned it in advance. Moreover, the evidence is that he acted alone in a fit of anger. As is the case with Oswald, the evidence shows that he took advantage of the opportunity that presented itself.

Why?

The evidence shows that Oswald assassinated the president from his place of employment primarily because the opportunity suddenly presented itself for him to become a central figure in his anticipated forthcoming Marxist revolution. The evidence is also telling us that Oswald was aware that JFK was bent on removing Castro from power and that this was also a factor in the decision. President Kennedy fell within Oswald's contorted definition of a Fascist. The evidence shows that Oswald was passionate enough about his political convictions to sacrifice his life for the cause.

By a cruel twist of fate, Lee Harvey Oswald was given the opportunity to leave his mark on world history as a radical Marxist revolutionary and took it.

15: Oswald Acted Alone

Figure 99
Hunter of Fascists: backyard photo CE-133A - This photo and two similar were recovered by the Dallas Police in the Ruth Paine garage in Irving, Texas on the Saturday following the assassination. Ms. Oswald was living with Ruth Paine at the time and Lee's meager belongings were stored there. Any doubts that the photos are authentic were eliminated when Oswald's former friend George DeMohrenschildt discovered a first-generation copy of Commission Exhibit CE-133A amongst his personal possessions upon his return to the U.S. from Haiti in early 1967. On the rear side of the photo, written in Oswald's hand in English is "To my friend George from Lee Oswald" 5/1V/63 and then in Russian in his wife's hand "Hunter of Fascists Ha-ha-ha." Ms. Oswald admitted taking the photos after originally denying she did. The photos were presumably taken soon after Oswald's mail-order weapons arrived at his P.O. Box in Dealey Plaza. As he intended, this picture in conjunction with his manifesto is telling us why he assassinated President Kennedy and attempted to kill General Walker (Marina Oswald, Dallas Police Department photograph, R.W. "Rusty" Livingston Collection/Sixth Floor Museum at Dealey Plaza www.jfk/org).

Figure 100
White House Photographer Cecil Stoughton's picture of President Kennedy's casket being taken aboard Air Force One - (Cecil Stoughton, John F. Kennedy Library, via David Von Pein's blog site "The Kennedy Gallery").

Conclusions and Recommendations

Given my collective findings and from everything else I have read or seen on video or TV, I am 100 percent convinced that Oswald planned and performed this horrible deed all by himself in spur-of-the-moment fashion.

I found no credible evidence of conspiracy, but did find solid grounds for allegations of such

I found no credible evidence of shots fired from anywhere else than the TSBD sniper's nest. I only found evidence of three shots and this same evidence indicates that they were all from the TSBD sniper's nest.

While I do see some evidence of the FBI attempting to limit the scope of the investigation and hurry it along, I see reasons other than trying to participate in a JFK assassination conspiracy. From my view, J. Edgar Hoover and others involved with the investigation were justifiably convinced that Oswald acted alone for the same reasons I am so convinced. The records of the news coverage show that within hours of the assassination it was obvious to everyone involved including the countless unbiased journalists covering the event that Oswald had assassinated President Kennedy and murdered Officer Tippet. As far as I can tell, there was not a shadow of doubt among local, state and federal investigators and journalists in the weeks and months that followed that Oswald was guilty and had likely acted alone.

FBI and WC critics tend to overlook the fact that when it is plainly obvious that an individual is guilty of premeditated cold-blooded murder, it is the primary job of law enforcement personnel assigned to the case to diligently assemble the evidence needed to convict him of the crime. It is not their job to look for evidence to exonerate a murderer when it is abundantly clear he is guilty. That would be the job of his defense team. Although the WC was obligated to take a much more judicial view than the FBI, its primary task was to build a case against Oswald since it was so obvious that he committed the crime. I do not see a rush to judgment.

The police and FBI investigations immediately revealed that Oswald had a very limited window of opportunity to shoot his rifle at the president from his place of employment and that the opportunity had arrived completely by chance within a period of a few days. Under these circumstances, even if evidence were ever found that Oswald had discussed presidential assassination with some other person at some point in the past, this is not evidence they had anything to do with what happened on an ad hoc basis at Oswald's place of employment on November 22, 1963. There was no opportunity for anyone to frame Oswald for shooting from the SE corner sixth floor window, since there was no way of knowing this shooting location would be available to Oswald at the time. The evidence is clear that TSBD employees inadvertently constructed the "assassin's lair" just a day or two before the assassination in the process of laying floor. It was available for Oswald's use that Friday simply by chance.

On this basis, in my view, Hoover and other government officials were justified in attempting to conduct a limited investigation that made the public aware of his lack of opportunity to carefully plan the event and involve others. Since Oswald had earlier defected to Russia, there were legitimate concerns that investigating possible Soviet involvement in anything more than a cursory manner would needlessly escalate Cold War tensions. There were also the same justifiable concerns that more than cursory investigations into Oswald's possible connections with anti or pro-Castro factions or the Mafia would needlessly compromise covert CIA operations to bring down Castro and other communist regimes. Beyond all this, Hoover was conspicuously sensitive to criticism of the FBI's failure to treat Oswald as a serious threat and was exercising damage control. In appointing chief Justice Warren to head up an independent investigation rather than relying on the FBI, President Johnson took all the above factors into consideration.

The U.S. Congress established the Rockefeller Commission in 1975 for the specific purpose of fully investigating and responding to allegations that the CIA took part in the JFK assassination. The Senate established the Church Committee in 1975 to look for evidence of Oswald's possible involvement in conspiracies and the government's involvement in cover-ups. The reports were somewhat critical and called for reforms but found no evidence of government involvement, conspiracy or cover-up. The HSCA took a hard second look in 1978 and reached the same conclusions.

I agree with the conclusions of these reports.

By the same token, however, as long as the government and its supporters continue to assert that there is definitive evidence of a first shot miss and that there is medical evidence that the Z313 inshoot wound to the president's head was in the cowlick area rather than slightly above the EOP, there are solid grounds for critics to raise allegations of conspiracy and cover-up. According to the evidence, if indeed there were a missed first shot and/or a Z-313 cowlick entry, there had to have been multiple shooters and a conspiracy and cover up.

Similarly, so long as the government and its supporters continue to assert a single bullet caused the governor's forearm and wrist wounds in addition to the governor's three other wounds, critics are justified in accusing the government of concocting evidence for the purpose of proving Oswald acted alone. According to my findings, the geometry does not work and the evidence that has been used to date to prove the single bullet theory is concocted to some extent.

The above comments do not apply to the Warren Commission and its report since the report leaves it open as to which shot missed and prudently states that a single bullet might not have caused all the governor's wounds. The WC had nothing to do with the cowlick entry.

I found no credible evidence of a government cover-up or any attempt to frame Oswald, but did find solid grounds for allegations of such

I found that all dubious conclusions and oversights in the collective government reports were without exception due to oversights and innocent mistakes by the experts the government retained to conduct the investigations. Unfortunately, however, when the government issues reports of the JFK assassination investigations that draw dubious conclusions in the face of conflicting evidence, or leave stones unturned, there is no assumption by the public of innocent oversights and mistakes. Instead there is unending controversy and rampant speculation.

The qualified comments I just made above on conspiracy, also apply to cover-up. In addition, I conclude that the WC should not have left so many open issues and so many stones unturned because it led to unending controversy and rampant speculation. The WC should have kept the investigation open until every single detail was resolved. As I have pointed out in this book, there is/was plenty of evidence available at the time to figure out exactly what happened.

I encountered a few loose ends.

In the puzzling absence of evidence to the contrary, I have concluded that the Secret Service possibly remains in possession of audio evidence that the last two shots were fired just a second apart. I am referring here to the missing recordings (if any) of the radio communications between Agents Kellerman and Lawson as the last two shots rang out. I am assuming there were recordings because it defies reason that the communications were not recorded. In any event, because there is nothing in the collective government reports that explains what happened to the recordings (if any), as far as I am concerned, the Secret Service still has some explaining to do.

While I found no credible evidence of a medical cover-up, the collective evidence suggests to me that there were additional autopsy photos taken looking inside the body and cranial cavity that are not currently available to assassination researchers. If this is the case, it would be helpful if the government or Kennedy family provided an explanation.

In view of the findings relating to CE-567 tissue samples reported in 1998, why has there been no follow-up nuclear DNA testing of "extraordinarily" well-preserved samples of cell nuclei in tissue specimen # 3? Under the circumstances, I recommend the government conduct the testing to avoid the appearance of covering up or subverting evidence refuting the single bullet theory.

The government's investigation were rigorous if not completely successful

I am satisfied that the U.S. Government conducted a rigorous if not completely successful investigation into the JFK assassination with the best of intentions. The FBI, Warren Commission and HSCA relied on consultants and experts to resolve and present all the evidence. In their rush to meet deadlines in making the case against Oswald, the consultants and experts made the honest and understandable mistakes and oversights that I have exposed in this book. The FBI and WC investigations of the shooting sequence were doomed to failure by the disastrous expert testimony that the minimum-firing time for Oswald's rifle was 2.3 seconds rather than 0.8 second. Whatever the mistakes, the investigations correctly confirmed what was obvious from the start: they identified Oswald as the lone assassin who fired the three shots from the TSBD sniper's nest.

Recommendations to the Department of Justice

In view of my findings, I am recommending that the FBI Crime Lab in Washington, D.C. go through the abundant new photographic, scientific and ballistics evidence I have presented in this book and formulate their own conclusions. I recommend the current head of the FBI direct his staff to prepare a long overdue addendum to the original FBI report that paints a clear picture for the public of exactly what happened during the JFK assassination. I note that the HSCA made a similar recommendation to the Department of Justice in 1979.

View of Dealey Plaza from Reunion Tower's GeO-Deck in 2004 - Von Pein, via the David Von Pein blog site "The Kennedy Gallery."

References Cited

Government reports cited

Secret Service Report 1963: U.S. Secret Service. *Report of the U.S. Secret Service on the Assassination of President Kennedy*. Secretary of the Treasury, Washington D.C., December 18, 1963.

FBI Report 1963: U.S. Federal Bureau of Investigation. *Investigation of the Assassination of President John F. Kennedy, November 22, 1963*. 5 vols. Federal Bureau of Investigation, Washington D.C., December 1963.

Warren Report 1964: President's Commission on the Assassination of President John F. Kennedy. Hearings before the President's Commission on the Assassination of President John F. Kennedy. 26 vols. U.S. Government Printing Office, Washington D.C., 1964.

_____. *Report of the President's Commission on the Assassination of President John F. Kennedy*. U.S. Government Printing Office, Washington, D.C., 1964.

Clark Panel Report 1968: U.S. Department of Justice, Ramsey Clark Panel. *Panel Review of Photographs, X-Ray Films, Documents and Other Evidence Pertaining to the Fatal Wounding of President John F. Kennedy, on November 22, 1963, in Dallas, TX*. U.S. Government Printing Office, Washington, D.C., 1968.

Rockefeller Commission Report 1975: U.S. Senate, President's Commission on CIA Activities within the United States. Investigation of the Assassination of President John F. Kennedy, Book 5, *Final Report of the Select Committed to Study Government Operations with Respect to Intelligence Activities*. U.S. Government Printing Office, Washington D.C., 1975.

HSCA Reports 1978-79: U.S. House Select Committee on Assassinations. Appendix to Hearings before the Select Committee on Assassinations. 12 vols. 95th Congress, 2d session. U.S. Government Printing Office, Washington, D.C., 1979.

_____. *Final Report of the Select Committee on Assassination, Summary of Findings and Recommendations* (including nine appendices). U.S. Government Printing Office, Washington, D.C., 1979.

Debunking the HSCA's conclusion on grassy knoll shooter 1982: National Academies of Sciences, Committee on Ballistics Acoustics, National Research Counsel. *Report of Committee on Ballistics Acoustics*. National Academies Press, Washington D.C., 1982.

ARRB Report 1998: Assassinations Records Review Board. *Final Report of the Assassinations Records Review Board*. U.S. Government Printing Office, Washington D.C., 1998.

NARA Press Releases 1999-00: National Archives and Records Administration press release, December 14, 1999, "Further Scientific Examination of the JFK Assassination Evidence."

_____. Press release, January 21, 2000, "Lab Tests on Kennedy Assassination Now Complete."

Books cited

Bugliosi, Vincent. *Reclaiming History: The Assassination of President John F. Kennedy*. Norton & Company, NY, NY, 2007.

Connally, Nellie and Herskowitz, Mickey. *From Love Field: Our Final Hours with President John F. Kennedy*. Rugged Land LLC, NY, NY, 2003.

Fetzer, James H., (editor). *Assassination Science: Experts Speak Out on the Death of JFK*. Catfeet Press, Chicago, IL, 1998.

Grodin, Robert J. *The Killing of a President: The Complete Photographic Record of the JFK Assassination, the Conspiracy, and the Cover-Up*. Viking Penguin, NY, NY, 1993.

Halvach, Laura and Payne, Darwin (editors). *Reporting the Kennedy Assassination*. Three Forks Press, Dallas, TX, 1996.

Holloway, *Diane. The Mind of Oswald*. Trafford Publishing, Victoria, BC, 2000.

Jackson/Nix, Gayle. *Orville Nix: The Missing JFK Film*. Semper Ad Meliora Publishing, TX, June 2014.

Life. The Day President Kennedy Died: 50 Years Later Life Remembers the Man and the Moment. Life Books, NY, NY, 2013.

Myers, Dale. *With Malice: Lee Harvey Oswald and the Murder of Officer J.D. Tippit*. Oak Cliff Press, Inc., Milford, MI, 1998.

National Research Counsel, Committee on Scientific Assessment of Bullet Lead Elemental Composition Comparison. *Forensic Analysis Weighing Bullet Lead Evidence*. National Academies Press, Washington D.C., 2004.

Posner, Gerald. *Case Closed: Lee Harvey Oswald and the Assassination of JFK*. Bantam Doubleday, NY, NY, 1993.

Savage, Gary. *JFK First Day Evidence*. The Shoppe Press, Monroe, LA, 1993.

Sneed, Larry A. *No More Silence*. University of North Texas Press, Denton, TX, 1998.

Sturdivan, Larry M. *The JFK Myths: A Scientific Investigation of the Kennedy Assassination*. Paragon House, St. Paul, MN, 2005.

Tague, James T. *The Truth Withheld: A Survivor's Story*. Excel Digital Press, Dallas, TX, 2003.

Trask, Richard B. *Pictures of the Pain: Photography and the Assassination of President Kennedy*. Yeoman Press, Danvers, MA, 1994.

_____. *That Day in Dallas: Three Photographers Capture on Film the Day President Kennedy Died*. Yeoman Press, Danvers, MA, 1998.

United Press International and American Heritage Magazine. *Four Days, the Historical Record of the Death of President Kennedy*. New York: American Heritage Publishing Company, 1967.

White, Stephen and CBS. *Should We Now Believe the Warren Report?* MacMillan Company, NY, NY, 1968.

Wrone, David R. *The Zapruder Film: Reframing JFK's Assassination.* The Sixth Floor Museum at Dealey Plaza and University Press of Kansas, Lawrence Kansas, 2003.

Articles cited

Alvarez, Luis W. "A Physicist Examines the Kennedy Assassination Film." *American Journal of Physics*, September 1976.

A*ssociated Press*, Press Release November 21, 2002, J F Kennedy Assassination: http://aptm.com/aptn/web site (regarding Muchmore film).

Connally, John. "Why Kennedy Went to Texas." *LIFE*, November 24, 1967.

Dumond, et al. "A Determination of the Wave Forms and Laws of Propagation and Dissipation of Ballistic Shock Waves." *Journal of the Acoustical Society of America*: California Institute of Technology, September 27, 1945.

Joe Durnavich titled "Making Sense of the Head X-rays." mcadams.posc.mu.edu/xray, April 2000.

Itek Corp. "Nix Film analysis." Lexington, MA 1967.

_____. "John Kennedy Assassination Film Analysis." Lexington, MA, 1976

Kosinski, Robert. "A Literature Review on Reaction Time." Clemson University, Clemson, SC, last updated September 2013. On-line: biae.clemson.edu/bpc/bp/lab/110/reaction.htm

Life staff writers. "Last Seconds of the Motorcade Together with Unpublished Pictures by Nine Bystanders." *LIFE*, November 24, 1967.

Maher, Robert and Shaw, Steven, "Deciphering Gunshot Recordings," rob.maher@montana.edu, Montana State University.

Myers, Dale. "Secrets of a Homicide: JFK Assassination" (explanation of methods used to construct computer animation of shooting sequence and presentation and discussion of findings and conclusions). Dale Myers, 1995-2008. www.jfkfiles.com.

_____. "Epipolar Geometric Analysis of Amateur Films Related to Acoustics Evidence in the John F. Kennedy Assassination." Dale Myers, 2007-2010. www.jfkfiles.com/jfk/html/acoustics.htm.

Oliver, Alfred and Dziemian, Arthur. "Wound Ballistics of 6.5-mm Mannlicher-Carcano Ammunition." U.S. Army Edgewood Arsenal Chemical Research and Development Laboratory Technical Report CRDLR 3264, March 1995.

Patoski, Joe. "The Witnesses: what they saw then, who they are now." *Texas Monthly*. Austin, TX, November 1998.

Towner, Tina. "View from the Corner." *Teen*, June 1968.

Rahn, Kenneth A., and Larry Sturdivan, "Neutron activation and the JFK Assassination: Part I. Data and Interpretation," *Journal of Radiological and Nuclear Chemistry*, vol. 262, No. 1, 205-213, 2004.

Shonfield, Maurice. "The Shadow of a Gunman." *Columbia Journalism Review*. July/August 1975.

Sturdivan Larry, and Kenneth A. Rahn, "Neutron activation and the JFK Assassination: Part II. Extended Benefits," *Journal of Radiological and Nuclear Chemistry*, vol. 262, No. 1, 215-222, 2004.

Zimmerman, M. R., and Spencer, J.D., Maimonides Medical Center "Final Report of John F Kennedy Assassination Evidence," September 16, 1998.

Audio/video cited

DVD titled "JFK Death in Dealey Plaza." *Discovery Communications, Inc.*, Silver Springs, MD, 2003.

DVD titled "Image of an Assassination: A New Look at the Zapruder Film." *MPI Video*, Orland Park, Ill, 1998.

DVD titled "JFK Assassination Films: The Case for Conspiracy." *Delta Entertainment Corporation*, Los Angles, CA, 2003.

DVD titled "The Kennedy Assassination Part 2, November 22, 1963" which includes a recording of the original *NBC TV News* broadcast and in particular Dave Wiegman's complete uncut Dallas footage which aired 4:05 p.m. eastern time. *Mad Phat Enterprises*, Pahromp, NV, 2009, copyright 1983.

DVD titled "The Story Behind the Story," *Dallas Morning News/WFAA-TV and Belo Interactive*, Dallas, TX, 2003.

Video tape titled "The Men Who Killed Kennedy, the Truth Shall Make You Free" *History Channel*, 2008.

Sixth Floor Museum at Dealey Plaza, Dallas TX. Oral History Program video/audio taped interviews: Marilyn Sitzman on June 29, 1993; James Tague on March 30, 1999; Earnest Brandt on May 12, 1993; and John Templin on June 28, 1995.

Recreation of Oswald rapid firing his rifle posted on YouTube in 2010 by Mag30th titled "Rapid Firing the Mannlicher-Carcano Rifle: 6 Shots in 5.1 Seconds," www.youtube.com/watch?v=h4c5Zr7hzzA.

Recreation of Zapruder's startle reactions to shot noise posted on YouTube in 2011 by Assassinationtruth titled "CBS News Inquiry, Should we now Believe the Warren Report," June 25, 1967, Part 6: 6:35-7:55 out of 8.14 minutes, www.youtube.com/watch?v=P8p9UoQIe8.

Chapter Index

1. Introduction and Summary   1

1.1 At long last!   1

1.2 Some insights on my thought processes and approach and why I am so confident in my conclusions   2

1.3 Official investigations and their findings in brief   5

1.4 Something is wrong   6

1.5 Overall findings and some words about the realities of subtle bias in presenting or assessing evidence in a judicial setting   7

1.6 My detailed investigation findings in brief   8

1.7 Extracting and piecing together the evidence showing exactly what happened   9

1.8 Summary of motion-picture evidence as to the sequence and as to the effects of the three shots (Chapters 2-7)   10

1.9 Summary of motion-picture evidence as to the source of the three shots (Chapter 8)   12

1.10 Summary of evidence as to minimum-firing time (Chapter 9)   13

1.11 Key corroborating evidence as to the source of the shots (Chapter 10)   14

1.12 Summary of key witness testimony on where the president was located on Elm as the first shot rang out (Chapter 11)   15

1.13 Summary of key witness testimony on where the president was located on Elm as the final two shots rang out (Chapter 12)   15

1.14 Summary of findings on the fate of the Z328-third-shot: (Chapter 13)   17

1.15 Summary of findings on wound locations (Chapter 14)   17

1.16 Summary of findings on who did it and why (Chapter 15)   20

1.17 Summary tables   20

2. The Zapruder Assassination Sequence   31

2.1 The camera and the filming speed   32

2.2 The film and camera timelines   33

2.3 First interview and testimony   33

2.4 The images   34

2.5 Pre-first-shot movements   35

2.6 Reactions to the Z221 shot   37

2.7 Movements between the Z221 and Z310 shots	39
2.8 Reactions to the Z310 shot	41
2.9 Reactions to an apparent third shot	42
2.10 Conclusions	44

3. The Wiegman Assassination Sequence — 57

3.1 Camera car 1	57
3.2 Interviews and testimony	58
3.3 Film timeline	59
3.4 Available versions and camera recording speed	60
3.5 Zapruder film correlation	61
3.6 The first 150 frames/6 seconds	62
3.7 Expected timing of reflex and alarm reactions	64
3.8 Distinguishable reactions to the Z310/W073 shot	65
3.9 Distinguishable reactions to the Z328/W098 shot	66

4. The Dorman Assassination Sequences — 77

4.1 Inside the TSBD	78
4.2 Interviews and testimony	78
4.3 Film and camera timelines and available versions	78
4.4 Camera recording speed	79
4.5 Zapruder-film correlation	79
4.6 Fourth-sequence images: D336 to D376 (Z181-227)	80
4.7 Fifth-sequence images: D377 to D494 (Z291-425)	81
4.8 Expected timing of reflex and alarm reactions	82
4.9 Distinguishable reactions to the Z221/D371 shot in the fourth sequence	83
4.10 Distinguishable reactions to the Z310/D394 shot in the fifth sequence	84
4.11 Distinguishable reactions to the Z328/D409 shot in the fifth sequence	84
4.12 Also relevant	85

5. The Muchmore Assassination Sequence — 97

Chapter Index

5.1 The Justin McCarty women — 98

5.2 Interviews and testimony — 98

5.3 The film and camera timelines and available versions — 99

5.4 Zapruder-film correlation and camera recording speed — 100

5.5 The assassination sequence — 100

5.6 Signature jolting, cranial eruptions and reflex reactions to the Z310 (M39) shot — 101

5.7 Alarm reactions to the Z310 (M39) shot — 101

5.8 Signature jolting, cranial eruptions and reflex reactions to the Z328 (M57) shot — 102

6. The Nix Assassination Sequence — 111

6.1 The three sequences — 111

6.2 Interviews and testimony — 112

6.3 The film and camera timelines and available versions — 113

6.4 Zapruder film correlation and camera recording speed — 114

6.5 The assassination sequence — 114

6.6 Signature jolting, cranial eruptions and reflex reactions to the Z310 (N020) shot — 115

6.7 Alarm reactions to the Z310 (N020) shot — 116

6.8 Signature jolting, cranial eruptions and reflex reactions to the Z328 (N038) shot — 116

6.9 Alarm reactions to the Z328 (N038) shot — 118

6.10 The Nix film's alleged "Station-Wagon Man" — 118

6.11 The Nix film's alleged "Gunman in the Shadows" a.k.a. "Flying Tackle Man" — 118

7. The Bronson Assassination Sequence — 127

7.1 Interviews and testimony — 127

7.2 Available versions — 128

7.3 Zapruder film correlation and camera recording speed — 128

7.4 The assassination sequence — 128

7.5 Reactions to the Z310 (B10) shot — 129

8. Jiggle Analysis — 134

8.1 Shock-wave-induced camera movement — 134

8.2 Shot-noise-induced human-reflex-reaction analyses (jiggle analysis) — 136

8.3 Conclusions — 138

8.4 The Alvarez and *CBS-News* studies — 142

8.5 The HSCA jiggle investigations — 143

8.6 The HSCA acoustics investigations — 143

9. Evidence on Minimum Firing Time and Marksmanship — 149

9.1 MC rifle test firing/minimum firing times/accuracy — 149

9.2 Oswald's marksmanship and bolt-operating proficiency — 151

10. Key Evidence as to the Location of the Assassin — 153

10.1 Key witness Howard Brennan — 153

10.2 Three key witnesses Jarman, Norman, and Williams on the fifth floor of the TSBD — 154

10.3 Three key witnesses Cabell, Couch and Jackson — 154

10.4 The observations and actions of Motorcycle-Officer Marion Baker — 154

10.5 Photographic evidence that supports all three shots came from the TSBD — 154

10.6 Ballistics evidence relating to the shooter's location — 156

10.7 Key ear/eyewitness testimony to the source of the shots — 156

10.8 One witness at the southwest corner of Houston and Elm — 156

10.9 Three witnesses on the fifth floor of the TSBD — 156

10.10 Three witnesses in the motorcade that saw the rifle extending from the sniper's nest — 157

10.11 Marion Baker's observations and actions — 158

11. Key Witness Testimony for the First Shot — 163

11.1 Conclusions — 163

11.2 Key stationary ear/eyewitness testimony to the first shot — 165

11.3 Nine along the north side of Elm from Z190 to Z215 — 166

11.4 Six along the north side of Elm from Z215 to Z250 — 167

11.5 Five along the north or south side of Elm from Z250 to Z310 (grassy knoll) — 167

11.6 Four key stationary witnesses that took pictures of the limo between Z133 and Z350 — 168

11.7 Key-motorcade-eyewitness testimony to the first shot — 169

11.8 Five in the presidential limo — 169

11.9 Four motorcycle-escort police — 170

11.10 Eight in the Queen Mary   171

12. Key Witness Testimony for the Final Two Shots   177

12.1 Conclusions   177

12.2 Key stationary ear/eyewitness testimony to the second and third shots   180

12.3 Seven along the north side of Elm from Z250 to Z370   180

12.4 Five along the south side of Elm from Z280 to Z355   182

12.5 Six others who testified to seeing the head shot   184

12.6 Key-motorcade-eyewitness testimony to the second and third shots   185

12.7 The five survivors in the presidential limo   185

12.8 The four motorcycle-escort police   188

12.9 Ten in the Queen Mary   189

13. Tracking Down the "Lost Bullet"   197

13.1 The initial discovery and investigation of the catch-basin gouge   198

13.2 The initial discovery and investigation of the scar on the curb near Tague   199

13.3 The Secret Service and FBI fail to find the catch-basin gouge   199

13.4 A more-careful look at the evidence of the two curb strikes   200

13.5 The true significance of the wounding of James Tague's LEFT cheek   200

13.6 Identification of the exact location of the missing Z328 bullet   201

13.7 Fate of the missing portions of the Z310 bullet   202

14. Resolving the Evidence on Wound Locations   209

14.1 Vertical trajectory analysis shows the Z310 shot caused the wounds to the president's head and governor's right forearm and wrist and that the Z221 shot caused the rest of the wounds   209

14.2 Additional evidence that the single bullet theory needs to be revised with respect to the governor's forearm and wrist wounds   210

14.3 The Z310 bullet entry hole is in the right occipital bone   212

14.4 Unraveling misunderstood autopsy photo view 6   212

14.5 Unraveling the perplexing autopsy photo view 7   213

14.6 Lateral and anterior/posterior autopsy X-rays show two inshoot wounds and one outshoot wound   215

14.7 Resolving the 6.5 mm fragment   216

14.8 The Z310 bullet's exit point in the parietal bone and the greater defect 216

14.9 Lateral trajectory analyses for the Z221 and Z310 shots confirms that both shots came from the TSBD sniper's nest and caused all the wounds except the Z331 wounds 217

14.10 Vertical and lateral trajectory analysis for the Z328 shot proves that Oswald fired the shot 220

14.11 Notes on illustrations

15. Oswald Acted Alone **239**

15.1 Oswald was a self described radical Marxist seeking out others of similar vein 239

15.2 Oswald shot the president from his place of employment and had no need to participate in a conspiracy or any opportunity to 240

15.3 Oswald's admitted presence alone on the upper floors during the shooting and obvious guilt 240

15.4 The evidence that Oswald did all the shooting is overwhelming 242

15.5 Why? 242

Name Index

Abernathy, Joe	112
Adams, Victoria	78
Agronski, Martin	170
Allen, William	201, 206
Allman, Pearce	85
Alonzo, Aurelia	166
Altgens, James	3, 16, 38, 43, 44, 49, 50, 115, 122, 154, 160, 165, 168, 172, 173, 178, 183, 191-193, 195, 196, 218, 235
Alvarez, Luis	10, 11, 135, 142, 143
Arce, Danny	157, 240, 241
Atkins, Tom	57, 58, 196, 207
Aynesworth, Hugh	180

B

Babushka Lady	4, 23, 41, 46 50, 97, 100, 101, 104-107, 129-131, 202
Baker, Marion	15, 20, 64, 154, 155, 158, 159, 162
Barger, James	143, 144
Barrett, SSA	200
Bell, Mark	58
Bennett, Glen SSA	16, 16, 55, 129, 132, 164, 172, 173, 178, 192, 193, 195
Berry, Jane	16, 166, 173, 176
Betzner, Hugh	16, 29, 79, 80, 81, 92, 119, 130, 147, 168, 173, 175, 176, 178, 184, 192, 193, 218
Black Dog Man	119, 155, 175, 176
Blakey, U.S. Army	150, 151
Boswell, Dr. Thorton	4, 213, 214, 216, 227, 231
Bothun, Richard	26, 44, 49, 50, 55, 115, 117, 121, 122, 125, 126, 129
Brandt, Earnest	130, 131, 166, 173, 176
Brehm, Charles	4, 16, 41, 50, 101, 106, 129-132, 152, 167, 173, 178, 182, 193, 201, 202, 206
Brennan, Howard	14, 153, 154, 156, 159, 174
Bronson, Charles	10, 13, 24, 27, 28, 57, 97, 100, 127-132, 168, 173, 180, 110-192
Bronson, Francis	127, 134, 137, 140, 141, 143-147
Brown, Margaret	166
Bugliosi, Vincent	6
Burney, Peggy	16, 130-132, 165, 176, 180, 181, 193
Burrows, Francine	4, 46, 97

C

Cabell, Earle	157
Cabell, Mrs. Earle	14, 81, 154, 157, 159
Calvary, Gloria	39, 129-131, 167, 169, 173, 175, 176
Campbell, O.V.	62-64, 66, 67, 71, 74, 75, 241
Cancellari, Tom	196, 204
Canning, Thomas	217, 218, 224, 234, 235
Castleberry, Vivian	180

Castro, Fidel 151, 239, 240, 242, 246
Chaney, James 16, 22-26, 38, 39, 47, 55, 97, 101-103, 105, 109, 110, 115-126, 138, 142, 155, 160, 171, 173, 178, 181, 188, 189, 193-195
Chisms, Arthur and Faye 38, 59, 129-131, 167, 173, 176, 186, 196
Chronkite, Walter 142
Cisco Walt 56
Clark, Ramsey 5
Clay, Billie 166, 173
Connally, John 1, 3, 5, 6, 9, 10, 16-19, 21, 23, 25, 35-55, 100, 101, 104-108, 115, 120-122, 141, 148, 156,164, 165, 170, 178-181, 183-190, 192, 193, 197, 209-212, 218-225, 235-238, 242
Connally, Nellie 3-5, 9-11, 16, 17, 22, 23, 25, 35-45, 47-55, 97, 101-105, 106-110, 111, 113-117, 119-126, 164, 165, 170, 173, 178-181, 183-188, 190, 193, 197, 237, 238, 242
Cornwall, Gary 150, 151

Conway, Deborah 178
Costella, John 10

Couch, Malcolm 14, 64, 154, 155, 157-159, 162
Craven, Tom 57, 59, 196
Croft, Robert 29, 147, 148, 169, 174

D

Day, Carl 161
Decker, Bill 16, 185, 193
DeMohrenschildt, George 243
Dickerson, Mary Sue 166
Dillard, Tom 17, 153, 154, 155, 158-160, 202, 204, 206, 207
Dishong, June 39, 129-131, 167, 169, 173, 175, 176
Donaldson, Ann 166, 173
Dorman, Elsie 4, 9-13, 21, 22, 24, 25, 27-29, 37, 57, 58, 71, 77-95, 96, 133-140, 141, 155, 160, 174

Dorman, John 79
Dox drawing 212, 226, 231, 232
DuMond, Jessie 135
Durnavich, Joe 229

E

Elliot, Joe 136
Euins, Amos 153

F

Finke, Dr. Pierre 4
Flying Tackle Man 24, 26, 42, 100-107, 109, 110, 118, 119, 122, 155, 160, 176, 182, 188
Foster, James 16, 178, 185, 193, 198-200, 202, 203, 207
Foster, Toni . . . . See Running Woman

Franzens, Mr. and Mrs. Jack 114
Frazier, Robert 149, 151
Fritz, Will 151

G

Name Index

Garner, Dorothy. 78
Gemberling, Robert. 200
Geraldo. 118
Givens, Charles. 157, 240, 241
Greer, William SSA. 16, 21, 23, 25, 36, 38-41, 44, 47-56, 101-107, 109, 115-117, 120-123, 125, 148, 163, 164, 169, 173, 186, 190, 193, 237, 242
Gregory, Dr. Charles Francis. 210, 211
Groden, Robert. 60-62, 79, 99, 113, 117, 118, 119, 128, 201, 212, 215

H

Hanes, Jerry. 50
Hargis, Bobby. 3, 11, 16, 22, 23, 25, 26, 38-44, 46, 47-55, 97, 100-110, 111, 114-120-126, 153, 155, 170, 173, 176, 178, 182, 183, 188, 189, 193-195
Harris, Jones. 118
Hartmann, William. 143
Hawkins, Peggy. 165
Haygood, Clyde. 196, 201
Hendrix, Ruth. 166, 173
Hesters, Charles and Beatrice. 32, 33, 58, 70, 129-131, 176, 181, 196
Hickey, George SSA. 16, 37-39, 47, 55, 129, 132, 154, 165, 172-174, 178, 192
Hicks, Karen. 39, 167, 173
Hill, Clint SSA. 3, 4, 11, 16, 22-24, 38, 39, 42-44, 46, 47, 50, 51, 54, 55, 99-109, 111, 113-115, 117, 122, 124, 125, 129, 132, 171, 173, 178, 188-192, 193, 195
Hill, Jean. 16, 23, 41, 50, 100, 103-107, 109, 110, 114, 122, 129-132, 178, 183, 185, 193
Hoefin, John. 57, 59
Holloway, Diane. 239
Holmes, Harry. 240
Hoover, J. Edgar. 200, 246
Hudson, Emmett. 16, 24, 26, 100-107, 109, 110, 115, 119, 122, 176, 178, 182, 188, 189, 193
Hughes, Robert. 57, 85
Humes, Dr. James. 4, 215, 216, 218, 230
Hunt, John. 230

I

Itek Optical Solutions. 46, 118

J

Jackson, D.L.. . . . . 16, 22-26, 115-118, 119, 120-126, 132, 155, 171, 173, 175, 176, 181, 188, 189, 193
Jackson, Robert. 12, 154, 157-159, 207
Jarman, James. 14, 154, 157, 159, 241
Johns, Lem SSA. 58, 59
Johnson, Lyndon. 246

K

Kellerman, Roy SSA. 16, 21, 23, 325, 6, 36, 38-41, 44, 47-56, 97, 101-107, 109, 115, 117, 120-123, 148, 164, 169, 170, 173, 179, 186, 187, 190, 193, 194, 247

Kennedy, Jackie. 4, 9-11, 16, 21, 23-26, 35-49, 51-55, 100-102, 106, 107, 113-118, 120-126, 128-130, 132, 138, 148, 165-167, 170, 172, 173, 176, 178, 180-184, 186, 187, 190-192, 193, 195, 207, 242

Kennedy, John. 1, 7, 18, 19, 21, 23, 31, 35-48, 51-55, 100-104, 114-117, 119, 120, 122-124, 128-130, 132, 141, 148, 153, 163, 164-169, 170, 172, 175, 176, 177, 178-195, 199, 209, 212-224, 226-238, 240, 242, 245-247

King, Larry. 179

Kinney, Sam SSA. 25, 98, 100, 103, 105, 109, 115, 117, 121, 122, 125, 132, 171, 173, 190, 193

Kosinsky, Robert. 13, 20, 64, 82, 85, 137

L

Landis, Paul SSA. 16, 38, 39, 47, 55, 119, 154, 172, 173, 175, 178, 190, 191, 193, 195

Lawson, Winston SSA. 185, 186, 247

Livingston, Rusty. 161

Lord, Bill 171, 189

Lovelady, Billy. 157, 240, 241

M

Maher, Robert. 134

Martin, B.J. 11, 22, 23, 25, 26, 38-41, 47-49, 51, 55, 97, 100-110, 115-126, 132, 155, 160, 171, 173, 176, 182, 188, 193

Martin, John. 199

McAdams, John. 6, 152, 218, 229

McCormick, Harry. 34

McIntyre, William SSA. 16, 22, 23, 25, 38, 39, 47, 51, 55, 98, 100, 103, 105, 109, 122, 171, 178, 191, 193, 195

McKinnon, Cheryl. 59, 70, 130-132, 176, 196

McLain, Hollis. 82, 85, 97, 143, 158

Miller, U.S. Army 150

Millican, A.J. 166, 173, 176

Moorman, Mary. 16, 23, 24, 26, 41, 50, 97, 100, 103-107, 109, 114, 122, 129-132, 182, 183, 185, 193, 194

Morley, Jefferson. 206

Muchmore, Marie. 10, 11, 9-12, 24, 26, 28, 29, 42, 44, 45, 57, 79, 97-110, 111, 118, 119, 133-141, 143-147, 155, 160

Mudd, F. Lee. 16, 38, 39, 50, 130, 131, 165, 176, 180, 186, 193, 196

Murphy, Charles. 59, 60

Murray, Jim. 203

Myers, Dale. 6, 80, 217-219, 224, 234, 239

N

Newmans, Bill and Gayle 16, 24, 26, 29, 50, 59, 70, 100, 106, 114-117, 118, 120-126, 129-132, 147, 167, 173, 176, 178, 180, 185, 187, 193, 196

Newman, Jean. 130, 131, 165, 166, 169, 173

Nix, Gayle/Jackson. 113, 118

Nix, Orville. 10, 24, 28, 29, 43-45, 57, 97, 99, 111-113, 120-126, 127, 133, 137, 140, 141, 143-147, 155

Nix, Orville, Jr. 112

Norman, Harold. 14, 154, 156, 157, 159, 241

Name Index

O

O'Brien, Lawrence	207
O'Donnell, Kenneth	16, 172, 173, 178, 191-193
Ockham, William of	2
Oswald, Lee Harvey	2, 5-10, 13, 14, 16, 17, 20, 32, 142, 149-152, 153, 161, 197, 201, 220, 239-247
Oswald, Marina	151, 242, 243

P

Paine, Ruth	243
Patoski, Joe Nick	85
Payne, Darwin	34, 167, 180, 181
Pinkston, SSA	200
Porter, Bob	166, 184
Posner, Gerald	6, 97, 239
Powell, James	153, 154, 155, 159, 160
Powers, David	16, 172, 172, 180, 187, 192, 193, 218, 235

R

Rahn, Kenneth	211
Ready, John SSA	16, 25, 26, 38, 39, 47, 110, 115, 117, 118, 121, 122, 125, 129, 132, 154, 172, 173, 175, 190, 191, 193, 195
Red Shirt Man	24, 26, 42, 100-107, 109, 110, 122, 126, 176, 182
Reed, Carol	167
Reid, Geraldean	63
Rickerby, Art	196
Roberdeau, Don	29, 50, 70, 71, 91, 106, 122, 130, 147, 159, 165, 173, 193, 205, 233, 237
Roberts, Emory SSA	16, 101, 109, 132, 171, 173, 178, 190, 191, 193
Robinson, Duane	218, 235
Rotkin, Charles	30
Ruby, Jack	240, 242
Running Man	50, 97, 102, 118, 122
Running Woman	23, 24, 26, 42, 48, 50, 52, 55, 97, 101, 114-118, 120-123, 125, 126, 129-132, 178
Ryan, Cleve	57
Rydberg drawing	20, 213, 216, 231

S

Sawyer, H.J.	153, 198
Scott, Frank	143
Shaw, Dr. Robert	17, 218, 220, 236
Shaw, Steven	134
Shelley, Bill	157, 240, 241
Sitzman, Marilyn	16, 31-34, 50, 115, 122, 129-132, 168, 173, 175, 176, 178, 181, 193, 196
Skaggs, Jay	58, 70
Skelton, Royce	198, 200
Sneed, Larry	152, 182, 184, 198
Sorrels, Forrest SSA	156, 185, 199

Staley, US Army	150
Station Wagon Man	118
Stetson Hat Man	62, 64, 66, 71, 74, 75, 162
Stoughton, Cecil	76, 244
Stubblefield, Mrs. William	130, 131, 185
Sturdivan, Larry	6, 136, 211
Styles, Sandra	78
Summers, Malcolm	16, 26, 44, 49, 50, 115, 118, 122, 129, 183, 184, 193

T

Tague, James	4, 17, 29, 197, 199-207
Templin, John	130, 131, 166, 173, 176, 178, 184, 193
Thompson, Josiah	152
Tippet, J.D.	239, 245
Towners, James, Mrs., and Tina	82, 85, 87, 94, 95, 155
Trask, Richard	50, 57-59, 97, 99, 106, 113, 122, 128, 148, 159, 168, 181, 199
Truly, Roy	26, 62-64, 66, 67, 74, 75, 162, 241
Turner, Nigel	119
Turning Man	74, 75

U

Umbrella Man	58, 70, 129-131, 180, 195, 196
Underwood, James	204
Unger, Robin	203, 207

V

Von Pein, David	6, 30, 55, 60, 76, 148, 195, 196, 248
Vu, Phuong	202, 208, 230

W

Walker, Edwin	20, 151, 239, 243
Wallace, Mike	179
Walthers, Buddy	198-200, 202, 203, 206
Watson, Jay	31, 50, 168, 181
Westbrook, Karen	39, 129-131, 167, 169, 173, 175, 176
Wiegman, Dave	9, 12, 13, 23-29, 33, 57-76, 77, 79, 80, 168, 173, 176, 178, 181, 185, 77, 79, 91, 134, 138-141, 143-147, 155, 157-159, 160, 169, 180, 196, 207
William of Ockham	2
Williams, Mary Lee	166
Williams, Bonnie Ray	14, 153, 154, 157, 159, 240, 241
Williams, C.F.	198
Willis, Linda	16, 37, 80, 92, 165, 174, 184, 193
Willis, Marilyn	16, 131, 178, 185, 193
Willis, Phil	29, 37, 92, 119, 131, 147, 169, 171, 173, 174, 176, 178, 185, 192
Willis, Rosemary	37, 80, 92, 164, 165, 174, 184
Woodward, Mary	35, 148, 165, 166, 173, 175, 176

Name Index

Wrone, David 33
Wycoff, Charles 33, 142

Y

Yarborough, Ralph 119

Z

Zahm, James 151
Zapruder, Abraham 3, 4, 6, 8-13, 16, 22, 24, 27-29, 31-34, 39, 44, 46-50, 57, 61, 64, 68-71, 77-80, 88-90, 92, 97-99, 102, 111-118, 122, 127-132, 133-137, 140-148, 154, 159, 163, 168, 169, 173-176, 178, 180-182, 184, 193, 195, 196, 221-223, 236, 238
Zimmerman, M. R. 210

Brian Kelleher / Phuong Vu, 2014

www.ingramcontent.com/pod-product-compliance
Lightning Source LLC
Chambersburg PA
CBHW041150290426
44108CB00002B/27